# The Law of Green and Social Procurement in Europe

Roberto Caranta & Martin Trybus (eds)

# The Law of Green and Social Procurement in Europe

DJØF Publishing Copenhagen
2010

*Roberto Caranta & Martin Trybus (eds)*
The Law of Green and Social Procurement in Europe
European Procurement Law Series vol. 2
First Edition 2010



DJØF Publishing is a company of the
Association of Danish Lawyers and Economists



Cover design: Bo Helsted
Print: Scandinavian Book, Aarhus
Printed in Denmark 2010
ISBN 978-87-574-2325-9

Sold and distributed in North America by:
International Specialized Book Services (ISBS)
Portland, OR 97213, USA
www.isbs.com

Sold in all other countries by:
DJØF Publishing Copenhagen
Denmark
www.djoef-forlag.dk

The research for this book has benefited from a PRIN 2008-2010 grant
'Self regulation and self administration'

DJØF Publishing
17, Lyngbyvej
P.O.Box 2702
DK-2100 Copenhagen
Denmark

Phone: +45 39 13 55 00
Fax: +45 39 13 55 55
E-mail: forlag@djoef.dk
www.djoef-forlag.dk

# Table of Contents

# Foreword by the Editors of the European Procurement Law Series

After the first volume on *The In-House Providing in European Law* we tackle here another core issue in European Public Procurement Law. What was originally the European Economic Community law focused very much on the elimination of barriers to trade among Member States. Public procurement legislation was one tool in the fight against protectionism. Its aim was to open public procurement markets to European-wide competition. The principal objective of the European rules in the field of public procurement is also today to ensure the free movement of goods and services and the opening-up to undistorted competition in all the Member States (e.g. Case C-454/06, *pressetext*). However, different policy considerations have acquired growing relevance in the past years. Environmental and social issues are being recognised as something deserving consideration along with concerns for wider competition. Fair and open competition may still be the primary consideration in public procurements, but other considerations now figure as of potential relevance, hence the expressions 'secondary considerations' in public procurement and sustainable public procurement – SPP.

So far this area has attracted very limited attention in the case law of the European Court of Justice. A couple of seminal cases (Case 31/87, *Beentjes*, and Case C-513/99, *Concordia Bus Finland*) provides the sketchy foundations upon which the new 2004 public procurement directives have based a number of provisions allowing for SPP. On the same basis the Commission has drafted its guidelines, at times an uneasy compromise between market integration and sustainability considerations. At the same time, particularly in the field of the environment, EU institutions have adopted measures to commit procuring entities to the cause of sustainable public procurements. Against this contradictory background, the practice in the Member States is quite diverse and evolving fast. The different trends need to be strengthened through a rigorous analysis of the legal possibilities open to sustainable public procurement.

The subject has already received scholarly attention. However, publications in this series are the result of the collaboration within a European research group made of academics specialized in procurement law who consider a comparative approach both valuable and necessary. The starting point is that European institutions have developed common principles and rules which are applicable all over the EU. However, uniform application cannot be taken for granted. European principles and rules superimpose themselves unto the pre-existing (and at times divergent) national provisions. Once they penetrate the domestic legal orders, the sources of EU law interact with national law. They are there to alter domestic law, but they also run the risk of being read in ways that minimise their innovative impact on the national legal order. They may be easily misunderstood by practitioners and academics alike whose frame of mind was cast in the moulds of national law.

The Commission and the Court of Justice are out there to redress false readings and misunderstandings. Comparative knowledge may however help to avoid mistakes as well, exposing domestic courts and other actors to possibly different approaches to what are in the end the same principles and rules. Comparative information and analysis of procurement law and practice in the various Member States is therefore an important tool for the development of procurement regulation and practice in the EU. More specifically, it is valuable for practitioners in the Member States to be aware of practices, regulation, case law, and interpretations of procurement law throughout the EU as this can assist them both in understanding the rules applicable and in developing best practices. As the European Court of Justice reminds us on its official website, the courts of the Member States are the 'ordinary courts in matters of EU law'. National courts may, and in some cases must, refer questions to the Court of Justice. With more and more Member States leading to increased delays in the preliminary reference procedures, national courts will more often have to look for answers elsewhere. Precedents from other national courts giving application to the common European rules and principles are a precious source of inspiration. Finally, it should no be overlooked that the Court of Justice too is aware of the value of the comparative approach and its rulings are from time to time influenced by a development or a trend in regulation or practice at national level. Increased comparative knowledge of the case law of different Member States may alert the Court of justice to the difficulties national courts are facing in giving full effect to European law. In some cases, it may make EU institutions aware of common trends developing at national level, a spontaneous *jus commune* which it is better to follow than just to oppose or even worse: to ignore.

It is our hope that the European Procurement Law Series will contribute to a strengthened dialogue between the various legal cultures in the field of procurement and that it will become a well-known source of inspiration.

This year we have extended the country coverage of the series, including France, a leading model for social clauses in public procurement, and Romania, one of the most relevant new EU members. As a third topic, we will address remedies and focus on the new remedies in Directive 2007/66/EC.

We would like to thank Dr. Sara Richetto for organising our most successful Orta meeting and for helping us in editing this volume, and our most helpful publisher, Vivi Antonsen, always ready to forgive our many shortcomings.

*Roberto Caranta*
Professor
University of Turin

*Steen Treumer*
Professor
University of Copenhagen

# I. Sustainable Public Procurement in the EU

*by Roberto Caranta*

## 1 Introduction

International and regional public procurement legal instruments adopted in the past have been prompted by a concern for opening up the national procurement market to competition from tenderers established abroad.[1] The Government Procurement Agreement (GPA), a plurilateral Treaty signed in 1994 in the framework of the World Trade Organisation (WTO) Uruguay Round, is very open as to the reasons having moved its signatories to action. Right at the beginning of the preamble, it states:

> […] "that the need for an effective multilateral framework of rights and obligations with respect to laws, regulations, procedures and practices regarding government procurement with a view to achieving greater liberalization and expansion of world trade and improving the international framework for the conduct of world trade; […] that laws, regulations, procedures and practices regarding government procurement should not be prepared, adopted or applied to foreign or domestic products and services and to foreign or domestic suppliers so as to afford protection to domestic products or services or domestic suppliers and should not discriminate among foreign products or services or among foreign suppliers;"

*In the same vein is the preamble for a national law on public procurement suggested, again in 1994, by the UNCITRAL Model Law on Procurement of Goods, Construction and Services:*

> 'WHEREAS the [Government] [Parliament] of ... considers it desirable to regulate procurement of goods, construction and services so as to promote the objectives of:

1. See generally S. Arrowsmith and P. Kunzlik 'Public procurement and horizontal policies in EC law: general principles' in S. Arrowsmith and P. Kunzlik (eds.) *Social and Environmental Policies in EC Procurement Law* (Cambridge, Cambridge University Press, 2009) 30 ff; Ch. McCrudden *Buying Social Justice. Equality, Government Procurement & Legal Change* (Oxford, UPO, 2007) 97 ff.

> [...] (b) Fostering and encouraging participation in procurement proceedings by suppliers and contractors, especially where appropriate, participation by suppliers and contractors regardless of nationality, and thereby promoting international trade;"

Originally, Community legislation issued from the same concern. Article 1 of Council Directive 71/304/EEC of 26 July 1971, concerning the abolition of restrictions on freedom to provide services in respect of public works contracts and on the award of public works contracts to contractors acting through agencies of branches, provided for the abolition of restrictions affecting the right to enter into, award, perform or participate in the performance of public works contracts on behalf of the State, or regional or local authorities or legal persons governed by public law. This general provision was given more detail in Article 3. Member States had to abolish both the restrictions preventing beneficiaries from providing services under the same conditions and with the same rights as nationals of that country and the practices which result in treatment being applied to beneficiaries that is discriminatory by comparison with that applied to nationals.[2] To this day, the European Court of Justice (ECJ) reiterates that 'the principal objective of the Community rules in the field of public procurement is to ensure the free movement of services and the opening-up to undistorted competition in all the Member States'.[3]

This does not mean that public procurement law has ever existed fully isolated from other policy areas. Suffice it here to recall that environmental impact assessment has for a long time been a necessary procedural step for the realisation of many public works projects and that social legislation ranging from security at the workplace to accessibility for all is relevant for both the design and implementation of public works contracts. It is worth noting that a

2. Unsurprisingly, the case law was intended to strike down legislative scheme aimed at protecting national manufacturers – or manufactures established in specific areas: e.g. Case C-21/88 *Du Pont de Nemours Italiana* [1990] ECR I-889; see case note R. Caranta 'In contrasto con il diritto comunitario le riserve a favore di imprese del Meridione', in Giust. civ. 1991, 1369; the case is discussed again by S. Arrowsmith 'Application of the EC Treaty and directives to horizontal policies: a critical review' in S. Arrowsmith and P. Kunzlik (eds.) *Social and Environmental Policies in EC Procurement Law* above fn. 1, 152 ff.
3. Case C-454/06, *pressetext* [2008] ECR I-4401, paragraph 31; see also Case C-513/99, *Concordia Bus*, [2002] ECR I-7213, paragraph 81: 'the duty to observe the principle of equal treatment lies at the very heart of the public procurement directives, which are intended in particular to promote the development of effective competition in the fields to which they apply and which lay down criteria for the award of contracts which are intended to ensure such competition'.

fair number of these rules stemmed from international or regional legal sources quite often close to those governing the opening up of public procurement markets. In the past decade or so, however, different policy considerations have acquired growing relevance with reference to public procurement legislation proper.[4] Environmental and social issues are being recognised as something deserving consideration along with concerns for wider competition.[5] Fair and open competition may still be the primary consideration in public procurement, but other considerations now figure as of potential relevance, hence the expression 'secondary considerations'.[6] Sustainable public procurement (SPP) has become a term of art.[7]

The evolution is more remarkable in EU law. Both the GPA and the UNCITRAL Model Law have failed so far to be modernised.[8] In the former, secondary considerations mainly take the form of a special regime for less and least developed countries (which anyway have so far failed to be enticed to enter into the Agreement).[9] Rules on qualification may even curtail the ability

4. More to the point, this has always been the case at national level: S. Arrowsmith 'The E.C. procurement directives, national procurement policies and better governance: the case for a new approach' (2002) 27 E.L.Rev. 6 f.; Ch. McCrudden *Buying Social Justice*, above, fn. 1, 25 ff.; regional instruments are starting to take note too.
5. In 2002 the OECD issued a Recommendation of the Council on Improving the Environmental Performance of Public Procurement – 23 January 2002 – C(2002)3 http://webdomino1.oecd.org/horizontal/oecdacts.nsf/linkto/C(2002)3; a progress report was later published http://www.olis.oecd.org/olis/2006doc.nsf/linkto/env-epoc-wpnep(2006)6-final ; a detailed discussions of the considerations militating for and against secondary considerations in Ch. McCrudden *Buying Social Justice*, above, fn. 1, 114 ff.
6. See J. Arnould 'Secondary policies in public procurement: The innovations in the new directives' (2004) 13 P.P.L.R. 187; P. Charro 'Case note to *Concordia Bus Finland*' 40 [2003] C.M.L.Rev. 179: S. Arrowsmith and P. Kunzlik 'Public procurement and horizontal policies in EC law: general principles' above fn.1, at 13 f, rightly point out that 'secondary' conveys the mistaken assumption that these considerations only come after best value and suggest to use 'horizontal'; there is some merits however in sticking to established terminology.
7. It is doubtful whether other, more political, considerations could also be relevant; a negative reply focusing on a very specific issue comes from H-J. Prieß – C. Pitschas 'Secondary Policy Criteria and Their Compatibility with E.C. and WTO Procurement Law. The Case of the German Scientology Declaration' (2000) 9 P.P.L.R. 171 ff.
8. As to the GPA see the remarks by S. Arrowsmith 'Reviewing the GPA: The Role and Development of the Plurilateral Agreement after Doha' (2002) *Journ of Int.l Economic Law*, 779 ff.
9. See Art. V.

to rely on secondary considerations.[10] Generally speaking, the whole exercise is still about opening up national public procurement markets to competition. As was rightly remarked, the *Myanmar* case, one of the very few cases brought under the GPA, saw the then European Community (EC) and Japan complaining about a US – Massachusetts legislative provision blacklisting companies doing business with what was once known as Burma.[11] This is hardly the way to uphold human rights through public procurement.[12] The Model Law, in line with the mandate of UNCITRAL to promote international trade, suggests as a general rule to open up national procurement markets to international bidders. However, in conformity with its non-binding nature, it cannot but recognise 'that enacting States may wish in some cases to restrict foreign participation with a view in particular to protecting certain vital economic sectors of their national industrial capacity against deleterious effects of unbridled foreign competition'. To minimize restrictions, the Model Law also offers the less disruptive alternative of the 'margin of preference' in favour of local suppliers and contractors.[13]

It is to be noted that neither the GPA nor the UNCITRAL Model Law expressly refer to environmental considerations. The provisions briefly referred to revert to old style protectionism, albeit maybe justified by a situation of underdevelopment. The following analysis will therefore centre on EU law, and more precisely on public procurement Directives 2004/17/EC and 2004/18/EC. These Directives, however, hardly fill the pictures in so far as sustainable procurement is concerned. These days a growing number of secondary EU law measures actually impose buying green – and to a lesser extent buying social – requirement on procuring entities.[14]

The development of sustainable public procurement rules in the case law and in the legislation will be described along with relevant policy initiatives taken by the EU Commission. More specifically, the possible place for sustainability considerations in the different stages of the procuring process will

10. Art. VIII(b); see Ch. McCrudden *Buying Social Justice*, above, fn. 1, 103 and 48 ff.
11. P. Charro 'Case note to *Concordia Bus Finland*' 40 [2003] C.M.L.Rev. 188 ff.; see also S. Arrowsmith 'Application of the EC Treaty and directives to horizontal policies: a critical review' above fn. 2, at 247 f.
12. The case WT/DS88/1 was later dropped, because the statute at issue was quashed by the US Supreme court.
13. See Art. 8, 27, 34 and 39; se also paras. 24 ff. of the Guide to the enactment.
14. The development is underlined by S. Arrowsmith and P. Kunzlik 'Preface' to S. Arrowsmith and P. Kunzlik (eds.) *Social and Environmental Policies in EC Procurement Law* above fn. 1, already at xviii; at 40 ff discussion as to which legal bases is appropriate for these measures.

be examined along with the problems these considerations may cause for fair and open competition.

**1.1 From the first tentative steps in the case law ...**

The leading case is often said to be *Beentjes*.[15] The judgment stemmed from a preliminary reference arising in proceedings between Gebroeders Beentjes BV and the Netherlands Ministry of Agriculture and Fisheries in connection with a public invitation to tender for a public works contract (land consolidation). The awarding authority considered that Beentjes lacked sufficient specific experience for the work in question, that its tender appeared to be less acceptable and that it did not seem to be in a position to employ long-term unemployed persons. Beentjes claimed that the decision of the awarding authority rejecting its tender, although it was the lowest, in favour of the next-lowest bidder had been taken in breach of the provisions of Directive 71/305/EC, the first Public Works Directive. The employment of the long term unemployed is a classical social inclusion award criterion. In general terms it is fair to say that the ECJ trod very carefully. It accepted that the most economically advantageous tender criterion 'leaves it open to the authorities awarding contracts to choose the criteria on which they propose to base their award of the contract', their choice being 'limited to criteria aimed at identifying the offer which is economically the most advantageous'.[16] The Court accepted that the Directive did (and does) not lay down a uniform and exhaustive body of Community rules; consequently, within its framework the Member States remain free to maintain or adopt substantive and procedural rules in regard to public works contracts; however, it stressed that this freedom is conditioned on full compliance 'with all the relevant provisions of Community law, in particular the prohibitions flowing from the principles laid down in the Treaty in regard to the right of establishment and the freedom to provide services'.[17] Even if the issue was left to be finally determined upon by the national court, the ECJ voiced some concern that

> 'The obligation to employ long-term unemployed persons could inter alia infringe the prohibition of discrimination on grounds of nationality laid down in the second paragraph of Article 7 of the Treaty if it became apparent that such a condition could be satisfied only

15. Case 31/87, [1988] ECR 4635.
16. Paragraph 19.
17. Paragraph 20.

by tenderers from the State concerned or indeed that tenderers from other Member States would have difficulty in complying with it.'[18]

Moreover, the ECJ held that 'in order to meet the directive's aim of ensuring development of effective competition in the award of public works contracts, the criteria and conditions which govern each contract must be given sufficient publicity by the authorities awarding contracts'.[19] In the end, 'the condition relating to the employment of long-term unemployed persons is compatible with the directive if it has no direct or indirect discriminatory effect on tenderers from other Member States of the Community. An additional specific condition of this kind must be mentioned in the contract notice'.[20]

One could hardly read *Beentjes* as an unconditional show of support for sustainable public procurement. The traditional Community concerns as to non-discrimination and free movement are very much at the heart of this judgement.

The situation was not much changed a number of years later when *Beentjes* was discussed in an infringement procedure against France.[21] The Nord-Pas-de-Calais Region had published 14 contract notices as part of the 'Plan Lycées' programme. The notices set out the award criteria, including an 'additional criterion' relating to the promotion of employment. Relying on *Beentjes*, the Commission claimed that such a requirement could be used only as a contract performance condition, not as an award criterion, because Community law allowed two award criteria only, namely the lowest price and the economically most advantageous tender. The French Government, on the other hand, considered that *Beentjes* specifically allowed additional award criteria in case of an award to the economically most advantageous tender. Siding with the Commission, Advocate General Alber reasoned that 'In

18. Paragraph 30; an easier case was the well known *Storebaelt* case: C-243/89, *Commission* v *Denmark* [1993] ECR-I 3353; the contract included a clause binding the contractor 'to use to the greatest extent possible Danish materials, consumer goods, labour and equipment'; the defendant Government conceded that the clause was breaching the free movement rules in the Treaty (paragraph 26).
19. Paragraph 21; the transparency requirement was reiterated in Case C-324/93, *Evans Medical Ltd* [1995] ECR I-563, paragraph 46, with reference to an award criterion considering 'reliability of supplies', which by itself cannot be considered as referring to sustainable public procurements.
20. Paragraph 37.
21. Case C-225/98 *Commission* v *France* [2000] ECR I-7445; see J. Arnould 'A Turning Point in the Use of Additional Award Criteria? (2001) 10 P.P.L.R. NA13; Ch. Lambert 'note' Act. Jur. Dr. Adm. 2000, 1055; S. Arrowsmith 'Application of the EC Treaty and directives to horizontal policies: a critical review' above fn. 2, at 240 ff.

*Beentjes* the Court ruled that an employment criterion (in that case a condition relating to the employment of long-term unemployed persons) had no relation to the criteria for the award of contracts',[22] and that 'The Directive would not be infringed if the requirement to promote employment were expressed as a condition – as in *Beentjes* – and in that respect assumed the character of a performance criterion, as was stated by the Commission'.[23]

The ECJ's reasoning differed markedly from these conclusions. It held that the procurement Directives do not 'preclude all possibility for the contracting authorities to use as a criterion a condition linked to the campaign against unemployment provided that that condition is consistent with all the fundamental principles of Community law, in particular the principle of non-discrimination flowing from the provisions of the Treaty on the right of establishment and the freedom to provide services'. However, 'even if such a criterion is not in itself incompatible with [Community law], it must be applied in conformity with all the procedural rules laid down in that directive, in particular the rules on advertising [...]'.[24] Having disproved the Commission's main argument, the ECJ found the Commission's action wanting: 'the Commission criticises only the reference to such a criterion as an award criterion in the contract notice. It does not claim that the criterion linked to the campaign against unemployment is inconsistent with the fundamental principles of Community law, in particular the principle of non-discrimination, or that it was not advertised in the contract notice'.[25] Rejection was the only option left by the self-defeating attack strategy chosen by the Treaties' watchdog.[26]

Again, the ECJ could hardly be said to be promoting or even endorsing sustainable public procurement. At about the same time, the then EC Commission had started accepting the possibility for taking environmental and social consideration into account.[27] It recognised that the legal framework needed some clarifications, and in 2001 it adopted two Interpretative Com-

22. Paragraph 43.
23. Paragraph 48.
24. Paragraphs 50 f.; critically J. Arnould 'A Turning Point in the Use of Additional Award Criteria? above nt. 21, at NA15 f.
25. Paragraph 53.
26. See paragraph 54: 'In those circumstances, the Commission's complaint relating to the additional award criterion linked to the campaign against unemployment must be rejected'; for a defence of the Commission's position see however J. Arnould 'A Turning Point in the Use of Additional Award Criteria? above nt. 21, at NA16.
27. Among a vast grey literature see the communications on *Public Procurements in the European Communities* COM (1998) 143 final; *Integrated Product Policy*, COM (2001) 68 final.

munications devoted to the Community law applicable to public procurement and the possibilities for respectively integrating environmental and social considerations into public procurement.[28]

Soon after the ECJ came back to environmental considerations in public procurement and *Concordia Bus Finland* was indeed a much more forthcoming case.[29] In the procurement proceedings aimed at outsourcing the urban transport bus network of the Municipality of Helsinki, the decision was taken to award the contract to the undertaking whose tender was economically most advantageous overall to the city. In assessing overall economic advantage, account was be taken of three types of criteria, namely the overall price of operation, the quality of the (bus) fleet and the operator's quality and environment management. The second and third criteria are relevant here. Regarding the quality of the vehicle fleet, additional points were to be awarded for the use of buses having limited nitrogen oxide emissions and external noise, while in relation to the operator's quality and environment programme, additional points were to be awarded for a body of certified qualitative criteria and for a certified environment programme. Concordia Bus was not given points under the second criterion, while as to the third took fewer points than the successful bidder, who was awarded the contract even if the overall price it offered was higher. Claiming that the second criterion was discriminatory, since only one operator was in the position to offer buses meeting the standards set for the award of the additional points, Concordia Bus brought a case in front of the national court, which referred it to the ECJ. A number of national governments intervened in the proceedings. Advocate General Mischo upheld the Municipality of Helsinki's stance. In his opinion,

> 'The emissions criteria are irretrievably linked to the configuration of the fleet with which the city of Helsinki wishes to see the bus service operated. A contracting authority cannot be prohibited from requiring the use of a fleet having 'state of the art' characteristics, even if it gives prime importance to one of the qualities of such a fleet, namely its characteristics in relation to gas emissions and engine noise.'[30]

In more general terms, and referring to *Beentjes* and to a few other precedents,[31] he strongly emphasised that 'an environmental criterion may be in-

28. COM (2001) 274 final and COM (2001) 566 final.
29. Case C-513/99, *Concordia Bus*, [2002] ECR I-7213.
30. Paragraph 77.
31. Notably to Case C-324/93, *Evans Medical Ltd* [1995] ECR I-563, and Case C-225/98 *Commission* v *France* [2000] ECR I-7445, both discussed above.

cluded in the criteria for the award of a public service contract',[32] provided that it is 'applied in conformity with the fundamental principles of Community law, in particular the principle of non-discrimination and the four freedoms, and with all the procedural rules laid down in the relevant directive, in particular the rules on advertising'.[33]

The Advocate General's conclusions were in the main followed by the ECJ. The Court held that words 'for example' used by the directive 'read together with Art. 6 then EC Treaty lead to the conclusion that public procurement law does not exclude the possibility for the contracting authority of using criteria relating to the preservation of the environment when assessing the economically most advantageous tender'.[34] In other words, strictly economic considerations are not the only ones relevant in public procurement. At the same time, however, the risk is quite relevant that sustainability considerations, especially those concerning social matters, might be a disguised way to allow a return to discriminatory and protectionist award practices. The ECJ, in line with the submission of the then EC Commission, which were stricter on this point than the conclusions by the Advocate General,[35] felt the need to state that

> 'However, that does not mean that any criterion of that nature may be taken into consideration by the contracting authority [...]. Since a tender necessarily relates to the subject-matter of the contract, it follows that the award criteria which may be applied in accordance with that provision must themselves also be linked to the subject-matter of the contract.[36]

32. Paragraph 91; as P. Charro 'Case note to *Concordia Bus Finland*' 40 [2003] C.M.L.Rev. 181, points out, the Advocate general 'sees no reason why secondary considerations should be treated with greater suspicion than purely economic criteria'.
33. Paragraph 123.
34. Paragraph 57.
35. Paragraphs 100 ff.; AG Mischo accepted that the ECJ had not followed him in *Concordia Bus* in his conclusions to Case C-448/01 *EVN and Wienstrom* [2003] ECR I-14527, paragraphs 66 f: 'In my opinion in the *Concordia Bus Finland* case [...], referring to the judgment in Case C-225/98 *Commission* v *France*, in which the Court found that an award criterion relating to employment, connected with a local campaign against unemployment, was in principle valid, I said that such a requirement was not apparent. However, in the *Concordia Bus Finland* judgment [...], the Court expressed its clear opinion on that question when it observed [...] that 'the contracting authority ... may take into consideration ecological criteria ... *provided that they are linked to the subject-matter of the contract* ...'.'
36. Paragraphs 58 ff.

In a way, the ECJ is here treading a median line between the strict position entertained by the Commission, which pretended that only criteria resulting in a direct benefit of an economic nature to the procuring entities could be held admissible, and a more relaxed view considering any potential benefit to some public interest.[37]

Summing up the conditions already laid down in the precedents with the necessity of a link with the subject-matter of the contract, and holding that all the relevant requirements were met in the case at hand, the ECJ concluded that

'where the contracting authority decides to award a contract to the tenderer who submits the economically most advantageous tender [...], it may take criteria relating to the preservation of the environment into consideration, provided that they are linked to the subject-matter of the contract, do not confer an unrestricted freedom of choice on the authority, are expressly mentioned in the contract documents or the tender notice, and comply with all the fundamental principles of Community law, in particular the principle of non-discrimination'.[38]

Sustainability considerations are here carefully balanced with the primary concern for fair competition: 'While the Court confirms that secondary criteria can be referred to at the award stage of a tender process, it sets a number of conditions that must be fulfilled to ensure that no preference is given to national suppliers to the detriment of suppliers from other Member States'.[39]

The limits to the possibility to refer to environmental criteria were laid bare a few years later in *EVN*.[40] The Republic of Austria had invited tenders for the supply of electricity in an open procurement procedure. Under the heading 'award criteria', the invitation stated that the economically most advantageous tender was to be assessed according to different criteria, including the price and the 'effect of the services on the environment in accordance with the contract documents', which was weighted at 45 per cent. The supplier was to undertake to supply the Federal offices, so far as technically possible, with electricity from renewable energy sources and in any case not know-

37. According to P. Charro 'Case note to *Concordia Bus Finland*' 40 [2003] C.M.L.Rev. 185, 'The *Concordia Bus Finland* case opens the way to for interpreting what constitutes a sufficient degree of economic measurability more generally, with the public authorities potentially referring to benefits that accrue not only directly to public authority but also to a larger portion of society'; this may be a slightly too loose reading of the case law, especially when the *EVN* judgment – discussed below – is considered.
38. Paragraph 64.
39. P. Charro 'Case note to *Concordia Bus Finland*' 40 [2003] C.M.L.Rev. 179.
40. Case C-448/01 *EVN and Wienstrom* [2003] ECR I-14527; see Th. Gliozzo 'L'admissibilité d'un critère environnemental au regard de la réglementation communautaire des marchés' Act. Jur. Dr. Adm. 2004, 334 ; S. Arrowsmith 'Application of the EC Treaty and directives to horizontal policies: a critical review' above fn. 2, at 180 ff.

ingly to supply electricity generated by nuclear fission. However, the supplier was not required to submit proof of his sources of supply. In the event of a breach of the undertaking to supply electricity from renewable energy sources or the undertaking not to supply electricity generated by nuclear fission, it would be open to the contracting authority to terminate the contract and to impose a penalty. Moreover, in the introduction to the tender documents it was stated that the contracting authority was aware that for technical reasons no supplier could guarantee that the electricity he supplied to a particular customer had actually been generated from renewable sources. Finally, the award criterion referred to the electricity provided not to the procuring entity, but to the public at large. Unsurprisingly, an unsuccessful bidder brought an action in the national courts complaining that the environmental criterion breached Community law. The case having been referred to the ECJ, Advocate General Mischo, while in principle ready to uphold the legality of environmental criteria, considered *inter alia* that only those award criteria which permit the accuracy of the information given by suppliers to be actually checked are admissible.[41]

Closely following *Concordia Bus*, the ECJ reiterated the principle stipulating that

> 'Community legislation on public procurement does not preclude a contracting authority from applying, in the context of the assessment of the most economically advantageous tender for a contract for the supply of electricity, a criterion requiring that the electricity supplied be produced from renewable energy sources, provided that that criterion is linked to the subject-matter of the contract, does not confer an unrestricted freedom of choice on the authority, is expressly mentioned in the contract documents or the contract notice, and complies with all the fundamental principles of Community law, in particular the principle of non-discrimination.'[42]

On the facts of the case, however, the review of the legality of the invitation to tender, while leaving some margin of appreciation to the referring court, turned out differently when compared to that in *Concordia Bus*. The ECJ ac-

41. Paragraphs 40 ff.; the Advocate general conceded the difficulty in determining the precise origin of any energy supplied to the final customer; he pointed out however that 'even though it is not easy to determine the source of the electricity supplied, there are means of doing so, for example, by requiring certificates or, as the Netherlands Government observes, 'by requiring tenderers to prove the quantity of electricity which is generated or purchased by them and comes from renewable sources, as well as the quantity from renewable sources which is intended, in accordance with the contracts they have made, for customers other than the contracting authority'.'
42. Paragraph 34.

cepted that, 'provided that they comply with the requirements of Community law, contracting authorities are free not only to choose the criteria for awarding the contract but also to determine the weighting of such criteria, provided that the weighting enables an overall evaluation to be made of the criteria applied in order to identify the most economically advantageous tender'.[43] However, it also held that the principle of equal treatment implies 'that tenderers must be in a position of equality both when they formulate their tenders and when those tenders are being assessed by the contracting authority'.[44] As a consequence, 'where a contracting authority lays down an award criterion indicating that it neither intends, nor is able, to verify the accuracy of the information supplied by the tenderers, it infringes the principle of equal treatment, because such a criterion does not ensure the transparency and objectivity of the tender procedure'.[45] The tender invitation was also found wanting under the link to the subject-matter requirement in that the additional criterion relating to the energy source referred to energy which was supplied to customers different from the procuring entity. The ECJ held that 'in so far as it requires tenderers to state how much electricity they can supply from renewable energy sources to a non-defined group of consumers, and allocates the maximum number of points to whichever tenderer states the highest amount, where the supply volume is taken into account only to the extent that it exceeds the volume of consumption expected in the context of the procurement, the award criterion applied in the case at issue is not compatible with the Community legislation on public procurement'.[46]

While most of the reasoning closely follows *Concordia Bus*, reiterating the main rules resulting from the precedent, the last dictum, although arising from a most unfortunate drafting of the award notice, strengthens the need for

43. Paragraph 39; see also paragraph 40 'As regards the award criterion at issue in the main proceedings, the Court has already held that the use of renewable energy sources for producing electricity is useful for protecting the environment in so far as it contributes to the reduction in emissions of greenhouse gases which are amongst the main causes of climate change which the European Community and its Member States have pledged to combat (Case C-379/98 *PreussenElektra* [2001] ECR I-2099, paragraph 73)'.
44. Paragraph 47.
45. Paragraph 51; see also, concerning another element of uncertainty in the tender invitation we don't need to discuss here, paras 56 ff.
46. Paragraph 71; Th. Gliozzo 'L'admissibilité d'un critère environnemental au regard de la réglementation communautaire des marchés' above nt. 40, at 337, remarks that anyway local procuring entities could not have the capacity to check the truthfulness of complicate technical and scientific information.

a link with the subject-matter of the contract, general interest considerations not being enough to vouchsafe the recourse to award criteria based on secondary considerations.[47]

### 1.2 ... to consecration in the legislation

Directive 2004/18/EC followed the lead of the case law. Already in its first recital, the Directive points out

> 'This Directive is based on Court of Justice case-law, in particular case-law on award criteria, which clarifies the possibilities for the contracting authorities to meet the needs of the public concerned, including in the environmental and/or social area, provided that such criteria are linked to the subject-matter of the contract, do not confer an unrestricted freedom of choice on the contracting authority, are expressly mentioned and comply with the fundamental principles mentioned in recital 2.'[48]
>
> In recitals 5 and 6 the Directive pays homage to environmental and (some) social considerations. Recalling that under Article 6 EC Treaty, environmental protection requirements are to be integrated into the definition and implementation of all Community policies and activities, the Directive is said to clarify 'how the contracting authorities may contribute to the protection of the environment and the promotion of sustainable development, whilst ensuring the possibility of obtaining the best value for money for their contracts.'[49] At the same time, nothing in the Directive should prevent the imposition or enforcement of those measures necessary *inter alia* to health and human and animal life, 'in particular with a view to sustainable development, provided that these measures are in conformity with the Treaty.'[50]

The new legislation has, however, failed to clarify all the issues arising from the possible reference to sustainability considerations in public procurement. Moreover, general procurement rules have to be read in conjunction with a growing number of regulations and directives specifically enrolling procuring entities to the cause of green public procurement. This major legislative production has come at a time when, sadly, the case law seems to have dried up. A number of problems are therefore still on the table and are being addressed through soft law interventions by the Commission.

Following the structure (itself not without problems as it will be shown) provided by the Commission in a number of Communications, the analysis

47. See M. Dischendorfer 'The Rules on Award Criteria Under the EC Procurement Directives and the Effect of Using Unlawful Criteria: The EVN Case' 13 (2204) PPLR NA83, and Th. Gliozzo 'L'admissibilité d'un critère environnemental au regard de la réglementation communautaire des marchés' above nt. 40, at 336.
48. See also Directive 2004/17/EC, recitals 1 and 12.
49. 5th recital.
50. 6th recital.

will follow the different stages marking the procurement process. Indeed, 'the introduction of environmental criteria is more problematic in some of the stages of a tender process than in others.'[51]

## 2 Definition of the subject-matter of the contract and technical specifications

Probably the most relevant opportunity for taking sustainability considerations into account manifests itself at the stage of the definition of the subject-matter of the contract through the drafting of the technical specifications.[52] Indeed, as was remarked, this freedom of choice is implied in democratic systems – basically a preference setting mechanism – and EU law could hardly curtail it.[53]

In its interpretative Communications, the then European Commission actually distinguishes the definition of the subject-matter of the contract from the drafting of technical specifications.[54] This distinction does not seem particularly helpful. Of course, it is up to the procuring entities to decide what to procure, but it is when technical specifications are laid down that the problem of consistency with European law may first arise.[55] In the end, as the Commission itself admits, 'The choice of the subject-matter of the contract made by the contracting authority is initially reflected in the technical specifications.'[56] The insistence maintained in this distinction is probably to be linked

51. P. Charro 'Case note to *Concordia Bus Finland*' 40 [2003] C.M.L.Rev. 184.
52. See Commission interpretative Communication on the Community law applicable to public procurement and the possibilities for integrating environmental considerations into public procurement COM(2001) 274 final, points 6 and 7 of the executive summary.
53. S. Arrowsmith and P. Kunzlik 'Public procurement and horizontal policies in EC law: general principles' in S. Arrowsmith and P. Kunzlik (eds.) *Social and Environmental Policies in EC Procurement Law* above fn. 1, at 17.
54. COM(2001) 274 final, points I and II.1 respectively; the difference is somewhat less marked in the Communication on integrating social considerations COM(2001) 566 final: see points 1.1 and 1.2 respectively.
55. COM(2001) 274 final, point I, is content with claiming that the definition of the subject-matter of the contract cannot result in restricted access to the contract in question for firms from other Member States, but this limitation is spelt out by the detailed rules on technical specifications.
56. COM(2001) 566 final, last paragraph of point 1.1; see also, ending with an homage to Monsieur de Lapalisse, COM(2001) 274 final, point II.1: 'Technical specifications include all characteristics required by the contracting authority in order to ensure that

to a further – itself quite weak – distinction between technical specification and contract performance conditions, to be discussed below.[57]

The big question as far as the definition of the subject-matter of the contract is concerned, is the extent to which (if indeed this is possible) procurement contracts may accommodate different considerations. For instance, one could ask, and *Bentjees* was probably such a case, whether a public contract may include both procurement and other considerations, such as providing work for the unemployed. The case law on mixed contracts, including both mixed procurement contracts and contracts which are partly procurement and partly non-procurement, has been analysed by Advocate General Sharpston in her conclusions for the *Loutraki* case.[58] In any case of mixed contracts, the analysis must follow certain steps: the first step is to enquire whether a separate treatment of the different elements making up the mixed contract would be possible. 'If so, any element which, taken on its own, falls within the scope of a particular procurement directive must be awarded in compliance with the provisions of that directive.'[59] If a separate treatment of the different element is not possible, it must be decided as a second step which rules apply to the whole. To this end, both the legislation concerning mixed contracts and the case law, the *Gestión Hotelera Internacional* case first and foremost, points to a criterion distinguishing on the basis of the main purpose of the contract. Therefore, where a mixed contract relates to both a transaction within the scope of a procurement Directive and a transaction otherwise outside its scope, the contract as a whole will not fall within the scope of the Directive if the former is merely incidental to the latter; reciprocally, 'if a con-

the product or service fulfils the use for which it is intended. These technical specifications give objective and measurable details of the subject-matter of the contract and therefore are to be linked to the subject-matter of the contract'.

57. See paragraph 6. The impression is that the Commission sees the definition of the subject-matter of the contract as linked not just to technical specifications, but also to contract performance conditions (see also COM(2001) 566 final, point 1.1, 2nd paragraph); as it will be shown below, however, the discrete nature of the latter notion too is not devoid from doubts.
58. Joined Cases C-145/08 and C-149/08, *Club Hotel Loutraki*, nyr; the contract at stake, as described in paragraph 6 of the conclusions, was a mixed contract in which: a public authority sells 49 % of the shares in a public casino at a price offered by the highest bidder, to whom it hands over management of the casino and the right to appoint the majority of its directors; that management is remunerated by a percentage of the operating profits; the successful bidder undertakes to implement an improvement and modernisation plan; and the public authority, if it operates any other casino in future within the region concerned, undertakes to compensate the successful bidder.
59. Paragraph 54.

tract contains elements relating to different types of public contract, it is the main purpose or object which determines which directive is to be applied.'[60]

The main/incidental object distinction is not always easy to establish. Relative value would be much easier (and objective). However, according to Advocate General Sharpston, 'since the application of the Community directives is triggered at different value thresholds for different types of contract, [relative value] cannot be the only criterion, or there could be a danger of manipulation in order to remove certain contracts from the scope of the procurement rules.'[61]

It is however doubtful whether this approach is entirely satisfactory. A logic conclusion would be that many public works or services contracts could be seen as having as their main object giving jobs to the unemployed and could therefore be considered as falling outside the provisions of EU law. One wonders whether the Court of Justice would be easily ready to uphold such a claim or to leave it to the national courts. A relevant consideration would be whether the contract itself or some of its element are at odds with some EU law provisions (such as for instance those on State aids).[62] Breach of EU law could lead to rule out the legality of some mixed contracts, therefore solving the problem before even reaching the procurement question. Still lawful mixed contracts are possible and the question whether, as the Court of Justice clearly feared in *Bentjees*, this could lead to discrimination on grounds of nationality will still be lingering.

Viewed from the point of possible inclusion of sustainability considerations in the procurement process, two further problems arise in connection with the drafting of technical specifications: the relevance of the production processes on the one hand and, on the other hand but also more generally, the reference to environmental and social standards.

As to the first question, the position of the Commission has been marked by a very cautious approach. In its Communication focusing on the possibilities for integrating environmental considerations into public procurement, the Commission, while avowing that the legislation then in force was silent on the point, opined that reference to a specific production process was possible only if this did not restrict competition and helped 'to specify the performance characteristics (visible or invisible) of the product or service'. According

60. Paragraphs 55 f.
61. Paragraph 59.
62. See generally H-J. Prieß and M. von Merveldt 'The impact of the EC State aid rules on horizontal policies in public procurement' in S. Arrowsmith and P. Kunzlik (eds.) *Social and Environmental Policies in EC Procurement Law* above fn. 1, at 249 ff.

to the Commission, such criteria could be possibly (if no discrimination were entailed) met by environmentally sound production processes (e.g. organically grown foodstuff and green electricity), but not by requirements relating to the way the prospective contractor is run (e.g the use of recycled paper in office or the engagement of specific groups of workers).[63] However, as it has been rightly pointed out, it is hard to see how production processes could influence the characteristics of energy, and recourse to the idea of 'invisibly' seems a poor trick to mask a distinction without a difference through reference to an impalpable concept.[64]

More complex is the general question as to the incorporation of sustainability considerations in the technical specifications. From the outset it is to be remarked that, while most of the time procuring entities may, under certain conditions, refer to secondary considerations when drafting technical specifications, in some cases binding European rules incorporate these considerations in all and any (public) contracts.

Already in its preamble Directive 2004/18/EC declares the power of contracting authorities to 'lay down the environmental characteristics, such as a given production method, and/or specific environmental effects of product groups or services.' To this end, reference to the specifications defined in eco-labels is possible, but not compulsory. Moreover, '[c]ontracting authorities should, whenever possible, lay down technical specifications so as to take into account accessibility criteria for people with disabilities or design for all users.'[65]

Article 23 (3) (b) of the same Directive allows technical specifications to be formulated 'in terms of performance or functional requirements, including environmental characteristics, provided that such parameters are sufficiently precise to allow tenderers to determine the subject-matter of the contract and to allow contracting authorities to award the contract.'[66] The Commission's *Communication on Implementing the Community Lisbon programme: Social services of general interest in the European Union* suggested that technical

63. COM(2001) 274 final, point II.1.2.; see also COM(2001) 566 final, point 1.2.
64. For a critical appraisal see P. Kunzlik 'The procurement of 'green' energy', in S. Arrowsmith and P. Kunzlik (eds.) *Social and Environmental Policies in EC Procurement Law* above fn. 1, at 392 ff, and S. Arrowsmith 'Application of the EC Treaty and directives to horizontal policies: a critical review' above fn. 2, at 173 f, and 217 ff.
65. See cons. 29; see also Directive 2004/18/EC, cons. 42; for a comment R. Boyle 'Disability issues in public procurement' in S. Arrowsmith and P. Kunzlik (eds.) *Social and Environmental Policies in EC Procurement Law* above fn. 1, at 320 ff.
66. See also Art. 34 (3) (b) of Directive 2004/18/EC.

specifications drafted in terms of performance or functional requirements would be particularly appropriate in case of social services contracts: 'the contracting or awarding authorities may decide to define just the aims to be achieved by the service provider. This way of defining technical specifications should guarantee the necessary flexibility and, at the same time, sufficient precision to identify the subject of the contract.'[67] According to the Commission, allowing variants may be another way to allow sustainable considerations.[68] It is submitted, however, that this possibility, when not coupled with incentives through favourable award criteria, is unlikely to stimulate the voluntary adhesion to environmental and social solutions which tend to be more expensive than neutral ones. A big issue anyway is whether procuring entities are capable to draft and implement these more complex kinds of technical specifications. Quite opportunely the Commission is at present working to establish common green public procurement criteria as technical specifications for the purchase of specific product groups.[69]

Eco-label requirements may be referred to as a benchmark. Regulation 2010/66/EC on the EU Ecolabel, having just replaced 2000/1980/EC of the European Parliament and of the Council on a revised Community eco-label award scheme.[70] As its predecessors, it is aimed at promoting products which have the potential to reduce negative environmental impacts, as compared with the other products in the same product group, thus contributing both to the efficient use of resources and to a high level of environmental protection. To this end, a voluntary certification scheme has been devised providing guidance and accurate, non-deceptive and scientifically based information to consumers on such products. The recitals of the Regulation prod Member

67. COM(2006) 177 final, at. 2.2.1.
68. COM(2001) 274 final, point II.1.4.; see also COM(2001) 566 final, point 1.2.
69. COM(2008) 400 final, points 3.2. ff.; a distinction is traced between 'core' and 'comprehensive' criteria: 'The core criteria are designed to allow *easy* application of GPP, focussing on the key area(s) of environmental performance of a product and aimed at keeping administrative costs for companies to a minimum. The 'comprehensive' GPP criteria take into account more aspects or higher levels of environmental performance for use by authorities that want to go further in supporting environmental and innovation goals. Since 'core' criteria form the basis of the 'comprehensive' criteria, this distinction between 'core' and 'comprehensive' will reflect differences in terms of ambition and availability of green products whilst at the same time pushing markets to evolve in the same direction.'
70. Detailed analysis in D. Wilsher 'Reconciling national autonomy and trade integration in the context of eco-labelling' in S. Arrowsmith and P. Kunzlik (eds.) *Social and Environmental Policies in EC Procurement Law* above fn. 1, at 408 ff.

States to use eco-labels to buy green: 'Member States should consider guidelines when they establish their national Green Public Procurement Action Plans and could consider the setting of targets for public purchasing of environment friendly products.'[71]

According to Article 23 (6) Directive 2004/18/EC, reference to the eco-label is possible only provided that *a*) the specifications referred to are appropriate to define the characteristics of the supplies or services that are the object of the contract; *b*) the requirements for the label are drawn up on the basis of scientific information, *c*) the eco-labels are adopted using a procedure in which all stakeholders, such as government bodies, consumers, manufacturers, distributors and environmental organisations can participate, and finally, *d*) they are accessible to all interested parties. In any case, '[c]ontracting authorities may indicate that the products and services bearing the eco-label are presumed to comply with the technical specifications laid down in the contract documents; they must accept any other appropriate means of proof, such as a technical dossier of the manufacturer or a test report from a recognised body.'[72]

As the Commission quite appropriately remarked, the eco-label scheme is voluntary and adopted by a small percentage of market participants. Making it compulsory would be tantamount to discriminate between potential bidders.[73] Procuring entities are therefore allowed to refer to other labels, even if Regulation 2010/66/EC clearly signals that patience with so many certification schemes, indeed a source of uncertainty, is running short.[74]

Article 23 Directive 2004/18/EC allows procuring entities to refer to a wide variety of technical standards, eco-labels being but one of them. Similar to the eco-label, meaning that adoption of the standards laid down in the applicable regulation is not compulsory is the philosophy behind Regulation 2008/106/EC of the European Parliament and of the Council of 15 January 2008 on a Community energy-efficiency labelling programme for office equipment (also known ad Energy Star). Under Article 4 (3) of that Regulation, participation in the program is indeed voluntary. However, in this case a

71. Recital 14.
72. Identical rules are found in Art. 34 (6) of Directive 2004/18/EC.
73. COM(2001) 274 final, point II.1.2.
74. Recital 14; under Art. 12(3) on promotion of the EU Ecolabel 'Member States shall encourage the use of the 'Manual for authorities awarding public contracts', as specified in Annex I, Part A, point 5. For this purpose, Member States shall consider, for example, the setting of targets for the purchasing of products meeting the criteria specified in that Manual'.

number of European and national procuring entities are forcibly enlisted in sustaining the environmental friendliness of their office equipment procurement. Under Artcile 6, 'the Commission and the other Community institutions, as well as central government authorities within the meaning of Directive 2004/18/EC [...], shall, without prejudice to Community and national law and economic criteria, specify energy-efficiency requirements not less demanding than the Common Specifications for public supply contracts having a value equal to or greater than the thresholds laid down in Article 7 of that Directive.'

Especially concerning the environment, the EU has adopted a number of legislative measures not just to encourage, but to require procuring entities to buy green.[75] A recent instance where EU law enforces environmental standards is now provided by Directive 2009/33/EC of the European Parliament and of the Council on the promotion of clean and energy-efficient road transport vehicles. The Directive

> '[...] aims to stimulate the market for clean and energy-efficient road transport vehicles, and especially – since this would have a substantial environmental impact – to influence the market for standardised vehicles produced in larger quantities such as passenger cars, buses, coaches and trucks, by ensuring a level of demand for clean and energy-efficient road transport vehicles which is sufficiently substantial to encourage manufacturers and the industry to invest in and further develop vehicles with low energy consumption, CO2 emissions, and pollutant emissions.'[76]

As is made plain in Article 1 of the Directive, it 'requires contracting authorities, contracting entities as well as certain operators to take into account lifetime energy and environmental impacts, including energy consumption and emissions of CO2 and of certain pollutants, when purchasing road transport vehicles with the objectives of promoting and stimulating the market for clean and energy-efficient vehicles and improving the contribution of the transport sector to the environment, climate and energy policies of the Community.' Under Article 3, the Directive is applicable to both contracting authorities or contracting entities in so far as they are under an obligation to apply the procurement procedures set out in Directives 2004/17/EC and 2004/18/EC, and to operators for the discharge of public service obligations under a public service contract within the meaning of Regulation 2007/1370/EC of the European Parliament and of the Council of 23 October

75. See instances and discussion in P. Kunzlik 'The procurement of 'green' energy' above fn. 64, at 382 ff.
76. Cons. 11.

2007 on public passenger transport services by rail and by road. When purchasing road transport vehicles procuring entities must take into account the operational lifetime energy and environmental impacts of the vehicles. Under Article 5 (3), this may be done 'by setting technical specifications for energy and environmental performance in the documentation for the purchase of road transport vehicles on each of the impacts considered, as well as any additional environmental impacts'; the impacts considered concern at least the energy consumption; the emissions of CO2; and the emissions of NOx, NMHC and particulate matter.

Environmental standards are anyway compulsory in other and more traditional ways through technical harmonisation at European level. One example is provided by Directive 2009/125/EC establishing a framework for the setting of eco-design requirements for energy-using products (also known as the Eco-design Directive). The Directive, the last of a sequel which is already quite long, is one example of full harmonisation, in that only appliances manufactured according to is prescription may be sold in the EU and procuring entities have no choice but to buy compliant goods.[77]

As it will be shown when dealing with the criteria for the selection of bidders, 'social-labels' referring to various aspects of corporate social responsibility (CSR) are more problematic, because their requirements rarely have a direct impact on the subject-matter of the contract.

However, the protection of workers' rights is at the core of Directive 96/71/EC of the European Parliament and of the Council concerning the posting of workers in the framework of the provision of services.[78] To avoid social dumping, seen as a distortion of the internal market, the Directive provides that workers temporarily posted abroad enjoy the same eventually more generous rights as local workers.[79] The Directive is not specific to public procurements but was at issue in *Rüffert*, a recent public contracts case.[80]

Mr Rüffert, acting in his capacity as liquidator of the assets of Objekt und Bauregie GmbH & Co. KG had brought an action in a German court against the Land Lower Saxony concerning the termination of a works contract for the structural work in the building of Göttingen-Rosdorf prison. The contract contained a declaration of compliance with the collective agreements and, more specifically, with the one regarding payment to workers employed on

77. See to this effect Art. 3 (1) of the Directive.
78. COM(2001) 566 final, point 3.2.1.2.
79. The Directive itself has lately been subject to a measure of criticisms: see A.R. Ganesh 'Appointing Foxes to Guard the Henhouse: The European 'Posted Workers' Directive' 15 (2009) *Columbia Journ. Eur. Law*, 123.
80. C-346/06, *Rüffert* [2008] ECR I-1989.

the building site of at least the minimum wage in force at the place where those services were to be performed. Objekt und Bauregie used as a subcontractor an undertaking established in Poland which came under suspicion of having employed workers at a wage below that provided for in the 'Buildings and public works' collective agreement. After investigations had commenced, both parties terminated the contract which they had concluded with one another. The *Land* based the termination *inter alia* on the fact that the contractor had failed to fulfil its contractual obligation to comply with the collective agreement. A penalty notice was also issued by the *Land*. At first instance, the Landesgericht Hannover held that the contractor's outstanding claim under the contract for work was offset in full by the contractual penalty in favour of the Land Lower Saxony. The Oberlandesgericht Celle considered that the resolution of the dispute depended on the question whether it was precluded from applying the *Land*'s procurement law incompatible with the freedom to provide services laid down in Article 49 of the then EC Treaty and referred the case to the ECJ.

The Court, in a classical internal market reasoning, considered that the protection afforded by Directive 96/71/EC is limited to terms and conditions of employment which are fixed by laws, regulations or administrative provisions and/or by collective agreements or arbitration awards which have been declared universally applicable, meaning those rules which must be observed by all undertakings in the geographical area and in the profession or industry concerned. Lacking such declaration, Member States may refer to collective agreements or arbitration awards which are generally applicable to all similar undertakings in the profession or industry concerned or to agreements which have been concluded by the most representative employers' and labour organisations at national level and which are applied throughout the national territory. The collective agreement referred to by the Land Niedersachsen, however, could not be considered as falling under any of the two options, since the collective agreement referred to covered only a part of the construction sector falling within the geographical area of that agreement, being specific to public contracts and not having been declared universally applicable.[81]

Unsurprisingly, workers could not be said to be entitled to the protection afforded by the Directive, and the termination of the contract could not be considered lawful. Indeed, 'Directive 96/71 expressly lays down the degree of protection for workers of undertakings established in other Member States

81. Paragraph 29.

who are posted to the territory of the host Member State which the latter State is entitled to require those undertakings to observe.'[82] Given the presence of a measure of harmonisation, which, in the words of the ECJ, 'seeks in particular to bring about the freedom to provide services, which is one of the fundamental freedoms guaranteed by the Treaty',[83] the judgement naturally concluded that provisions such as those present in the *Land*'s legislation could not be justified by the objective of ensuring the protection of workers or by other overriding policy considerations, since the harmonisation measure already satisfied those needs.[84]

Another relevant piece of legislation is Council Directive 2001/23/EC on the approximation of the laws of the Member States relating to the safeguarding of employees' rights in the event of transfer of undertakings, businesses or parts of undertakings or businesses.[85] The ECJ has constantly held that the fact that the transfer of undertaking as a consequence of a public procurement procedure does not affect the application of the Directive just mentioned.[86] This option has been reiterated by the Regulation of the European Parliament and of the Council 2007/1370/EC on public passenger transport services by rail and by road, whose Article 4(5) provides that

> 'competent authorities may require the selected public service operator to grant staff previously taken on to provide services the rights to which they would have been entitled if there had been a transfer within the meaning of Directive 2001/23/EC. Where competent authorities require public service operators to comply with certain social standards, tender documents and public service contracts shall list the staff concerned and give transparent details of their contractual rights and the conditions under which employees are deemed to be linked to the services.'[87]

More generally, under Article 27 Directive 2004/18/EC, procuring entities may – or shall if the national legislation so provides – state in the contract documents 'the body or bodies from which a candidate or tenderer may ob-

82. Paragraph 33.
83. Paragraph 36; see the analysis by S. Klumpp 'Dienstleistungsfreiheit versus Tariftreue' *Neue Juristische Wochenschrift*, 2008, 3475 f.
84. Paragraphs 38 ff; see also S. Arrowsmith and P. Kunzlik 'Editors' Note' in S. Arrowsmith and P. Kunzlik (eds.) *Social and Environmental Policies in EC Procurement Law* above fn. 1, at 7.
85. COM(2001) 566 final, point 3.2.1.2., referring to Directive 77/187/EEC, then in force.
86. Case C-172/99, *Oy Liikenne* [2001] ECR I-, paras 19 ff.
87. See G.S. Ølykke 'Regulation 1370/2007 on Public Passenger Transport Services' in *Public Procurement Law Review*, 2008, NA84.

tain the appropriate information on the obligations relating to taxes, to environmental protection, to the employment protection provisions and to the working conditions which are in force in the Member State, region or locality in which the works are to be carried out or services are to be provided and which shall be applicable to the works carried out on site or to the services provided during the performance of the contract.' If so, procuring entities may ask potential bidders 'to indicate that they have taken account, when drawing up their tender, of the obligations relating to employment protection provisions and the working conditions which are in force in the place where the works are to be carried out or the service is to be provided.'[88]

## 4 Selection of candidates

Because of the principle of non discrimination, Member States are not allowed to set aside contracts to the benefits of particular companies. An exception is spelt out in Article 19 of Directive 2004/18/EC, which provides that

> 'Member States may reserve the right to participate in public contract award procedures to sheltered workshops [...] where most of the employees concerned are handicapped persons who, by reason of the nature or the seriousness of their disabilities, cannot carry out occupations under normal conditions.'[89]

Some uncertainties still linger as to the legal possibilities to directly award public contracts whose object is the provision of social services to social organisations and NGOs. The Commission's Communication on 'Implementing the Community Lisbon programme: Social services of general interest in the European Union' points to the application of the general public procurement rules and principles: 'In such cases, the public body delegating a social mission of general interest to an external organisation must, at the very least, respect the principles of transparency, equal treatment and proportionality. Moreover, in certain cases, the public contracts directives impose more specific obligations.'[90] Another question is whether NGOs participation in a contracting authority rules out the applicability of the *in house* exception to the

88. See also Art. 39 of Directive 2004/17/EC.
89. See also Art. 27 of Directive 2004/17/EC; see R. Boyle 'Disability issues in public procurement' above fn. 65, at 333 ff; the history of sheltered workshop is outlined by Ch. McCrudden *Buying Social Justice*, above fn. 1, 4 and 56 ff.
90. COM(2006) 177 final, at. 2.2.1.

application of procurement rules.[91] A recent judgement following an infringement procedure initiated because of the award of service contracts in the health sector by an Italian regional authority to some NGOs, while not really addressing the issue squarely, seems to indicate that NGOs are not different from enterprises.[92]

The rules on the selection of candidates allow a wide scope for Member States minded to foster sustainable procurements anyway. Two different kinds of provision may be relevant: those listing possible reasons for exclusions from the procurement procedures and those concerning the technical capacity of bidders.[93]

Professional misconduct is one of the possible reasons for exclusion under Article 45(2) Directive 2004/18/EC. Indeed, any economic operator must be excluded from participation in a contract if he has been convicted by a judgment which has the force of *res judicata* in accordance with the legal provisions of the country of any offence concerning his professional conduct or, which is less burdensome for the procuring entity, has been guilty of grave professional misconduct proven by any means which the contracting authorities can demonstrate.[94]

A margin of discretion seems to be left to the Member States when defining professional misconduct, provided that the general principles of European

91. In her conclusions to Case C-324/06, *Coditel* [2008] ECR I-, note 31, Advocate general Verica Trstenjak remarked: 'It remains unclear how the involvement of private persons or non-profit organisations, for example in the social or cultural fields, is to be regarded'.
92. Case C-119/06, *Commission v. Italy*, [2008] ECR I-, paragraphs 34 ff.; see A. Brown 'Application of the Directives to Contracts to Non-for-profit Organisations and Transparency under the EC Treaty: A Note on Case C-119/06 Commission v Italy', *Public Procurement Law Review*, 2008, NA96; R. Caranta 'Attività pubblica, attività no-profit, e disciplina dei contratti pubblici di servizi', *Urbanistica e appalti*, 2008, 293; M. Mattalia 'Convenzionamento diretto o procedure concorsuali nell'affidamento del servizio di trasporto sanitario?' *Foro amm. CdS*, 2008, and A. Albanese 'L'affidamento di servizi socio-sanitari alle organizzazioni di volontariato e il diritto comunitario: la Corte di giustizia manda un monito agli enti pubblici italiani', *Riv. it. dir. pubbl. comunitario*, 2008, 1453.
93. COM(2001) 566 final, point 1.3.
94. See S. Arrowsmith 'Application of the EC Treaty and directives to horizontal policies: a critical review' above fn. 2, at 228 ff.

Union law (proportionality included thereby) are complied with.[95] According to one of the recitals of the same Directive,

> 'If national law contains provisions to this effect, non-compliance with environmental legislation or legislation on unlawful agreements in public contracts which has been the subject of a final judgment or a decision having equivalent effect may be considered an offence concerning the professional conduct of the economic operator concerned or grave misconduct. Non-observance of national provisions implementing the Council Directives 2000/78/EC(15) and 76/207/EEC(16) concerning equal treatment of workers, which has been the subject of a final judgment or a decision having equivalent effect may be considered an offence concerning the professional conduct of the economic operator concerned or grave misconduct.'[96]

These are just examples. Breaches of the rules concerning minimum wages,[97] rules on the security at the workplace, or rules on the compulsory hiring of people with special needs or disadvantages,[98] may all qualify as grave professional misconduct, in the end depending on choices made by national legislation.[99] In fact, among the other reasons for exclusion expressly listed in Article 45, one more may be linked to secondary considerations: when the bidder has not fulfilled his obligations relating to the payment of social security contributions in accordance with the legal provisions of the country in which he is established or with those of the country of the contracting authority.[100] A real problem here is how to apply these rules to prospective contractors coming from other countries and especially from outside the EU.[101]

Coming to technical capability, the most relevant provision is Article 48. Under this provision, technical and/or professional abilities of the economic operators shall be assessed and examined considering past experiences, as evidenced by certificates of satisfactory execution which shall specify

95. See S. Williams 'Coordinating public procurement to support EU objectives – a first step? The case of exclusions for serious criminal offences' in S. Arrowsmith and P. Kunzlik (eds.) *Social and Environmental Policies in EC Procurement Law* above fn. 1, at 492 ff.
96. Recital 43.
97. A long tradition of forcing wage compliance through public procurements extends outside Europe: see Ch. McCrudden *Buying Social Justice*, above, fn. 1, 37 ff.
98. R. Boyle 'Disability issues in public procurement' above fn. 65, at 318.
99. See also COM(2001) 566 final, point 1.3.1.
100. Art. 45(2)(e).
101. See for instance S. Arrowsmith 'Application of the EC Treaty and directives to horizontal policies: a critical review', in S. Arrowsmith and P. Kunzlik (eds.) *Social and Environmental Policies in EC Procurement Law* above fn. 1, at 170 ff.

whether the contracts awarded were carried out according to the rules of the trade and properly completed;[102] by information regarding the tenderer's quality standards, procedures and measures,[103] and as to his managerial staff and manpower.[104] The Commission insists that these requirements have a direct link with the object of the contract.[105]

In this way, a watchful procuring entity may gather many indications as to the business practices of the concerned bidders and gather evidence possibly pointing at breaches of social and environmental legislation. At the same time, the possible adherence by the bidders to voluntary corporate social responsibility – CSR – rules can be turned into a professional capability condition only with reference to contracts whose object has a social component.[106]

Specific attention is paid to environmental management. Under Article 48(2) (f) Directive 2004/18/EC, for public works contracts and public services contracts, and only in appropriate cases, procuring entities may ask for 'indication of the environmental management measures that the economic operator will be able to apply when performing the contract.' The provision is specified by Article 50, the title of which reads 'Environmental management standards', under which

> 'Should contracting authorities, in the cases referred to in Article 48 (2) (f), require the production of certificates drawn up by independent bodies attesting the compliance of the economic operator with certain environmental management standards, they shall refer to the Community Eco-Management and Audit Scheme (EMAS) or to environmental management standards based on the relevant European or international standards certified by bodies conforming to Community law or the relevant European or international standards concerning certification. They shall recognise equivalent certificates from bodies established in other Member States. They shall also accept other evidence of equivalent environmental management measures from economic operators.'[107]

Pending new legislation, EMAS are ruled by Regulation 2001/761/EC allowing voluntary participation by organisations in a European Eco-Management

102. Art. 48(2)(a and b).
103. Art. 48(2)(c and d).
104. Art. 48(2)(e and g); see also (i) with reference to the proportion of the contract which the services provider intends possibly to subcontract.
105. COM(2001) 566 final, point 1.3.2.; see also Art. VIII(b) of the GPA.
106. COM(2001) 566 final, 1.3.2. The Commission also considered that, 'In view of the references which may currently be required in order to assess the economic and financial standing of tenderers, it is not possible for social considerations to be included in such references' (point 1.3).
107. Same provision in Art. 52(3) of Directive 2004/17/EC.

and Audit Scheme. The Scheme is established for the evaluation and improvement of the environmental performance of 'organisations' whose activities has an impact on the environment. To this end, the environmental management system of the organisation is audited to check its compliance with environmental law and policy by independent bodies.[108]

As usual, to avoid placing limits on the competition, requirements concerning the proof of a condition for the participation in procurement procedures are not formalised. A potential bidder may demonstrate that it satisfies the procuring entity's requirements otherwise than by having EMAS.

The problem here is that very little guidance is provided in the Directive as to the situations which justify such a requirement. What is plain from Article 48(2)(f) is that this is never the case with supply contracts.[109] For the other contracts, procuring entities are left with the difficulty to find out which cases are 'appropriate'. Of limited assistance are the recitals, referring again to 'appropriate cases', but adding that these are cases 'in which the nature of the works and/or services justifies applying environmental management measures or schemes during the performance of a public contract.'[110]

What is sure is that the recital quoted above confirms the difficulty in rigorously distinguishing supposedly discrete categories, since a selection of candidates issue is mixed up here with a performance condition.

Finally, as was confirmed in the *Contse* case, a requirement concerning the place where economic operators have their offices and production centres will normally be considered discriminatory and not proportionate to any public interest invoked.[111] A similar fate would normally befall selection criteria based on the carbon footprint of a product (but the same would be true if they were worded as technical specifications or – and more probably – award criteria).[112]

108. See also COM(2001) 274 final, point II.2.2.2
109. COM(2001) 274 final, point II.2.2.2., also referred to the 'quality of the supplies', but this seems inconsistent with the wording of Art. 48(2)(f) of the new directive.
110. Recital 44; COM(2001) 274 final, point II.2.2.2., stipulates that, in order to be relevant, the EMAS requirements should have an impact 'on the capacity of a company'; this hardly helps.
111. Case C-234/03 *Contse and Others* [2005] ECR I-9315, paragraph 45 and 79.
112. See the discussion in S. Arrowsmith and P. Kunzlik 'EC regulation of public procurement' in S. Arrowsmith and P. Kunzlik (eds.) *Social and Environmental Policies in EC Procurement Law* above fn. 1, at 65, and S. Arrowsmith 'Application of the EC Treaty and directives to horizontal policies: a critical review', in the same collection, at 176 s.

## 5 Award criteria

Award criteria have been the battleground over which sustainability considerations have fought for recognition. The rules laid down by the ECJ in *Concordia Bus* have been codified in Article 53(1) (a) Directive 2004/18/EC. Under this provision,

'[...] when the award is made to the tender most economically advantageous from the point of view of the contracting authority, various criteria linked to the subject-matter of the public contract in question, for example, quality, price, technical merit, aesthetic and functional characteristics, environmental characteristics, running costs, cost-effectiveness, after-sales service and technical assistance, delivery date and delivery period or period of completion, or.'[113]

The link to the subject-matter of the contract is clearly spelt out. The corresponding recital in the Directive stresses the need that contract 'be awarded on the basis of objective criteria which ensure compliance with the principles of transparency, non-discrimination and equal treatment and which guarantee that tenders are assessed in conditions of effective competition.' As a consequence, the criteria chosen,

'[...] taken as a whole, must make it possible to determine the most economically advantageous tender for the contracting authority. The determination of these criteria depends on the object of the contract since they must allow the level of performance offered by each tender to be assessed in the light of the object of the contract, as defined in the technical specifications and the value for money of each tender to be measured. In order to guarantee equal treatment, the criteria for the award of the contract should enable tenders to be compared and assessed objectively. If these conditions are fulfilled, economic and qualitative criteria for the award of the contract, such as meeting environmental requirements, may enable the contracting authority to meet the needs of the public concerned, as expressed in the specifications of the contract. Under the same conditions, a contracting authority may use criteria aiming to meet social requirements, in response in particular to the needs – defined in the specifications of the contract – of particularly disadvantaged groups of people to which those receiving/using the works, supplies or services which are the object of the contract belong.'[114]

The last indent is particularly restrictive. Taken literarily, it could lead to the conclusion that meeting the needs of disadvantaged people cannot be an additional object of the contract itself, being at best a side effect of contract per-

113. Same provision in Art. 55(1)(a) of Directive 2004/17/EC.
114. Those recalled are the most relevant passages of an inordinately long recital 46; see also recital 55 of Directive 2004/17/EC.

formance. To make it clearer by way of an giving an example, hiring long term unemployed for gardening services could hardly be considered to fall under the definition, since they cannot be said to be people 'using the works'.

As remarked by Charro: 'The need for some sort of relationship between the award criteria and the contract that is being attributed should prevent the use of overbroad secondary criteria, such as a vague reference to the environmental soundness of a product. It might also lead to a difference of treatment between environmental and other secondary criteria (such as social, political and human rights provisions), as with the latter the link to the specific nature of the product/service appears to be more tenuous. While ecological criteria can be subject to consideration by public authorities if carefully crafted, it will be more difficult – although certainly not unconceivable – to develop means of integrating social considerations at the award stage, apart from the narrow number of cases where the service that is going to be provided is specifically intended for a given category of disadvantaged persons. The exercise will be even more burdensome with relation to political/human rights provisions, which are rarely contract-specific.'[115]

This position is evidently shared by the Commission, which has always been and to some extent still seems to be quite suspicious of the use of secondary award criteria.[116] The position of the ECJ, as shown in *EVN*, is ambiguous at best.[117]

115. P. Charro 'Case note to *Concordia Bus Finland*' 40 [2003] C.M.L.Rev. 187; see also P. Braun 'Selection of Bidders and Contract Award Criteria: The Compatibility of Practice in PFI Procurement with European Law' (2001) 10 P.P.L.R. 9; another facet of the same problem is whether some aspects which are relevant in the selection phase of bidders could also be considered at the award stage; generally speaking the case law is still uncertain on this issue: S. Treumer 'The Distinction between Selection and Award Criteria in EC Public Procurement Law: A Rule without Exception?' (2009) 18 P.P.L.R. 103.

116. In the communication 'Public Procurement in the European Union' (COM(1998) 143 final) the Commission considered it legitimate to take environmental considerations into account for the purpose of choosing the economically most advantageous tender overall, if the organiser of the tender procedure itself benefits directly from the ecological qualities of the product. See also COM(2001) 274 final, point II.3. and COM(2001) 566 final, 1.4.1., which further maintained that an 'economic advantage' to the procuring entity was required. The Commission has partially softened its stance in COM(2008) 400 final, point 3.2. 'Award criteria, if given a significant weighting, may however give an important signal to the market place. Depending on the type of product and the number and importance of the other – non environmental – award criteria, a weighting of 15 % or more could be considered 'significant'.'

117. *Supra.*

More generally, as already remarked, the limits to the admissibility of mixed contracts and the rules applicable to them has yet to be determined satisfactorily by the case law. From this perspective, an indication as to the legality of trying at killing two birds with just one contract could be drawn from Directive 2009/33/EC on the promotion of clean and energy-efficient road transport vehicles.[118] Different recitals point at diverging policy considerations. One is clearly in the mainstream of the better value for money philosophy, claiming that 'Including energy consumption, CO2 emissions, and pollutant emissions in the award criteria does not impose higher total costs but rather anticipates operational lifetime costs in the procurement decision.'[119] The autonomous policy value of emissions reduction is however quite plain in another recital, quite honestly admitting that 'Clean and energy-efficient vehicles initially have a higher price than conventional ones. Creating sufficient demand for such vehicles could ensure that economies of scale lead to cost reductions.'[120]

Under Article 5 (3), as an alternative to setting technical specifications for energy and environmental performance, procuring entities may either use environmental impacts as award criteria or monetise them for inclusion in the purchasing decision, according to the methodology for the calculation of operational lifetime costs set out in Article 6. Of the impacts that must be considered, however, only one is evidently benefiting procuring entities not institutionally responsible for the protection of the environment and human health, namely energy consumption. The other two, emissions of CO2 and of NOx, NMHC and particulate matter have nothing to do with lifetime costs as traditionally understood.[121]

118. The preamble to the Directive makes it clear that 'Mandatory application of criteria for the procurement of clean and energy-efficient vehicles does not preclude the inclusion of other relevant award criteria. It also does not prevent the choice of retrofitted vehicles upgraded for higher environmental performance. Such other relevant award criteria may also be included in procurements subject to Directives 2004/17/EC or 2004/18/EC, provided they are linked to the subject-matter of the contract, do not confer an unrestricted freedom of choice on the contracting authority or contracting entity, are expressly mentioned and comply with the fundamental principles of the Treaty' (Rec. 24).
119. Rec. 20.
120. Rec. 13; see also COM(2008) 400 final, point 1.1.
121. See COM(2008) 400 final, point 1.1., fn. 4: 'Life cycle costs should cover the purchase price and associate costs (delivery, installation, commissioning ...), operating costs (including energy, spare parts, maintenance) and end-of-life costs such as decommissioning, removal and disposal». Accordingly, COM(2001) 274 final, point

In any case, the provisions on contract performance to be analysed in the next chapter clearly show that public procurement contracts may include a secondary object besides the works, supplies, and services being at their core. This being so, and considering that Directive 2009/33/EC stands for the propositions that secondary considerations may be indifferently taken into account at both contract drafting stage and as award criteria, the suspicion with which the Commission sees the reference to these considerations in the award stage is probably excessive.

Finally, under Article 55 (1) (d), bidders whose tender is suspected of being abnormally low must give convincing evidence to the contrary, also having regard to 'the compliance with the provisions relating to employment protection and working conditions in force at the place where the work, service or supply is to be performed.'[122]

Contractors have to comply with binding rules concerning the environment and the welfare of workers of general application in a given Member State or in a part thereof, even when not expressly recalled in the technical specifications. If binding rules were breached in the past, the bidder may be disqualified. In case of abnormally low offers, the high risk of future breach may lead to the immediate exclusion of the bid. As it will be shown below, the Commission considers respecting these rules as contract performance conditions.

## 6 Contract performance conditions

Since *Beentjes* the EU Commission has tried setting aside contract performance conditions as a separate issue,[123] distinguished from technical specifications as a way to mitigate the possibly disruptive effect of taking secondary considerations into account.[124] The Commission went so far as to intimate

II.3.3., concluded that 'As a general rule, externalities are not borne by the purchaser, but by society as a whole and therefore do not qualify as award criteria.'

122. See also Art. 57(1)(d) of Directive 2004/17/EC.

123. The whole discussion centers around a short paragraph in *Beentjes*. The Court held that 'A condition such as the employment of long-term unemployed persons is an additional specific condition and must therefore be mentioned in the notice, so that contractors may become aware of its existence' (paragraph 36).

124. According to J. Arnould 'A Turning Point in the Use of Additional Award Criteria? above, at NA16, however, 'The Commission's distinction between selection and award criteria on the one hand, and performance conditions on the other hand, has

that such clauses or conditions 'should not be (disguised) technical specifications.'[125]

In this conceptual framework, Artcile 26 Directive 2004/18/EC, stipulates that

'Contracting authorities may lay down special conditions relating to the performance of a contract, provided that these are compatible with Community law and are indicated in the contract notice or in the specifications. The conditions governing the performance of a contract may, in particular, concern social and environmental considerations.'[126]

The provision benefits from some clarification in the preamble which, apart from cautioning against direct or indirect discrimination, indicates that these conditions may

'[...] be intended to favour on-site vocational training, the employment of people experiencing particular difficulty in achieving integration, the fight against unemployment or the protection of the environment. For instance, mention may be made, amongst other things, of the requirements – applicable during performance of the contract – to recruit long-term job-seekers or to implement training measures for the unemployed or young persons, to comply in substance with the provisions of the basic International Labour Organisation (ILO) Conventions, assuming that such provisions have not been implemented in national law, and to recruit more handicapped persons than are required under national legislation.'[127]

It is doubtful whether contract performance conditions are really distinguishable from technical specifications and if the distinction – if any – has the consequences the Commission pretends to draw from it.[128] Under Article 23(1), 'The technical specifications as defined in point 1 of Annex VI shall be set out in the contract documentation.' Annex VI stipulates that in the case of public works contracts 'technical specification' means 'the totality of the

been rejected by the Court' in Case C-225/98 *Commission* v *France* [2000] ECR I-7445.

125. COM(2001) 566 final, point 1.6.; the Communication goes on: 'They should not have any bearing on the assessment of the suitability of tenderers on the basis of their economic, financial and technical capability, or on the award criteria'; see also COM(2001) 274 final, point 4.
126. See also Art. 38 of Directive 2004/17/EC.
127. See Rec. 44 of Directive 2004/17/EC.
128. 'Public Procurements. Regional and social aspects' COM(1989) 400 final, at IV.2; see critically P. Kunzlik 'The procurement of 'green' energy', above fn., 393 f; S. Arrowsmith 'Application of the EC Treaty and directives to horizontal policies: a critical review' above fn. 2, at 207 f.

technical prescriptions contained in particular in the tender documents, defining the characteristics required of a material, product or supply, which permits a material, a product or a supply to be described in a manner such that it fulfils the use for which it is intended by the contracting authority. These characteristics shall include levels of environmental performance, design for all requirements (including accessibility for disabled persons) and conformity assessment, performance, safety or dimensions, including the procedures concerning quality assurance, terminology, symbols, testing and test methods, packaging, marking and labelling and production processes and methods. They shall also include rules relating to design and cost, the test, inspection and acceptance conditions for works and methods or techniques of construction and all other technical conditions which the contracting authority is in a position to prescribe, under general or specific regulations, in relation to the finished works and to the materials or parts which they involve.'[129]

This definition is all encompassing. It includes not just environmental performances, but also production processes and methods. The distinction is even more blurred now when, as was recalled above, Article 23 (3) (b) Directive 2004/18/EC allows technical specifications to be formulated in terms of performance requirements.[130] In case of service procurements, for instance, performance of the contract and performance of the service cannot be distinguished anyway. It is therefore far from clear why contract performance conditions should be differentiated from technical specifications, also considering that both are subject to the same requirements as to transparency and non discrimination.[131]

The Commission seeks to differentiate technical specifications and contract performance conditions as if the breach of the latter could only be relevant during the execution of the contract. This is a prospective rather than retrospective approach, meaning that in the event of a breach of these rules the

129. A similar definition is then given for the technical specification in supplies and services contracts.

130. See also Ch. McCrudden *Buying Social Justice*, above, fn. 1, 539 ff.; the Author, however, accepts 'contract conditions' as a discrete entity (at 563 ff.).

131. See also Art. 4(6) of Regulation of the European Parliament and of the Council 2007/1370/EC on public passenger transport services by rail and by road, 'Where competent authorities, in accordance with national law, require public service operators to comply with certain quality standards, these standards shall be included in the tender documents and in the public service contracts'; see COM(2001) 566 final, last paragraph of point 3.2.1.2.

contracting authority will have recourse to remedies ranging from penalties to termination of the contract.[132]

Again, the distinction may hold good in some cases of supplies procurements, when goods already manufactured are purchased. In these cases, the conformity of the goods to the technical requirements could be measured *ex ante*. But this is not the case with works, services, and other supply contracts. Breaches of technical specifications usually occur during contract implementation.[133]

Whatever might be the right characterisation of contract performance conditions, it is plain that, just as with technical specifications, their legality will depend on a balance between the need to respect the freedom of choice of procuring entities as to what they want to purchase and the necessity to strike down clauses meant to protect national or local economic operators.[134] In this respect, the clauses concerning the employment of long term unemployed persons or other disadvantaged groups will presumably continue to be problematic.[135]

## 7 Conclusions

European Union law is trying to strike a delicate balance between competition and secondary objectives.[136] Sustainable procurement is not just a passing fashion. It makes sense to spend taxpayers' money having in mind not just what procuring entities may buy but also how they may at the same time pursue other deserving objectives in both protecting the environment and so-

132. COM(2001) 566 final, point 1.6., states that 'the contract conditions need not be met at the time of submitting the tender'.
133. The same limits seems to affect the attempt made by S. Arrowsmith and P. Kunzlik 'EC regulation of public procurement' in S. Arrowsmith and P. Kunzlik (eds.) *Social and Environmental Policies in EC Procurement Law*, above fn. 1, at 60 ff. (but see also in the same collection S. Arrowsmith 'Application of the EC Treaty and directives to horizontal policies: a critical review', at 164 ff.) to equate contract performance conditions with sales arrangements as defined under the well-known Joined Cases C-267/91 and C-268/91 *Keck and Mithouard* [1993] ECR I-6097 to lessen the risk that they be qualified as restrictions to trade.
134. The already mentioned clause relevant in *Storebaelt* case: *C*-243/89, *Commission* v *Denmark* [1993] ECR-I 3353, would clearly not be permissible.
135. See e.g. S. Arrowsmith and P. Kunzlik 'EC regulation of public procurement', above fn., at 78 f.
136. On the 'linkage' between different policy objectives see Ch. McCrudden *Buying Social Justice. Equality, Government Procurement, & Legal Change* above, fn. 1

cial rights. The danger of hidden protectionism, of beggar thy neighbour policies, is however always present and European institutions, the Commission foremost among them, are not ready to lower their attention. Public procurement law is still about the freedom to provide goods and services in other Member States, and national rules purportedly protecting other overriding public interests must be in conformity with the Treaty on the Functioning of the European Union.[137]

The new generation of Directives has built on the case law and the Commission's Communications allowing Member States to refer to environmental and social considerations when designing their procurement policies. At times, specific European legislation compels reference to these considerations. Most of the time, however, it is just an option left to Member States. To pursue environmental and social goals and to allow sustainable development, the Commission is working hard – but not without some missteps – to give procuring entities indications as to what is permissible and what is not because it infringes EU Treaty rules on free movement.[138]

It should not come as a surprise to find out that Commission's efforts are more advanced when it comes to the environment. In 2003 the Communication on Integrated Product Policy recommended to Member States to adopt a national action plan on Green Public Procurements by the end of 2006.[139] More recently, to help Member State to more easily navigate GPP, a handbook on environmental public procurement (buying green) was published.[140]

In 2008 a Communication on Public procurement for a better environment was issued as part of the Action Plan on Sustainable Consumption and Production and Sustainable Industrial Policy (SCP/SIP).[141] The potentially conflicting policies involved in sustainable procurements are clearly articulated:

> 'The basic concept of GPP relies on having clear and ambitious environmental criteria for products and services. A number of national criteria and national approaches to GPP have been developed. However, as the use of GPP increases, the criteria used by Member States should be compatible to avoid a distortion of the single market and a reduction of EU-wide competition. Having a single set of criteria would considerably reduce the administrative burden for economic operators and for public administrations implementing GPP. Com-

137. COM(2001) 566 final, point 3.2.1.1.
138. The 'institutional schizophrenia' affecting some of the Commission's efforts are underlined by S. Arrowsmith and P. Kunzlik 'EC regulation of public procurement' above fn., at 94
139. COM(2003) 302 final.
140. http://ec.europa.eu/environment/gpp/pdf/buying_green_handbook_en.pdf
141. COM(2008) 400 final.

mon GPP criteria would be of a particular benefit to companies operating in more than one Member State as well as SMEs (whose capacity to master differing procurement procedures is limited).'[142]

The Commission is now working 'to endorse the existing and establish further common GPP criteria for more product groups, in close cooperation with the Member States and relevant stakeholders. Common GPP criteria have the advantage of avoiding market distortions and reduced competition which could arise as a result of differing national GPP criteria.'[143] A communication on integrating social aspects in public procurement is eagerly awaited.[144] These initiatives by the EU Commission show how much further clarification of the legal issues surrounding sustainable public procurements is needed.

## Bibliography

S. Arrowsmith, 'The E.C. procurement directives, national procurement policies and better governance: the case for a new approach' (2002) 27 E.L.Rev. 3.

S. Arrowsmith and P. Kunzlik (eds.), *Social and Environmental Policies in EC Procurement Law* (Cambridge, Cambridge University Press, 2009).

P. Charro, 'Case note to *Concordia Bus Finland*' 40 [2003] C.M.L.Rev. 184.

M. Dischendorfer, 'The Rules on Award Criteria Under the EC Procurement Directives and the Effect of Using Unlawful Criteria: The EVN Case' 13 (2204) PPLR NA83.

Th. Gliozzo, 'L'admissibilité d'un critère environnemental au regard de la réglementation communautaire des marchés' Act. Jur. Dr. Adm. 2004, 334.

Ch. McCrudden, *Buying Social Justice. Equality, Government Procurement, & Legal Change* (Oxford, UPO, 2007).

142. Point 1.3.
143. Point 3.2.
144. http://ec.europa.eu/social/main.jsp?langId=it&catId=89&newsId=417

# II. Green Public Procurement and Socially Responsible Public Procurement: An Analysis of Danish Regulation and Practice

*by Steen Treumer*

## 1 Introduction

Denmark is amongst the Member States in the European Union (EU) with the highest level of Green Public Procurement (hereafter GPP)[1] and an analysis of Danish regulation and practice is of particular interest for this reason. The interest of the reader should also be triggered by the fact that this high level of GPP is *not* the result of widespread national regulation imposing GPP in the field of public procurement. This fact makes it relevant to consider why the level of GPP is so high in Denmark which is one of the issues that will be addressed in this article. Socially Responsible Public Procurement (hereafter SRPP) is another hot issue in Denmark. However, the use of social considerations is clearly more limited and hesitant than the use of environmental considerations.[2] This fundamental difference in the level of application is rather surprising as these types of considerations both imply that the procuring entity takes non-economic advantages into account and for this reason they

1. See 'Collection of statistical information on Green Public Procurement in the EU' which can be found on the following webpage http://www.ecofys.nl. This study covered ten product groups in the seven best Member States in the European Union including Denmark.
2. See also the study of Martin Trybus on social considerations in public procurement in Denmark where he concludes that 'It can be said that Denmark is only at the beginning of integrating SRPP in procurement contracts'. The study can be found on the webpage of the European Commission and is a part of a 'Legal and Policy Review of SRPP frameworks in selected EU Member States' at http://ec.europa.eu/social/main.jsp?catId=331&langId=en&newsId=417&furtherNews=yes and the study of Trybus on Denmark was completed in June 2008.

have typically been referred to as 'secondary considerations'.[3] It appears relevant to consider the background for the fundamental difference between GPP and SRPP which will also be a part of the analysis in this chapter.

The purpose of this chapter is to analyse the regulation and practice with regard to GPP and SRPP in Denmark and to identify trends, problems and challenges. Section 2 of this article considers regulation of the area in the broadest sense and includes also circulars and guidance where the latter has a very high impact in Denmark in practice especially when it comes to environmental considerations. Section 3 concerns self-regulation with focus on partnerships for the promotion of GPP which is an interesting phenomenon and apparently not widespread in the Member States of the EU. It could therefore possibly be a source of inspiration in other countries. Section 4 provides an analysis of Danish procurement practice in this area which is primarily based on tender notices in the Official Journal of the EU and the data has been supplemented by interviews with various contracting authorities. This part of the analysis is presumably of general interest also to non-lawyers. Section 5 is about disputes related to the use of environmental and social considerations. The Danish case law is relatively limited in this area which appears to be in conformity with the general trend in other Member States of the EU. Nevertheless, several of the Danish cases are excellent examples of the problems and breaches that are likely to materialise when these considerations are taken in a concrete procedure. Finally, section 6 contains the conclusion of the analysis.

## 2 Regulation (legislation, circulars and guidance)

As pointed out in the introduction above a contracting entity applying environmental considerations and/or social considerations will as a clear starting point[4] not gain a direct economic advantage. It therefore becomes relevant to consider whether the application of this type of considerations is legal where

3. As opposed to the primary considerations closely linked to the economic advantages such as price, quality and service costs.
4. This is the main rule and it is of cause possible to identify exceptions. As an example some environment friendly products have lower energy consumption and longer life span compared to traditional products and you will therefore gain an economic advantage from buying these instead.

there is not a clear legal basis for the use of secondary considerations.[5] GPP and SRPP will normally infer extra costs on the contracting entity and a tax payer could therefore question whether such an approach is in accordance with the requirements of administrative law and more specifically the principle of legality. The answer to this question of a more general nature is – in a Danish context – that there is no doubt that a contracting entity can lawfully include environmental or social considerations as they are in the general interest, even though this implies a higher price for needed products or services.[6] A duty to apply environmental considerations on equal terms with other considerations even follows explicitly from the legislation concerning some contracting authorities, cf. section 2.1 of this article.

The public procurement Directives leave considerable discretion to the Member States and thereby room for national regulation in the field of public procurement. In some Member States the national legislator has used this discretion to a large extent whereas the approach in other Member States has been cautious and the supplementary regulation at national level limited. The Danish public procurement regulation clearly falls in the latter category which also can be seen from the implementation of the public procurement Directives. The Danish legislator has used an atypical approach when the public procurement Directives were implemented. The exact text of the Directives was maintained when they were implemented and the legislator thereby basically refrained from making any substantial changes to the text of the Directives. It is important to be aware of this fundamental aspect of the Danish regulation of the area of public procurement.

However, this does not imply that there is no legislation or other sorts of regulation in the area which has decisive or considerable impact on the behaviour of contracting authorities in Denmark. One sort of regulation is legislation that *indirectly* regulates the area of public procurement for instance by establishing environmental or social requirements that must be complied with. Like in other Member States, there are numerous examples of provi-

5. The application of environmental or social considerations will in some instances follow from the law i.e. where the law requires a public building to be accessible for a handicapped person or where the law imposes a specific standard in order to protect the environment.
6. See also Simon Evers Hjelmborg, Peter Stig Jakobsen, Sune Troels Poulsen, *Public Procurement Law – the EU directive on public contracts*, 2006, 1. ed. p. 207.

sions of this type[7] but the analysis in the following subsections of the article will be on *direct* regulation of the area of public procurement even though the word regulation is used in a the broadest sense and includes public policy and guidance from public authorities. As there are fundamental differences in the level of application of environmental and social considerations the regulation of these two types of considerations will be divided in two subsections.

### 2.1 Environmental considerations

It follows from §6 of the Environmental Protection Act that all public authorities shall act to promote the purpose of this law when they undertake public works, run public companies, *procure* or consume. Furthermore, it follows from §51(7) of the same act that all State entities and State owned or controlled companies must take environmental considerations into account when they procure goods and services and that these considerations must be applied on equal terms with other economic considerations such as price, quality, conditions of delivery etc. The relevant Ministry[8] issued Circular no. 26 of 7 February 1995 on considerations of the environment and use of energy in public procurement. It follows from this Circular that the state institutions or companies addressed by the Circular must formulate a deliberate environmental and energy policy, elaborate an action plan for the implementation of this policy and must be able to document the achieved results. It also follows from this Circular that institutions must consider both the use of energy and costs of investments when they procure goods that consume energy and that the most energy effective[9] goods should be given preferential treatment, cf. §3 of the Circular. Recently a Circular on energy effectiveness in State institutions replaced an older version of a Circular on the same subject-matter. The aim of the Circular is to implement the decision of the government according to which the energy consumption of the State must be reduced by at least 10 per cent in 2011 compared to the level in 2006 and to reduce the water consumption of the State. All ministries and related institutions must procure energy efficient products unless this will not be 'profitable' from an assessment of considerations for the society and environmental considerations, cf. §6 of the Circular. The formulation of this provision is rather blurred whereas the formulation in the old version of the Circular

7. For instance provisions that establish that a public building must have a toilet for handicapped persons or provisions regulating the working environment at a building site.
8. At that time 'Miljø- og Energiministeriet'.
9. The term 'Energirigtige' in Danish is applied in the Circular.

seemed to give a clearer indication of the relevant assessment. It was stipulated in the former version of the Circular that the relevant institutions should buy energy efficient products unless they could establish that such products did not live up to substantial requirements as regards function, quality, environment and cost effectiveness. As follows from the above, the Danish regulation on environmental considerations is more developed as regards State institutions whereas local and regional authorities enjoy a wider discretion.

The Competition Authority issued a guide on green public procurement in 2002 in collaboration with the Ministry of the Environment.[10] This guide takes its point of departure in the Interpretative Communication from the European Commission in COM (2001)274[11] on the EU law applicable to public procurement and the possibilities for integrating environmental considerations into public procurement.

Furthermore, the Ministry of the Environment has issued a number of so-called Environmental Guidances[12] on its website.[13] These Guidances are of the utmost importance in practice as they appear to be the preferred source of inspiration when Danish contracting authorities draft environmental requirements, cf. also the analysis of a recent study monitoring the current level of GPP in the seven best performing Member States.[14]

### 2.2 Social considerations

The direct regulation of public procurement and social considerations appears to be very limited. However, it follows from the public procurement Directives that a tenderer may be excluded from the tender procedures where he has not fulfilled obligations relating to the payment of social security contributions or taxes in accordance with the legal provisions of the country in which he is established or with those of the country of the contracting authority.[15] It also follows from the public procurement Directives that the Member States shall specify, in accordance with their national law and having regard

10. The guide has the following title: 'Offentlige grønne indkøb – en vejledning i mulighederne for at varetage miljøhensyn i forbindelse med afholdelse af udbud', 2002, 16 pages.
11. 'Community law' in the title of the communication.
12. In Danish called 'miljøvejledninger'.
13. http://www.mim.dk
14. Cf. 'Collection of Statistical information on Green Public Procurement in the EU' which is a study published in 2008 available on the website of the European Commission, *supra* note 2. According to this study the environmental guidances were used by 69 % of the correspondents in the survey.
15. See the Public Sector Directive Art. 45(2)(e) and 45(2)(f).

for Community law, the implementing conditions for this paragraph. It follows from the Danish legislation[16] that the contracting authority shall consider whether the relevant taxes or social contributions have been paid in Denmark or in the country where the tenderers are established. As will be further elaborated below in section 5.2 of this chapter this legislation has given rise to an interesting dispute involving a cross-border tenderer.[17]

The Danish Competition Authority issued a Guide outlining the possibilities of taking social considerations in public procurement in 2004.[18] Like the guidance on environmental considerations mentioned in section 2.1 the Guide on this area was also heavily inspired by the Interpretative Communication of the European Commission.[19] This follows explicitly from the introduction to the Guide on p. 3. and there are several explicit references to the interpretation of the European Commission in the Guide. As will be further elaborated below in section 4 of this chapter the use of social considerations at the award stage of the tender procedures is a clear exception in Danish public procurement practice which might be connected to certain wordings in the Guide of the Competition Authority.

## 3 Self-regulation

As mentioned above in section 2 the Danish regulation on environmental considerations is more developed as regards State institutions whereas local and regional authorities enjoy wider discretion. Nevertheless, the use of environmental considerations is widespread also when the contracting entity is a local or regional authority and the local authorities in general appear to promote in particular environmental consideration to a higher degree than they are obliged to according to the Danish regulation of the area.

A recent and very interesting Danish phenomenon is self-regulation based on partnerships for the promotion of GPP. This appears not to be common in

16. Cf. Law no. 336 of 13 May 1997 § 1 read in conjunction with § 2(2).
17. See the remarks in section 5.2. to the case dated 29 October 2009, *Swedlock AB's klage over Servicestyrelsens udbud af låseenheder* which was based on a complaint to the Competition Authority from a Swedish company.
18. The guide has the title 'Sociale hensyn ved offentlige indkøb – en vejledning i mulighederne for at tage sociale hensyn ved udbud'.
19. Com (2001) 566. Communicative interpretation on the Community law applicable to public procurement and the possibilities for integrating social considerations into public procurement.

Europe but could possibly be a source of inspiration in other Member States of the EU. The Danish Ministry of the Environment and the 3 largest municipalities in Copenhagen, Aarhus and Odense concluded a partnership for the promotion of Green Public Procurement in 2006. The parties to this agreement committed themselves to a green public procurement policy and to implement a number of concrete measures for the procurement of environmentally friendly goods. Subsequently a number of other municipalities have joined the partnership and other municipalities are encouraged to join. The partnership, its aim and obligations, current participants etc. is described in further detail on a webpage.[20] The parties of the partnership are all committed to a procurement policy where environmental considerations are a priority and obliged to publicise their policy on their webpages. A number of concrete obligations are also stipulated in the agreement and related to a variety of goods i.e. computers, copy paper, cleansing agent and toys and are quite far-reaching.

Another partnership is called 'Dogme 2000' and is also a partnership between municipalities which was formed as early as 2000. The participating municipalities agreed to be frontrunners in the efforts for the creation of a better environment and agreed on a set of rules for the co-operation. There are currently 8 municipalities in the partnership and it is based on the following dogmas: You should measure the impact of humans on the environment, you shall elaborate a plan for improvement of the environment and the work with the environment shall have a local foundation.

Finally, it is quite evident that many contracting authorities, on their own initiative, ensure the observance of environmental considerations to an extent that they are not obliged to by legal or administrative regulation. The background for this seems to be a general attitude of politicians and decision-makers in favour of environmental considerations. A clear majority of the citizens are also in favour of this approach according to various polls.

## 4 Application

A part of the study behind this article has been a structured analysis of the Danish practice with regard to the use of environmental and social considerations. The basis for this has been the collection and analysis of Danish tender

20. See 'Partnerskabet for offentlige grønne indkøb' on http://www.mst.dk

notices from the Tender Electronic Daily (hereafter TED)[21] supplemented with interviews with 15 contracting authorities.

### 4.1 Environmental considerations

In order to identify procedures where environmental considerations had been taken, a catalogue of search words[22] related to environmental considerations were applied with regards to Danish tender notices in TED from more than the past five years.[23] The total number of these notices was 7,790 and 2,261 of these notices contained the search words relating to environmental considerations. As it was not possible to analyse such a large number of notices in further detail 100 recent tender notices were selected.[24] Subsequently another 100 tender notices from 2007[25] was analysed to detect whether there was significant differences between the trends in the tender notices from the two periods of time. The following figures explicitly refer to the most recent tender notices in 2009.

Thirteen of the tender notices proved to be irrelevant for various reasons. The task in itself was of an environmental nature in 21 of the tender notices for example consultancy on reduction of the use of energy or the collection of waste and assessment of the degree of pollution on a piece of land. There were contract clauses relating to the environment in nine of the notices establishing requirements for a sworn declaration of compliance with the environmental legislation, active efforts in order to reduce the negative impact on the environment or references to more detailed contract clauses on environmental protection in the supplementing tender documentation. However, it should be noted that apparently such standard clauses are very common according to the interviewed contracting authorities and in accordance with the from above this could not be established on the basis of the selected tender notices. A couple of frequently applied standard contracts also contain environmental contract clauses.[26]

21. http://ted.europa.eu
22. The following words in Danish: 'environment', climate, green, environmental consideration(s), sustainability, ecological and ecology'.
23. From 1 January 2005 until 9 March 2010.
24. The first 100 tender notices after 1 September 2009 which appeared relevant based on the selected search words.
25. From Januar 2007 until April 2007.
26. The contracts of SKI and of IKA (see §20, 24 and 25 of this contract on environment, social responsibility and ethics).

1,999 of these contained the search words relating to social considerations. As it was not possible to analyse such a large number of notices in further detail 100 recent tender notices were selected.[33] Subsequently another 100 tender notices from 2007[34] were analysed to detect whether there were significant differences between the trends in the tender notices from the two periods. This was not the case and the following figures explicitly refer to the analysis of the most recent tender notices in 2009.

A very large part of these tender notices proved to be of minor interest. 40 of the tender notices had as the only social consideration the requirement of a payment of social security contributions and another 27 were not of interest for other reasons.

In twelve of the tender notices the contract was of a social nature but without explicit reference to social considerations. These tender notices, for instance, related to transportation of disabled persons or the building of an old people's home. Seven tender notices contained a requirement of information on elements of a social nature for instance compliance with working environmental regulation or a personnel management policy. In some instances such a policy was clearly a qualification requirement.

Social considerations were in general not part of the award criteria except for considerations of the working environment which was a sub-criterion in two tender notices with a relative weighting of 8 per cent and 10 per cent. The fact that social considerations are exceptional at the award stage was confirmed by the interviews. The uncertainty of the state of law with regard to social considerations appears to be one of the elements behind this practice. It should also be noted that the guide of the Danish Competition Authority outlining the possibilities of taking social considerations into account in public procurement does not encourage contracting authorities to take social considerations into account at the award stage.[35]

Eleven tender notices contained references to contract terms or requirements of sworn declarations of a social nature. It was remarkable that about 80 per cent of the tender notices with social clauses related to cleaning services. These clauses appeared to be inspired by the Guide from The Danish

33. The first 100 tender notices after 1 September 2009 which appeared relevant based on the selected search words.
34. From Januar 2007 until April 2007.
35. It is recommended that social considerations at the award stage is only applied where the contracting entity is certain that this is legal, cf. p. 4 of the guide from 2004 with the title 'Sociale hensyn ved offentlige indkøb – en vejledning i mulighederne for at tage sociale hensyn ved udbud'.

Competition Authority outlining the possibilities of taking social considerations into account in public procurement in 2004.[36]

As mentioned above, a number of interviews were conducted with the aim of shedding further light on the practical application and its challenges. The contracting authorities were asked about the cost of social considerations. The answers were very different. Contracting authorities without experience with the application of social clauses estimated that this would increase the price whereas the municipality of Copenhagen which frequently applies social clauses considered that this by and large did not have an impact on the price. However, none of the interviewed had made concrete studies of the economical consequences of social clauses. When asked about the background for the more limited use of social considerations various answers were given. Many stated that they knew that social considerations could be taken even though they had not done this so far. The majority were uncertain of how to do this except in the form of a standard clause. One contracting authority explicitly stated that taking social considerations into account would increase the price and this was incompatible with an obligation to reduce the budget. The overall impression was that the state of the law was considered blurred and that it was troublesome to integrate social considerations in concrete tender procedures.

The Municipality of Copenhagen is, as mentioned above, very experienced with the use of social considerations. The application of these has given rise to a number of problems and challenges. As an example it can be troublesome to integrate a clause about employment of apprentices. The clause can only relate to the task tendered out itself, whereas the apprentice needs to get a broader working experience and the duration of the apprenticeship has to fit the duration of the public contract. It was also mentioned that the other parts of the administration of the Municipality were sceptical about the link between public contracts and social considerations. Nevertheless, the experiences in some areas were very positive. Social clauses on long-time unemployed with regard to cleaning services were mentioned as an example with the addition that this is assessed so as not to increase the price.[37]

36. The guide has the title 'Sociale hensyn ved offentlige indkøb – en vejledning i mulighederne for at tage sociale hensyn ved udbud'.
37. This assumption is supported by an interview referred in the article 'Sociale klausuler har kun lille betydning for prisen' [Social clauses have only little impact on the price], written by journalist Annemette Schultz Jørgensen and published on http://www.udbudsportalen.dk.

# 5 Disputes

There is only a limited number of Danish public procurement cases involving environmental and social considerations. However, some of these cases are very interesting because they illustrate fundamental problems and the outcome of several of these cases has been surprising and even questionable. Nevertheless, the lack of case law in the area and the character of the breaches in the limited case law indicate that the abuse of environmental and social considerations by Danish contracting authorities is clearly the exception.

## 5.1 Environmental considerations

There are a limited number of cases involving environmental considerations but the majority of these cases are not of particular interest for the purposes of this chapter. They concern public procurement issues of a more general nature and are not linked to a problem that is specific and exclusively linked to the fact that the contracting authorities have applied environmental considerations. As an example, many Danish disputes partly concerned the separation of selection and award criteria[38] and confusion of the criteria is common in European and Danish practice. A recent example of a breach of the EU public procurement rules in this respect can be found in the ruling of 15 December 2005, *Air Liquide Danmark A/S against Roskilde Amt, Storstrøms Amt and Vestsjællands Amt* from the Danish Complaints Board for Public Procurement. The contracting authority had applied a criterion 'environmental considerations' as a sub-criterion in the award criterion 'economically most advantageous tender', even though it was a selection criterion.

A recent and rather surprising development is a number of challenges of the bid evaluation of various contracting authorities relating to environmental sub-criteria. As the contracting authorities enjoy a wide discretion when it comes to the award and evaluation of the contract it was not to be expected that several tenderers would complain about the evaluation as such. The argumentation in this case law has essentially been that the bid of the complaining tender should have been given a higher score. As could be expected this argument has in general been rejected by the Complaints Board for Public

38. For a general analysis of this classical but also very interesting theme please see the Special Issue of the Public Procurement Law Review (PPLR 2009 no. 3 pp. 103-164) with an overview article by the undersigned and articles on the issue from Germany, France, Italy, Belgium, Norway and Denmark.

Procurement.[39] However, in the ruling of 14 July 2009, *Updata Danmark A/S mod Lyngby-Taarbæk Kommune* the Complaints Board established that the contracting authority had violated the principle of equal treatment by having evaluated the bid of the complainant as inferior to the other bids in relation to the sub-criteria 'environmental and energy circumstances'.

### 5.2 Social considerations

There is only a very limited number of Danish public procurement cases involving social considerations. Nevertheless, many these few cases are very interesting because they illustrate fundamental problems and, as with the cases on environmental consideration discussed above, the outcome of several of these cases has been surprising and even questionable.

There is hardly any case law where social considerations relating to goods or services have been challenged so the ruling of 16 October 1996, *Danske Vognmænd against Stevns Kommune* from the Danish Complaints Board for Public Procurement is an exception. A municipality had tendered out the refuse collection in the municipality and had taken special considerations with regard to the working environment of the refuse collectors into account. One reason for the tender was the increased requirements regarding the working environment in the Danish legislation but the municipality had clearly gone beyond the requirements of the law. The complainant, a professional organisation representing haulage contractor, contested various elements in the tender procedures including the use of the considerations regarding working conditions. First, the complainant argued rather surprisingly that the municipality was not entitled to take the working environment into account. Second, the complainant argued that the contracting authority was not entitled to establish requirements based on considerations regarding the working environment beyond what followed from the Danish legislation or Community legislation. The municipality had required the use of a specific product or similar which the Complaints Board found was a violation of the public procurement rules. Furthermore, the municipality had chosen a system regarding the treatment of the refuse bags with a number of advantages for the refuse collectors. The collectors should not carry the refuse bag, the opening and closure of the bags could take place without physical contact to the bags and the

39. See Ruling of 10 December 2008, *Nordjysk Kloak- og Industriservice A/S against Aalborg Kommune*, Ruling of 26 August 2009, *Barslund A/S against Københavns Kommune* and ruling of 1 October 2009, *Cimber Air A/S against Forsvarskommandoen*.

placement of a new bag could take place without strains on the backs of the collectors.

The Complaints Board held that the contracting authority had been entitled to establish considerations regarding the working environment beyond the requirements of the legislation and that the requirements were also not a violation of the Treaty provisions on the free movement of goods and on non-discrimination. The latter was interesting as the only producer of a vehicle for the collection of refuse that fulfilled the requirements based on considerations regarding the working environment was located in Denmark. This coincidence could make you wonder whether there in fact was an element of discrimination in the concrete case but the contracting authorities enjoy the widest discretion when it comes to deciding on which product or service it requires. The same phenomenon occurred in the well-known case from the ECJ in C-513/99, *Concordia Bus Finland* where the contracting authority's own transport undertaking was one of the few undertaking able to offer buses satisfying the environmental criteria established by the contracting authority or perhaps even the only tenderer which had a real possibility, cf. para 72 of the judgment. The ECJ concluded in this case that this fact was not in itself constituting a breach of the principle of equal treatment, cf. para 85 of the judgment.

The public procurement Directives ensure that the contracting authorities may take some social considerations into account when it comes to exclusion and assessment of the suitability of the tenderers, even though social considerations usually play a limited role in this phase of the tender procedure. There are hardly any Danish cases regarding the use of social considerations at this stage but one should be mentioned as it is both illustrative and concerns a fundamental issue. The case dated 29 October 2009, *Swedlock AB's klage over Servicestyrelsens udbud af låseenheder* was based on a complaint to the Competition Authority from the Swedish company Swedlock AB. This company had applied for qualification but had been rejected by the contracting authority as it had not attached a sworn declaration on fulfilment of obligations relating to the payment of social security contributions and taxes *in Denmark.* Instead the company had attached a declaration from the Swedish authorities concerning the fulfilment of its obligations regarding social security obligations and taxes in Sweden. It follows from the public procurement Directives that a tenderer may be excluded from the tender procedures where the tenderer has not fulfilled obligations relating to the payment of social security contributions or taxes in accordance with the legal provisions of the country in which he is established or with those of the country of the contracting authority.[40] It also follows from the public procurement Directives that the Member States shall specify, in accordance with their national law and having regard for Community law, the implementing conditions for this paragraph. It follows from the Danish legislation[41] that the contracting authority shall consider whether the relevant taxes or social contributions have been paid in Denmark or in the country where the tenderers are established. The contracting authority had complied with its obligations according to this legislation and had stipulated that the tenderers should present documentation with regard to the payment of taxes and social contributions in the country where it is established and in Denmark. The Danish Competition Authority considered that the contracting authority was entitled to reject the request for qualification as the Swedish company had not in time forwarded the sworn declaration as stipulated in the tender conditions. This approach will surely be perceived as very formalistic by many but it is in accordance with the general understanding of EU public procurement law in Denmark.

A recent complaints case from the Competition Authority regarding services of a social nature covered by Annex II B in the Public Sector Directive[42] gives another illustration of the usually very restrictive approach. However, contrary to the above-mentioned case it relates to the award phase of the tender procedure. In this case dated 3 December 2008, *Jobcenter Odenses udbud af beskæftigelsesopgaver* a tenderer had been rejected because it did not comply with a formal tender condition according to which each tender should have a maximum of six pages plus front page and annexes. Furthermore, it was stipulated that all questions and columns in the electronic tender form should be answered and filled out. The tenders of the complainant were all six pages. However, one page had been added to the electronic tender as a file with a scanned copy of the relevant signatures had been added. The Competition Authority assessed that the contracting authority had been both entitled and obliged to reject the tender as the condition followed explicitly from the tender conditions. Before reaching this conclusion the Authority quoted the an Interpretative Communication from the European Commission[43] and a case from the Danish Complaints Board[44] as a basis for this

40. See the Public Sector Directive Art. 45(2)(e) and 45(2)(f).
41. Cf. Law no. 336 of 13 May 1997 § 1 read in conjunction with §2(2).
42. A job centre's tender of various services including placement service to employment on flexible terms.
43. Commission interpretative communication on the Community law applicable to contract awards not or not fully subject to the provisions of the Public Procurement Directives (2006/C 179/02).

harsh and literal interpretation of the tender conditions according to which it is irrelevant whether the exceeding number of pages is due to content or pure formalities such as signature or date. It is submitted that this is a too restrictive interpretation of the principles underlying the public procurement rules which goes beyond what is necessary and a breach of the principle of proportionality. When a contracting authority stipulates that the tenders must not exceed a given number of pages, the underlying reason is that it has estimated that the given number of pages is sufficient and that it does not have or wish to use resources on considering more content – measured in pages. Surely it will not take any contracting authority more than a couple of minutes to print and relate to an extra page with a signature and it appears that the tenders of the complainant should not have been rejected on these grounds. It should also be pointed out that the tenderer in question did not get a competitive advantage as it did not have more pages to promote its services. Furthermore, the acceptance of such a restrictive approach gives the contracting authority that wishes to discriminate another tool and discourages tenderers in general from participating in tender procedures. The latter is the case regardless of whether the approach in general is extremely formalistic or if this is only the case if you are 'unlucky' to have your tender considered by a very cautious or pedantic contracting authority.

Social considerations also played a crucial role in a controversial case concerning termination of a tender procedure without an award as the contracting authority allegedly had based its decision on social considerations regarding its own employees. This case, *ISS Facility Services A/S and Danish Industri against Silkeborg Kommune*,[45] was recently considered by the Danish Court of Appeal (Vestre Landsret) and is now pending before the Danish Supreme Court. The case started with a complaint to the Competition Authority[46] and was then followed up by a ruling from the Danish Complaints Board for Public Procurement.[47]

44. Ruling of 6 August 2001, *Oxford Reseach against Faaborg Kommune*.
45. Judgment of 15 May 2009 from the Court of Appeal (V.L. B-0257-08).
46. Complaint of 5 April 2006 concerning the municipality of Silkeborg's termination of a tender procedure without an award. See the webpage of the Competition Authority under the date 22 November 2006 (the date of the completion of the initial treatment of the case within the Competition Authority).
47. The Competition Authority chose to submit a complaint to the Complaints Board for Public Procurement in continuation of the complaint it had received. This has only happened in very few cases, and the Competition Authority based this decision on the fundamental questions raised in the case.

The contracting authority was a municipality, and the tender related to the cleaning of a public school. The city council of the municipality terminated the tender procedures, as it assessed that the tender which was the economically most advantageous and fulfilled the stipulated contract terms concerning working environment, cleaning standard and quality could not satisfy the working conditions that it desired for the employees that currently undertook the cleaning and was presupposed to be employed by the winning tenderer. The tenderer had assessed that the cleaning could be done much faster than what was currently done and the city council estimated that it was completely unrealistic that the service could be rendered with this speed and quality while at the same time securing the desired working conditions for the employees. The city council therefore decided to opt for a new modernised type of in-house solution. It is worth stressing that the municipality had submitted an internal offer in this case and that this offer had been evaluated as the second least advantageous tender out of a total of six submitted tenders. Furthermore, the head of school, a committee on education in the municipality and apparently also the financial committee of the municipality had instead suggested the acceptance of the economically most advantageous tender. The case is an excellent example of the fundamental challenges regarding equal treatment and transparency that may occur when a tender procedure involves both an internal offer and external offers.

The Complaints Board held in its ruling of *24 April 2007, Konkurrencestyrelsen against Silkeborg Kommune* that the contracting authority had violated the principles of equal treatment of tenderers and transparency by termination of the tender procedure without an award. However, according to the judgment of 15 May 2009 of the Danish Court of Appeal, the municipality (Silkeborg Kommune) had not violated the EU principles of equal treatment of tenderers and of transparency when it terminated the tender procedures as outlined above. The implications of this ruling are far-reaching as it leaves contracting authorities an extremely wide discretion when it comes to the termination of the tender procedures without an award. The reasoning of the Court of Appeal has various weaknesses and is on some points at least highly questionable and, as mentioned above, the case is now pending before the Supreme Court.

## 6 Conclusion

Environmental and social considerations are considered as important and so-called hot topics[48] in Denmark. However, there are various fundamental differences between these two types of considerations. Public procurement and environmental considerations are regulated in greater detail than social considerations in Denmark and the practical application of these two different types of considerations is very different. The use of environmental considerations is widespread whereas the use of social considerations is rather limited. Another very important difference relates to the role of these types of considerations at the award stage of the tender procedure. The use of social considerations as sub-criteria in the award criterion the economically most advantageous tender is the exception, whereas many examples of environmental considerations as award criteria can easily be found. Furthermore, the relative weighting of the environmental sub-criteria is relatively high (10-20 per cent) which is noteworthy as environmental considerations as a starting point are not of direct economical value to the contracting authority. One of the interviewed contracting authorities even gave examples of a relative weighting of up to 40-50 per cent on tenders relating to toys. This illustrates the importance attributed to environmental considerations of at least some Danish contracting authorities.

The background for these fundamental differences is not evident from the research this article is based on. Nevertheless, it seems that there is considerable legal uncertainty regarding the use of social considerations which was stressed by several of the interviewed contracting authorities. Such legal uncertainty will surely have an impact in practice in Denmark, which is one of the countries in the EU where the EU public procurement rules are interpreted strictly and where the enforcement system ensures a very high degree of efficient enforcement.[49] In addition, many of the contracting authorities

48. Just like the closely related CSR – Corporate Social Responsibility.
49. The efficiency and restrictive approach could be illustrated in many ways. It only takes an extremely modest fee of about 500€ to bring a complaint before the Danish Complaints Board for Public Procurement and if the complainant loses the case it cannot be imposed to pay the legal costs of the contracting authority. The Complaints Board can also grant damages for a breach of the procurement rules even though it is not a court or tribunal within the Danish judiciary system. The Board has granted damages for the loss of profit in various cases whereas you have to search long for precedents of this in other national systems. The reader who is interested in documentation for the restrictive interpretation could read section 5.2 again as this section contains a couple of examples.

had the impression that social considerations are costly whereas this is not necessarily the case for a contracting authority buying green. In many instances it will pay off economically or at least not cost much to buy energy efficient products as for instance a light bulb which lasts longer and consumes less energy. This is not evident when it comes to a social clause concerning the long-time unemployed which also might scare relevant service providers away.

There could also be a difference in attitude to the two types of considerations. Environmental considerations in public procurement procedures are likely to be considered more relevant and important than social considerations by many Danish decision-makers. The reader should bear in mind that Denmark is one of the countries in the world with the highest taxes partly because of the so-called Danish welfare state that ensures a high degree of equality and a high degree of protection of the weakest in society. The existence of Danish partnerships for the promotion of GPP covered in section 3 above and the apparent lack of partnerships for the promotion of SRPP could be seen as an element confirming the difference in attitude as regards environmental and social considerations. These partnerships are a recent and very interesting Danish example of self-regulation which appears not to be common in Europe and it could possibly be a source of inspiration in other Member States of the EU.

There are only a limited number of Danish public procurement cases involving environmental and social considerations. In spite of their limited number some of these cases are very interesting because they illustrate fundamental problems and the outcome of several of these cases has been surprising and even questionable. Nevertheless, the lack of case law in the area and the character of the breaches in the limited case law indicate that the abuse of environmental and social considerations by the Danish contracting authorities is a clear exception.

## Bibiliography

Simon Evers Hjelmborg, Peter Stig Jakobsen, Sune Troels Poulsen, *EU-udbudsretten – Udbudsdirektivet for offentlige myndigheder*, Jurist- og Økonomforbundets Forlag: Copenhagen, 1st ed. 2005, pp.191-213.

Simon Evers Hjelmborg, Peter Stig Jakobsen, Sune Troels Poulsen, *Public Procurement Law – the EU directive on public contracts*, Jurist- og Økonomforbundets Forlag: Copenhagen, 2st ed. 2006, pp. 204-226.

Annemette Schultz Jørgensen, 'Sociale klausuler har kun lille betydning for prisen', 27 October 2009, http://www.udbudsportalen.dk

Ruth Nielsen, *Udbud af offentlige kontrakter*, Jurist- og Økonomforbundets Forlag: Copenhagen, 3rd ed. 2005, chapter 11, pp.291-314.

Jeppe Lefevre Olsen, 'CSR-hensyn i offentlige og udbudspligtige kontrakter', 4 December 2009, http://www.udbudsportalen.dk

Michael Steinicke and Lise Groesmeyer, *EU's Udbudsdirektiver med kommentarer*, Jurist- og Økonomforbundets Forlag: Copenhagen, 2nd ed. 2008.

# III. Public Contracts and Sustainable Development in France

*by Laurent Vidal*

## 1 Introduction

The steps that have led France to make public procurement an instrument of sustainable development have been numerous and have been marked by disputes between the national and (then) Community authorities.[1] These steps are part of a regulatory framework which has enabled the development of tools dedicated to the promotion of sustainable development within the public order and the effects of which are beginning to be felt. From a technical perspective, taking into account sustainable development in public procurement is present at all stages of the contract: the launch of the procedure, examination of applications and bids and performance of the contract.

## 2 The stages of consideration of sustainable development in public procurement

The stages of consideration of sustainable development in public procurement will be distinguished mainly according to the different versions of the Public Procurement Contracts Code.

### 2.1 First steps: before the Public Procurement Contracts Code of 2001

The commitment of France to a green purchasing policy found its origins in Agenda 21, adopted by the United Nations on the occasion of the Conference on Environment and Development held in Rio de Janeiro from 3 to 14 June

1. Development that '*meets the needs of the present without compromising the ability of future generations to meet their own needs*' (Our Common Future, Report of the World Commission on Environment and Development of the UN, chaired by Gro Harlem Brundtland, April 1987).

1992.[2] Referred to in the signatory countries as 'Agenda 21',[3] the objectives of this program have found a first translation in the Guidance Law No. 95-115 of 4 February 1995 for management and development planning.[4]Again, in the mid-1990s, some local governments have engaged in the development of green public procurement procedures after the signing of the 1994 Aalborg Charter (Charter of European Cities for Sustainability adopted in Aalborg, Denmark, 27 May 1994). For its part, in 1996 the French Republic has adopted a policy of '*greening the administration*'.

This process was then supported by the European Commission, especially by two Interpretative Communications (EC Comm., comm. No. 2001/C-333/07, 4 July 2001 on the *Community law applicable to public procurement and possibilities for integrating environmental considerations into public procurement*, and EC Comm., comm. No. 2001/ C-333/08, 15 October 2001 on the *Community law applicable to public procurement and the possibilities for integrating social considerations into public procurement*).

## 2.2 The Public Procurement Contracts Code of 2001

It is in this context that the 2001 French Public Procurement Contracts Code was first drafted. The possibilities of taking sustainable development into account, especially in the guise of protecting the environment, were very limited under this Code. It established a distinction as to the inclusion of environmental interests at the stage of either the definition of the subject-matter of the contract or at that of its implementation. Sustainable development could not be taken into account at the award stage. Thus, besides that Article 53-II of the Code on award criteria contained no specific reference to the concept of sustainable development, no specific reference was made in the Code to social or environmental criteria. Deprived of being able to decide on the question of whether such criteria could be included among the traditional criteria, the administrative courts showed themselves very restrictive.

2. S., especially, Chapter 4, paragraph 23: '*Governments should therefore review the (...) purchasing policies of their agencies and departments to improve if possible the environmental content of government procurement policies, without prejudice to principles of international trade.*'
3. The fourth session of recognition of '*territorial projects of sustainable development and Local Agenda 21*' has just ended. It enabled the Ministry of Sustainable Development to distinguish 34 new projects, plus three parks.
4. S., Articles 2, 6 and 88-1. Article 2: '*The national planning and development of the territory fixed basic guidelines on planning, environment and sustainable development.*'

For the administrative courts, criteria other than those listed in Article 53 could be considered. However, additional criteria, such as environmental or social criteria, could be considered at the award stage only if it was justified by the subject-matter of the contract. However, under the principle of neutrality of public procurement rules, only criteria aiming at achieving best value for money were considered justified by the subject-matter of the contract. Such an interpretation seriously reduced the possibilities of taking into account such criteria when awarding contracts.

The Council of State had to rule on an Interdepartmental Circular of 29 December 1993 urging the State services and local authorities to promote the involvement of tenderers in the fight against exclusion and long-term unemployment.[5] To this end, the circular called for the use of an additional criterion, beside the criteria of price, technical merit cost of use and turnaround time. However, the circular also stated that this additional criterion did not compensate for the deficiency of a candidate's tender under the first four criteria. The intention of the circular was to make the criterion for the inclusion of social interest a secondary criterion. The national federations of public works and building appealed to the Council of State. While not taking a direct position on the illegality of such a criterion, the Council of State however neutralised its application by denying the contested Circular any regulatory nature.[6]

The illegality of an additional criterion unrelated either to the subject-matter of the contract or to the performance conditions was also criticised by the Administrative Tribunal in Strasbourg in a case referred to it by the Prefect concerning a cleaning contract awarded by the Urban Community of Strasbourg. In this case, the call for tenders and tender regulations contained among predetermined award criteria a criterion linked to providing job opportunities for the unemployed.[7]

This position was confirmed by the Council of State in similar circumstances: it was a contract for clearing ditches and cleaning up debris. The Council of State considered that an award criterion referring to the 'socially highest bidder' was not legal, since it was unrelated to the subject of the contract and its performance conditions.[8]

5. This case can be easily transposed to environmental criteria.
6. Council of State, 10 May 1996, *National Federation of Building*, Appl. No. 159.979, conclusions by Stephane Fratacci.
7. Strasbourg Administrative Tribunal, 30 November 1999, *Prefect of Bas-Rhin and Urban Community of Strasbourg*)
8. Council of State, July 25 2001, *Municipality of Gravelines*, Appl. No. 229.666.

The situation was different with reference to contract performance conditions. The 2001 code included an Article 14 providing for the possibility to include in the specifications conditions for promoting employment of people experiencing particular difficulty, in the fight against unemployment or protection of the environment.

In summary, under national law, the environmental and social requirements could not be considered until the implementation stage of the contract. Moreover, this refusal to take into account considerations related to sustainable development at the stage of the award was in addition to the great difficulty in distinguishing between award criteria and conditions of performance. It was indeed paradoxical to allow the introduction of environmental criteria in the contract implementation stage, while excluding them at the stage of the selection of tenders. Indeed, for a tenderer to be selected, he must be able to meet the requirements of the specifications. However, compliance with the requirements of the specifications is one of the first selection criteria, since it determines the eligibility of the tender. It is therefore likely that the measures introduced in the specifications were already considered in the 'cahiers des charges', introducing a real risk of discrimination.

Shortly afterwards a new summit was held under the auspices of the United Nations in 2002. The Plan of Action adopted at the Earth Summit in Johannesburg planned

> '[...] to encourage relevant authorities at all levels to take into account sustainable development when making decisions relating to particular awarding (...) procurement'.[9]

The early 2000s was also the time of the first relevant judgments of the Court of Justice, in particular *Concordia Bus*.[10] The question before the ECJ was whether the economically most advantageous bid could be assessed in light of environmental criteria, in this case the reduction of nitrogen oxide emissions and noise levels of vehicles. On this occasion, the Court adopted a rather liberal position of principle in considering, first, that the list of criteria contained in the then Services Directive is not exhaustive and, secondly, that the guidelines should not be interpreted as meaning that each of the award criteria used by the contracting authority to identify the economically most advantageous bid must necessarily be purely economic. This position was

9. Report of the World Summit for Sustainable Development, Johannesburg, 26 August to 4 September 2002, United Nations. The 18th session of the Commission on Sustainable Development of United Nations was held from 3 to 14 May 2010.
10. Case C-513/99, *Concordia Bus*, [2002] ECR I-7213.

also shared by Advocate General Mischo, who strongly emphasised that it is not necessary that the environmental criteria included in the award stage provide an economic advantage to the contracting authority, such a test being acceptable when it appears useful in the light of the general interest.

This decision was upheld by the judgement in the *EVN* case. Thus we can summarise the position of the ECJ stating that the Court did not oppose the inclusion of sustainable development in public procurement – nor at the award stage nor at the stage of implementation –, and its position is more liberal than that of the Commission as expressed in its Interpretative Communications. The position of the ECJ, however, was taken by the Commission as the opportunity to redesign the procurement Directives, including some criteria related to sustainable development as part of the award criteria.

In France, the effort to reduce the impact of government operations on the environment has continued from 2003 onwards through the National Strategy for Sustainable Development (NSSD), adopted on 3 June 2003 by the Interdepartmental Committee for Sustainable Development (ICSD), including Section 26 devoted to the development of environmentally responsible procurement. In this context, a Public Procurement Contracts Research Group for '*Sustainable Development and the Environment*' was created (Interdepartmental Order of 9 January 2004, Official Journal of 28 January 2004). It is now placed within the Economic Observatory of Public Procurement (Order of 10 November 2005, made under Article 136 of the Public Procurement Contracts Code and on the Economic Observatory of Public Procurement, Official Journal of 13 November 2005).

### 2.3 The Public Procurement Contracts Code of 2004

The French Public Procurement Contracts Code was the subject of a second major ammendment in 2004. Environmental concerns extended their reach beyond contract performance conditions (PPCC 2001, Article 14) to award criteria (PPCC 2004, Article 53). In essence, if the new version of the Procurement Code issued from Decree No. 2004-15 of 7 January 2004 made no direct reference to the concept of sustainable development, environmental considerations might be taken into account from the point of the award criteria for assessing the most economically most advantageous offer. The provision in Article 53-II, which takes into account the environmental criterion, is reinforced by Article 45, on the the selection of candidates. As for the performance of the contract, the protection of the environment is explicitly taken into account in Article 14.

In addition, since March 1st, 2005, the Environmental Charter is part of the French Constitution.[11] Article 6 thereof provides that

> '[...] public policies must promote sustainable development. To this end, they reconcile the protection and enhancement of the environment, economic development and social progress'.

In the same year, the European Commission published a Handbook on Green Public Procurement entitled '*Buying Green*'.

## 2.4 The Public Procurement Contracts Code of 2006

It is in this context that Decree No. 2006-975 of August 1st, 2006 was issued, amending again the Public Procurement Contracts Code and marking a new stage in the consideration of sustainable development through public procurement. Through its Articles 5, 6, 14, 45, 50 and 53, the Procurement Code as amended in 2006, allows the contracting authority to take into account environmental requirements in accordance with general principles related to public contracts, and this at several stages of the procurement process and the implementation of the contract.

Article 5 on the definition of requirements imposes on the contracting authority to take concerns for sustainable development into account. This first stage of the public procurement process gives the contracting authority the opportunity to consider all possibilities to incorporate requirements in terms of protection of the environment, working conditions and overall costs of the purchase.[12]

11. Constitutional Act No. 2005-205 of 1 March 2005, *Official Journal of March* 2, 2005.
12. According to a ministerial answer of January 11, 2007: '*The provisions of Article 5 of the Public Procurement Contracts Code state that 'the nature and extent of needs to meet (...) are determined precisely by taking into account the objectives of sustainable development.' This section imposes an obligation on the contracting authority to consider the definition of its needs with regard to sustainable development objectives. The concept of sustainable development is interpreted broadly as it includes three pillars that should be combined if possible: economic efficiency, social equity and ecologically sustainable development. Thus, for each of its purchases, the contracting authority has the obligation to consider the possibility of integrating its contract (technical specifications, specifications, conditions of implementation) or in the procurement procedure (selecting applications or selection criteria of tender) requirements in terms of sustainable development, from one or all three pillars. To the extent that this obligation is incumbent on the contracting authority in defining its needs, that is to say prior to the launch of the proce-*

Article 6 on the technical specifications allows to define environmental requirements in the documents required for the prospective bidders' consultation. In this framework, the contracting authority may refer to eco-labels awarded by independent bodies. Eco-labels are statements of compliance to pre-established criteria for the use and environmental quality that take into account the life cycle and environmental impacts of products and which are established by governments in consultation with stakeholders such as distributors and manufacturers, consumer associations and environmental protection organisations.[13]

The possibility of variants provided for in Article 50, is another means of integrating environmental protection at the technical specifications stage without the contracting authority necessarily having to specify its requirements too precisely. Thus, the contracting authority may specify that it is willing to accept offers that meet certain greener variants, for example, as to the content of hazardous substances. Environmental concerns will also be integrated into the procurement process at later stages.

Indeed, Article 45 concerning the selection of bidders and candidates allows public purchasers to consider their skills in terms of environmental protection through the assessment of their technical capabilities.

Article 53 enables public purchasers to refer to environmental criteria in relation to all other criteria for selection of the offer. This criterion will nevertheless have to be related to the object of the contract or its performance conditions, be expressly stated in the call for tenders or consultation regulations and respect the principles laid down in Article 1 of the Code. Like the other criteria, this criterion should not be worded as to give unlimited discretion to the public purchaser in selecting the best offer.

*dure, it does not justify vis-à-vis traders its inability to take into account the objectives of sustainable development in the consultation files of the procurement. However, insofar as it is an obligation that is imposed by the Code, the authority must be able to justify at any time with respect to control bodies of the contract that it is impossible taking into account such objectives of sustainable development. The contracting authority may in particular use the report for presentation specified in Article 79 to explain its decision.'* Min. Answ. No. 25167: OJ Senate Q, 11 Jan. 2007, p. 75 (Q. 9 November 2006, Mr. Bernard Piras).

13. S., Min. Answ. No. 92699: JOAN Q, July 18, 2006, p. 7569. In this context, the government has established a procedure for recognition of individuals or entities that ensure compliance with Fairtrade conditions, a committee whose composition and powers are defined by Decree (see Act No. 2005-882 of August 2, 2005, Art. 60, Official Journal of 3 August 2005).

Moreover, regarding the performance of a public procurement contract, public purchasers may, in accordance with the provisions of Article 14, provide for environmental implementation requirements in the public call for competition or in the consultation regulations. These conditions should not have a discriminatory effect either. These environmental requirements must be met by the potential contractor. For example, you may find the following conditions: delivery/bulk packaging rather than in small containers, recovery or reuse of packaging, delivery of goods in reusable containers, collection and recycling of waste products.

These tools enable public purchasers to determine for themselves the level of environmental requirements they wish to meet through their contracts. They cover the whole field of public procurement, whatever the value or object. Finally, under Article 132 of the Code and the Order of August 28, 2006 made thereunder, it was planned to establish a specific study panel on public contracts called '*Sustainable Development and the Environment*' whose mission is to produce guides and documentation addressed to all those involved in order to take into account public concerns related to sustainable development and the environment.

### 2.5 The National Action Plan for Sustainable Public Procurement

Following the 2006 Public Procurement Contracts Code, the Interdepartmental Committee for Sustainable Development (ICSD) held on 13 November 2006, decided to implement the approach in developing a National Action Plan for Sustainable Public Procurement (NAPSPP) for the next three years (2007-2009).[14] A draft was submitted for public consultation until 25 January 2007 before being adopted by the Government; a final plan was then released in March 2007 after transmission to the Commission (DG Environment). The plan contains twenty identified actions. This includes reducing carbon dioxide emissions by 10 per cent by 2008 (by the renewal of the fleet of the State). Efforts should also focus on specific areas such as wood and energy.

Based on the National Strategy for Sustainable Development (NSSD) and proposals of '*The Grenelle Environment Round Table*',[15] successive prime

14. '*Is sustainable public procurement while integrating in one way or another, requirements, specifications and standards for the protection and enhancement of the environment, promoting social progress and economic development including research of efficiency, improving service quality and full value for costs (immediate and deferred).*'
15. V. Statement by the President of the Republic at the end of '*The Grenelle for Environment*' 1 November 2006. At the close of '*The Grenelle for Environment*', Presi-

ministers adopted several circulars on the policy of State services in the field of eco-responsible procurement. See Circular 5 April 2005 on ways to implement the procurement of timber products to promote sustainable forest management, Journal Officiel of 8 April 2005; Circular of 28 September 2005 on the exemplary role of the State with regard to energy savings, unpublished; Circular of 2 May 2008 on the exemplary State policy on the use of products from organic farming in catering, Official Journal of 20 May 2008 and Circular 3 December 2008 which aims to encourage the State to take into account sustainable development objectives in the operation of its services and its public institutions, Official Journal of 12 February 2009.

To take just two examples, the Circular dated 5 April 2005 sets out recommendations applicable to the three stages of the procurement process, namely definition of the requirements, selection of tenderers, and contract award. As such, for example, at the selection stage, it is stated that the public purchaser may ask the applicant to produce either a certificate guaranteeing its adherence to a professional charter providing that the supply of wood products are made with regular and sustainable sources, or a certificate by an independent certification body attesting the compliance of the chain of control implemented to ensure the traceability of wood-based products. However, the public purchaser must also accept other evidence of equivalent measures to guarantee the quality produced by the applicants if they do not have access to such certificates or no possibility of obtaining them within the deadlines set. Tenderers may also be requested to provide samples of descriptions and photographs of supplies. In a Circular dated 3 December 2008, each of the departments is asked to establish a '*Plan for an Exemplary Administration*' in which provisions will be included to ensure the inclusion of sustainable development objectives in the operation of public institutions and services. This plan involves everyday purchases – corresponding to the portion of ordinary procurement for the operation of any administration – the measures of eco-responsibility and social responsibility of the State as an economic operator and as an employer. The specific arrangements of these actions were identified in twenty sheets attached to the Circular and setting

dent of the Republic expressed the wish that the Public Procurement Contracts Code was reformed so that environmental clauses are no longer an option but an obligation. Among the measures announced at the time, it will be noted as follows: the obligation to bring forward in the specifications of the catering or labelled products from certified farms, the announcement of a reform of the Public Procurement Contracts Code from 2008 to the environmental clauses are no longer an option but an obligation.

deadlines and common objectives, strategies and means of action for implementation. Some also provided an 'indicator monitoring'. The plan had to be submitted by the end of first quarter 2009 and be subjected to an annual monitoring report as of 2009.

For its part, the General Review of Public Policies (GRPP) planned in its chapter on the reform of state procurement to 'promote economic and socio-responsible public procurement within the framework of sustainable development'.[16]

This eco-responsible procurement was supported by the Commission Communication of 16 July 2008 on public procurement for a better environment.[17]

## 2.6 The French Environmental Guidelines Act of August 3, 2009

The French Environmental Guidelines Act was passed on 3 August 2009 implementing the 'The Grenelle Environment Round Table' and should be followed by a law of implementation, known as 'Grenelle II'.[18] It provides that

> '[...] all government buildings and public buildings will be audited by 2010' to 'engage their renovation as of 2012 with the treatment of those surfaces which are less efficient in terms of energy savings. This renovation will aim to reduce by at least 40 % energy consumption and at least 50 % reduction in greenhouse gas emissions from these buildings within eight years' (Article 5).

16. Council of Modernization of Public Policies December 12, 2007. To make clearer the information offered to the public, the Ministry of Economy, Ministry of Sustainable Development and the various players in the fair trade sector have decided to establish the National Commission on Fair Trade.
17. COM (2008) 400/2.
18. The Annual Report to Parliament on the implementation of the commitments of '*The Grenelle for Environment*' was submitted to Parliament October 10, 2009 pursuant to Article 1 of the Act of August 3, 2009. On April 16, 2010, the National Committee on Sustainable Development and the Grenelle for Environment (NCSDGE) succeeded to the monitoring committee which essentially repeats the composition organized into five colleges: State elected officials, business representatives, organizations of union workers, associations and foundations to protect the environment. Finally, after the Senate decided adopted on October 8, 2009, the draft law on national commitment to the environment, called '*Grenelle 2*', has been adopted May 11, 2010 by the National Assembly. The text will then be reviewed in joint committee.

Moreover,

> '[...] the State will encourage local authorities, with respect to their self-government, to initiate a program to renovate their buildings' energy savings under the same conditions and at the same pace'.

The text adds that

> '[...] if the conditions defined by Ordinance No. 2004-559 of 17 June 2004 on the partnership agreements are met, it may be required in partnership contracts to carry out renovation work in the field of saving energy, covering respectively 50 and 70 million square meters of government buildings and key public institutions.'

More generally,

> '[...] the public procurement regulations must take into account the objective of reducing energy consumption [...], by allowing the contracting authority to use an energy performance contract, particularly in the form of a global contract combining design, implementation and operation or maintenance, since the improvements in energy efficiency are contractually guaranteed.'

Note also that '*the State's goal is the renovation of the entire public housing stock*' with a rate of 40,000 in 2009, 60,000 in 2010 and 70,000 in 2011 and 2012. The goal is still set that all new construction subject to a claim filed for building permits from the end of 2012 have a average primary energy consumption below a threshold of 50 kilowatt hours per square meter per year. This requirement is effective from the end of 2010 with regard to public buildings (Article 4). A Title IV, entitled *Exemplary State*, provides that

> '[...] the State must, as any public authority, take into account in the decisions it is considering, their impact on the environment, including their share in global warming and their contribution to the preservation of biodiversity, and explicitly justify the attacks that these decisions may occasionally cause to the environment' (Article 48).

As regards public procurement, this principle of public action comes in stating that

> '[...] the State shall promote respect for the environment in public procurement by the increasing use in government procurement and services under its authority, of environmental criteria and environmental variations.'

In this regard, the State's objective, from 2009, is 'to purchase, regarding new passenger cars for use by civilian administrations of the state, only vehicles eligible for 'environmental bonus', except service needs'; beginning in 2010, 'to buy only certified wood or wood from forests managed sustainably'; as of 2012, 'to significantly reduce paper consumption of its administrations, widespread recycling of paper used by its government and to this date, only use recycled paper or paper from forests managed sustainably'; to use

> 'for the supply of its catering services organic products representing 15 % of orders in 2010 and 20 % in 2012 and, in same extent, seasonal products, products with low environmental impact with regard to their conditions of production and distribution, products whose quality and origin can be certified or products from farms engaged in an environmental certification process' (Article 48).

Pursuant to Act No. 2009-967 of August 3, 2009, Decree No. 2010-273 of 15 March 2010 requires minimal amounts of wood to be incorporated in new building constructions except those for which the public owner proves the incompatibility of the use of wood with the regulatory requirements for safety or health reasons or reasons relating to a building's function. These quantities of wood are measured by the volume of wood being used as compared to the reported net ground floor area (NGFA) of this construction according to minimal amounts specified in the text.

Finally, Directive 2009/33/EC, which requires public or private persons to whom a public service mission has been assigned to include in the criteria for the award of a contract the cost of energy consumption and CO2 and pollutants emissions from vehicles used for public transport services, has not yet been implemented in France.,.

Today, it is this regulatory framework which governs the consideration of sustainable development through public procurement.[19]

19. First French Conference on sustainable public procurement held May 12, 2010 in Paris. The European Commission has set a target of 50 % of GPP from 2010. In this perspective, France is responsible for implementing a comprehensive communication plan on green public procurement for which a vector is organizing a conference. This conference, jointly organized by the General Commission on Sustainable Development and the State Public Procurement Service was held May 12, 2010 at the Ark south of Defense. Beyond the aspect of 'green', the presentations were geared toward a wider acceptance in dealing with 'responsible' purchases. They discussed the Public Procurement Contracts Code, eco-labels, plans for exemplary administration, support tools for buyers, etc. Two round tables on sustainable procurement practices have enabled the sharing of good practices and perspectives in this field.

### 2.7 The Law for national commitment to the environment of July 12, 2010, Law No. 2010-788

This Act aims of implementing the broad guidelines of the Planning Act on the implementation of the

This Act aims of implementing the broad guidelines of the Planning Act on the implementation of the "Grenelle for Environment" (Grenelle 1).

The law on national commitment to the environment was published in the Official Journal of 13 July 2010. The draft text was finally decided by the senators and MPs, respectively 28 and 29 June 2010.

Its component comes with the implementation of six major projects:

- The fight against global warming,
- Preservation of biodiversity,
- Development of sustainable agriculture,
- Biosafety,
- Protection of Health,
- The implementation of a sustainable waste management,
- The establishment of appropriate governance to the changing ecological society and the economy.

The text thus closes the Grenelle Environment Forum, whose conclusions were endorsed by the President of the Republic in October 2007. Many orders will however be necessary to ensure that the provisions of the Act can apply.

If any section of the law is specificall dedicated to public procurement, whether, for example, improving the energy performance of buildings, sustainable waste management or measures to preserve biodiversity, many provisions of the Act are intended to be taken into account by those involved in public procurement.

## 3 The tools for promoting sustainable development in public procurement and their first result

The first results of the tools for promoting sustainable development in public procurement are beginning to show results.

### 3.1 The tools for promoting sustainable development in public procurement

These tools can be divided into four categories: institutional tools, documentation tools, technical tools and communication tools.

#### *3.1.1 Institutional tools*

##### *3.1.1.1 The Economic Observatory on Public Procurement (EOPP)*

Under the National Action Plan for Sustainable Public Procurement (NAPSPP), it was decided that each contracting authority had to implement the plan for its own purchases. The EOPP must monitor its implementation and measure the relative share in sustainable public procurement contracts awarded each year by French contracting authorities, the objective being to publish, after the first revision of the Action Plan, a reliable and representative indicator of sustainable public procurement. At the end of the last year of the Plan, it is planned to organise a national conference to learn from the practices implemented and gather input from stakeholders in preparation of the first revision of the plan.

Placed with the Minister responsible for the economy, the EOPP was created by Order of 10 November 2005 and entered into force on 14 November 2005. The Legal Affairs Directorate of the Ministry of Economy shall provide the Secretariat General. Representing all the institutions involved on the demand side for public contracts, organisations responsible for implementation of economic policies and representatives of buyers, the EOPP was given three missions: to collect and collate data on accounting, financial and economic information relative to public contracts, including the economic census of public procurement, to establish on the basis of these data the relevant economic analysis, and to provide a forum for dialogue among stakeholders in public procurement about the technical and economic aspects of public procurement, thanks in particular to study groups on contracts (SGC) and reflection workshops.

##### *3.1.1.2 Study groups on contracts (SGC)*

Section 132 of the Public Procurement Contracts Code of 2006 provides that

> '[...] the Economic Observatory on Public Procurement can create study groups on contracts responsible for developing, in particular, technical recommendations, specifications and technical terms or technical guides to facilitate the award procedures and performance of public contracts. The missions, composition, organisation and methods of operation of study groups of contracts are determined by order of the Minister for the Economy.'

This device interfaces with that provided by the Decree of 10 November 2005 on the EOPP which in Article 1 states that the Observatory

> '[...] is a permanent forum for consultation and as such sets up and operates working groups involving public purchasers and economic stakeholders to review all technical and economic aspects of public procurement.'

Article 2 of the Decree states that the Observatory should

> '[...] determine the technical documentation developed by the technical working groups that it sets up. It validates the technical documents prepared. The technical documents prepared by technical working groups are subject to the advice of a Scientific Advisory Board prior to their submission by the Executive Committee [...]'.

The Decree of 28 August 2006 provides for the mission of the study groups on contracts, the needs they meet, the type of documents they produce and their validation methods. It also outlines their composition and working procedures. Thus, it is the Observatory's Executive Committee that creates the study groups on contracts by a decision which also sets their missions and appoints their members. The Decree of 28 August 2006 was amended by the Decree of 10 April 2009, which states that the Director of Legal Affairs of the Ministry of the Economy and the Director of the Purchasing Department of the State are *ipso jure* members of each study group of contracts. They replace the permanent study groups on contracts (PSGC), the first of which, dedicated to 'Food Supplies', was created by Decree of 11 December 1952, and the most recent relating to sustainable development and environment, by Order of 9 January 2004.

There are currently 11 study groups on contracts with a group devoted to 'Sustainable Development and Environment' (SGC-SDE). The SGC-SDE has been established by the Executive Committee of the EOPPP by Decision No. 2006-1 of 1st March 2007. It is chaired by the Assistant of the Interdepartmental Delegate to the Sustainable Development section of the Department of Ecology. The SGC-SDE's mission is to develop materials to help public purchasers to integrate sustainable development into public procurement, in the award procedures as well as in the performance of public contracts.

#### *3.1.1.3 The reflection workshops (RW)*

As part of its mission to set up task forces designed to study all technical and economic aspects of public procurement, involving public purchasers and economic stakeholders, the EOPP set up workshops for reflection. These are places that evoke topics of discussion that may not have a direct relationship with the regulations. The contributions they have to make have a character that is both forward looking and innovative. For its contribution to this debate, EOPP has set up a workshop on 'Economic Impact of Sustainable Public Procurement', whose works began in June 2007. In a complementary logic with the work performed under the SGC-SDE, the brainstorming workshop intended to develop a tool to quantify the economic impact of green procurement. It is initially to provide all public purchasers with a simple method for computing full cost, total cost of use during the life cycle or of use of the product or service or even full cost overall, which may be incorporated into their specifications and provide a criterion for selecting tenders.

*3.1.1.4 The operational committees (OPCOM)*

Operational committees (OPCOM) were introduced at the end of 2007 to propose to the Government, in view of the Environmental Guidelines Act, concrete measures for implementing the conclusions of the various committees organised under '*The Grenelle for Environment*'. On 26 December 2007 the OPCOM No. 4, entitled '*Exemplary State*' was thus established. It was composed of several working groups, one group dedicated to '*Sustainable Public Procurement*'. It reported its findings on 28 March 2008 and on this occasion proposed the text of what would become the aforementioned Circular of 3 December 2008 aiming at encouraging the State to take into account sustainable development objectives.

*3.1.1.5 The State Public Procurement Service (SPPS)*

Proposed in 2006 by an interdepartmental audit, the reform of the procurement organisation of the State found its true momentum in 2007 under the General Review of Public Policies (GRPP), spearheaded by the General Head for State Modernisation (GHSM). According to the 12 December 2007 Council for the modernisation of public policies, this reform meets several objectives: to reduce the cost of procurement operations while coordinating and organising more purchasing functions of ministries, but also promoting eco-responsible and socio-responsible public purchases in the context of sustainable development, and facilitating access of SMEs to public procurement. This reform also aims at professionalising the 'purchasing' function, by developing skills and improving decision-making tools.

Announced by the Minister for Budget during the first meeting of the Council for the modernization of public policies, the '*Agency for State Public Procurement*' has still not been created. It is finally a '*State Public Procurement Service*' (SPPS), a national agency midway between central and devolved administrations, which will implement the current procurement policy of the State. In fact, a comparison of the draft Decree on the creation of a '*Procurement Agency of the State*' with the Decree No. 2009-300 of 17 March 2009 establishing the '*State Public Procurement Service*' does not show significant differences in the organisation and powers of these two structures. And like what was planned for the Agency, the SPPS is promoting a new practice of promoting public procurement performance targets, sustainable development, social development, and wider access for SMEs to public procurement. The skills and mode of operation of the SPPS were specified by a decree of 19 March 2009.

On 14 April 2010, a new tool has been established, based on the organisation of the large companies in the field of procurement. It is to develop the use of best practices for national and interdepartmental contracts, and to professionalise the procurement process in all ministries. The objective is to achieve a saving of € one billion by 2012 in an area of current purchases amounting to €10 billion.

The SPPS is working with the head officials for procurement (DHOP) of each department. Specifically, it determines the level at which needs are assessed within the meaning of Article 5 of the Public Procurement Contracts Code; it develops purchasing strategies by using, *inter alia*, economic contracts analysis, the most efficient modes of contracting, and standardisation and globalisation of procurement procedures at the appropriate level; to ensure the optimization of procurement policies, it can sign agreements with national and EU procuring entities giving them the power to act as central purchasing bodies.

#### *3.1.1.6 The Advisory Commission on Public Procurement Contracts (ACPPC)*

The ACPPC continues its institutional transition: already passed from an audit to an advisory role to the benefit of State administrations, it sees its expanded mission in serving local authorities, which are offered the option, but are not under the obligation to use its services. It is governed by Decree No. 2009-1279 of 22 October 2009 on the Advisory Commission on Public Procurement Contracts and its implementing Order of 22 October 2009 on assistance to local authorities by the ACPPC for developing and awarding contracts and framework agreements. Its mission is to advise and assist contracting authorities from the start of procedures for the award of contracts and framework agreements and, under certain conditions, throughout the award process.

### *3.1.1.7 The Interdepartmental Mission for the Quality of Public Buildings (IMQBP) and the Agency for the Environment and Energy Management (AEEM)*

We recall finally the existence of the Interdepartmental Mission for the Quality of Public Buildings (IMQPB) and the Agency for Environment and Energy Management (AEEM), which contribute in specific areas to sustainable public procurement. They have a role to play in the energy quality of public buildings.

The IMQPB was created by a Decree (Decree No. 77-1167 of 20 October 1977 establishing an interdepartmental mission for the quality of public buildings). Placed with the Minister in charge of architecture, its purpose is to promote architectural quality in the field of public buildings, whether new or rehabilitated structures. This area includes buildings, infrastructures, public spaces, which are the responsibility of the State or local governments. The IMQPB is playing a role of coordination, leadership and information in conjunction with State administrations, public institutions of the State and national undertakings. It can take on similar missions in agreement with local authorities, their public institutions and relevant professions. The IMQPB follows especially experimental programs whose implementation will be undertaken in departments in which a pilot project will be conducted for this purpose, which will be financed by a fraction of the investment credits for construction of buildings in each of the departments involved. It encourages and assists in such pilot projects. The IMQPB led, directly or indirectly, the training of the officials responsible for the public works. Research programs which may affect the architectural quality of public buildings are reviewed annually with the General Delegation for the scientific and technical research, under the auspices or with the participation of the mission.

As for AEEM, it participates in the implementation of public policies in the areas of environment, energy and sustainable development. It was present in 21 of the 34 operational committees for the operational commitments of '*The Grenelle for Environment*'.

### *3.1.2 Documentation tools*

In addition to these institutional tools, France has placed many documentation tools at the disposal of stakeholders taking part in sustainable development in public procurement. Many guides have been written: '*Eco-responsible Public Procurement Guide*' by the SGC-SDE of EOPP of February 2005 or 2007 on '*Eco-responsible Public Procurement of Wood, Eco-responsible Authorities Guide*' from the Department of Environment and AEEM in October 2005, '*Good Practices Guide: Raise Relevant Offers in*

*Public Procurement. Help for the Expression of Needs*' in February 2008 of EOPP, '*Guide for Sustainable Procurement*' in 2008 of the Department of Research and Higher Education, etc.

Similarly, many websites include sections on sustainable public procurement, see European Commission.[20]

Also worth of note is the existence of training activity undertaken by the Training Institute for the Environment (TIFE), the Institute of Public Management and Economic Development (IPMED) or AEEM.

### *3.1.3 Technical tools*

Among the technical tools created for sustainable procurement one may recall the sheets attached to the Circular of 3 December 2008 for general purchases of goods and services. For the most part, they add detail to the guidelines set out in paragraphs 93-108 of the National Action for Sustainable Public Procurement; the various indicators developed by the EOPP, the AEEM, the SPPS, the IMQPB, the ACPPC; the progress reports for each department as part of implementing its policy of eco-responsible procurement, and, finally, eco-labels. As to the latter, we can recall the existence of a European Eco-label,[21] the Nordic Ecolabel (The Swan) and national eco-labels, including the French eco-label (FS Environnement).

### *3.1.4 Communication tools*

Finally, the promotion of sustainable development in public procurement is conducted through communication tools such as the organisation of Fairs.[22]

20. GPP – Green Public Procurement (http://ec.europa.eu/environment/gpp/index_en.htm) and EMAS – The Eco-Management and Audit Scheme (http://ec.europa.eu/environment/emas/about/summary_en.htm) Department of Ecology, Energy, Sustainable Development and Planning (DEESDP) (http://www.ecologie.gouv.fr/-Marches-publics-.html and http://www.ecoresponsabilite.ecologie.gouv.fr/index.php), the Economic Observatory on Public Procurement (http://www.minefe. gouv.fr/directions_services/daj/oeap/index.htm) and the Agency for the Environment and Energy Management (http://www2. ademe.fr / servlet / KBaseShow? sort =- 1 & cid = 96 & m = 3 & catid = 13 750), the French Association for Standardization (FAST) (http://www.boutique.afnor.org/NEL1AccueilNormeEnLigne.aspx).
21. See Regulation (EC) No 1980/2000 of 17 July 2000 establishing a revised Community system for awarding eco-labels, OJ L 237 of 21 September 2000.
22. E.g. '*Buy & Care*' (http://www.pollutec.com/site/FR/Buy_and_care/index.php), '*Sustainable Planet*' (http://www.planete-durable.com) or '*Ecorismo*' (green products and environmental solutions for the hotels, camping, catering and tourism – http://www.ecorismo.com/)

Sustainable development through public procurement also brings together several networks.[23]

## 3.2 First results of the tools for promoting sustainable development in public procurement

### *3.2.1 The latest figures on public procurement by the EOPP*

The first results of the promotion of sustainable development in public procurement have become published recently. In its newsletter of 15 January 2010, the EOPP delivered the latest figures on public procurement. Contracts including social clauses represent only 1.5 per cent of all contracts. The environmental clauses appear to have more success: not only such clauses are found in 2.1 per cent of the contracts, but progress over the last year is quite high, over 33 per cent.

### *3.2.2 The ACPPC's latest reports*

In its activity report for 2008 the ACPPC points out that several tools are available in the Public Procurement Contracts Code for promoting sustainable development, including those listed in Article 6 (technical specifications), 14 (contract performance conditions), 15 (set aside) 45-II (information on qualification provided by applicants), 53-53-I.1 and IV (award procedures). However, the ACPPC prefers recourse to environmental performance clauses because if sustainable development is the subject of a weakly weighted award criterion, there is no guarantee that the objectives can be achieved in the contract.

In its annual report for 2009, the ACPPC advised procuring entities to ask economic operators for the description of the means implemented to ensure environmental quality; potential tenderers are allowed to prove their environmental quality by producing an ISO 14001 certification. However services must assess whether this requirement is not likely to limit competition. Most often these concerns are taken into account in the technical specifications or the award criteria, environmental criteria being valued in a range from 5 to 10 per cent. The Committee calls on the services to consider whether it is preferable to provide for award criteria or technical requirements. The answer de-

23. '*The Club of Eco-responsible Public Institutions*' led by the Department of Ecology, Energy, Sustainable Development and Regional Planning, Territorial Networks such as '*Ordre Public and Sustainable Development*' (http://www.achatsresponsables.com and http://www.achatsresponsables-bdd.com), the Network '*Ethical Public Procurement*' (http://www.cites-unies-france.org / html / home / index.html) and, finally, the Network '*Fair Public Procurement*' (http://www.achatspublicsequitables.com/.

pends on both the desire to achieve good results and the state of competition. A requirement in the technical specification is the best way to achieve the desired results in terms of sustainable development. It is also necessary that a sufficient number of economic operators are able to respond. If this is not the case, it is preferable to introduce environmental requirements into the award criteria. Finally, the report states that while environmental concerns are addressed fairly by the public purchasers, this is not the same for social measures.

All this shows that taking into account sustainable development is making progress and that procuring entities are aware of the need of maintaining a competition between operators at the same time. The balance can be found at all stages of the contract.

## 4 Sustainable development in public procurement and the stages of the contract

The inclusion of sustainable development is reflected in all stages of the contract but in different ways.

### 4.1 The launch of the procedure

At this stage, the procuring entity should first of all precisely define its needs, and then go and see which goods or services could satisfy the needs. It will then purchase pursuant thereto. Therefore, everything must be mentioned in the call for tenders and the tender documents. What has not been mentioned may not be required later on. This rigidity is due to the application of fundamental principles of public procurement (free access, equal treatment and transparency). The provisions of Article 5 of the Public Procurement Contracts Code state that

*'[...] the nature and extent of needs to be met (...) are determined precisely by taking into account the objectives of sustainable development.'*

This novelty of the Public Procurement Contracts Code in 2006 has no basis in EU law because there is no corresponding definition of requirements in the Directives 2004/17/EC and 2004/18/EC. The scope of this Article has been specified by the Head of Legal Affairs at the Ministry of Economy and Finance in reply to a written question from Senator Piras.[24] It appears that if the

24. Min. Answ. No. 25,167: OJ Senate Q 9 November 2006, p. 2793.

contracting authority has an obligation to introduce sustainable development at the time of the definition of its requirements, this obligation does not extend to the adoption of specific measures. For each purchase, the contracting authority has an obligation to consider the possibility of integrating it in its contract (technical specifications, and contract performance conditions), or in the procurement procedure (selection of applicants or award criteria) requirements concerning one or all aspects of sustainable development. To establish the link to the object of the contract of the social or environmental clause is difficult, and any solution will depend on the specific facts of each case.

As part of the definition of the subject-matter of the contract, it is for the contracting authority to translate its requirements in a contractual document, 'the special technical terms and conditions'. To do this, Article 6 of the Public Procurement Contracts Code in 2006 allows the contracting authority to 'make reference to standards or other equivalent documents' or, and this is new, 'to speak in terms of performance or functional requirements'. In this case, the contracting authority may include environmental characteristics, which can be defined by reference to an eco-label. Again, the technical assessment of the requirements in the contractual documents must be consistent with the purpose of the contract. Otherwise, the technical requirement may be challenged on the grounds that it constitutes a factor of unfair discrimination in respect of prospective applicants. The buyer must be able to justify to the control authorities the requirements of the specifications relating to the subject-matter of the contract. The reference to eco-labels and other ecological labels should be proportionate to the subject of the contract.

### 4.2 Examination of applications

Regarding the admissibility of its application, the applicant must prove that it is in good standing with respect to its fiscal and social obligations. On the basis of Directives 2004/17/EC and 2004/18/EC, a company guilty of repeated breaches of environmental provisions under administrative law and subject to penalties in this respect, may be excluded for serious professional misconduct. In its 2005 Handbook on Green Public Procurement, the Commission states that an offer may be regarded as unacceptable if it fails to comply with a statutory requirement.

As to the experience of tenderers, Article 45 of the Public Procurement Contracts Code gives the contracting authority the possibility to ask them to produce certificates of quality. In environmental matters, the Code refers to the EU eco-management and audit scheme and the European or international standards for environmental management (mainly the ISO standards 14,000).

Besides the global environmental management systems (EMS) certified by a third party, some quality certificates are dealing only with an environmental theme or a corporation.[25] Some certificates are dealing only with one step of the composition of an EMS. Concerning this last category, the French Association for Standardization now offers a so-called approach '1-2-3 environment' to certify the successive stages of the implementation of an EMS.

When asked for certificates of qualification, the Code specifies that the purchaser must specify that evidence of the ability of the company may be provided by any means. The lack of specific mention of these terms does not affect the legality of the contract if it is still provided that this capacity 'can be evidenced by certificates of qualification or other evidence considered as equivalent'.[26] Like the terms of reference in the technical specifications, the contracting authority must consider whether the quality certificates submitted by applicants other than those mentioned by the contracting authority are their equivalents.

Beyond the formal rules, a request for information about the skills of the applicants 'must be objectively necessitated by the subject-matter of the contract and the nature of the services to be performed' when it has the effect of restricting market access to certain undertakings.[27] To assess the qualifications of bidders in terms of work or services that require environmental management measures, the authority may ask for the register of contracts carried out previously (e.g. reference in terms of high environmental quality building sites or in terms of 'low nuisance construction sites', etc.). This requirement must still comply with Section 52 of the Public Procurement Contracts Code, which states that

> 'the lack of references to the performance of similar contracts does not justify the elimination of a candidate and does not relieve the contracting authority of the duty to examine the professional, technical and financial expertise of applicants'.

### 4.3 Examination of bids

Pursuant to Article 53 (1) of the Public Procurement Contracts Code, the procuring entity has a real freedom as to the criteria and weighting that will determine its choice of the most economically advantageous offer. The adminis-

25. For example, the Imprim'vert approach – National Plan of Action for Sustainable Public Procurement, p. 7.
26. Council of State, January 25, 2006, *Department of Seine-Saint-Denis*, Appl. No. 278115.
27. Council of State, May 10, 2006, *Society Bronzo*, Appl. No. 281976.

trative courts perform a control limited to manifest mistakes of assessment. The benefit of inserting an environmental criterion must relate directly to the contracting authority. The only satisfaction of the public interest is not sufficient to justify the legality of a criterion. However, the use of environmental criteria is not restricted only to contracts specifically designed to protect the environment. A link to the subject-matter of a contract will exist when execution of a contract includes an environmental impact and when the ecological criterion tends to mitigate this impact. For example, the relevance of environmental criteria is obvious in terms of construction contracts. It is indeed easily deduced that there is a link between environment and buildings when looking for the type of heating and/or cooling, the materials used, the future management costs of and the wastes from the building both during its lifetime and afterwards. In the context of construction contracts, environmental criteria can therefore certainly be considered routinely justified by the subject of these contracts. We can consider that this is also true for purchases of vehicles contracts if we take into account the rate of CO2 emissions, the rate of recyclable materials or noise, etc. We might add printing contracts (impact on air pollution and water), products from the forest, including 'old' forests (impact on biodiversity), cleaning products (impact on users' health and indoor air pollution), electrical and electronic equipment (impact on soil pollution), etc. The criterion must be evaluated objectively and transparently.

In a case concerning a street furniture advertising contract, the Council of State held that the buyer 'could, having regard to the subject of the contract, retain the aesthetic criterion'. But setting this criterion at a predominant level (50 per cent) 'without giving any indication of its expectations in this regard, the buyer was given a discretionary choice, contrary to the principle of equal treatment and transparency'.[28] Similarly, the ecological criteria must be quantifiable and reducible to numerical values that lend themselves to objective comparison. The requirement of objectivity and transparency also means that the tender committee is able to verify the accuracy of information provided.

In a recent case, the Administrative Tribunal of Caen has concluded that the lack of information in the consultation files on the conditions of implementation of a criterion relating to '*environmental quality*' made the procedure for the award of a public contract illegal.[29] In this case, the buyer had committed to a specific procedure for concluding a contract for the treatment of residual household waste. Concerned about the environmental impact of

28. Council of State, April 28, 2006, *City of Toulouse*, Appl. 280197.
29. Administrative Tribunal of Caen, injunction, January 5, 2010, No. 0902741, *Company Les Champs Jouault*.

the contract, it had planned that among the two criteria, one would refer to the price of the service, the other would be dedicated to the '*environmental quality*' and would have a weighting of around 30 per cent. The applicant company, which saw its bid rejected, did not contest this criterion in principle. However, it maintained that it was too vague to enable it to make an offer in full knowledge of the facts. The defendant procuring entity claimed it had included in the specifications of the contract a whole series of requirements that were likely to help the applicants to understand the expected material and content of the criterion for environmental quality. The court held that these factors were not sufficient to inform applicants about the conditions of implementation of environmental criteria: one thing is to include in a contract stipulations for environmental purposes and another is to judge the bids on the basis of environmental criteria. In doing so, the court has applied recent case law of the Council of State which is worth considering for the demands it placed on the definition of award criteria, including special procedures. The case law allows the implementation of environmental award criteria provided they do not give the contracting authority an unrestricted freedom of choice. It requires, moreover, that these criteria are brought to the attention of the tenderers, not only the criteria for evaluating tenders, but also, even in special procedures, their conditions of implementation [30] However, it considers that, contrary to what is prescribed in the formal proceedings, the criteria for evaluating tenders have not to be weighted by the contracting authority in special procedures.[31]

From an even more recent Ministerial Answer it is clear that selection criteria, based on performance on the protection of the environment, if permitted, are however subject to certain conditions: they cannot ignore the fundamental principles governing public procurement, foremost among them the equal treatment of tenderers, and must be related to the subject-matter of the contract. The proximity of a company, for example, in order to reduce C02 emissions, cannot be integrated as such among the criteria for the selection of tenders: such a criterion is discriminatory to the detriment of more remote companies. Account must be taken of the fact that environmental concerns in the Public Procurement Contracts Code are not limited to the award of the contract but extend to all stages of the procedure, from formulating technical specifications to writing contract performance clauses. In particular, Article 14 of the Code allows contracting authorities to require, as a condition of per-

30. Council of State, Section, January 30, 2009, *National Agency for Employment*, Appl. No. 290236.
31. Min. Answ. No. 25,186: OJ Senate Q 4 Jan. 2007, p. 27.

formance, limiting emissions of greenhouse gases, which does not necessarily imply a need for proximity to a favour particular company but rather an environmental approach in the implementation of the contract in terms of setting up of construction or the means of transport used.[32]

Another recurring theme is the use of products from organic farming in catering. Based on the National Strategy for Sustainable Development (NSSD) and the proposals of '*The Grenelle for Environment*', several circulars have been adopted on the eco-responsible public procurement by departments including the aforementioned Circular of May 2, 2008, on the exemplary role of the State in the use of products from organic farming in catering. In order to approach the goal of the exemplary State, the Government wanted to create a sustainable demand for organic products, by encouraging the introduction of foods from organic farming in catering with a target of 15 per cent in 2010 to reach 20 per cent in 2012. Like any public procurement, procuring entities purchasing products from organic farming, or catering based on products from organic farming, are under an obligation to respect the principles of freedom of access to public procurement, equal treatment of tenderers and transparent procedures. The local and national organic production cannot be privileged as such.

In a Ministerial Answer of 30 September 2008, the Ministry of Economy, however, advises catering managers to have a sustainable development approach, incorporating the carbon cost of transportation of goods, encouraging a balanced occupation of the territory, and keeping jobs in the agricultural sector. To go in this direction, it is essential that public procurement officers lead an upstream reflection on the supply capacity of the local organic industry. Again according to the Minister, the procurement contract conditions may then be specified so as to promote local sourcing, also by dividing the contract into lots, and deciding to publish the contract notice in a local paper or in a specialised paper on environment, or by specifying that the subject of the contract will take into account sustainable development, or considering environmental variations. It may also be requested that the bidder demonstrates its capabilities and know-how on sustainable development when bids are selected. For example, the bidder may be rated on the environmental impact generated by his proposal, particularly in terms of transportation. According to the Ministry, within the possibility of introducing environmental criteria, it will be possible to require specific techniques such as 'fruits or vegetables in season', or introducing a quality product demands in terms of

32. Min. Answ. No. 10874: Q OJ Senate, January 21, 2010, page 130.

freshness which ensures short periods between harvest and delivery. To support the contracting officers, the Government will train its staff on these issues, emphasising the overall coherence necessary to ensure for sustainable development.[33]

In short, if a contracting authority decides to examine the tenders on the basis of environmental criteria (or, apart from the price, of any other criterion), it must ensure sufficient transparency with respect to the applicants, stating, in consultation files and, more particularly, in tender regulations, the evidence on which it intends to rely when assessing that criterion.

### 4.4 Execution of the contract

We have already indicated that under Article 14 of the Public Procurement Contracts Code:

> '[...] the conditions for the execution of a contract or a framework agreement may contain elements of a social or environmental nature, taking into account the objectives of sustainable development balancing economic development, protection and the enhancement of environmental and social progress'.

The bidders must undertake to respect these conditions; otherwise their offer will be rejected as irregular. These conditions should not, however, affect the fundamental principles that govern public procurement, and in particular should not have the effect of breaking the equal treatment of applicants. However, it would be contrary to the principle of contractual freedom if the procuring entity pretended to dictate all the practical details of contract implementation. Within these limits buyers use the conditions of implementation and are not required to assort them according to specific selection criteria. The use of selection criteria and contract performance conditions may legally be done independently. However, when a contracting entity uses Article 14 alone, it is liable to receive bids which, although complying with the terms of social or environmental performance, are very differentiated on these points, with the ensuing difficulties in selecting the most interesting offer. By combining Articles 53-1 and 14, the contracting entity encourages traders to submit a sustainable development process more elaborate than would be required by simple compliance with the contract performance clause. It is therefore recommended, where possible, to coordinate the two instruments.[34] To illustrate the provision in Article 14, the circular dated 3 August 2006 pro-

33. Min. Answ. No. 19,090: Senate Q OJ, 30 September 2008, page 8376.
34. Min. Answ. No. 00,422: OJ Senate Q, 8 October 2009, page 2365.

vides, as an indication, some examples of contract performance: shipping/packing in bulk rather than small containers, recovery or reuse of packaging, delivery of goods in reusable containers, collection and recycling of waste products. These specifications will find their place in the special administrative terms and conditions document and the special technical terms and conditions document, to supplement the general administrative terms and conditions document and the general technical terms and conditions document, which aim to define the terms of the contract. Applicants are required to submit tenders in accordance with all these specifications.

Recently, the Administrative Tribunal of Nimes considered a sub-criterion of the 'internal control of the implementation of procedures relating to environmental quality and sustainable development'. This does not relate to the tenderer's technical capacity to execute the contract, but to the criterion of the quality of service offered. As such, it is obviously linked with the contract, and cannot be regarded as indefinite or incapable of being economically quantifiable. Indeed Article 5-6 of the special technical terms and conditions states that applicants must define the control measures which they intend to implement for real time monitoring services, management arrangements and monitoring of claims, the implementation of measures related to environmental quality in the context of sustainable development policy of the company. Accrding to the Tribunal, neither the reference to a framework of guiding principles for sustainable development, nor the fact that respect for the environment is also taken into account under the criterion of the technical merit of the offers, through the choice of the vehicles to be used and their pollution levels, are such as to invalidate the sub-criterion.[35]

## 5 Conclusion

As a conclusion, it can be emphasised that if France has taken many steps in the consideration of sustainable development in public procurement, the major environmental challenges facing it now impose taking yet a further step. In this sense, it is expected that the Council of State, following the example of what it already did with reference to Article 7 of the Charter of the Environment[36] will decide on the possibility for claimants of invoking Article 6 of the Charter directly which states: 'Public policies must promote sustainable

35. Administrative Tribunal of Nimes, injunction, July 10, 2009, *Ocean Company*, No. 091712.
36. Ass., October 3, 2008, *City of Annecy*, Appl. No. 297931.

development. To this end, they reconcile the protection and enhancement of the environment, economic development and social progress.'

# IV. Secondary Considerations in Public Procurement in Germany

*by Martin Burgi*

## 1 Introduction: the go-ahead for secondary considerations*

Describing and analyzing the multi-faceted landscape of secondary considerations in German public procurement law, it should be noted that they remain of growing importance, irrespective of former and undeniably controversial discussions in the past. In the light of the Commission's initiatives, a vast array of dissertations, legal essays and scientific papers in this context can be found, establishing quite different terms: secondary considerations, secondary policies, secondary criteria or aspects, sustainable public procurement (SPP), green procurement or socially responsible public procurement (SRPP) are frequently used keywords when talking about additional political aims in public procurement law.

The application of procurement law results from the public purchaser´s decision to purchase goods or services from an external entity in order to fulfil administrative tasks (such as the services for the public).[1] Generally speaking, the public entity has always been operating on the premise of a cost-efficient purchase. The award process in Germany is completely governed by the towering principle of competition, enshrined in §§ 97 I, II of the German Competition Act (GWB).[2] Due to the multiple and often dendritic administra-

* The author wishes to express his thanks to research assistant *Frauke Koch* for her valuable support in the preparation and publication of this paper.

1. Hans-Peter Kulartz, Fridhelm Marx and others (eds), *Kommentar zur VOL/A* (Werner Verlag Köln 2007) para 7 fns 30ff; Jan Ziekow, *Die Berücksichtigung sozialer Aspekte bei der Vergabe öffentlicher Aufträge* (Studien zum öffentlichen Wirtschaftsrecht, Carl Heymanns Verlag, Köln 2007) 2.
2. § 97 I GWB 'Contracting entities shall procure goods, works and services in accordance with the following provisions through competition and by way of transparent award procedures.'
   § 97 II GWB 'The participants in an award procedure shall be treated equally unless discrimination is expressly required or allowed by this Act.'

tive services and in view of a complicated financial situation (paucity of public resources), cost-efficient award decisions are increasingly important. Given the current credit crunch, the public entity is held to economise more than ever.

Nevertheless, a huge quantity of supplemental and deserving political goals are taken into consideration.[3] The spectrum of secondary policies ranges from environmental[4] to social or political-economical criteria. The purchase of ecologically-friendly or fair trade products, the promotion of long-term unemployed or handicapped employees tend to alter the characteristics of award processes, which are no longer seen exclusively from the economic angle. The idea of charging the award procedure with additive criteria has given rise to long and encompassing debates ever since the existence of procurement law. Reasons arguing for a 'buy better"-campaign are as manifold as refutations and fears in existence. Both the pros and cons of secondary criteria will be discussed later in this article.

Taking the nature of a typical German awarding procedure into account, it should be noted that secondary criteria come into play at different stages. To clarify: The public entity's decision to call for tender or the definition of the subject-matter of the contract bear relation to certain criteria.

These may exert influence as suitability criteria or help to determine the most economically advantageous tender. It is also possible that they appear at the performance stage. That keeping in mind, the legal conditions regarding the admissibility of secondary considerations may, of course, vary. As the more or less complex German procurement system stipulates, the character of the concern in question (either ecological or social) should be considered when exposing the requirements de lege lata. The German procurement framework is coined by a trichotomy: GWB,[5] Procurement Order (VgV)[6] and the three procurement regulations, beginning with the regulation for supplies and services (VOL/A 2009),[7] followed by the regulations for the award of in-

3. Jakob Steiff, 'Vergabefremde Aspekte – eine Zwischenbilanz' (2009) VergabeR 290 ff.
4. Friederike Mechel, *Die Förderung des Umweltschutzes bei der Vergabe öffentlicher Aufträge* (Nomos, Baden-Baden 2006) 2ff.
5. 'Neufassung des Gesetzes gegen Wettbewerbsbeschränkungen' (2005) BGBl. I 2114.
6. Bundesministerium für Wirtschaft und Technologie, <http://www.bmwi.de/BMWi/Redaktion/PDF/Gesetz/VgV,property=pdf,bereich=bmwi,sprache=de,rwb=true.pdf> accessed March 2010.
7. Bundesministerium für Wirtschaft und Technologie <http://www.bmwi.de/BMWi/Redaktion/PDF/Gesetz/verdingungsordnung-fuer-leistungen-vol-a-2009>accessed March 2010.

dependent contractor services (VOF)[8] and for public works (VOB/A 2009).[9] Rules and norms referring to secondary considerations may therefore be subject to different legal instruments.

In order to give effect to the different aspects flanking the award procedure, the Germann legislator is currently trying to establish norms or work out guidelines for administrative bodies referring to questions of application and integration of secondary considerations.[10]

## 2 The quest for the subject-matter of the public procurement contract

### 2.1 Definition of secondary criteria

Secondary criteria still remain a conundrum, despite the amplitude of scientific essays and several court rulings dealing with this issue. The main questions are not completely settled yet, though the national (German) legislator has recently taken further steps in this direction (with the creation of § 97 GWB, especially the implementation of § 97 IV 2 GWB).

At the outset of this report stands the search for a definition of secondary considerations. Though most legal practitioners do have examples in mind when thinking about secondary aspects, discovering an accurate definition for secondary considerations turns out to be a very problematic concern, as neither EU nor national procurement law provide a legal definition or a useful explanation one (bidders or contracting authorities) could work with. The definition of a public contract contains no indication about secondary criteria and their characteristics either. For this reason, a specification of secondary considerations can only be worked out by carefully analysing the characteristics and purposes of a typical award process.

8. Bundesministerium für Wirtschaft und Technologie <http://www.bmwi.de/BMWi/Redaktion/PDF/Gesetz/vergabeordnung-fuer-freiberufliche-leistungen-vof,property=pdf,bereich=bmwi,sprache=de,rwb=true.pdf>accessed March 2010.
9. Bundesministerium für Verkehr, Bau und Stadtentwicklung, <http://www.bmvbs.de/Anlage/original_1102253/VOB-Teil-A-und-B-Ausgabe-2009.pdf>accessed March 2010.
10. Deutscher Städtetag, 'Die Berücksichtigung sozialer Belange im Vergaberecht' (2009) <http://www.staedtetag.de/imperia/md/content/schwerpunkte/fachinfos/2009/22.pdf> accessed March 2010.

## 2.2 Difference between secondary and primary criteria

In view of the non-existent legal definition of secondary criteria, the difference between the latter and primary considerations could possibly be of importance. Recapitulating the central targets of an award procedure, the public entity aims at the cost-efficient satisfaction of demands.[11] In order to fulfil comprehensive administrative tasks (welfare, basic infrastructure, danger defence), the public entity needs to buy goods and services externally, provided that the body is not able to produce the needed goods itself. The procuring entity is generally free in its decision if and what good to procure – as long as the procurement procedure helps to perform administrative tasks (margin of discretion). The supply with products, services and works[12] is regarded as the main purpose (the so-called primary criterion) of an average procurement procedure.

Secondary considerations, however, concentrate on the pursuit of other public aims. Taking account of the provisions, treaties, conventions and decisions in force, the ban of child work or the promotion of the employment of women constitute public interests, for example. The only and yet the decisive question is whether these additional considerations may be implemented into public procurement law and how the implementation should be arranged.

By means of awarding a contract, the fostering of enterprises with a socially sound organisation (employing handicapped or long-term unemployed, improving the status of women) or of those acting in correspondence with ecological standards enables the procuring body to pursue (other) important political interests existing within a welfare state. Having a closer look at the issue, it is noteworthy that the public body finds itself in the role of a 'consumer' as far as primary considerations are concerned. In case of primary considerations, the contracting authority asks for goods or services and minimum standards which are obligatorily needed and for guarantees for the functioning of the procured product or service.

By way of encapsulating the procurement process with additional clauses, the procuring body acts rather like a 'regulator', trying to fight for general public concerns such as a better, clean environment, fair, healthy and equal working conditions, reflation or fair trade, for instance. Taking an analytical approach, secondary considerations, not necessarily required for a successful execution of the contract or the satisfaction of demands, make an appearance

11. Albert Bleckmann, Stefan Pieper, Volker Epping (eds), *Öffentliche Auftragsvergabe und Umweltschutz* (Carl Heymanns Verlag, Köln 2003) 8.
12. Stefan Hertwig, *Praxis der öffentlichen Auftragsvergabe* (4th edn, CH Beck, München 2009) 8.

as subventions.[13] They resemble instruments of navigation and control and as such they should be navigated and controlled. The procuring body seeks to boost certain enterprises because they fulfill specific requirements.

Attached to this difference between primary and secondary considerations is the undeniably delicate question of determining a dividing line. The protection of the environment or the aim for social interests might also be considered as primary considerations. This might be the case if a public entity calls for tender and seeks to purchase the construction of a sewage plant or a home for the handicapped. This bearing in mind, the procurement of ecologically or socially friendly services or works itself constitutes the main purpose of the award process and cannot be characterised as secondary considerations in a strict sense.

Certainly, an entity seeking to favor manufacturers using ecologically-friendly or newly developed technologies intending to facilitate its market entry, is applying secondary criteria as an instrument of policy. Even if the picked criterion is formative or of modifying effect as regards the main purpose of satisfying demands,[14] the characterisation of the aspect turns out to be quite complicated. Generally speaking, the transition between purely primary and secondary considerations is definitely smooth.

Due to the fact that the clarification does not constitute the heart of this chapter, but concentrates on laying down the main rules for the integration of secondary considerations instead, there will be no further remarks on this matter.

### 2.3 Reasons for implementing secondary criteria

Why exactly do secondary considerations deserve to find their way into award procedures?

All hopes of an easy and simple answer are dashed immediately. A short presentation of arguments accentuates that the State is – due to the ongoing privatisation and greater liberalization – losing important means of control as

13. Stefan Hertwig, *Praxis der öffentlichen Auftragsvergabe* (4th edn., CH Beck, München 2009) 4.
14. Bundesministerium für Wirtschaft und Technologie, 'Öffentliches Beschaffungswesen' (2007) 11 < http://www.bmwi.de/BMWi/Redaktion/PDF/Publikationen/gutachten-2-2007,property=pdf,bereich=bmwi,sprache=de,rwb=true.pdf> accessed March 2010.

regards the performance of state services and political tasks.[15] From the State's backing out follows that public purchasers are continuously searching for alternative and yet effective ways of rendering public governance possible. Pursuing additional political aims by way of using the potential of procurement law as a policy instrument is tantamount to gaining control over private enterprises involved in administrative tasks. In view of the State's considerable power of demand, secondary desiderata can be used as politically effective and influential instruments of control.

Notwithstanding, numerous important administrative tasks (such as public welfare) still remain the responsibility of the State. Public entities, trying to concentrate on the purchase of eco-friendly goods or fair trade products, serve as archetypes not only for the private sector but also for consumers. Bearing in mind that private entities are already working on the establishment of exemplary, ecologically and socially friendly corporate structures (family-friendly concepts), public entities are meant to adjust and open the door for secondary considerations in procurement law.

Secondary considerations encourage economic enterprises to focus on specific political aims they would not have thought about otherwise (mainly because of a restricted budget). This way, the state ensures the pursuit of political goals. The awarding bodies use award procedures as incentives.[16] Competing entities try to match certain standards (promoting the protection of the environment, for instance) in order to be paid homage in shape of being granted the contract. Taking the subsidising character of secondary considerations into account, the winning enterprise can afford to center on inventing new technologies, adhere to environmental or social standards and is thereby enabled to fulfil politically desirable interests.[17] In fact, integrating secondary aspects into the award procedure helps launching better products, though these might be more expensive due to the augmented requirements the product should fulfil. In the long term, however, ecologically as well as so-

15. Martin Burgi, '*Vergabefremde' Kriterien*' in Eberhard Grabitz, Meinhard Hilf (eds), *Das Recht der Europäischen Union* (40th edn., CH Beck, München 2010) B 13 fns 1-65.
16. Friederike Mechel, *Die Förderung des Umweltschutzes bei der Vergabe öffentlicher Aufträge* (Nomos, Baden-Baden 2006) 18.
17. Bundesministerium für Wirtschaft und Technologie, 'Öffentliches Beschaffungswesen' (2007) 9 < http://www.bmwi.de/BMWi/Redaktion/PDF/Publikationen/ gutachten-2-2007,property=pdf,bereich=bmwi,sprache=de,rwb=true.pdf>accessed March 2010; Friederike Mechel, *Die Förderung des Umweltschutzes bei der Vergabe öffentlicher Aufträge* (Nomos, Baden- Baden 2006) 19.

cially friendly production processes can pay off thanks to the amortisation of the initially higher acquisition and production costs.

Thus, the integration of secondary considerations can be used as a means to boost cross-border trade and the development of new and better technologies. Foreign enterprises, working with newly developed machines or improved techniques or companies specialized in eco-friendly goods might apply for an award in another Member State. This helps promoting competition, known to be one of the most important targets in general EU and procurement law.

What is more, with view to international and European treaties (climate protection, ILO conventions) and the binding obligations resulting thereof, the state should demonstrate and proof its serious concern in protecting the environment, for instance.[18]

Summing up, various and numerous reasons are fighting for the implementation of secondary criteria into the award process.

### 2.4 Problems and fears

Despite these legitimate though quite ambitious joint goals, fears and counterarguments are put forward. In order to prevent abuse, barriers and constraints are set up. Additional parameters, be they in the shape of environmental targets or social, might certainly be employed in a way aiming at treating certain bidders preferentially. Not surprisingly, critical voices raise concern that green or social procurement may collide with fundamental EU principles and lead to favoritism or cronism.[19] The inclusion of secondary considerations into the process of an award could potentially serve as a way of disguised protectionism and might allow the return of discriminatory conduct. The procuring body might, for instance, define the subject-matter of the contract in a way allowing only certain bidders to participate. The determination of the procured good can also be phrased in a manner which intentionally enables just one single bidder to match the requirements. This way, by picking the entity's favourite bidder,[20] the public purchaser eludes the strict and

18. Bündnis 90/ Die Grünen, 'Für ein transparentes, mittelstandsfreundliches, innovationsoffenes und soziales Vergaberecht' (2007) BT-Drs. 16/6786.

19. Deutscher Städtetag, 'Die Berücksichtigung sozialer Belange im Vergaberecht' (2009) 9 http://www.staedtetag.de/imperia/md/content/schwerpunkte/fachinfos/2009/22.pdfaccessed March 2010.

20. Jan Ziekow, *Die Berücksichtigung sozialer Aspekte bei der Vergabe öffentlicher Aufträge* (Studien zum öffentlichen Wirtschaftsrecht, Carl Heymanns Verlag, Köln 2007) 2.

mandatory procurement rules. Secondary criteria bear a 'minefield-potential' allowing manipulation to the detriment of other competitors. Bidders, fulfilling the desired secondary facets might be chosen although their bids would not have been identified economically most advantageous without the set up of secondary considerations.

The entity might be acting preferentially by way of choosing specifically fitting award or suitability criteria, too. In order to substantiate: the awarding body requires the delivery of the procured good to be cheap (low costs of transport) and low in pollutants, which indirectly and intentionally favors local enterprises (due to a shorter distance).[21] Strictly speaking, this call for tender is nothing but an inadmissible hidden protectionist measure. Most awarding bodies are interested in promoting small local enterprises because – as a rule – these companies are financially disadvantaged and would otherwise (due to financial and staff equipment) not be awarded the contract. This way, public purchasers use public procurement as a means to influence the local job-market. Whilst local supplier's earnings are likely to be spent in the local economy, public entities will still tend to give preference to regional competitors.

Furthermore, possible breaches of European law or other problems and fears connected to the implementation of secondary criteria are – having a closer look on the issue – dependent on the respective aspect. Due to the primary interest in a fair and unrestricted, non-discriminatory competition, each criterion has to be in line with European law. As far as environmental considerations are concerned, problems may not arise that frequently. First, the protection of the environment constitutes one of the most important goals of the Union and is – as a consequence – covered by different guiding provisions of EU law (for example Art. 11 of the TFEU, Art. 53 of Directive 2004/18/EC or the preamble of the Treaty). In light of the ECJ rulings on the matter, laying down the core requirements for the integration of secondary criteria, considerations should be directly linked to the subject-matter of the contract. The stage where the aspect comes into play (suitability or award criterion or criterion relevant at the performance stage) governs the question whether or not a link is necessary. As a matter of fact, a link with the object of the tender is

21. Meinhard Dreher, 'Vergaberecht im Wandel: *Die Sicht der Wissenschaft*' in Rainer Pitschas, Jan Ziekow (eds), '*Vergaberecht im Wandel*' (Duncker & Humblot, Berlin 2006) 34; Stefan Hertwig, *Praxis der öffentlichen Auftragsvergabe* (4th edn, CH Beck, München 2009) 6; Albert Bleckmann, Stefan Pieper, Volker Epping (eds.), *Öffentliche Auftragsvergabe und Umwelt* (Carl Heymanns Verlag, Köln 2003) 300; VK Südbayern, Ruling of 17th June 2009, Z 3-3-3194-22-05/09.

(more) easily given in case of ecological considerations, since they exert a direct influence on the product – at least in most cases (see remarks below).

In addition, bidders have to match more and more complex conditions if applying successfully for a public contract including secondary aspects. This leads to an increased workload, which firstly prevents bidders to participate and secondly results in more expensive products in the longer run.[22]

Another problem entwines around secondary considerations: questions relating to the actual correspondence with environmental laws, of monitoring,[23] surveillance and control are pending. A solution is asked for, in order to guarantee fair and healthy competition and the practical realisation of the public body's aims. Attaching environmental or social conditions to a procurement process is, of course, desirable. Still, sustainable procurement decisions are only meant to work if effective means to safeguard compliance with law on the one hand and sanctions (if the worst comes to the worst) on the other hand are available, which requires government departments and local authorities to get behind it wholeheartedly. The German legislator is asked to pass adequate provisions.

Of course, not only European law restricts the integration of secondary targets. The principle of equal treatment, as enshrined in Article 3 I Basic Law (GG), the German Constitution, constitutes a limitation for manipulative, protective and (direct or indirect) discriminatory award practices.[24] Tender procedures above and particularly below the thresholds should be compliant with the demands of the German Constitution. Unless a legitimate reason is available and the principle of proportionality is complied with, discriminatory procedures are strictly forbidden. Due to a ruling of the Federal Constitutional Court (BVerfG), constitutional requirements (Articles 3 I, 12 I, 9 III GG) generally do not prevent a contracting body from introducing social con-

22. Jan Ziekow, *Die Berücksichtigung sozialer Aspekte bei der Vergabe öffentlicher Aufträge* (Studien zum öffentlichen Wirtschaftsrecht, Carl Heymanns Verlag, Köln 2007) 2.
23. Bündnis 90/ Die Grünen, 'Vergaberecht reformieren-Rechtssicherheit schaffen-Eckpunkte für die Reform des Vergaberechts' (2008) BT- Drs. 16/8810; Deutscher Städtetag, '*Die Berücksichtigung sozialer Belange im Vergaberecht*' (2009) 13, <http://www.staedtetag.de/imperia/md/content/schwerpunkte/fachinfos/2009/22.pdf>accessed March 2010; Stefan Hertwig, *Praxis der öffentlichen Auftragsvergabe* (4th edn, CH Beck, München 2009) 6.
24. Burgi, '*Vergabefremde Zwecke und Verfassungsrecht*' (2001) NZBau 69, 70.

siderations. The ruling of the BVerfG dealt with the admissibility of collective agreements.[25]

Taking everything into account, the inclusion of secondary considerations, as desirable as it may seem at first sight, should not and does not go unrestricted. Regulations provided by European as well as by national, that is constitutional law, are necessary.

## 3 Green and social considerations facing existing legislation

### 3.1 Green considerations

As the ECJ noted,[26] the possibility of integrating secondary aspects into procurement processes is not excluded by European law. In any case, multiple restrictions are drawn by this field of law.

One criterion in particular has acquired relevance and is the main subject of recent discussions in Europe. Article 11 TFEU and the mentioning of the protection of the environment as an important goal in both the preamble of Directive 2004/18/EC and of the then EC Treaty demonstrate its undeniably increasing importance. Environmental concerns currently struggle their way into award procedures. The terms 'sustainable public procurement' and 'green procurement' have become paramount keywords, sending a strong signal for future awards. Given the prevalent opinion that European law is taking priority over federal law, the German legislator is asked to transform European provisions into national law. European rules relating to the integration of 'green characteristics' have become an affaire nationale, a subject of transposition. It remains undisputed that German institutions should act in full compliance with EU law.

The concept of establishing ecology-minded buying patterns appears almost consuetudinary in Germany, judging solely by the amount of intensified antipollution measures taken since the end of the 1980's respectively the beginning of the 90's[27] and having special regard to the national objective of 'environmentalism' in Article 20 a GG.[28]

25. Rainer Noch, Vergaberecht kompakt (4th edn, Werner Verlag, Köln 2008) 656, 657; BVerfG, Ruling of 11th July 2006, (2007) VergabeR 42.
26. Case C-513/99- *Concordia Bus Finland* [2002] ECR I-7213.
27. Deutscher Städtetag, '*Die Berücksichtigung sozialer Belange im Vergaberecht*' (2009) 9 <http://www.staedtetag.de/imperia/md/content/schwerpunkte/fachinfos/2009/22.pdf> accessed March 2010; Albert Bleckmann, Stefan Pieper, Volker Epping

*3.1.1 Examples of sustainable procurement*

First of all, the concept of sustainable procurement requires an explanation: eco-friendly procurement is a process whereby the public authority seeks to purchase goods, services and works with reduced ecological impacts throughout their life-cycle when compared to goods, services or works with the same function that would otherwise be called for by the public entity.[29] Environmental characteristics should go beyond what is obligatorily needed on the basis of national environmental legislation.[30] The tableau on German rules on green procurement is mainly a result of the Member State's obligation of transposition.

Different ways to foster the preservation of the environment are conceivable : eco-friendly and re-usable packing,[31] recycling, eco-friendly waste disposal, training staff in ecological or energy-effective aspects, inventing clean and energy-efficient vehicles[32] (low carbon-dioxide-emissions, gas-powered busses), preferably with a tolerable noise level,[33] road pavements built with natural stones, cultivation of organic cotton, eco-friendly construction of buildings due to the use of regenerative materials, usage of renewable energy, inventing and purchasing electricity-saving products. The fight against the green house effect, for example, might rather be won by concentrating on conservation-conscious product processes or the invention of products with lower fuel consumption and pollution, thinking predominantly about cars. By way of example, fruit and vegetable purchased by a public entity for the purpose of hosting an important (charity) event, should preferably hail from the region. Thereby the public purchaser is able to keep itineraries short and $CO_2$-

(eds), *Öffentliche Beschaffung und Umweltrecht* (Carl Heymanns Verlag, Köln 2003) 8.

28. Albert Bleckmann, Stefan Pieper, Volker Epping (eds), *Öffentliche Beschaffung und Umweltrecht* (Carl Heymanns Verlag, Köln 2003), 331,335.
29. Albert Bleckmann, Stefan Pieper, Volker Epping (eds), *Öffentliche Beschaffung und Umweltrecht* (Carl Heymans Verlag, Köln 2003), 13; Stefan Hertwig, *Praxis der öffentlichen Auftragsvergabe* (4th edn, CH Beck, München 2009) 22.
30. European Commission, 'Study on the Collection of statistical information on Green Procurement' 12 <www.ec.europa.eu/environment/gpp/studies_en.htm> accessed February 2010.
31. Jens-Peter Schneider, '*Umweltschutz im Vergaberecht*' (2009) NVwZ 1059.
32. Case 513/99- *Concordia Bus Finland* [2002], ECR I-7213; Jens-Peter Schneider, '*Umweltschutz im Vergaberecht*' (2009) NVwZ 1058.
33. Jan Ziekow, '*Vergabefremde Kriterien nach der Neufassung der Vergaberichtlinien*' in Rainer Pitschas, Jan Ziekow (eds), *Vergaberecht im Wandel* (Duncker & Humblot, Berlin 2006) 159.

emissions will be reduced.[34] When procuring a cleaning-contract, the governmental buying concept should require the use of ecologically-friendly, allergenic and non-irritating cleansing agents, for example.

In fact, the State can call for a comprehensive and sustainable ecological concept of each enterprise,[35] in order to foster the preservation of the environment.[36] The examples just mentioned deserve fair attention within an award procedure. Nevertheless, the introduction of green considerations is-especially in the light of European court rulings – dependent on multiple legal requirements.

### *3.1.2 Standards necessary for the work, the product or the service*

One of the main phenomena in public procurement law is that the public purchaser is generally free in his decision if and what to procure, thus enjoys freedom of choice. Of course, the European concern for unrestricted and fair competition is an immensely important benchmark. While defining the object of the contract, the procuring body may include several varying environmental aims. As a matter of course, the aims and requirements differ in their influence on the procured product and should therefore be dealt with differently with regard to the legal point of view. The purchasing body might refer to these indispensable requirements by way of including green criteria in the definition of the contract[37] or by describing technical specifications.

Some standards demanded by the public purchaser are simply indispensable for the successful fulfillment of administrative tasks (example: purchase of $CO_2$-friendly buses[38]). Referring to this, the State is requiring essential minimum standards guaranteeing the functioning of the procured good or service, which is in itself an issue beyond legal admissibility. At exactly this point, the difference between primary and secondary considerations is blurred because it is difficult to determine whether the quest for ecological criteria

34. Albert Bleckmann, Stefan Pieper, Volker Epping (eds), *Öffentliche Auftragsvergabe und Umweltschutz* (Carl Heymanns Verlag, Köln 2003) 308.
35. Jan Ziekow, '*Vergabefremde Kriterien nach der Neufassung der Vergaberichtlinien*' in Rainer Pitschas, Jan Ziekow (eds), *Vergaberecht im Wandel* (Duncker & Humblot, Berlin 2006) 159.
36. Jens-Peter Schneider, '*Umweltschutz im Vergaberecht*' (2009) NVwZ 1059; Albert Bleckmann, Stefan Pieper, Volker Epping (eds), *Öffentliche Beschaffung und Umweltschutz* (Carl Heymanns Verlag, Köln 2003) 300; Jan Ziekow, '*Vergabefremde Kriterien nach der Neufassung der Vergaberichtlinien*' in Rainer Pitschas, Jan Ziekow (eds), *Vergaberecht im Wandel* (Duncker & Humblot, Berlin 2006) 159.
37. OLG Düsseldorf, Ruling of 16th April 2003, (2003) ZfBR 721.
38. Rainer Noch, *Vergaberecht kompakt* (4th edn, Werner Verlag, Köln 2008) 640.

results from a secondary objective (even if laws recommending the integration of green criteria exist) or from the simple necessity to buy a functioning product.

Legal rules, enabling the public purchaser to integrate green considerations exist on the European and, due to the Member State's obligation of implementation, on the national (German) level as well. Directive 2004/18/EC contains the basic rules on the European platform, whereas the complex German system offers three different kinds of legal acts: GWB, VgV and the three procurement regulations.

Article 23 (3) (b) of the said Directive provides rules on technical specifications. According to the annex to the Public Procurement Order for Supplies and Services (VOL/A) 2009, ecological considerations and guidelines are put into the category of technical specifications. The public contractor may integrate green considerations helping to specify the procured good. The aspects required relate to its function and performance. German counterparts to Article 23 (3) (b) can be found quite easily: §§ 7 XI, 8 II VOL/A-EG and §7 III Public Procurement Order for Works (VOB/A) (2009) render possible the inclusion of environmental characteristics in technical specifications. Environmental certificates can be used as such. In compliance with the obligations resulting from the Directive, the chosen parameters must be designed to describe the subject-matter of the contract and allow the award decision to be made.

*3.1.3 Green considerations required by EU and national procurement law*

The procuring body may also introduce green procurement criteria. Firstly, the contracting authority may ask for green qualitative selection – considerations which are required by EU or national procurement legislation. These rules solely relate to the field of procurement. Or (secondly) the purchaser wants to introduce ecological criteria required by EU or national law other than public procurement law (see 2.1.4.).

Beginning with green criteria required by the European or national procurement legislator, the most important European norm can be found in Article 45 of the Directive. This article deals with green selection criteria, to be more precise with reasons for the exclusion from the bidding process. A competitor convicted by a judgment with the force of res judicata because he acted in breach of legal provisions concerning his professional conduct (Article 45 (3) (c) or a bidder who demonstrably committed grave professional misconduct (Article 45 (2) (d) is necessarily excluded from the on-going award procedure. The violation of fundamental European or national environmental legislation might be considered grave professional misconduct and therefore serves as a reason for the exclusion of the economic operator. At this point it should be briefly noted that the national legislator is free to work out detailed rules for professional misconduct, at least as long as no discrimination is entailed and European law principles are complied with. The German procurement system contains regulations on the exclusion of bidders as well: §§6 V lit c VOL/A 2009, lit d, 6 lit c, lit d VOL/A-EG, 16 II no.2 VOB/A (2009).

Under § 97 IV 1 GWB the picked bidder should necessarily be reliable:

'Contracts shall be awarded to skilled, efficient and reliable undertakings.'

In case of professional misconduct or a conviction the reliability of the bidder cannot be verified any more, which is the reason for exclusion from the ongoing award process.

The most important question is, whether green criteria required by European or national law are used as an indication for the bidder´s reliability. All in all, there are two different ways of legally required green criteria indicating the bidder´s reliability. Pursuant to Article 45 (2) (c) of the Directive, a bidder could be considered unreliable if he has been convicted because of an infringement of binding ecological norms. This, however, implies that the infringement itself bears relation to the award in question and that the bidder has been already and officially declared guilty. Only if a relationship between award and norm is given, a safe prognosis about the bidder´s reliability for the performance of the procured contract can be made.

The other and possibly better way of using legally obligatory green criteria as reliability indication is to verify grave professional misconduct, meaning that the bidder has infringed important environmental rules bearing relation to his profession.

Thinking about laws capable of evoking a negative reliability diagnosis, one is to find norms in the Penal Code (StGB), some rather sporadically spread within the code, others even in a specific paragraph dealing with deeds involving environmental damage. The provisions of §§ 300 ff. StGB center on deeds constituting a public danger. They refer to the use and impacts of detrimental substances (explosion). §§ 324 ff StGB cover criminal acts with negative impacts on the environment[39]. Under § 324 StGB, water pollution is a punishable offence. § 325 StGB declares air pollution punishable and §

39. Rainer Noch, Vergaberecht kompakt (4th edn, Werner Verlag, Köln 2008) 231, 373.

330 StGB is enlisting cases of especially serious damages caused to flora and fauna.

In conclusion, these criminal provisions can be either taken as an instrument to justify exclusion or, taking the recently amended provision of § 97 IV 1 GWB into account, as an indication of the bidder´s missing reliability due to his lack in law-abidance. Consequently, such a bidder is not capable of winning the contract.

### *3.1.4 Green considerations required by EU or national law other than public procurement law*

Most public authorities welcome environmental aims, especially in times of an on-going debate on climate change. In general, it can be said that environmental aspects or closely related topics are frequently mentioned in guidelines, administrative regulations, documents or notes as well as in guidance or performance papers and manuals. The scope of these norms is not exclusively focusing on procurement law, but covers all fields of 'green' state action. With a view to the amplitude of national strategies on sustainability, focus is laid on some exemplary measures.

Article 48 Directive 2004/18/EC contains important regulations on the technical and professional ability of the bidder. The focus is laid on methods available to prove the technical abilities to perform the contract. German norms dealing with the same matter can be detected in § 97 IV 1 GWB, which is only applicable in case of pan-European contract awards and in §§ 8 II,V VOL/A-EG, 16 II VOB/A (2009). Certificates help to give credible and sufficient evidence of the bidder´s capability to vouchsafe a satisfactory and successful execution of the contract, for example. They regard comparable (previous) contracts or the enterprise´s environmental concept in general and can be used as indices for the bidder´s capability.

§ 97 IV 1 GWB does not focus on listing all methods available. On the contrary, this norm leaves a margin of discretion to the procuring body. As long as the certificates allow the examination of the bidder´s technical capability and render possible the assessment, the public authority is free to decide on the needed certificates or methods of evidence.

By far the most important rules are laid down in the procurement regulations VOL/A and VOB/A. In correspondence with Article 48 (2) (f), § 7 XI VOL/A-EG, § 8 II VOL/A-EG and § 7 VII VOB/A (2009) relate to the bidder´s ability (concerning green procurement) which might be proven by means of an indication of environmental management measures. If the buying agent asks for certificates issued by independent institutes or agencies, reference to the environmental management system EMAS or comparable systems based on European guidelines such as DIN EN ISO 14 001, for example, might be made. The rules laid down in Article 48 (2) (ii) of the Directive have been transposed into national law as well. § 8 IV,VI VOL/A-EG and – as far as public works contracts are concerned – § 16 II No.1 VOB/A (2009) contain detailed rules on the bidder's ability to perform contracts to be proven through certificates drawn up by impartial and official quality control institutes or agencies of recognized competence. These certificates provide evidence that products are built in conformity with the specifications or standards asked for. The bidder's reliability is demonstrated as well; the procuring entity gathers indications and information concerning the bidder, his business practices or his (continuing) compliance and intention to act in accordance with European environmental legislation. Undeniably, this point is liable to be mixed up with performance conditions.

The German Constitution covers an independent rule relating to the aim of preserving the environment: Article 20 a GG. This provision officially proclaims environmental protection as a national objective. Despite its importance, further-reaching consequences for procurement law and questions of integrating green considerations cannot be separated from this constitutional implementation. Even in case of buying goods externally, the State is held to act in awareness of the current situation in climate and environment questions. Its enormous buying potential should be used as a means to create a better environment.[40]

Article 27 (2) of the Directive stipulates that bidders seeking further information about the environmental requirements they should meet, are obliged to give proof of having taken account of all environmental obligations in force when drawing up the tender. Carefully examining the German provisions, a rule equivalent to the European regulation does not exist at the moment. Nevertheless, national procurement-related laws[41] provide that the contracting authority can ask the bidder to give indications of his acting in accordance with certain obligations (such as the Regulation on the procurement of energy-efficient products/services[42] or the National Action Plan on the Procurement of Wood,[43] for example)

40. Bundesministerium für Wirtschaft und Technologie, 'Allgemeine Verwaltungsvorschrift zur Beschaffung energieeffizienter Produkte und Dienstleistungen' (17 January 2008) [12] *Bundesanzeiger* 198.
41. §§ 8 Nr.3 I,4 VOB/A; 7 Nr.4, 21 Nr.1 VOL/A.
42. Bundesministerium für Wirtschaft und Technologie, 'Allgemeine Verwaltungsvorschrift zur Beschaffung energieeffizienter Produkte und Dienstleistungen' (17th

*3.1.5 Green considerations left to the discretion of the procuring body*

Some rules bearing reference to environmental protection are not obligatorily required – neither by EU nor by national law. The procuring bodies are granted a margin of discretion as regards the decision to introduce green procurement conditions, the rules (covering administrative regulations as well) – provided they exist – are therefore of an 'additional' character. The standards demanded by the contracting authority are higher than the required legal standards.

An example of national legislation with an environmental impact (federal level) is the administrative regulation on the procurement of energy-efficient products and services, adopted in January 2008. This legal work enacted by the Federal Ministry of Economics and Technology on the basis of Article 86 GG as legal authorisation lays down the noticeable importance of green procurement once again. This regulation is closely linked to procurement law, but it is – strictly speaking – not a provision stemming from procurement law itself (understanding 'procurement law' in its true sense, namely solely GWB, VgV and the procurement regulations) but rather from administrative law. The administrative regulation finds itself in line with the core rules of the ECJ for the implementation of ecologically based criteria set up in the cases *Beentjes* and *Concordia Bus Finland.* After a brief overview of its articles, it can be concluded that reference to specifications defined in Eco-labels ('Blauer Engel', 'European Ecolabel' or 'Energy star' indicating the tenderer´s technical and professional capacity) or by way of other comparable environmental certifications is possible. The regulation adheres to every single contract award stage where green criteria come into play.

The regulation and its focus on secondary environmental considerations is just one piece in the ramified puzzle of the German strategy on cultivating sustainable procurement. Another interesting and ecology-related act concerns the purchasing of wood products.[44] As the common action of the Federal Ministry of Economics and Technology and the Federal Ministry for the Environment, Nature Conservation and Nuclear Safety envisions, the procurement of sustainable wood is legally obligatory for all administrative bod-

January 2008) [12] *Bundesanzeiger* 198; Olaf Otting, 'Grünes Vergaberecht – Die Beschaffung energieeffizienter Produkte und Dienstleistungen nach der Vergaberechtsreform' (2009) CUR 44 ff.

43. 'Gemeinsamer Erlass zur Beschaffung von Holzprodukten' (17th January 2007) GMBl. 67.
44. 'Gemeinsamer Erlass zur Beschaffung von Holzprodukten' (17th January 2007) GMBl. 67.

ies. Certificates may provide sufficient proof of its origin or ecologically sound converting.

Another rule allowing secondary environmental considerations is Article 26 of Directive 2004/18/EC, relating to the conditions for the performance of contracts. In Germany, the Law on the Modernisation of Procurement Law,[45] in force since April 20th 2009, enables the contracting authority to lay down additional green requirements as far as the performance of the contract is concerned (use of re-useable packing). Environmental along with social or innovative characteristics might be considered now, provided that a link to the subject-matter of the contract is given and the aspects are expressly mentioned in the specifications. The latter is a requirement going far beyond the European guidelines.

Secondary criteria can be introduced discretionarily at the stage of contract award criteria, too. Two award criteria only are applicable (due to Article 53(1) of Directive 2004/18/EC) in order to determine the 'best bidder'. Either the award is made to the economically most advantageous tender or to the tender offering the best price. As far as the first alternative is concerned, ecological considerations (among with other explicitly enlisted secondary considerations) may find their way into the award procedure, provided that – recalling the findings of the ECJ in the case *Concordia Bus Finland* – a link to the subject-matter of the contract can be proven. The German counterpart of Article 53 can be seen in § 97 V GWB:

'The award is made to the economically most advantageous tender'.

Although secondary considerations are not explicitly mentioned in the wording,[46] it is – after long and intense discussions in literature – widely acknowledged that the most economically advantageous tender can be determined by implementing additional characteristics such as ecology-minded characteristics.

Though ecological requirements may possibly render the procured good more expensive, long-term costs might possibly be lower and the public entity might derive advantage from it (profit).

As domestic law stipulates, the chosen criterion should allow the determination of the economically most advantageous offer and should enable the tenders to be compared and assessed objectively – two requirements the ECJ is still and quite consistently demanding.

45. 'Gesetz zur Modernisierung des Vergaberechts' (20th April 2009) BGBl. I, 790.

Furthermore, the procuring entity is meant to define the weighting of the chosen criteria. Thanks to this obligation, the entity is obliged to decide which criterion constitutes the most important one. To exemplify: when procuring a contract relating to the environmentally sound construction of a school (non-usage of tropical wood), the public entity has to determine the weighting of different criteria such as price, quality or the origin of the wood used (example: price 50 %, quality 30 %, origin 20 %).

Apart from § 97 GWB, laying down the rules for contracts above the thresholds, the public procurement regulations contain general rules on environmentally-friendly award criteria, too (§19 IX VOL/A-EG), §16 VI No.3 VOB/A [2009]). Below the thresholds, plenty of room is given to the purchaser regarding the decision to apply green considerations.

### 3.2 Social Considerations

Unsurprisingly, not only ecological aims are considered during the award process. Additional remarks, focusing on social considerations, have to be made as well. An analysis of the German situation is capable of demonstrating the large number of various social concerns struggling and sometimes successfully having fought their way into public procurement law.[47] The most important social aims are subject to the following remarks.

#### *3.2.1 Examples of social procurement*

Social aspects do cover a broad range of subjects concerning work, social security, employment, social policy and human rights. This paragraph seeks to present some examples of a socially friendly procurement procedure, with an emphasis on the social concerns used most frequently.

As a longtime member of the International Labour Organisation, Germany has ratified numerous conventions which are to be implemented. In order to ensure the backing of international labour standards, Germany pursues aims covered by conventions and recommendations published by the ILO when procuring public contracts. Therefore, the list of social criteria is led by lots of employment-related considerations concerning the maximum hours of a working day, the protection of workers against sickness, injuries or disease arising out of employment, equal remuneration for work of equal value or

47. Jochen Mohr, *'Soziales Vergaberecht?'* (2009) *VergabeR 543*; Zsofia Varga, 'Berücksichtigung sozialpolitischer Anforderungen nach dem neuen §97 IV 2 GWB-europarechtskonform?' (2009) *VergabeR* 535ff.; Jan Ziekow, *Die Berücksichtigung sozialer Aspekte bei der Vergabe öffentlicher Aufträge* (Studien zum öffentlichen Wirtschaftsrecht, Carl Heymanns Verlag, Köln 2007) 5.

equal working conditions and payment for women and men. Other social aspects relate to the ban of child work (production of footballs for school sport or smocks for public servants without employing children), the compliance with collective wage agreements (minimum and fair wages), the establishment of fair and family-compatible structures within an enterprise, the promotion of the long-term unemployed, the aid for adolescents making entry into the labor force or the fight against poverty.[48] Corporate social responsibility might also imply the promotion of apprentices or vocational training. Sometimes, socially responsible procurement processes focus on the production of goods which may be used by handicapped persons, sometimes contract awards are offered preferentially to workshops for the handicapped.

Not rarely, the fostering of small and medium-sized enterprises, so-called SME's, is put into the same category (social) when talking about secondary considerations. This subject, however, will be dealt with separately in this paper.

Despite their manifold character and their deserving consideration, social criteria cannot that easily be integrated into an award process. The conditions set up by the ECJ are difficult to match, many fears and critical voices are raised. In fact, social criteria bear a potential for conflict – when compared to ecological criteria. This is mainly due to the fact that – as a rule – social criteria do not directly influence the procured good, service or work. The linkage to the subject-matter of the contract (the most essential requirement spelt out by the ECJ) is more difficult to prove. Notwithstanding, a multi-faceted framework, generously encompassing all kinds of legal acts and fields of law (notifications, petitions, decisions of the city council, administrative regulations) is or will be available soon.

In general parlance: the implementation of social ideas into procurement law embarks on a 'Great Quest'.

*3.2.2 Standards necessary for the work, the product or the service*

Recalling the remarks on green considerations necessarily picked by the procuring entity in order to be supplied with a working product or a useable service, comparable consequences or observations cannot be made here. It is hard to think about either a service or a good which simply has to fulfil social criteria because appropriate use and function would not be guaranteed other-

48. Jan Ziekow, *Die Berücksichtigung sozialer Aspekte bei der Vergabe öffentlicher Aufträge* (Studien zum öffentlichen Wirtschaftsrecht, Carl Heymanns Verlag, Köln 2007) 5.

wise.[49] This is mainly due to the fact that social criteria are not as product-related as environmental or other concerns. Provided that the public entity wants to procure a works contract regarding the construction of a home for the handicapped, the bidder should necessarily pay heed to its accessibility by wheelchair users. In this case, the definition of the subject-matter of the contract bears relation to social secondary criteria.

As far as Article 23 of the Directive is concerned, technical specifications might also cover social criteria in addition to ecological ones. Article 23 (3) (d) allows the inclusion of 'other criteria' necessarily needed to purchase a fully functional product. Hence the norm is offering an extensive possibility of embedding social concerns as well. As long as the chosen social aspect is applied in order to describe the functional requirements of the product, of course. The social criterion has to be an integral component of the subject-matter of the contract. The following example is meant to match these requirements: A public purchaser calls for a public works contract wanting to construct a building accessible for handicapped persons or a home for the handicapped.[50] Or a good is produced which should be useable by handicapped or blind persons, for example. Only general requirements bearing no relation to the product or service itself or to its function and use are not covered by Articled 23 of the Directive.

The German implementing provisions are §§ 7 IV VOB/A (2009) and 8 VOL/A-EG and 6 II No.3 VOF/A.

*3.2.3 Social Considerations required by EU or national procurement law*

Some social considerations are required by European or national law with specific reference to the field of procurement law.

As already stated above, Article 45 of the Directive focuses on reasons legitimizing the exclusion of a bidder from the ongoing award procedure. In case of a criminal act for which the bidder has been convicted and which is able (Article 45 (2) (c)) to question his professional reliability or in case of grave professional misconduct (Article 45 (2) (d)), a tenderer can be excluded. Transposing these abstract cases into the 'social criteria language', the breach of standards worked out by the ILO, such as the employment of children, for example, results in the bidder's exclusion from the procurement procedure. Criminal acts like fraud (§ 263 StGB), theft (§ 242 StGB), tax

49. Rainer Noch, *Vergaberecht kompakt* (4th edn, Werner Verlag, Köln 2008) 641.
50. If the public contractor decides to build a home for the handicapped, the social criterion of accessibility by the chairbounded is self-evident. In this case, the category of 'essential considerations' might be taken into view.

fraud (§ 370 AO) or illegal employment (SchwarzArbG) may serve as justification to exclude a bidder.[51] The comparable German provisions offering a list of relevant criminal law provisions governing the bidder's exclusion are found in § 6 IV VOL/A-EG and § 6 b VOB/A 2009.

As far as social criteria are concerned, Article 45 (2) (e) provides for the exclusion of any bidder who has not fulfilled his or her obligations relating to the payment of social security contributions.

German procurement rules concerning the exclusion of a tenderer because of his failure to pay social contributions are §§ 16 II No 2 lit d VOB/A (2009), 6 V lit d VOL/A-EG.

Furthermore, § 97 IV 1 GWB comes into play again. The public purchaser might diagnose missing reliability if the bidder either has been convicted due to his infringement of norms stemming from criminal law, because he has been acting contrary to norms and thereby has committed grave professional misconduct or because he did not pay social contributions or taxes.

### *3.2.4 Social Considerations required by EU or national law other than public procurement law*

Again, the aforementioned remarks about environmental considerations should be kept in mind when reporting about the legal situation of social criteria given on both the European and the German law level. It goes without saying that some of the provisions also applicable to fields other than public procurement may vary or differ as social and environmental criteria do not share the same character. But in case of identical norms, namely those which deal with ecological and social concerns at the same time, a short summary will be sufficient as the consequences affecting the award procedure will be roughly the same. Many German provisions exist especially on the level of the Länder and influencing the socially-friendly award of contracts.

Beginning the analysis with Article 19 Directive 2004/18/EC, it provides that Member States may reserve public contracts including the performance of such to sheltered workshops carrying out employment programs. Special regard should be given to the fact that the majority of the employees concerned are handicapped and due to the nature or seriousness of their disabilities not able to work under 'normal' conditions. Their preferential treatment is an adequate and understandable aim. Furthermore, the Federal Ministry of Economics and Technology passed guidelines relating to the consideration of

51. As regards the illegal employment of workers, see Hans-Peter Kulartz, Friedhelm Marx and others (eds.), *Kommentar zur VOL/A* (Werner Verlag, Köln 2007) para 2 fn 47.

sheltered workshops for unemployed respectively blind persons. These decrees require federal procurement agencies to reserve a considerable budget for contracts awarded to workshops for the disabled.[52] This might even include large contracts. Beginning with the sub-constitutional provisions of §§ 141 and 143 Social Code IX (SGB IX),[53] the preferential treatment of workshops for handicapped or blind persons is dealt with. In transposition of these obligations, the Federation has enacted a directive, dating from 2001 and laying down specific rules for the consideration of the said workshops when procuring a public contract.[54] It is worth to notice that comparable laws are in force at the level of the Länder.[55] In Rheinland Palatinate[56] or Hesse,[57] for example, preference within an award process can be given to the handicapped.

Furthermore, most Länder have enacted impressive legal frameworks banning child work. They provide notifications, petitions, decisions of the city council or administrative regulations, seeking to avoid the employment of children in need of special care and protection. With view to 158 million children aged between 5-14 years and being engaged in child labor, many German municipalities seek to advocate the non-negotiable childrens' rights as enshrined in several international treaties and conventions. The fight against slavery, inhuman and hazardous working conditions (working with chemicals or dangerous machines), illegal or unethical kinds of work (prostitution or drug dealing), exploitation, bondage or child trafficking may be promoted by setting up the requirement to act in accordance with international standards. Of course, the abidance by international norms on child work can also be used in the context of reliability criteria (Artcile 45(2) (d)).

On the federal level §§ 5, 8 or 22 of the Youth Working Protection Act (JArbSchG) seek to establish fair and appropriate working conditions. These

52. Martin Trybus, ITC, Study Contract, '*Social considerations in Public Procurement*' 4 <www.ec.europa.eu/social>accessed February 2010.
53. Horst Hopf, 'Gesetz zur Modernisierung des Vergaberechts' (2009) Apf 227.
54. Federal Decree on Contracts for workshops for the disabled' (2004) MBl. NRW 437; Bundesministerium für Wirtschaft und Technologie (10th May 2001) [109] Banz 1174.
55. As the relevant provisions are not subject to either of the procurement laws (GWB, VOL/A, VOB/A, VOF and the VgV), the presentation of these norms is made within this paragraph despite the actually non-fitting superscription.
56. §8 Verwaltungsvorschrift Rheinland Pfalz (29th July 2004), MWVLW Rheinland-Pfalz 8205 381015.
57. Gemeinsamer Runderlass für die Berücksichtigung bevorzugter Bewerber bei der Vergabe öffentlicher Aufträge' (14th October 1994).

provisions contain a ban for the employment of children (§ 5) and regulations on the working hours of juveniles (strictly considering the juvenile's age, see § 8). § 22 entails that juveniles are not allowed to be employed if the work carried out is of detrimental or noxious consequences.

The public purchaser is often asking for socially-friendly business structures in an award procedure, too. One of the leading interests is to bring bidders to provide and accomplish affirmative action programs for women. Inter alia to reach this aim, the national legislator enacted the General Equal Treatment Act (AGG) in 2006. Pursuant to §§ 6, 7 AGG, any kind of discriminatory conduct towards employees on the basis of sex is prohibited. From § 12 AGG follows the employer's obligation to take all actions necessary, including preventive measures, to protect (female) workers from discrimination.

Other national legal acts bearing reference to employment are the Law on Working Hours (ArbeitszeitG), detailed rules on night work or the Posted Workers Act (AentG).[58] The latter sets out minimum standards regarding working conditions. Questions about (minimum) wages, holiday entitlement, health protection or work safety are addressed.

Taking the suitability stage of a procurement procedure into account, Article 48 of Directive 2004/18/EC plays a major role. This provision envisages methods to prove the bidder´s technical and professional ability. § 97 IV 1 GWB constitutes the German counterpart, additional rules stem from §§7, 8 VOL/A-EG, which are also applicable below the thresholds. Declarations and certifications (SA 8000:2001[59]) give evidence of the bidder´s successful performances in comparable past contracts. An economic operator working in the fashion or sports fashion industry might, for instance, be asked to declare and prove that he has not employed children when producing clothes or football shoes.[60]

Future-related declarations or the evidence of a general business interest in the ban of child work are not admissible (due to a vague terminology) and in the latter case not sufficient. Following the rulings of the ECJ and focusing

58. Deutscher Städtetag, 'Die Berücksichtigung sozialer Belange im Vergaberecht' (2009) 7, http://www.staedtetag.de/imperia/md/content/schwerpunkte/fachinfos/2009/-22.pdf accessed March 2010.
59. Global certification system for companies not expressly referred to in German provisions on public procurement law.
60. Deutscher Städtetag, 'Die Berücksichtigung sozialer Belange im Vergaberecht' (2009) 23, <http://www.staedtetag.de/imperia/md/content/schwerpunkte/fachinfos/2009/22.pdf>accessed March 2010.

on the wording of all relevant procurement rules, the considerations should all be closely related to the actual contract award.[61]

Taking everything into account, it can be noted that each public entity interested in introducing social criteria into public procurement law, is aiming high due to the multiple and complex conditions. Nevertheless, a pot-pourri of different legal acts and a wide range of social aims exist at the level of both the Länder and the Federation.

### *3.2.5 Social considerations left to the discretion of the procuring body*

It is important to note that the inclusion of social criteria – apart from the requirements that have been presented above – is voluntary; there is no legal obligation to introduce this kind of measure. Therefore, the public purchasers are free to integrate social criteria such as the employment of long-term unemployed, educating trainees or fostering the equatlity of women. The demand to act in accordance with collective agreements has been written into procurement provisions by the Länder, too.[62] The negatory ruling of the ECJ in the case Rüffert (contradicting the estimation of the BVerfG in this matter)[63] dating from 3.4.2008,[64] however, led to the fact that most Länder declared their collective agreement provisions non-applicable, at least for the time being. In its decision relating to Directive 96/71/EC the court found that collective agreements which are not universally applicable are not compatible with the fundamental freedom to provide services, laid down in then Article 49 EC Treaty. In consequence, the German legislator noted (in its explanation to the Law on the Modernization of Procurement Law[65]) that the findings of the ECJ should be followed as far as the public works sector is concerned. At the moment, the implementation of social aspects relating to collective agreements is therefore put to rest.

Contracting authorities consider social aspects mostly at the award stage, a fact which is mainly due to political considerations. Nevertheless, German correspondents can be found at every other stage of the awarding process.

61. Deutscher Städtetag, 'Die Berücksichtigung sozialer Belange im Vergaberecht' (2009) 22, <http://www.staedtetag.de/imperia/md/content/schwerpunkte/fachinfos/2009/22.pdf>accessed March 2010.
62. Although, the Länder have enacted provisions in the field of procurement law, remarks about their contents are made within this paragraph of the paper because – strictly speaking – the norms of the Länder cannot be categorized into GWB, VgV or the procurement regulations, which is defined as procurement law in this article.
63. BVerfG, Ruling of 11th July 2006, (2007) VergabeR 42.
64. Case C- 346/06-*Rüffert* [2008] ECR I- 1989.
65. 'Gesetzentwurf zur Modernisierung des Vergaberechts' (2009), BGBl. 16/790.

Keeping the findings of the ECJ in mind and having explicit regard to the wording of the provision of § 97 V, for example, the integration of social criteria at the award stage turns out to be a bold venture. The inclusion of social aspects is only possible if the award is made to the economically most advantageous tender. The stipulation of a link to the subject-matter of the contract produces difficulties. Social criteria do not have an immediate influence on the procured product or service, they affect the subject-matter only indirectly.

Article 26 of Directive 2004/18/EC, relating to the conditions for the performance of a contract award, lists environmental and social considerations to the same extent. § 97 IV 2 GWB enables the public contractor to consider social criteria as regards the performance of the contract:

> 'Special conditions, such as social, environmental or innovative aspects, relating to the performance of a contract may be laid down, provided that these are linked with the subject-matter of the contract in question and are expressly mentioned in the specifications.'

At this point, the provisions of the ILO Conventions come into play again. The abidance by the Conventions within the process of production, the ban of child work, for example, are mainly regarded as performance conditions. In order to have means of supervision and control, the public entity can ask for the bidder's declaration to act in accordance with international labor standards.

As recent legal initiatives show, the purchaser also requires goods which have not been manufactured in workshops of the Church of Scientology. In this way, public entities use their power of demand in order to exert influence on the rise and fall of this frequently and publicly disputed sect, too.[66]

By way of drafting administrative regulations Germany is using its margin of discretion in this field.

## 4 Different Stages for the implementation of secondary criteria

### 4.1 Linked with the subject-matter of the contract

Basing the award of a contract on secondary criteria (social or ecological), nearly caused an academic sensation over the years. The 'fuss' about the integration of secondary criteria has calmed down a bit since the ECJ provided

66. Deutscher Städtetag, (by giving further and more detailed examples), 'Die Berücksichtigung sozialer Belange im Vergaberecht' (2009), 19ff, <http://www.staedtetag.de/ imperia/md/content/schwerpunkte/fachinfos/2009/22.pdf>accessed March 2010.

some guiding rules relating to this topic, though. Recalling the core findings in the leading cases *Beentjes* and *Concordia Bus Finland* for the implementation of secondary considerations, the chosen criterion has to be linked to the subject–matter of the contract. As each tender necessarily relates to the object of the contract, the criterion applied should be linked to the subject-matter of the contract too. Furthermore, Member States are obliged to act in full compliance with all relevant provisions (especially with all fundamental principles) stemming from EU law when calling for tender and integrating secondary considerations. The conditions governing the contract must be given sufficient publicity and shall ensure that no preference is given to national suppliers to the detriment of other bidders.[67]

Dwelling on the different stages of a procurement procedure where secondary considerations traditionally emerge, secondary criteria will be closely examined with respect to their linkage to the subject-matter of the contract. The first paragraph intends to cover the stages where secondary considerations are typically linked to the subject-matter, whereas the second paragraph focusses on stages without the required linkage.

#### *4.1.1 Technical specifications*

It is common knowledge that each tender process begins with the public entity's decision to call for tender. After the analysis of demands and needs follows the definition stage. The definition of the subject-matter of the contract is mostly accomplished through technical specifications; excellent opportunities for taking secondary considerations into account become manifest. Drafting technical specifications necessarily implies the specification of the characteristics, main features and functions of the procured good or service.

The procurement of reusable bottles, the deployment of Euro 4 standard buses (ecological criteria) or the construction of a barrier-free home for the handicapped or homeless are examples for secondary (social) criteria. The only aim of a procurement procedure might possibly be the employment of a certain percentage of the long-term unemployed. Examining these examples, a link to the object of the contract is given whenever the criterion constitutes an integral part of the product or service itself.[68]

67. Pablo Charro, '*Case note to Concordia Bus Finland*' (2003) 40 CMLRev 179; OLG Saarbrücken Ruling of 13th November 2002, 5 Verg 1/02.
68. *Deutscher Städtetag*, 'Die Berücksichtigung sozialer Belange im Vergaberecht' (2009) 13<http://www.staedtetag.de/imperia/md/content/schwerpunkte/fachinfos/2009/22.pdf>accessed March 2010.

### *4.1.2 Production Process*

Considering the production process, the quest for the link to the subject-matter of the contract seems to be a bit more complex. The production process asked of the tenderer has to be product- or service-related. In the case of ecological criteria (the purchase of organic food or green electricity), a linkage can be easily attested. It is important to accentuate that the criterion chosen has to refer specifically to the award in question, neither to former nor to future awards. Furthermore, general circumstances, for example that the construction of the place of production has been in conformity with ecological standards[69] or the use of recycled paper in the office, cannot be considered. As a rule, the production process should directly influence the procured product. Hence, a linkage to the subject-matter of the contract can be diagnosed. Regarding the ban of child work (production process), the employment of the long-term unemployed or social circumstances at the production stage in general, a linkage with the subject-matter cannot be ascertained (that easily) in all cases. Only if a better quality of the product is achieved in this way, for example, an influence of the production process on the product is given.[70]

### *4.1.3 Technical and professional capability or suitability*

At this stage, the capability or suitability of a tenderer is examined by the procuring entity. As the discussion above has shown, this stage relates to the selection of the candidates. Due to the breach of laws, rules with close connection to the product procured,[71] demonstrating the bidder's lack of professional reliability or by reason of grave professional misconduct, the competing tenderer is excluded from the award procedure. At this point, it should be briefly noted that the national legislator enjoys freedom concerning the enactment of detailed rules for professional misconduct. It should only be ensured that no discrimination is entailed and European law principles are complied with.

69. Horst Hopf, '*Gesetz zur Modernisierung des Vergaberechts*' (2009) Apf 226; Jan Ziekow, '*Vergabefremde Kriterien nach der Neufassung der Vergaberichtlinien*' in Rainer Pitschas, Jan Ziekow (eds), *Vergaberecht im Wandel* (Duncker & Humblot, Berlin 2006) 160.
70. Meinrad Dreher, '*Vergaberecht im Wandel: Die Sicht der Wissenschaft*' in Rainer Pitschas, Jan Ziekow (eds), *Vergaberecht im Wandel* (Duncker & Humblot, Berlin 2006) 32; Albert Bleckmann, Stefan Pieper, Volker Epping (eds), *Öffentliche Auftragsvergabe und Umweltschutz* (Carl Heymanns Verlag, Köln 2003) 202, 308; Jan Ziekow, *Die Berücksichtigung sozialer Aspekte bei der Vergabe öffentlicher Aufträge* (Studien zum öffentlichen Wirtschaftsrecht, Carl Heymanns Verlag, Köln 2007) 69.
71. Jens-Peter Schneider, 'Umweltschutz im Vergaberecht' (2009) NVwZ 1057.

Certificates (RUGMARK, SA 8000:2001), evidence of former comparable contracts and (optional) declarations help to give credible proof of the bidder's capability to vouch for a satisfactory and successful execution of the contract called for. Some municipalities ask bidders for declarations relating to their abidance by the core norms of the ILO, for example. They are possibly meant to declare their willingness to produce certain products without employing children. In other award procedures, entities are 'obliged' to fulfil conditions set up in eco-labels or they are to act in accordance with environmental agreements. Of course, the declarations given should be relevant to the performance of the contract award in question. Declarations relating to future measures do not aim at the concrete delivery of goods and are therefore regarded inadmissible.[72] Documents revealing information about past performances are partly held inadmissible too, as they tend to lose sight of new applicants trying to enter the market.[73]

#### *4.1.4 Contract Award Criteria*

Contract award criteria are often regarded as the perfect gateway for the inclusion of environmental or social aims in public procurement law. In compliance with European requirements, two ways of awarding a contract are offered.

Either the award is made to the tender with the best price or the award is made by ways of determining the economically most advantageous bid. The latter method, picked by the German legislator enables the use of secondary criteria. § 97 V GWB stipulates the following:

> 'The award is made to the economically most advantageous tender.'

The same obligation can be drawn from § 21 I 1 VOL/A-EG and § 3a VI VOB/A (2009).

It should be added that, departing from earlier case law, the selected criterion is not necessarily meant to produce economical advantages for the public authority. Therefore the criterion can be chosen freely. As a matter of fact, the link to the subject-matter of the contract in question and compliance with the

72. Jan Ziekow, *Die Berücksichtigung sozialer Aspekte bei der Vergabe öffentlicher Aufträge* (Studien zum öffentlichen Wirtschaftsrecht, Carl Heymanns Verlag, Köln 2007) 42.
73. Albert Bleckmann, Stefan Pieper, Volker Epping (eds), *Öffentliche Beschaffung und Umweltschutz* (Carl Heymanns Verlag, Köln 2003) 364.

basic principles of non-discrimination, transparency and competition (as enshrined in § 97 I and II GWB) must be ascertained.

Taking the requirement of using non-tropical wood, energy-efficient lamps or energy-saving devices (when procuring the construction of a public building), for example, a cost increase due to higher initial costs can of course be observed. But a profitability check, encompassing life cycle costs and a closer look on possible lifetime environmental impacts (taking into account costs of operation as well as costs during the utilization phase) might bring about the opposite result. Extra-costs, due to the expensive initial purchase will be amortised or even over-compensated in the longer run. A bidder not offering the best price but constantly acting in accordance with essential environmental provisions might be given preferential treatment since the ecological requirement is linked to the subject-matter of the contract (effectiveness). The bidder deserves approbation for his ecological conduct, the reason why secondary criteria resemble subsidies.

The same idea may be applied to social considerations. Complying with conventions on the ban of child work produces extra-costs for the competing entrepreneurs. An economic operator manufacturing clothes has to pay higher wages for his employees. This is a reason why his tender does not offer the best price. Nevertheless, his tender might be chosen as the requirement is directly product-related: quality, esthetics, technical superiority or durability of the product will be better.[74]

#### *4.1.5 Abnormally low tenders*

It is worth mentioning that a bidder who does not adhere to environmental or social provisions (when applying for the tender called for) is often able to offer the best price. The breach or neglect of certain standards enables the cutting of prices. If so, the bid might possibly be considered abnormally low. Therefore, the non-compliance with the relevant norms is directly connected to the purchased product (price, possibly lower quality because of lower standards). A fact which might result in the bidder´s exclusion from procedure (due to § 16 II No. 2 lit c VOB/A [2009] for example).

### 4.2 Not linked with the subject-matter of the contract

In contrast to the aforementioned stages and examples, the following remarks concentrate on the presentation of award stages where a linkage with the sub-

74. Jan Ziekow, *Die Berücksichtigung sozialer Aspekte bei der Vergabe öffentlicher Aufträge* (Studien zum öffentlichen Wirtschaftsrecht, Carl Heymanns Verlag, Köln 2007) 45.

ject-matter of the contract is not required. This is the case as far as sheltered workshops, reliability criteria or the performance criteria are concerned. Therefore, the inclusion of secondary considerations – as far as it is actually admissible – takes place under eased conditions.

*4.2.1 Sheltered workshops*

Turning attention to sheltered workshops, mainly dealt with in Article 19 of Directive 2004/18/EC on the European and §§ 41 and 43 SGB IX at the national level (apart from various administrative regulations), a relation between secondary criterion and subject-matter of the contract is nearly impossible to ascertain. A public body calling for tender and treating certain companies, so-called sheltered workshops (mostly for handicapped or blind persons), on a preferential basis is predominantly eager to promote the workshop and to get involved with community service. Normally, the public buyer does not make any references as to the characteristics or functions the product or service should comply with. On the contrary, the general fostering of sheltered workshops is the only aim the public agent has in mind. Therefore, a link to the procured good, service or works can hardly be diagnosed.

*4.2.2 Reliability as a part of suitability*

At this point, it should be stressed that the suitability criterion 'reliability' should not be mixed up with the other criteria (technical and professional ability) which have just been put into the category 'in linkage with the subject-matter'.

A bidder who has been acting in accordance with environmental or social standards and norms for a long time provides evidence of his or her reliability. As far as § 97 IV 1 GWB is concerned, the breach of certain norms demonstrates that the bidder is not abiding by the law (law-abidance as the newly implemented suitability criterion) and therefore not reliable.

Nevertheless the connection to the subject-matter of the contract cannot be detected if solely judging by the general compliance with the law. In fact, the economic operator has to prove and affirm that he is willing to comply with social or ecological conditions when it comes to the delivery of the procured good or service. This is rather a question affecting the level of technical and professional ability. The reliability criterion is in itself abstract and scarcely product related, no matter which criterion is applied. Therefore, the reliability stage is free from the requirement of a linkage with the subject-matter of the contract.

#### *4.2.3 Performance of contracts – necessarily linked with the subject-matter of the contract*

In most Member States, the performance stage renders possible the inclusion of secondary criteria which are not linked to the subject-matter of the contract. This appears to be the case if a public entity wants to achieve the participation of entities employing men and women pari passu or the abidance by social (ILO) norms.

§ 97 IV 2 GWB, however, enables German contracting authorities to lay down additional requirements relating to the performance of a contract only if the detection of a linkage to the subject-matter of the contract is possible and the characteristics are expressly mentioned in the specifications. This appears to be quite convincing. As the performance stage implies the execution of the contract and pertains to the behavior of the bidder after having won the contract, a relation to the product does normally exist when the purchasing body lays down certain conditions the enterprise has to comply with. The performance and execution of a contract marks a stage where a connection with the subject-matter (for example: eco-friendly packing, recycling of the used product, ecologically sound methods of transport or delivery or even abidance by working hours regulations or work safety norms concerning the transport of a product) of the contract is typically given. Performance itself refers to the product or service in question.[75]

## 5 What else? – Outlook on small and medium-sized enterprises – SME's

Another aspect worth of consideration is seen in the promotion of small and medium sized undertakings.[76] Although the promotion of SME's is mainly seen as a different issue, they are worth to be mentioned in this chapter as they are subject to frequent political debates. The Commission defines SME's as enterprises with up to 250 employees and an annual turnover of €50 million.[77] Due to the fact that these enterprises do not – generally speaking –

75. Jan Ziekow, *Die Berücksichtigung sozialer Aspekte bei der Vergabe öffentlicher Aufträge* (Studien zum öffentlichen Wirtschaftsrecht, Carl Heymanns Verlag, Köln 2007) 46 ff.
76. VK Saarland, Ruling of 7th September 2009, 3 VK 01/09.
77. Commission, 'Recommendation concerning the definition of micro, small and medium-sized enterprises' [2003] OJ L124/36; Christian Förster, '*Mittelstandsförderung auf Europäisch – Neue Definition der kleinen und mittelständischen Unternehmen*

possess the necessary means and capacities to fulfil complex and expensive contracts and given the fact that SME's are closely connected to the regions they are situated in, the national legislator desiring to boost sustainable economic growth, tries to improve their chances in an award procedure by means of using and developing SME-friendly measures. SME-friendly instruments (for example allowance for central purchasing bodies to bundle their demands, sub-contracting or grouping economic operators, division into lots) aim at creating equal chances for all participating bidders. SME-favouring measures on the other hand, are directed at improving the situation of small and medium-sized enterprises. They influence the result of an award and therefore go far beyond SME-fair instruments.[78]

Fears of disguised local promotion, unjustified discrimination or increasing prices are plain objections in this context. The ultimate benchmark for SME-favouring awards and the validity of respective instruments is represented by the fundamental freedoms emanating from European law.

Giving general preference to small and medium-sized local undertakings by considering their bid to be the economically most advantageous just because of their affiliation to this category (just because of what they are in comparison to major enterprises) is considered (in-)direct discrimination and therefore has to be justified. The integration of the goal to foster SME's is not free from legal problems and requirements: each award criterion should be directly linked to the subject-matter of the contract. Unfortunately, giving the character of this aim, the promotion of small and medium-sized undertakings is mostly not linked to the subject-matter of the contract in question.

The new Procurement Directives do not include any explicit provision for the promotion of SME´s, only the task to promote the access of SME's to public contracts.[79] The national legislator has used this discretion and explicitly incorporated the policy on fostering small and medium-sized undertakings: the provision of § 97 III GWB encourages and enables small and medium-sized undertakings to participate in complex award procedures:

*(KMU) zum 1.1.2005'* (2005) EWS 4; however the definition is only a recommendation and the Member States are allowed to shorten or expand the definition by taking into account specific features; VK Saarland, Ruling of 7th September 2009, 3 VK 01/09.

78. Martin Burgi, 'Small and medium-sized enterprises and procurement law', PPLR., (2007), 288.
79. See Recital 32 of the Public Sector Directive.

'The interests of small and medium-sized undertakings shall be primarily taken into consideration. Contracts may be divided into trade-specific and partial lots. If economic or technical reasons require so, several trade-specific or partial lots may be awarded in combination'.

Nowadays, lot awarding, constituting the preferable instrument, is made possible.

Nevertheless, the instrument of limiting lots has been adapted. Thereby, the national legislator hopes to counteract the award of all lots or most of them to one contractor and avoids the dependency of the purchaser on a single supplier.

§ 97 III GWB declares an obligation ('shall be') to take SME interests into serious consideration.[80] The second statement of § 97 III GWB says that contracting authorities are free to decide on the instruments applicable to achieve equality of opportunity for SMEs. Presenting this provision, it can be highlighted that it contains the obligation to award contracts in a SME-friendly and fair manner; SME-favouring measures integrating secondary policies, however, are in need of justification.

Furthermore, numerous Länder[81] enacted rules dealing with the promotion of small or medium-sized enterprises. As these instruments of local promotion mostly imply indirect discrimination, they are in need of a justification.[82]

## 6 Quantitative Data

Most public authorities are interested in pursuing environmental aims, especially in times of an ongoing debate on climate change. Bearing in mind that Germany constitutes the largest public and utilities market within Europe, the introduction of secondary considerations in Germany offers considerable potential. Nevertheless, ecological aspects remain the subject of rather careful considerations in practice. The most decisive criteria for green procurement

80. Bundesministerium für Wirtschaft und Technologie, 'Öffentliches Beschaffungswesen' (2007) 14 < http://www.bmwi.de/BMWi/Redaktion/PDF/Publikationen/ gutachten-2-2007, property=pdf,bereich=bmwi,sprache=de,rwb=true.pdf> accessed March 2010; Horst Hopf, '*Gesetz zur Modernisierung des Vergaberechts*' (2009) Apf 226.
81. Exemplary reference is given to the Mittelstandsrichtlinie in Thüringen, the Mittelstandsförderungsgesetze (MFG) and Mittelstandsrichtlinien (MRöA;öAMstR) in Baden-Württemberg or Bayern.
82. Martin Burgi, 'Small and medium-sized enterprises and procurement law' PPLR., (2007), 287.

are the question whether the product has any environmental impacts on the purchase (25 %), the availability of green alternatives (29 %) and the familiarity of such (20 %).

Green considerations in Germany incorporate a wide range, covering the purchase of cleaning products, construction, electricity as well as the fields of textiles, furniture and office equipment. About 74 per cent of the contracts awarded in the office-it-sector include green criteria. Therefore 96 per cent of the computers and monitors bought in Germany are considered 'green' – a fact, which helps to explain why Germany plays a model role as regards $CO_2$ – impacts of GPP.

The area of catering and food attains a score of 37 per cent for green procurement, whereas 68 per cent of the furniture contracts embrace ecologically friendly conditions.

The current public awareness on climate change is mirrored in the fact that 72 per cent of German organisations introduce environmental components within their procurement policy while 20 per cent of the organisations have action plans on green procurement.

In order to foster ecologically friendly procurements, public purchasers take different measures: 9 per cent of the procuring entities invest money in ecological education and staff training and about 6 per cent is spent on measures providing political support. Active communication (21 per cent) and above all (25 per cent) the appointment of formative powers (empowering responsible people to meet ecological demands) constitute the most important instruments.

Astonishingly, only 30 per cent of approximately 30,000 contracting authorities (13,000 announcements at the moment) consider secondary considerations when calling for tender.[83]

In order to give a concrete example: In Germany, about 3000 new vehicles are procured by local bodies in the local traffic sector each year. But judging by data from 2008, only 10 new busses, run with hybrid technology, were bought.[84] A closer view reveals quite a few understandable reasons.[85]

83. Jan Ziekow, *Die Berücksichtigung sozialer Belange bei der öffentlichen Auftragsvergabe* (Studien zum öffentlichen Wirtschaftsrecht, Carl Heymanns Verlag, Köln 2007) 12.

84. McKinsey-Survey, '*Potenziale der öffentlichen Beschaffung für ökologische Industriepolitik und Klimaschutz*' (2008) <http://www.bmu.de/files/na/application/pdf/mckinseystudie.pdf>accessed January 2010.

85. All data is extracted from: 'Green considerations, Collection of statistical information on Green Public Procurement in the EU-report on data collection results',

Although social considerations, on the other hand, are often taken by politicians as an instrument to raise their profile, their integration via procurement law remains rather an exception than the rule.

The reluctance to add requirements of social responsibility is due to the fact that social regards are mostly dealt with by special legal norms stemming from either constitutional, tax, child or social law, the law of occupational safety or health law. German municipalities use these norms preferably to achieve and establish socially friendly living and working conditions. Nearly every city in Nord Rhine-Westphalia, for example, tries to prevent the purchase of building material produced through exploitative child labour. Procurement rules are rarely used to achieve these aims due to legal uncertainty and the declaredly complex procurement framework.

## 7 Conclusion and outlook

Tackling the various secondary consideration affecting award procedures, it should be reiterated that the core rulings of the ECJ define the ultimate delimitations. Above the thresholds, compatibility with the findings of the ECJ and European Law (Directive 2004/18/EC) is of the highest priority. Implementing ecological or social criteria and aspects in the award process is only possible if a link to the subject-matter of the contract is given and if the fundamental rules of both EU and national procurement law are followed.

The interest of public authorities to implement additional considerations – important as they may be – does not get as much attention as one might possibly think. The devil is often in the detail, meaning that most procuring entities are afraid of violating fundamental provisions. Or, they do not exactly know how to introduce secondary considerations. In view of the legislator's ambition and obligation to foster the protection of the environment and in view of the on-going climate change, ecological considerations are going to be increasingly important, a reason why the national legislator is focusing on preparing useful guidelines.

All in all, a balance between the integration of secondary criteria on the one hand and the paramount principle of competition should be found.

First, the rules provided by the national and European legislators lack detail. The requirement of a link to the subject-matter, for instance, is spongy and nebulous. Second, public entities are afraid of violating complicated

<www.ec.europa.eu/environment/gpp/studies_en.htm>accessed March 2010.

European or national rules. Provided that a contracting authority does not abide by the governing rules, it might be obliged to pay large sums in compensation (damages system in public procurement law).

Third, the integration of secondary criteria results in extra work and an elongation of the procedure. Fourth, the procurement procedure is not on ly longer and more intricate,[86] the products called for are more expensive too. And fifth, public contractors want to prevent public criticism resulti ng from the fact that award procedures are frequently used to enable local protectionism or unfair treatment.

Therefore, municipalities and other procuring bodies are in need of guidelines and structures.

Worth mentioning is the fact that some regulations envisage the creation of task forces on GPP. By this means, fears of integrating secondary (ecological) criteria might be reduced. Relating to the administrative regulation on the procurement of energy-efficient products and services, for example, a task force chaired by the Federal Ministry should be created. The main purpose will be the monitoring and promotion of the national strategy on green procurement.

As the stage of award criteria constitutes (maybe) the most relevant stage[87] where secondary aspects might be taken into account, most contract awards include ecological conditions or the product´s life-cycle implications when it comes to determining the economically most advantageous tender.

In view of an amplitude of ILO norms and conventions in the matter of employment and work safety, municipalities and other public bodies should also be adamant and keen to try and implement the aims into practical life. Thereby the State would set an excellent example ('leading by example') for both private entities and citizens.[88] Up to now, German municipalities and other procuring entities preferred to abstain from social considerations in procurement law.[89] Hopefully, awarding bodies are going to abandon their reluc-

86. Tobias Traupel, '*Das Vergaberecht in der Reform*' (2007) Tagungsband des 8. Düsseldorfer Vergaberechtstages 15.
87. This constitutes the stage which enables the public body to integrate secondary considerations best.
88. Albert Bleckmann, Stefan Pieper, Volker Epping (eds*), Öffentliche Auftragsvergabe und Umweltschutz* (Carl Heymanns Verlag, Köln 2003) 26.
89. Deutscher Städtetag, 'Die Berücksichtigung sozialer Belange im Vergaberecht' (2009) 13, http://www.staedtetag.de/imperia/md/content/schwerpunkte/fachinfos/2009/22.pdf>accessed March 2010.

tance in this matter in view of the modernization of procurement law, enabling the insertion of various social criteria at different stages.

Therefore scientific observations about secondary considerations in Germany arrive at the conclusion, that politicians are emphatically pushing forward their inclusion whilst they build a source of serious concern and have created a climate of legal uncertainty at the same time. With a vengeance, both public entities and bidders try to funk the inclusion of secondary parameters. First and foremost social procurement practices are consistently avoided, a fact emphasising quite an imbalance between social and green procurements.

Lest there be significant inaction and less break-appliance-behavior, the legislative aim clearly must be to write down detailed provisions or guidelines dedicated to a 'can-do-approach' for secondary considerations.

## Bibliography

Albert Bleckmann, Stefan Pieper, Volker Epping (eds), *Öffentliche Auftragsvergabe und Umweltschutz* (Carl Heymanns Verlag, Köln 2003).

Martin Burgi, 'Small and Medium-sized Enterprises and Procurement Law – European Legal Framework and German Experiences' (2007) PPLR 288.

Martin Burgi, '*Vergabefremde Kriterien*' in Eberhard Grabitz, Meinhard Hilf (eds), *Das Recht der Europäischen Union*, fns 1-65.

Friederike Mechel, *Die Förderung des Umweltschutzes bei der Vergabe öffentlicher Aufträge* (Nomos, Baden-Baden 2006).

Jochen Mohr, 'Soziales Vergaberecht?' (2009) *VergabeR* 543.

Olaf Otting, 'Grünes Vergaberecht – Die Beschaffung energieeffizienter Produkte und Dienstleistungen nach der Vergaberechtsreform' (2009) CUR 44.

Jakob Steiff, 'Vergabefremde Aspekte – eine Zwischenbilanz' (2009) *VergabeR* 290.

Deutscher Städtetag, '*Die Berücksichtigung sozialer Belange im Vergaberecht*', 2009 (www.staedtetag.de/imperia/md/content/schwerpunkte/fachinfos/2009/22.pdf).

Zsofia Varga, 'Berücksichtigung sozialpolitischer Anforderungen nach dem neuen §97 IV Satz 2 GWB – europarechtskonform?' (2009) *VergabeR* 535.

Jan Ziekow, *Die Berücksichtigung sozialer Aspekte bei der Vergabe öffentlicher Aufträge*, (Studien zum öffentlichen Wirtschaftsrecht, Carl Heymanns Verlag, Köln 2007).

# V. Sustainable Procurements in Italy: Of Light and Some Shadows

*by Roberto Caranta and Sara Richetto*

## 1 Foreword

If green procurement is a new thing in Italy as elsewhere, Italy had a long tradition in using the power of the purse to try and achieve social goals, foremost among them the fight against unemployment generally and with specific attention to disadvantaged categories. This effort, however has quite often translated into open protectionism to the benefit of national contractors.

*Du Pont De Nemours* is an early instance as to how this attitude may conflict with European law imperatives. Law N. 64 of 1 March 1986 (Disciplina organica dell'intervento straordinario nel Mezzogiorno-system of rules governing special aid for Southern Italy), had extended to all public bodies and authorities, to bodies and companies in which the State had a shareholding, and to local health authorities, the obligation to purchase at least 30 % of their supplies from industrial and agricultural undertakings and small businesses established in Southern Italy. Du Pont De Nemours challenged the procurement notice and award decision taken by a local health authority in compliance with the statute. The case was brought to the European Court of Justice which, unsurprisingly, held that 'a system, which favours goods processed in a particular region of a Member State, prevents the authorities and public bodies concerned from procuring some of the supplies they need from undertakings situated in other Member States. Accordingly, it must be held that products originating in other Member States suffer discrimination in comparison with products manufactured in the Member State in question, with the result that the normal course of intra-Community trade is hindered'.[1] Indeed, what later become Art. 28 of the EC Treaty (now Art. 34 TfEU) 'must be interpreted as precluding national rules which reserve to undertakings estab-

1. Case C-21/88 *Du Pont de Nemours Italiana* [1990] ECR I-889; see R. Caranta 'In contrasto con il diritto comunitario le riserve a favore di imprese del Meridione' *Giust. civ.* 1991, 1369.

lished in particular regions of the national territory a proportion of public supply contracts'.[2]

The Constitutional court too had to fight local protectionism, quashing the statutory rules enacted by one Region that made participation into public works procurement conditional upon being listed in a regional list of potential contractors, a not too covert attempt at buying local.[3] However, the legislation still in force effectively closets regional markets for social services to the benefit of local NGOs.[4]

After sketching the institutional and legal environment for public procurement in Italy, the provisions fostering sustainable procurements enacted in Italy following Directives 2004/17/EC and 2004/18/EC will be analysed.

## 2 Institutional and legal environment

Although not (yet) in the shape of a federal State, Italy is in a process of gradual devolution of competences to the regional and local level. According to a controversial judgement by the Constitutional court, the State has exclusive competence in legislating and regulating public procurement in so far as issues of competition – read in a generous sense – may arise.[5] The State also has legislative competence, either exclusive or concurrent, with reference to many aspects of the social legislation, including the protection of workers' health.[6]

D.lgs. 12 aprile 2006, n. 163, 'Codice dei contratti pubblici relativi a lavori, servizi e forniture in attuazione delle direttive 2004/17/CE e 2004/18/CE', hereinafter the 'Code', already amended a few times, has taken the place of various pieces of legislation on works, supplies and services procurements.

2. Para 18.
3. Corte cost., 26 giugno 2001, n. 207, *Urbanistica e appalti*, 2001, 987.
4. The system is still being upheld in courts: Cons. Stato, Sez. V, 2 febbraio 2009, n. 558 www.giustizia-amministrativa.it .
5. Corte cost., 23 novembre 2007, n. 401, *Giorn. dir. amm.*, 2008, 624, note C. Lacava '*I contratti pubblici tra Stato e regioni e la tutela della concorrenza*'; see also R. De Nictolis 'La Corte Costituzionale si pronuncia sul codice dei contratti pubblici relativi a lavori, servizi e forniture' *Urbanistica e appalti*, 2008, 5.
6. Corte cost., 7 novembre 2003, n. 331, *Foro it.*, 2004, I, 1364, con nota di M. Miglioranza 'Inquinamento elettromagnetico e limiti alle competenze regionali: standard di protezione nazionali e legalità sostanziale'.

The provisions in Directives 2004/17/CE and 2004/18/CE opening up some room for social and environmental considerations in public procurements have found their way in the Codice. Art. 2(2) stipulates that, within the limits prescribed by the Code itself, the best value for money principle may make way to social, health, and environmental considerations if the contract notice so provides.

Community law provisions incorporating sustainable procurement rules usually are not mandatory, and as such they were transposed into the Italian legislation. Some considerations are, however, taken into account by general rules outside the Code and their incorporation in the contract specifications is normally mandatory. This is the case for instance with reference to the mandatory employment of disadvantaged people, social security and other benefits, working hours, sufficient and equal pay, occupational safety and health.

If the legislative environment is more or less the same all over Italy, the competence to manage public procurement procedures is very much decentralised. Consip s.p.a. is acting as a central purchasing entity for serial supplies and a few services. Most public law entities, however, manage their procurements themselves. At times, and this is not only the case with the State but also with the Regions and other sub-national entities, specific units within each entity procure autonomously what they need. In many Regions the units responsible for health care in any given districts manage their own procurements, even if a few Regions have created centralised purchasing bodies at times managing e-procurements.[7]

## 3 Definition of the subject-matter of the contract and technical specifications

Traditionally in Italy technical specifications are drafted in specific *capitolati*, sorts of *cahiers des charges*, laying down all sort of general and special rules applicable to any given contract.[8] A number of rules of general application, including environmental and social ones, may be expressly referred to in the capitolati, have at least some kind of general referral clause to any binding rules which may be applicable by way of legislation. However, according to

7. E.g. Art. 18 ff. L.R. Emilia Romagna, 24 maggio 2004, n. 11.
8. See S. Ponzio, *I capitolati negli appalti pubblici* (Napoli, Novene, 2006).

settled case-law, rules of general application must be complied with even if they are not expressly or impliedly referred to in the contract documents.[9]

Art. 68 of the Code lays down the rules concerning the definition of the subject-matter of the contract through technical specifications. Under its first indent, whenever possible technical specifications must be drafted so as to take into consideration the accessibility requirements for the handicapped, the need for a design adequate for all users, and environmental protection.[10] In any case, under Art. 68(2), technical specifications have to be drafted so as to allow equal opportunities to all potential bidders and may not hinder without proper justification the competition.[11]

Among the numerous pieces of legislation upholding social or environmental values, only a few may be brought to attention here.

Measures to promote accessibility for all have been part of Italian building legislation since l. 9 gennaio 1989, n. 13 and l. 27 febbraio 1989, n. 62, 'Disposizioni per favorire il superamento e l'eliminazione delle barriere architettoniche negli edifici private'. These days an extensive regulation is to be found in Art. 77 ff. D.P.R. 6 giugno 2001, n. 380, 'Testo unico delle disposizioni legislative e regolamentari in materia edilizia'. The legislation applies to both private and public buildings. All new public buildings must conform to accessibility for all standards to be taken into account when designing the works. Specific funds are set aside to upgrade both private and public buildings to the same standards.

Specific provisions have been enacted through l. 9 gennaio 2004, n. 4, 'Disposizioni per favorire l'accesso dei soggetti disabili agli strumenti informatici', to foster the accessibility of the websites of public administrations, including private firms entrusted with the provision of services of general interest. According to Art. 4(1), better accessibility is a reason for preference in case of otherwise equivalent bids. Under Art. 4(2), technical specifications in procurement for website design and supply must be drafted taking into ac-

9. With reference to the rules for employment of people with handicaps Cons. Stato, Sez. V, 19 giugno 2009, n. 4028, in *Giur. It.*, 2009, 456; Cons. Stato, Sez. V, 24 gennaio 2007, n. 256, in www.giustizia-amministrativa.it ; Cons. Stato, Sez. V, 18 novembre 2004, n. 7555, in *Foro Amm. CDS*, 2004, 3244.

10. See generally R. Invernizzi '*Specifiche tecniche*' in M.A. Sandulli, R. De Nictolis e R. Garofoli (curr.) *Trattato sui contratti pubblici* (Milano, Giuffré, 2008) vol. III, 2073 ff.

11. Cons. Stato, Sez. V, 12 luglio 2004, n. 5049, *Giur. it.*, 2005, 407, held to be unnecessarily discriminatory a provision in a notice for procurement of school meals published by a municipality which mandated that the meals had to be cooked and packed on its territory which was motivated by concerns for the freshness of the meals.

count specific rules enacted by the Government. The same applies to purchases by the private sector and NGOs when they are made possible thanks to public funds. These rules were enacted with d.p.r. 1° marzo 2005, n. 75. The CNIPA – Centro nazionale per l'informatica nella pubblica amministrazione, a technical unit entrusted with spreading IT use in the public sector, is charged with vigilance on the compliance with l. 9 gennaio 2004, n. 4. It adopted a decree listing the firms charged with certifying accessibility.[12]

Coming to green technical specification and eco-labels, Art. 25 of the D. Lgs. 5 febbraio 1997, n. 22, required public authorities to purchase and to use goods made of recycled elements.[13] Today Art. 68 (3)(b) and (9) of the Code are the result of copy and paste implementation of Art. 23 Comma 3(3)(b) and (6) of Directive 2004/18/EC. While it is doubtful whether procuring entities are capable of drafting specifications in terms of performance, the reference to eco-labels should not pose particular problems. Be that as it may be, so far the provisions in Art. 68 which were examined here have not lead to litigation adjudicated by courts.

## 4 Selection of candidates (and special provisions for NGOs active in the social sphere)

As elsewhere, in Italy many environmental standards are mandatory and a number of social considerations have evolved into social rights benefiting from protection at either Constitutional or legislative level. These provisions are imperative in the sense that they impose themselves on every contractor. As such, they deserve to be considered 'general' contract performance conditions. However, they are also relevant in relation to the selection of candidates, since their breach in the past may lead the delinquent contractors to be disqualified from taking part into award procedures.[14]

Before going to the details, it is necessary to point out some past rules and interpretations which actually limited the power of SMEs and NGOs to take part in procurement procedures thus breaching Art. 4, Directive 2004/18/EC,

12. It created a specific website www.pubbliaccesso.gov.it
13. See M. Occhiena '*Norme di gestione ambientale*' in M.A. Sandulli, R. De Nictolis e R. Garofoli (curr.) *Trattato sui contratti pubblici* (Milano, Giuffré, 2008) vol. II, 1474 ff.
14. See generally R. Greco '*I requisiti di ordine generale*' in M.A. Sandulli, R. De Nictolis e R. Garofoli (curr.) *Trattato sui contratti pubblici* (Milano, Giuffré, 2008), vol. II, 1267 ff.

which outlaws discrimination based on the form taken on by economic traders is forbidden. For instance, Art. 113(5)(a), of D. Lgs. 2000, n. 267 (Testo Unico degli Enti locali) limited competition for the award of local service procurement and concession to companies incorporated as *società per azioni* or *società a responsabilità limitata*. The Court of justice, in the *Frigerio case*, held that precludes national provisions EU law imposing specific legal form to candidates or tenderers.[15]

Clearly inconsistent with European law was also the case law excluding cooperatives and other non-profit organisation from public procurement procedures (different from those for which NGOs are preferred – as we shall see).[16] Apart from that the recent corporate law reform by D. Lgs. N. 3 of 2006 has equated cooperatives to other corporate entities,[17] Art. 34 of the Code, as modified due to the opening of an infringement procedure by the Commission,[18] today provides that individual traders, trading companies and cooperative societies all are allowed to award procedures in public contracts.[19] Art. 34 of the Code seems now to be in line with the case law of the Court of justice, which recently held that the provisions of Directive 2004/18/EC, in particular those in Article 1(2)(a) and (8), first and second subparagraphs, which refer to the concept of 'economic operator', must be interpreted as permitting entities which are primarily non-profit-making and do not have the organisational structure of an undertaking or a regular presence on the market – such as universities and research institutes and consortia made up of universities and public authorities – to take part in public tendering procedures.[20]

Coming to those provisions in the Code that give effect to the provisions on qualification found in Directive 2004/18/EC, under Art. 38 of the Code, implementing both Art. 27 and Art. 45(2)(e) of the directive, those firms having breached either security at work provisions or rules on social contributions in their home countries are excluded from all contracting procedures. The provision is reinforced in Art. 87(4-bis) of the Code, in theory dealing

15. Case C-357/06, *Frigerio*, [2007] ECR I-12311.
16. Cons. Stato, sez. V, 7 ottobre 2008, n. 4901 in *Ambiente e sviluppo*, 2009, 4, 374; TAR Lombardia Brescia, sez. I, 27 ottobre 2008, n. 1440 in www.giustizia-amministrativa.it.
17. Codice civile, Articles 2511, 2518 and 2519.
18. C(2008)108.
19. R. De Nictolis, Le novità del terzo (e ultimo) decreto correttivo del codice dei contratti pubblici, in *Urbanistica e appalti*, 2008, 1225.
20. Case C-305/08, *CoNISMa*, nyr.

with abnormally low offers but having become the locus for providing answer to social considerations, as added by Art. 1(909) l. 27 dicembre 2006, n. 296.[21]

Procuring entities are charged to check that social contribution rules and work security provisions are abided by. Art. 16-*bis*(10) of d.l. 29 novembre 2008, n. 185, as amended by l. 28 gennaio 2009, n. 2, give procuring entities the power to access the on-line databases of the institutions responsible for collecting social contributions.[22] Under Art. 9 of the Code, procuring entities may set up a single contact point to inform all potential bidders as to the rules concerning *inter alia* occupational safety; the provision is implementing Art. 27 of EC directive 2004/18/EC. The Autorità per la vigilanza dei contratti pubblici di lavori, servizi e furniture, the vigilance authority for public contracts, manages a data bank with information on potential contractors which are accessible to the procuring entities. The Osservatorio dei contratti pubblici relativi a lavori, servizi e forniture, a statistical technical unit attached to the vigilance authority, is charged with collecting data on, among others, workforce costs and security measures referred to in contract notices all over the Country with the aim of establishing standard performance costs (Art. 7 (4)(a) of the Code). It is also worth mentioning that a qualification system for works procurements has been set up under Art. 40(4)(d) of the Code, making it easier for procuring entities to become knowledgeable of past breaches of environmental or social rules.

It is doubtful that the present system is effective to counter breaches taking place outside Italy, even less so when breaches take place outside the EU. Procuring entities will not normally be in a position to know what are the social and environmental rules in force outside the country, let alone whether a firm has complied with them. At the same time, when applied without proper

21. Cons. Stato, sez. V, 19 novembre 2009, n. 7255, in www.giustizia-amministrativa.it, upheld the provision in a call for bids requiring participants to have regularly paid social contributions; the judgment also held that the date to consider to this effect is the date the bid is submitted; Cons. Stato, Sez. VI, 27 febbraio 2008, n. 716, www.giustizia-amministrativa.it, held that breaches of social contribution rules need to have been the object of a final decision (and this was not the case, since the decision taken by the competent institution had been challenged in court and judgeement was pending); according to T.A.R. Veneto, Sez. I, 26 maggio 2009, n. 1601 www.giustizia-amministrativa.it, serious breaches only are relevant, with the exclusion of merely formal irregularities.
22. The same statute introduced unemployment benefits for redundant workers which do not receive any other benefits. This provisions came into force with D.M. 19 maggio 2009, n. 46441 and Circular of INPS 26 maggio 2009, n. 73.

knowledge of foreign legislation, these kinds of rules could lead to imposing Italian standards to firms operating outside Italy. In this context, it may be relevant that the Code does not contain any express reference to the ILO standards. The possibility left open by paragraph 33 of the preamble to the Directive 2004/18/EC has not been embraced in the legislation, even if procuring entities may take into account social considerations by their own motion provided they abide by the Code.

Incidentally, it may be recalled that the question has also arisen as to whether it is possible to directly award a procurement contract to contractors proposing very advanced technology for the protection of the environment. Art. 57 of the Code has implemented Art. 31 of Directive 2004/18/CE on negotiated procedures without any prior publication of a contract notice. An interesting case concerned the application of Art. 57(2)(b) concerning the case when, for technical or artistic reasons, or for reasons connected to the protection of exclusive rights, the contract may only be entrusted to a specific economic operator. The municipality of Ugento intended to conclude a contract for a special and energy saving system for the street lighting. The City Council, whose decision was upheld by the local first instance administrative court, decided to directly award the contract to a specific economic operator, who in its view offered an advanced technology at low cost.[23]

It is doubtful whether such as decision is consistent with European law, since it is doubtful – and impossible to say without a proper competitive procedure – whether only one operator existed qualified to offer a smart lighting system.

Art. 52 of the Code implements Art. 19 of directive 2004/18/CE on sheltered workshops, at the same time keeping in force the more generous provisions related to procurement award to other entities employing disadvantaged categories.[24] The point is, that sheltered workshop are not known as such under Italian law and the pre-existent legislation lays down requirements for privileged access to public procurements which are divergent from those found in Art. 19 of the Directive. A recent interpretative document by the vigilance authority, while assessing this circumstance, has tried to shed some light on sheltered workshops and distinguish them from other entities em-

23. T.A.R. Puglia Lecce, Sez. III, 29 gennaio 2010, n. 372, in www.giustizia-amministrativa.it.
24. See A.M. Balestrieri 'Gli 'appalti riservati' fra principio di economicità ed esigenze sociali' *Urbanistica e appalti*, 2009, 789.

ploying persons issuing from many disadvantaged categories and not just handicapped people.[25]

It is to be assumed that the pre-existing and by far more generous provisions will continue to be applied across the country at least in so far as below the threshold procurements are concerned. The most relevant instance is that of social co-operatives. Art. 4 l. 8 novembre 1991, n. 381, amended a few times in the past, lays down the requirements a firm must meet to be considered a social cooperative. Two different kinds of social cooperatives are envisaged: 1) cooperatives operating in health and education, where the social objectives are mainly met by providing services to the most needy sections of the general public; 2) other social cooperatives which instead have as their mission to help disadvantaged people to work. In this case, disadvantaged people must amount to at least 30 per cent of their workforce. The charitable work of participants is possible and is not bound by the rules on working conditions, which are different from those relating to social security. Social Cooperatives at time are not paid but receive a reinborsement of their costs. Disadvantaged people are defined as handicapped, people formerly committed to psychiatric wards, drug users and alcoholics, minors of at least minimal working age with difficult familiar conditions.[26] Apart for the management of kindergartens, social cooperatives are entrusted with janitorial and cleaning services,[27] nursing services,[28] waste collection.[29] The work of volunteers being in principle gratuitous may only be partially counted against the costs reimbursed by the procuring entity.[30]

According to Art. 5, procuring entities may award social cooperatives below the threshold services contracts (services in the social and health and education areas being reserved to specific social cooperatives), following procedures divergent from usual public procurements rules;[31] Art. 5(4) fur-

25. Determinazione n. 2/2008, January 23rd, 2008.
26. Regions may however widen the scope of the provision, including more disadvantaged categories: see Cass. Lav., 14 marzo 2005, n. 5472, *CED Cassazione*, 2005.
27. Cons. Stato, Sez. V, 30 agosto 2001, n. 4580, *Foro Amm.*, 2001, 2044.
28. T.A.R. Veneto, Sez. I, 26 febbraio 2002, n. 957, *Foro Amm. TAR*, 2002, 425.
29. T.A.R. Puglia, Bari, Sez. I, 27 maggio 2000, n. 2307, *Riv. It. Dir. Pubbl. Comunitario*, 2000, 1485, but in this case the award was struck down because above the threshold.
30. T.A.R. Campania, Salerno, Sez. I, 3 luglio 2002, n. 641, *Foro Amm. TAR*, 2002, 2651.
31. The under the threshold limit has been stressed in the case law: e.g. Cons. Stato, Sez. V, 30 agosto 2001, n. 4580, *Foro Amm.*, 2001, 2044; T.A.R. Lazio, Latina, Sez. I, 15 novembre 2007, n. 1211, www.giustizia-amministrativa.it ; T.A.R. Puglia, Bari, Sez.

ther empowers procuring entities to state in the contract notice that the contract will have to be executed by employing disadvantaged people. Procurement procedures, when any recourse to them is had, may even be reserved to the participation of social cooperatives.[32] However this is not often the case. The administrative court have held that Art. 5(4) does not depart from the general rules of public procurement based on the general principles of transparency, competition and non-discrimination.[33]

In theory, regions and local authorities may not limit participation in the procurement procedures to social cooperatives having their main office in their jurisdiction.[34]

Regions have taken the lead from l. 8 novembre 1991, n. 381, adopting their own statutes on the matter. One instance is l.reg. Piemonte, 9 giugno 1994, n. 18 '"Norme di attuazione della legge 8 novembre 1991, n. 381 'Disciplina delle cooperative sociali''. According to Art. 7, when programming different social activities, the Region must foresee the specific contributions of social cooperatives, identifying those sectors where these cooperatives may play a relevant role thanks to their mix of public interest, entrepreneurship, and democracy; similar provisions are found in Art. 8 f., concerning vocational training and employment policies.

Art. 10 ff. l.reg. Piemonte, 9 giugno 1994, n. 18, deal with contracts between procuring entities and social cooperatives. The Regional government is given the power to draft standard contracts; in order to avoid interruptions in the service provision, contract duration must extend to more than one year, but to ensure proper vigilance, their implementation must be reviewed yearly. Given the type of activities concerned, Art. 12 rules out the award criterion

I, 7 maggio 2002, n. 2265, *Foro Amm. TAR*, 2002, 1731; T.A.R. Puglia, Bari, Sez. I, 27 maggio 2000, n. 2307, *Riv. It. Dir. Pubbl. Comunitario*, 2000, 1485; T.A.R. Marche, 7 aprile 2000, n. 521, *Urbanistica e appalti*, 2000, 6, 674.

32. E.g., with reference to management of kindergartens, Cons. Stato Sez. V, 17 aprile 2002, n. 2010, in *Foro Amm. CDS*, 2002, 929; T.A.R. Puglia, Lecce, 15 aprile 2009, n. 724, in *Urbanistica e appalti*, 2009, 1015, held that the well-established principle allowing procuring entities to introduce into the call for bids provisions aimed at restricting the participation to subjects being particularly qualified, applies provided that this choice does not limit the competition.
33. T.A.R. Lazio Roma, 9 dicembre 2008, n. 11093, in www.giustizia-amministrativa.it; T.A.R. Calabria, 24 novembre 2008, n. 1503, in www.giustizia-amministrativa.it.
34. T.A.R. Marche, 14 maggio 1999, n. 565, in *Trib. Amm. Reg.*, 1999, I, 2662; however, upholding the exclusion from the procedure of a co-operative which did not provide evidence as to its being included in the regional list established under Art. 2 l.reg. Piemonte, 9 giugno 1994, n. 18, Cons. Stato, Sez. V, 2 febbraio 2009, n. 558 www.giustizia-amministrativa.it .

based on the lowest price. The award is to take place in application of the most advantageous economic offer, taking into account the price, the quality of the proposes activities, the efficiency in meeting the objectives, and any other element relevant with reference to the specific services at issue. Art. 13 lays down more specific rules for public procurements awarded to social co-operatives having as their objective providing employment opportunities to disadvantaged categories. According to Art. 13(1), procuring entities must set aside a percentage of their procurement budget for contracts to be awarded to social cooperatives. Contract documents must foresee how many disadvantaged people are to be hired, with reference to which tasks and for how much time. A specific employment project must be drafted with reference to any disadvantaged person. The award criteria must take into account the consistency of the program of social inclusion; the sustainability of the work opportunities offered; the territorial links of both the disadvantaged people and the sphere of intervention of the social cooperatives. The l.reg. Piemonte, 9 giugno 1994, n. 18, further provides different aids and benefits to the different charitable activities performed by the social cooperatives.

Other measures have been taken pursuant to the horizontal subsidiarity principle now enshrined in Art. 118 of the Italian Constitution. They envisage a deeper involvement of civil society, NGOs included, in the design and delivery of social policies. The leading text at national level is l. 7 dicembre 2000, n. 383, 'Disciplina delle associazioni di promozione sociale'. NGOs corresponding to certain characteristics are listed in national and regional registers. They normally operate through the charitable work of their participants, but they may also hire workers. They enjoy different fiscal benefits and may be rented space for free by the State and other public law entities. Under Art. 30, they may pass agreements with public law entities designing the services they may provide to sections of the general public, forms of control on the provision of the same services by the public law entity concerned, and the ways the NGOs may ask for refund of the costs they have shouldered.

The Government adopted an instruction directed to the Regions and to the local authorities on the procedures to be followed when entrusting social services to NGOs.[35] Art. 5 and 6 stipulate that public law entities responsible for the provision of social services may both procure the social services from the NGOs or entrust them with the provision of the services. In both cases, the choice of the NGO must follow transparent and competitive procedures. Un-

35. D.P.C.M. 30 marzo 2001, 'Atto di indirizzo e coordinamento sui sistemi di affidamento dei servizi alla persona ai sensi dell'art. 5 della legge 8 novembre 2000, n. 328'.

der Art. 4, the award criteria must refer to the most economically advantageous offer having reference to the candidate's experience in the specific sector.[36]

Here too the Regions have followed the lead of State. We may take for instance l.reg. Piemonte, 8 gennaio 2004, n. 1, 'Norme per la realizzazione del sistema regionale integrato di interventi e servizi sociali e riordino della legislazione di riferimento'. Art. 31(1) again rules out the lowest price award criterion. The Regional government is given the power to enact instructions to the local authorities with the view to encourage civil society, NGOs, and charities participation in the provision of social services. Concerning the award criteria to be used, Art. 31(4) refers to the need to enhance the project capability of contractors, to take into account the costs foreseen in nationwide employment contracts, and to asses the quality standards of services provided to the public.

The Regional Government adopted the instructions foreseen by Art. 31 l.reg. Piemonte, 8 gennaio 2004, n. 1, with a decision taken on May 22nd, 2006. First of all it considers the huge variety of civil society organisations recognised by the national and regional legislation. Along with social cooperatives, we shall consider volunteers' organisations and the 'associazioni di promozione sociale' recognised under l. 7 dicembre 2000, n. 383, and l.reg. Piemonte 7 febbraio 2006, n. 7 'Disciplina delle associazione di promozione sociale', non profit organisations, and others. Concerning the award of procurement contracts for services, the instructions refer to the criteria listed in Art. 31 l.reg. Piemonte, 8 gennaio 2004, n. 1, mentioned above, and a preference for restricted and negotiated procedures. Best value for money can be considered a target as important as the quality of services provided to the general public or to specific sections thereof. Minimum wages as agreed upon at national level by trade unions and employers' organisations have to be complied with also in cases relating to workers associated in social cooperatives.

The document is relevant in two respects. On the one hand, it must consider the panoply of different civil society organisations that in the past two decades have found some form of legislative recognition and various benefits. It is suggested that clarity would very much benefit from any initiative

36. This could of course pose problems when considered under the case law distinguishing qualification and award criteria: see generally S. Treumer 'The Distinction between Selection and Award Criteria in EC Public Procurement Law: A Rule without Exceptions?' PPLR, (2008), 103, and for the position in Italy M. Comba 'Selection and Award Criteria in Public Procurement Law' PPLR, (2008), 122.

aimed at the simplification of this complex normative panorama. On the other hand, it shows that many social services, particularly those targeted to individuals in need, are now provided by NGOs and other organisations following special award procedures which are not open to all market participants and where best value for money is of limited relevance.

The situation in Italy mirrors the European Commissions remarks as to the peculiar position of social services in the Communication on Services of general interest, including social services of general interest: a new European commitment.[37] This is especially so when one considers the regional and local level, actually responsible for the provision of these services.

Indeed, NGOs play a relevant role in the provision of many social services. The legal position, however, will probably have to be somewhat reassessed following the Court of justice judgment in the *Misericordie* case.[38] In particular, direct contracting without any transparency and competition is probably to be held inconsistent with European law but for the very low value services. At the same time, it is doubtful whether procedures stressing value for money are appropriate for awarding contracts concerning social services.

In the past, the favourable treatment of NGOs with specific reference to the procurement services had to be contrasted with a trend in the case law generally excluding them from taking part in 'normal' public procurement procedures, which were considered a preserve of for profit organisations.[39] This trend has now been finally abandoned.[40]

37. COM(2007) 725 final, at 7 ff.
38. Case C-119/06, *Commission v. Italy*, [2008] ECR I-, points 34 ff.; see A. Brown 'Application of the Directives to Contracts to Non-for-profit Organisations and Transparency under the EC Treaty: A Note on Case C-119/06 Commission v Italy', PPLR, (2008), NA96; R. Caranta 'Attività pubblica, attività no-profit, e disciplina dei contratti pubblici di servizi', *Urbanistica e appalti*, 2008, 293; M. Mattalia *'Convenzionamento diretto o procedure concorsuali nell'affidamento del servizio di trasporto sanitario?' Foro amm. CdS*, 2008, 1976, and A. Albanese 'L'affidamento di servizi socio-sanitari alle organizzazioni di volontariato e il diritto comunitario: la Corte di giustizia manda un monito agli enti pubblici italiani', *Riv. it. dir. pubbl. comunitario*, 2008, 1453.
39. A recent judgment in this vein is T.A.R. Liguria, Sez. II, 15 maggio 2008, n. 1012, in www.giustizia-amministrativa.it .
40. Cons. Stato, Sez. VI, 16 giugno 2009, n. 3897, *Giur. it.*, 2009, 2787: the court did not consider relevant that the foundation has a special tax regime as this condition also applies to the social cooperatives (referred to in art. 34 of this Code) or to the non-profit organisations (regulated in D.lgs. 24 marzo 2006, n. 155); Cons. Stato, Sez. V, 8 luglio 2002, n. 3790, *Giust. Civ.*, 2002, I, 2956; T.A.R. Lazio, Sezione III *quater*, 18 luglio 2006, n. 5993, *Giur. It.*, 2006, 2421, and *Sanità pubbl.*, 2006, 6, 79, note C.

A specific discipline has been enacted by D. Lgs. 1 dicembre 1997, n. 468, 'Revisione della disciplina dei lavori socialmente utili', amended by D. Lgs. 28 febbraio 2000, n. 81, concerning the employment of redundant workers and long-term unemployed in the construction and maintenance of public buildings and in the provision of other services of general interest. The services are awarded on the basis of a project submitted by the workers concerned. The case law points out that the services in question being additional to those normally provided cannot be the same as those awarded in the past following public procurement procedures. Moreover, the concerned public law entities must be satisfied that the services in question could not be provided under normal market conditions.[41] The said conditions are very restrictive. The fact that considerable amounts of money are still allotted to these projects could, however, raise some suspicions as to the reality.[42]

The panorama must also include the provisions by D.lgs. 24 marzo 2006, n. 155, which is dedicated to 'social firm' (not necessarily but not excluding co-operatives). Social firms are empowered to operate in the most different social sectors, such as social welfare, health care services, education and learning, environmental protection, upgrading of cultural inheritance, social tourism, university instruction, research into cultural services and other instrumental services directed towards social companies. Accordingly, the case law has held that they may take part in public procurement procedures on the same footing as commercial companies.[43]

Finally, concerning technical capability, Art. 48(2)(f) and Art. 50 of Directive 2004/18/EC, on environmental management standards, have been respectively implemented through cut and paste in Art. 42(1)(f) and in Art. 44 of the Code.[44] These provisions have so far not been litigated in Italian courts. No-

Corbetta, 'La partecipazione delle ONLUS alle gare d'appalto per l'affidamento dei servizi alla persona'; T.A.R. Liguria, Sez. II, 23 dicembre 2002, n. 1206, *Urbanistica e appalti*, 2003, 703, note L. Fumarola 'Non profit e appalti di servizi', and *Foro Amm. TAR*, 2003, 85 (s.m.), nota L. Musselli 'Applicabilità dei principi concorrenziali e regime di convenzionamento tra pubblica amministrazione ed enti non profit: il caso dell'affidamento del servizio di trasporto malati da parte di un'azienda ospedaliera'.

41. See Cons. Stato, Sez. V, 28 aprile 2003, n. 2128, *Foro amm. CDS*, 2003, 1324; Cons. Stato Sez. V, 25 giugno 2002, n. 3451, *Foro amm. CDS*, 2002, 1470.
42. See http://www.lavoro.gov.it/Lavoro/md/AreeTematiche/AmmortizzatoriSociali/Lavori_Utili/ .
43. Cons. Stato Sez. V Sent., 25 febbraio 2009, n. 1128, *Giornale dir. amm.*, 2009, 532.
44. See M. Occhiena '*Norme di gestione ambientale*' above fn, 1478 ff.

tices published in TED were analysed in order to check whether Italian procuring entities took into account environmental considerations and, in particular, EMAS and Eco-label. Eco-label was not referred to in any tender notices, while EMAS or ISO 14001 was required on an average of 30-40 notices each year since 2005 as either a requirement or a way to provide information on the environmental management systems. This was normally the case with reference to contracts for sewage disposal, waste and garbage management, and public lighting. The overall impression is that we still have to see a marked improvement concerning environmental considerations in Italian public procurement practice.

## 5 Award criteria

Art. 53(1)(a) of Directive 2004/18/EC has been implemented in Art. 83 of the Code. After the amendments introduced with d.lgs. 31 luglio 2007, n. 113, award criteria may refer not just to environmental characteristics, but to the possible reduction in the use of energy and other natural resources by the works or the goods procured. The provision stresses the necessary link with the subject-matter of the contract to be passed.

A nice case concerned a procurement for school meals. Additional points were to be awarded with reference to a) gifts to the kids (5 points out of 100); b) sponsoring of a nutritional education program targeted to the same kids (5 points out of 100); c) sponsoring of formation classes targeted to the workers providing the service (5 points out of 100); d) hiring of additional personnel (10 points out of 100). The Sicilian section of the Council of State found the award criteria to be legal, holding as to a) that it is appropriate to think of a Christmas gift for young children; b) and c) are instrumental to a better quality of the service, and d) is good for encouraging employment and not without any link to the procurement at issue.[45]

The rules on abnormally low offers are of strategic relevance when considering environmental and social issues. Following some high profile accident on the workplace, the Italian Parliament has been particularly keen in re-drafting the provisions of the Code dealing with these offers with a view to buttress security at the work place.

45. Cons. Giust. Amm. Sicilia, 2 marzo 2007, n. 86, www.giustizia-amministrativa.it ; price was allotted up to 60 out of 100 points.

Art. 8 of l. 3 agosto 2007, n. 123, has amended Art. 86 of the Code, laying down criteria for deciding which offers may be considered to be abnormally low. A new provision (3-bis) was added stating that procuring entities, when drafting contract documents and checking abnormally low tenders, must make sure that the indicative price is adequate with reference to the appropriate pay-level for the workers and to cover security measures. The portion of the price referring to those items is specifically indicated referring to tables drafted and regularly updated by the Ministry for labour and pensions on the basis of the applicable collective agreements. Finally, security costs are non negotiable and bidders cannot take into consideration lower costs (3-ter).

Deeper modifications affected Art. 87 of the Code, dealing with the verification of abnormally low offers. Art. 87(2)(e), which copied Art. 55(1)(d) of Directive 2004/18/EC stipulating that justifications may refer to the respect of working condition, was repealed by Art. 1(909) l. 27 dicembre 2006, n. 296. Under Art. 87(2)(g), to exonerate what on their face appear to be abnormally low tenders with reference to costs relating to their workforce, candidates may refer to the tables prepared by the Ministry for labour and social policies [different provisions bear witness to the ever changing denominations of Italy's ministers] based on collective agreements between associations of employers and trade unions, account also being taken of the rules on social contributions. Art. 87(3) rules out the admissibility of justifications relating to minimum wages, which must be read as providing that any justification must tend to demonstrate that rules as to minimum wages have been complied with. Art. 87(4), which was amended twice in a matter of weeks by Art. 1(909) l. 27 dicembre 2006, n. 296, and by Art. 3 D.Lgs. 26 gennaio 2007, n. 6, provided that no justification is admissible with reference to the costs relating to security on the workplace, cost which have to be expressly indicated in the bid.

Furthermore, art 89(3) of the Code cast a duty upon procuring entities, when preparing calls for bids, to be satisfied that the economic value is adequate and enough to cover the labour cost, as stated in art. 87(2)(g).[46]

The problem with these provisions is how far the procuring entities may go in forcing wages, social and other security costs inevitably calculated against the Italian legislative background on firms coming from other countries, this even the more so if those firms come from EU Member States. Here again, it is much easier to check the respect of workers rights in public pro-

46. G. Ferrari and L. Tarantino, *Gara pubblica e costo del lavoro*, in *Urbanistica e appalti,* 2009, 248.

curement for works, since the security legislation applicable to the workers would normally be the Italian one. Especially when suppliers of goods and services are from the European Union, the desire to protect national firms and workers from social dumping has to be carefully balanced with the need not to set barrier to the free circulation of goods or services. The recent legislative amendments seem to go a long way towards imposing national standards even on goods and services supplied from outside the country. This way they follow a lead provided by the case law. The *Consiglio di Stato*, Italian highest administrative court, held that a French firm could not exonerate what appeared an abnormally low bid in a procurement for goods by referring to less strict – and onerous – security on the workplace legislation in force where the goods were manufactured.[47] It is doubtful whether this ruling is consistent with European law.[48]

The strict attitude just described is waived for cooperatives, which may benefit in procurement procedures from the special status and the benefits attached they enjoy on a more general level (and whose characterisation as State aid would deserve further analysis). A well established case law maintains that, while generally participants may not quote work costs below the legal minimum, cooperatives may well show that their members' costs are lower than the legal minimum thanks to more favourable social benefits rules exempting them from certain contributions.[49] The same applies to some SMEs benefiting from similar preferential treatment.[50] The same is true with regards to tenders jointly submitted by 'normal' firms and social cooperatives or other operators enjoying benefits such as lower labour costs. This means that the specific regime of social cooperatives will also be taken into account for the control on abnormally low offers.[51]

47. Cons. Stato, Sez. IV, 27 ottobre 2003, n. 6640, *Giur. it.*, 2004, 1285.
48. R. Caranta, *I contratti pubblici*, in F.G. Scoca, F.A. Roversi Monaco e G. Morbidelli (Dirr.) *Sistema del diritto amministrativo italiano* (Torino, Giappichelli, 2004) 376 f.
49. E.g. Cons. Stato, Sez. V, 15 giugno 2001, n. 3185, *Foro amm.*, 2001, 1561; justifications, however, must be specific, referring to the legal status as a co-operative not being sufficient: T.A.R. Campania, Salerno, Sez. I, 3 luglio 2002, n. 641, *Foro amm. TAR*, 2002, 2651.
50. Cons. Stato, Sez. V, 21 gennaio 2009, n. 278, *Giur. It, 2009.*
51. T.A.R. Piemonte, Sez. I, 11 dicembre 2008, n. 3130, in *Urbanistica e appalti*, 2009, 248, note G. Ferrari and L. Tarantino, *Gara pubblica e costo del lavoro.*

## 6 Contract performance clauses

The idea of contract performance clauses as a discrete entity from technical specification is something unheard of in Italy. This notwithstanding, Art. 26 of Directive 2004/18/CE, has been duly translated into Art. 69 of the Code. The Italian provision is just a little bit more talkative than the Community one. What is peculiar is that procuring entities willing to insert performance conditions targeted to social or environmental consideration may ask the advice of the vigilance authority, which is given 30 days to respond. In the first application of the provision, the provisional authority ruling the municipality of Pozzuoli, near Naples, whose elected council had been dissolved and the mayor removed because of links with the Camorra, the local Mafia denomination, asked the authority which special measures should be taken when awarding a contract. With an advice dated July 3, 2007, the Authority suggested the adoption of specific security rules when dealing with the tenders to make sure they are not tampered with nor opened before the jury starts its tasks. The Autorità further suggested the insertion of a clause empowering the jury charged with the selection of the best offer to ask the Autorità itself to investigate whether the qualifications of the participants were legally established. It is doubtful whether any of the given indications were really linked to social considerations relating to the performance of the contract. The criminal environment present in parts of Italy calls for very special considerations.

Concerning contract implementation, the general rules for the social inclusion of handicapped workers are relevant to public procurements as well. Art. 3 l. 12 marzo 1999, n. 68 'Norme per il diritto al lavoro dei disabili', mandates compulsory hiring of handicapped workers with regard to both public and private law entities. According to Art. 17, candidates in and bidders to public procurement procedures must show and be ready to prove that they comply with the provisions on mandatory hiring of handicapped workers, otherwise facing exclusion from the procedure.

A specific protection is offered to workers of cleaning services firms. Under the collective agreement passed between trade unions and employers' associations, the firm having been awarded a procurement has to hire the workers from the incumbent firm. In a way, rules on the transfer of undertakings are made applicable to this specific situation.

Under l. 3 agosto 2007, n. 123, a new kind of contract performance condition must necessarily be an integral part of any contract documents concerning supplies and services procurements. Procuring entities must draft the Documento unico di valutazione dei rischi (DUVRI), outlining the risks implied in the implementation of the contract due to the fact that the contractor's workers may operate on the premises and/or in contact with the procuring entity's own personnel and/or users served by the procuring entity (so called interference risks). The new provisions are not without difficulties, and the vigilance authority drafted an interpretative communication, pointing out that the new document is additional to itself and does not substitute the security document each firm has to elaborate with reference to the implementation risks falling under its sphere of responsibility.[52]

Also concerning contract implementation are the rules on subcontracting. Subcontracting is the easiest way for SMEs to take some share of the public procurement market. The Italian legislation, however, has always been and still is very strict on subcontracting, which is seen as a way for criminal organisations to infiltrate the procurement market. On the top of this, there is the fear that workers with sub-contractors may be more easily squeezed than workers with contractors, being usually big firms more open to dialogue with the trade unions. The first rules were laid down in Art. 18 l. 19 marzo 1990, n. 55 'Nuove disposizioni per la previsione della delinquenza di tipo mafioso e di altre gravi forme di manifestazione di pericolosità sociale'. The legislative aim was not so much to protect the subcontractor's workers – just an ancillary preoccupation – but to make sure that firms somehow linked to Mafia-like organisations could not get a share of the public procurement market.

These days, bowing to pressure from the European Commission, Art. 118 of the Code stipulates that it is up to the procuring entity to indicate in the contract documents whether or not subcontracting will be allowed and for which of the items of the contract. For works procurements, maximum 30 per cent of the main works may be subcontracting. For those works where the procuring entity is ready to allow subcontracting, candidates must state already in their bids which items they will subcontract to others. The contractor must then send the procuring entity a copy of the contract with the subcontractors, along with certificates showing that the subcontractor has all the necessary requisites to be part of a contract with a procuring entity. The bidder can satisfy what on their face may appear abnormally low offers when subcontracting to co-operatives and other firms benefiting from preferential fiscal and/or social contribution treatments.[53]

52. Determinazione n. 3/2008, March 5, 2008.
53. Cons. Stato, Sez. V, 21 gennaio 2009, n. 278, *Giur. It.*, 2009.

## 7 Conclusions

Directives 2004/17/EC and 2004/18/EC gave Member States some discretion in allowing room for sustainable considerations in public procurements. The Directives' provisions have been transposed, at times almost word by word in the Italian 'Code'. However, there is a lack of cases concerning both the most innovative provisions (such as those on ecolabel, EMAS, sheltered workshops, contract performance conditions), and some established possibilities (such as reference to environmental award criteria). Thinking of the many and different rules which could be linked to sustainable procurements, the case law is still very much focused on traditional issues, such as the breach of social contribution rules or reserved contracts to the benefit of social cooperatives. What is more relevant, the courts have yet to entertain doubts as to the consistency with European law of the legal rules applicable to awar to social cooperatives.

The possibility that everything is going well and the new provisions on sustainable procurements are applied smoothly, as indulgent as it may appear, does not seem very realistic. Public procurements are hugely litigated in Italy, and the new provisions do not lack problematic aspects which could give rise to very nice cases. The possibility is there that, notwithstanding a flurry of information activities following the entry into force of the new rules, procuring entities are slow if not reluctant to go into action and move into unchartered territories.[54]

Some signs that the situation is about to change are however discernible. The national central purchase entity, Consip, has laid down the measures it is taking in a specific document.[55] The former APAT (*Agenzia per la Protezione dell'Ambiente e per i Servizi Tecnici*, since 2008 part of ISPRA – *Istituto Superiore per la Protezione e la Ricerca Ambientale*) provided an important contribution to the project named 'Preparation and application of measures for the development of correct buying policies and environmentally sustainable from the Member States'.[56] In the meantime, the ministerial Behemoth is slowly switching into action mode with the approval of the GPP action plan –

54. Many events concerned green public procurements: e.g. http://www.arpa. piemonte.it/upload/dl/Sostenibilita_e_ecogestione/Appalti_Verdi/Locandina_48X68_OK.pdf; there is even a specific website-based journal on green procurements: www.appaltiverdi.it .
55. http://appaltiverdi.it/vsdata/documents/Consip.pdf .
56. R. Luciano, L. Andriola, M. D'Amico, quando la pubblica amministrazione acquista verde, in *Ambiente e sviluppo*, 2005, 9, 808

referred to as the environmental action strategy for the sustainable development.[57]

Given the fairly decentralised Italian procurement system, many activities take place at local level, but it is difficult for the lawyer to have more than anedoctical evidence.[58] Just to give one instance, already in 2003 the Regional Agency for the environmental protection of Piemonte started a project named 'APE' (which stands for bee in Italian) to develop green public procurement. The procuring entities participating in the 'APE' project commit themselves to introduce environmental criteria in the purchase of a number of goods, to the reduction of toxic chemicals and to the inclusion of environmentally elements in the award criteria; the commitment also include promoting environmentally consistent technologies and ecolabel (according to the recent Regulation 2010/66/EC on the European Ecolabel).[59]

## Bibliography

A. Albanese, 'L'affidamento di servizi socio-sanitari alle organizzazioni di volontariato e il diritto comunitario: la Corte di giustizia manda un monito agli enti pubblici italiani', in *Riv. it. dir. pubbl. comunitario*, 2008, 1453.

A.M. Balestrieri, 'Gli 'appalti riservati' fra principio di economicità ed esigenze sociali' in *Urbanistica e appalti*, 2009, 789.

R. Caranta, *I contratti pubblici*, in F.G. Scoca, F.A. Roversi Monaco e G. Morbidelli (Dirr.) *Sistema del diritto amministrativo italiano* (Torino, Giappichelli, 2004) 376 ff.

R. Caranta, *'Attività pubblica, attività no-profit, e disciplina dei contratti pubblici di servizi'*, in *Urbanistica e appalti*, 2008, 293.

M. Comba, 'Selection and Award Criteria in Public Procurement Law' in PPLR, (2008), 122.

R. De Nictolis, Le novità del terzo (e ultimo) decreto correttivo del codice dei contratti pubblici, in *Urbanistica e appalti*, 2008, 1225.

57. See Ministero dell'ambiente e della tutela del territorio e del mare, Decreto 11 aprile 2008 'Approvazione del Piano d'azione per la sostenibilità ambientale dei consumi nel settore della pubblica amministrazione'; for references to some previous policy documents also covering GPP aspects see M. Occhiena '*Norme di gestione ambientale*' above fn, 1473 f.
58. E.g. http://appaltiverdi.it/vsdata/documents/32-34 %20modena.pdf ; the ministerial decree mentioned in the next footnote, at point 4.1.1.1., refers to old studies, the more recent of 2005.
59. E. Degiorgis, M. Glisoni, Progetto APE: l'esperienza della provincia di Torino negli acquisti pubblici ecologici, in *Ambiente e sviluppo*, 2007, 5, 435.

G. Ferrari and L. Tarantino, Gara pubblica e costo del lavoro, in *Urbanistica e appalti,* 2009, 248.

R. Invernizzi, '*Specifiche tecniche*' in M.A. Sandulli, R. De Nictolis e R. Garofoli (curr.) *Trattato sui contratti pubblici* (Milano, Giuffré, 2008) vol. III, 2073 ff.

C. Lacava. 'I contratti pubblici tra Stato e regioni e la tutela della concorrenza' note Corte cost., 23 novembre 2007, n. 401, *Giorn. dir. amm.*, 2008, 624.

M. Miglioranza, 'Inquinamento elettromagnetico e limiti alle competenze regionali: standard di protezione nazionali e legalità sostanziale', note Corte cost., 7 novembre 2003, n. 331, *Foro it.*, 2004, I, 1364.

S. Treumer, 'The Distinction between Selection and Award Criteria in EC Public Procurement Law: A Rule without Exceptions?' in PPLR, (2008), 103.

# VI. Aggregate Models of Public Procurement and Secondary Considerations: An Italian Perspective

*by Gabriella M. Racca*

## 1 Relevance of aggregation of public demand on sustainable procurement policies

Aggregation of public demand may have positive effect on the demand for green and socially conscious goods. The exemplary role of procuring entities in fostering sustainable procurement is automatically accentuated by the mass of aggregated procurement. The economies of scale possible through the aggregation might also more than offset the possible higher cost of sustainable products and services compared with traditional ones. Moreover, sustainable procurement is fraught with difficulties, not least because of the legal uncertainties surrounding it. Small buyers might be discouraged to go down this path. Aggregating demand and procuring larger quantities makes it easier for the buyer to invest the resources necessary to draft contract documents which incorporate sustainable considerations without breaching general provisions protecting competition and free movement of goods and services.

These general considerations apply in Italy as well. However, a considerable emphasis on saving money through aggregated demand is not going without the risk of making it more difficult for individual procuring entities to pursue sustainable procurement policies.

## 2 Aggregated demand and central purchasing bodies under Directive 2004/18/EC

The urge to save costs led to the establishment of models of collaborative procurement and central purchasing bodies at national and regional levels. Many models of collaborative procurement can be used, such as joint procurements for the purchase of goods and services without any structural change, procurements awarded on the basis of a framework contract, or the setting up of a dedicated corporation. In the latter case, an entity with a separate legal personality, such as a central purchasing body, is created.[1]

A central purchasing body is a public purchaser from or through which other purchasers can acquire goods, works or services without having to comply with the public procurement rules.[2] The directive on public procurement[3] only recently took into account that certain centralised purchasing techniques have been developed in Member States. Several contracting authorities are responsible for making acquisitions or awarding public contracts/framework agreements on behalf of other contracting authorities.[4] In view of the large volumes purchased, those techniques favour the increase of competition and the streamlining of public purchasing.[5]

1. R. Caranta '*Le centrali di committenza*', in M. A. Sandulli – R. De Nictolis – R. Garofoli (edited by) *Trattato sui contratti pubblici*, (Milano, 2008), Vol. II, pp. 607 et seq.; G. Della Cananea '*Le alternative all'evidenza pubblica*', in P. Rescigno – E . Gabrielli (edited by) *Trattato dei contratti*, (Torino, 2007), Vol. I, pp. 381 et seq.; N. Dimitri – G. Piga – G. Spagnolo (edited by) *Handbook of Procurement* (Cambridge, 2006), pp. 47 et seq.; C. H. Bovis *EU Public Procurement Law* (Chaltenhan, 2008), pp. 94 and 315 et seq.; J. Chard – G. Duhs – J. Houlden, 'Body beautiful or vile bodies? Central purchasing in the UK' (2008) 1 PPLR NA26; for a global perspective see S. Arrowsmith *Reform of the uncitral Model Law on Procurement: Procurement Regulation for the 21st Century* (Danvers, 2009), pp. 204 et seq. and L. Knight – C. Harland – J. Telgen – K.V. Thai – G. Callender – K. McKen (edited by) *Public Procurement. International Cases and Commentary* (Oxford, 2007), pp. 176 et seq.
2. If the arrangement is between a purchaser and an 'in-house entity' which satisfies the Teckal line of ECJ case law, case 107/98 *Teckal v Comune di Viano* [1999] E.C.R. I-8121 at [51]; then the public procurement rules will not apply, otherwise, it will be necessary to consider whether the procuring entity can make purchases from a central purchasing body (CPB) or under a framework agreement. R. Cavallo Perin – D . Casalini 'Control over in-house providing organizations' (2009) 5 PPLR 227 et seq.; M. Comba – S. Treumer (edited by) *The In-House Providing in European Law* (Copenhagen, 2010), pp. 2 et seq. See art. 11 (2) of Council Directive (EC) 18/2004: 'Contracting authorities which purchase works, supplies and/or services from or through a central purchasing body in the cases set out in Article 1(10) shall be deemed to have complied with this Directive insofar as the central purchasing body has complied with it'. To the same effect art. 29 (2) Council Directive (EC) 17/2004.
3. Whereas n. 15, Council Directive (EC) 18/2004.
4. S. Arrowsmith 'Framework Purchasing and Qualification Lists under the European Procurement Directives' (1999) 8 P.P.L.R. 115-146 and 168-186.
5. L. Albano – L. arpineti – F. Dini – L. Giamboni – F. Russo – G. Spagnolo 'Riflessioni sull'impatto economico degli istituti innovativi del codice dei contratti pubblici relativi a lavori, servizi e forniture' (2007) 4 Quaderni CONSIP 13 et seq.

For the above reasons the Directive provided a Community definition of central purchasing bodies specifically directed at contracting authorities. A definition has also been given of the conditions under which, in accordance with the principles of non-discrimination and equal treatment, contracting authorities purchasing works, supplies and/or services through a central purchasing body may be deemed to have complied with the Directive.[6] The Directive allows Member States to choose whether to create central purchasing bodies and leaves them the choices on the use of these instruments.[7]

## 3 Aggregated demand and central purchasing bodies in Italy

In Italy, the process of centralization of demand began only recently and the country cannot not yet show the experience or the efficient results already achieved by other Member States.[8]

The Italian national central purchasing body (Consip s.p.a.) has been entrusted with the tasks of entering into contracts on behalf of other contracting authorities,[9] and only recently also into framework agreements.[10] Central

6. Art. 1, para. 10 Council Directive (EC) 18/2004: 'a 'central purchasing body' is a contracting authority which: – acquires supplies and/or services intended for contracting authorities or – awards public contracts or concludes framework agreements for works, supplies or services intended for contracting authorities'.
7. Whereas n. 23 Council Directive (EC) 17/2004.
8. For the UK System see: UK Government's Operational efficiency programme: collaborative procurement report, May 2009, which lists more than 40 central puchasing bodies; Uk Office of Government Commerce, 'Central Purchasing Bodies in the Public Contracts and Utilities Contracts Regulations' <http://www.ogc.gov.uk/ documents/OGC_Guidance_on_Central_Purchasing_Bodies.pdf> accessed March 2008; S. Arrowsmith 'Some problems in delimiting the scope of the Public Procurement Directives: privatisations, purchasing consortia and in-house tenders' (1997) P.P.L.R. 198 et seq.; J. Chard – G. Duhs – J. Houlden 'Body beautiful or vile bodies? Central purchasing in the UK' (2008) P.P.L.R. NA26; For the Italian system: G. M. Racca 'Collaborative procurement and contract performance in the Italian healthcare sector: illustration of a common problem in European procurement', (2010) P.P.L.R. 119. About the German experience see: Beschaffungsamt des Bundesministeriums des Innern 'Tätigkeitsbericht 2008/2009' <http://www.bescha.bund.de> accessed December 2009.
9. D.lgs. November 19, 1997, n. 414, about the foundation of Consip, but only with D.M. (Ministry of Tresaure) February 24, 2000 Consip S.p.A. has been mandated to stipulate conventions. For further reference see D. Broggi *Consip: il significato di un'esperienza, Teoria e pratica tra e-Procurement ed e-Government* (Roma, 2008), pp. 9 et seq.

purchasing bodies may recur to information and communication technology tools to carry out e-procurement and electronic auctions, besides ensuring full digitalisation of all procurement documents.[11] The implementation of e-auctions across a broad spectrum of public sector expenditure could be particularly useful. There is indeed scope for increased collaboration and regular recourse to e-auctions could provide a regular stream of benchmark data and a repository of re-usable tools.

Following the implementation of Financial Act 2006 (Law no. 266/05) Consip s.p.a. has to cooperate with a network of regional central purchasing bodies which are starting their activities.[12] This should assure interoperability with regional central purchasing bodies' platforms, as a basis for a wider co-operation in the procurement process. Moreover, 'Difesa servizi s.p.a.', a new national central purchasing body has recently been created for the military sector.[13]

10. L. December 29, 2009, no. 191 art. 2, para. 225, (l. n. 191/2009), *Disposizioni per la formazione del bilancio annuale e pluriennale dello Stato (legge finanziaria 2010).* See also: R. Caranta '*L'accordo quadro*' in M. A. Sandulli – R .De Nictolis – Garofoli (edited by)*Trattato sui contratti pubblici*, (Milano, 2008), Vol. III, pp. 1942 et seq.
11. L. Bertini, A. Vidoni, 'Il Mercato Elettronico della Pubblica Amministrazione – MEPA. Scenario, funzionalità e linee di tendenza' (2007) 6 Quaderni CONSIP 37 et seq. From an economic perspective G. Piga – K.V. Thai (edited by), *Economics of Public Procurement* (Palgrave Macmillan, 2007), pp. 63 et seq.; L. Knight – C. Harland – J. Telgen, K.V. Thai – G. Callender – K. McKen (edited by) *Public Procurement. International Cases and Commentary* (Oxford, 2007) pp. 216 et seq.; J. Bulow – P Klemperer 'Auctions versus Negotiations' (1996) 1 *American Economic Review* 180-194; P. Klemperer 'What Really Matters in Auction Design' (2002) 1 *Journal of Economic Perspectives*, 169-189; Y. K. Che 'Design Competition through Multidimensional Auctions' (1993) 4 *Rand Journal of Economics,* 668-680.
12. Art. 1, para. 158 of Law n. 266 of December 23, 2005.
13. L. no. 191 art. 2, para. 27, of December 29, 2009, envisages the establishment of the limited company 'Difesa Servizi Spa', in Rome, with the purpose of the acquisition of goods and services closely linked to the performance of institutional duties of the Defence Administration. Such activities shall not be directly related to military operations, except those of management and sale of military property. The share capital of the company is Euro 1 million. Any subsequent capital increases shall be ruled by decree of the Minister of Defence,. The company's shares are fully subscribed by the Ministry of Defence and cannot be released to third parties. See also Directive 2009/81/EC of the European Parliament and of the Council of 13 July 2009, *on the coordination of procedures for the award of certain works contracts, supply contracts and service contracts by contracting authorities or entities in the fields of defence and security, and amending Directives 2004/17/EC and 200 4/18/EC*. Member States have two years to transpose the Directive into national legislation. B. Heuninckx 'A

The network between all these central purchasing bodies is not yet operative in Italy,[14] and the number of contracts awarded by them is still very low in comparison with others counties,[15] reaching only around 8 % of all supplies and services.[16]

Recourse to framework contracts signed by central purchasing bodies is mandatory for State authorities, while other public administrations (such as regional or local) can chose whether to use this possibility or to carry out their own separate procurement procedure to buy the same product. But the real problem is that the central purchasing bodies' framework agreements still cover only a very limited range of goods and services.

Primer to Collaborative Defence Procurement in Europe: Troubles, Achievements and Prospects' (2008) PPLR 17.

14. Autorità per la Vigilanza sui contratti pubblici di Lavori, Servizi e Forniture 'Censimento ed analisi dell'attività contrattuale svolta nel biennio 2007-2008 dalle Centrali di Committenza Regionali e verifica dello stato di attuazione del sistema a rete' January 27-28, 2010, 7 et seq.
15. See: Government's Operational efficiency programme: collaborative procurement report, May 2009: the Government currently spends around £220bn on goods and services – that's about £1 in every £4 spent in total by the Exchequer. It is our aim to ensure that Government – both central Whitehall departments and the wider public sector – maximises the value it achieves from this expenditure through a variety of approaches: championing and facilitating collaboration across the major areas of third party spend; making the procurement process more efficient through the use of frameworks and e-procurement tools; reducing the negative environmental impact of goods and services purchased and working with suppliers to improve their sustainability performance; improving spend data to assist better decision making, and engaging with Government's strategic suppliers to foster greater innovation and value within the supply chain.
16. One possible strategy to build a 'centralization index' for the acquisition of goods and services is the following. Consip SpA is the Italian Public Procurement Agency awarding National Frame Contracts (NFCs), basically, Framework Agreements with one economic operator and all conditions laid down at the outset – and managing the Electronic Marketplace (MEPA) on behalf of the Ministry of Economy and Finance (MEF). One measure of centralization in year t can be defined as follows: CI_t = V_t / Max V_t where, V_t = value of purchases through (NFC + MEPA) in year t; Max V_t = public sector's overall purchases of goods and services that could be handled by the NFCs and MEPA system. By using raw data from the Italian National Statistical Institute (ISTAT) and MEF, Consip's Research Unit computed the following ranges for the 2007 and 2008 centralization indeces: CI_2007 is between 4.2 % and 5 %; CI_2008 is between 7.4 % and 8.9 %.

Thus the process of procuring commonly used goods and services across the Italian public sector is still dispersed, resulting in a very wide range of prices for similar goods and services.[17]

Italy is presently dealing with all the main difficulties in the enhancement of collaborative procurement, namely digital convergence, sharing of information and archives as well as the definition of needs. The joint management of aggregated demand, the creation of new tools for undertakings to access in an easier way public procurement and the definition of common procedures have yet to be achieved.[18] Nonetheless, the foreseeable and considerable advantages deriving from collaborative procurement will surely determine and guide future public policies in this direction.[19] The aim of limiting and rationalizing public expenditure, whilst ensuring the utmost quality, is to enhance and develop the different forms of collaborative procurement.[20]

The advantages of the collaborative procurement model becomes evident when the issue of sustainable procurement is taken into consideration. The incorporation of social and environmental clauses acquires greater importance when these clauses are incorporated by purchasing bodies that award many high value contracts. For a single contracting authority the incorporation of such clauses is not only complex but also has a limited effect. On the other hand, the incorporation of such clauses by Consip s.p.a. and other central purchasing bodies has a wider effect and can also influence the economic and production choices of bidders. Therefore, public organizations with their

17. R. Caranta 'Country Legal and Policy Review for SRPP in Italy – Study on social consideration in Public Procurement' March 20, 2008 2 et seq.
18. G.M. Racca 'Collaborative procurement and contract performance in the Italian healthcare sector: illustration of a common problem in European procurement' (2010) PPLR 119. Permanent Conference for Relations between State, Regions and the Autonomous Provinces of Trento and Bolzano, 24 January 2008 approved the 'Accordo tra Governo, Regioni e Province Autonome per la costituzione del sistema a rete'.
19. Forum for the future 'buying a better world' <http://www.forumforthefuture.org/> accessed December 2007, 7 et seq.
20. Uk Government's Operational efficiency programme: collaborative procurement report, May 2009, 4, 'it is realistic to achieve a total of around £6.1 billion of annual value for money savings by the end of 2013-14 *provided that the Government acts swiftly to implement the recommendations of this report.* This level of savings is compared to the 2007-08 baseline of the £89 billion government procurement spend that has been categorised to a commonly-procured commodity. A further £1.6 billion value for money savings could be achieved through the collaborative procurement of IT, and are included in the savings figures set out in the *Operational Efficiency Programme: back office operations and IT* report.4 This gives a total collaborative procurement savings figure of £7.7 billion by 2013-14'.

substantial purchasing power can influence sustainable procurement policies, thus also driving innovation from the demand side.[21]

Considering the recent new evaluation criteria for well-being in Europe, no more linked solely to the GDP growth,[22] more attention to social issues will also have to be paid in public procurement policies. This consideration led Europe to allow the incorporation of secondary considerations in public procurement, even limiting the emphasis on the value for money principle.[23] This implies that secondary considerations may be legally incorporated in public procurement, in compliance with the transparency and non-discrimination principles.[24]

Secondary considerations can entail additional costs that the contracting entities accept to pursue public interests that go beyond strictly economic considerations.[25] In the case of sheltered workshops, for instance, secondary

21. S. Arrowsmith – P. Kunzlik (edited by) *Social and Environmental Policies in EC Procurement Law: New Directives and New Directions* (Cambridge, 2009) 9 et seq. for an analysis of the implications about secondary consideration policy in public procurement.
22. J. E. Stiglitz – A. Sen – J. P. Fitoussi '*Measurement of Economic Performance and social Progress*' September 14, 2009. 'The Commission on the Measurement of Economic Performance and Social Progress' (CMEPSP) was made up of 21 members in addition to Prof. J. E. Stiglitz (Chair), Prof. A. Sen (Chair Adviser), Prof. J. P. Fitoussi (Coordinator of the Commission), and 9 rapporteurs. The Commission's aim has been: '- to identify the limits of gross domestic product (GDP) as an indicator of economic performance and social progress, including the problems with its measurement; – to consider what additional information might be required for the production of more relevant indicators of social progress; – to assess the feasibility of alternative measurement tools, and to discuss how to present the statistical information in an appropriate way'.
23. Whereas n. 46 Council Directive (EC) 18/2004, according to which 'In order to guarantee equal treatment, the criteria for the award of the contract should enable tenders to be compared and assessed objectively. If these conditions are fulfilled, economic and qualitative criteria for the award of the contract, such as meeting environmental requirements, may enable the contracting authority to meet the needs of the public concerned, as expressed in the specifications of the contract. Under the same conditions, a contracting authority may use criteria aiming to meet social requirements, in response in particular to the needs – defined in the specifications of the contract – of particularly disadvantaged groups of people to which those receiving/using the works, supplies or services which are the object of the contract belong'.
24. Case C-31/87, *Beentjes* [1988] ECR I-4635, Case C-324/98, *Telaustria Verlags GmbH and Telefonadress GmbH v Telekom Austria AG.* [2000] ECR I-10745.
25. C. McCrudden Buying social justice equality, government procurement, & legal change, (Oxford, 2007); S. Arrowsmith, P. Kunzlik (edited by), *Social and Environ-*

considerations may be considered as a subsidy to the benefit of those disadvantaged, with the view of improving their quality of life.

On the other hand, secondary considerations may be considered fully compatible with the value for money principle, when their incorporation does not involve additional costs compared to a 'normal' procurement. For example, a product with environmental characteristics does not necessarily cost more than a product without such features. The choice of the public administration to require such characteristics has the power to direct innovation and the spread of such kinds of products within the public procurement market and the general market as well.[26] The incorporation of social clauses in a framework agreement of considerable value[27] common to a relevant number of public administrations has significant policy consequences. Collaborative procurement becomes instrumental in the effort to spread the social effects of sustainable procurement as a whole, as the choice to incorporate such clauses becomes a model for the other public administrations.

This is particularly true in Italy where, as we will see, contracting authorities choosing not to adhere to framework agreements must attain a better quality/price ratio than the one found in the central purchasing bodies' framework agreements, to justify their choice.

*mental Policies in EC Procurement Law: New Directives and New Directions* (Cambridge University Press, 2009), 108 et seq.

26. For some examples of this choice in Italy see: 'Protocollo di intesa per la promozione della sicurezza sui luoghi di lavoro e possibili misure di intervento per le aziende dei pubblici servizi' Confservizi Piemonte e Valle d'Aosta e le organizzazioni sindacali confederali della Provincia di Torino, February 25, 2008; 'Protocollo di intesa tra il Comune di Roma e le organizzazioni sindacali CGIL, CISL e UIL in materia di appalti e di affidamento di lavori pubblici, forniture di beni e servizi', September 28, 2007; 'Patto per lo sviluppo territoriale – Provincia di Vercelli' December 2, 2005; 'Protocollo di intesa tra il Comune di Bologna e le organizzazioni sindacali CGIL, CISL e UIL in materia di lavori, servizi e forniture' November 24, 2005.
27. S. Arrowsmith, 'An Assessment of the New Legislative Package on Public Procurement' [2004] 41 CMLR 1.

## 4 Secondary considerations in the selection criteria of central purchasing bodies and the influence on the bidder's organization

It is commonly known that secondary considerations can be incorporated in the contract documents at different levels,[28] included in the definition of the technical or professional capacity of the bidder.[29] Secondary considerations may enter into the definition of the subject-matter of the contract, including the technical specifications of the product, work or service, and the contract performance conditions.[30]

The choice of requiring a specific quality of the bidder for the safeguard of social and environmental objectives must not infringe free competition and must be reasonable and proportionate to the subject-matter of the contract.[31]

When central purchasing bodies define such bidders' participation criteria they take into due account the reference market and may also issue a contract notice divided in lots so as to avoid the exclusion of SMEs.[32] All potential contractors, including both large and small and medium-sized enterprises, would benefit from a coherent approach to sustainable procurement.[33] Furthermore, the sustainability criteria required in procurement contracts may gradually increase with time, so that undertakings will gradually prepare themselves to satisfy the same, thus avoiding issues of limitation to free competition or discrimination. In the long term this will influence the bidder's organization towards aims of sustainable development.

28. Study on the incorporation of Social Considerations in Public Procurement in the EU, Proposed Elements for taking account of the Social Considerations in Public Procurement, 54 et seq.
29. S. Arrowsmith – P. Kunzlik (edited by) *Social and Environmental Policies in EC Procurement Law: New Directives and New Directions* (Cambridge, 2009), 109 et seq.
30. S. Arrowsmith – P. Kunzlik (edited by), *Social and Environmental Policies in EC Procurement Law: New Directives and New Directions* (Cambridge, 2009), 121 et seq.
31. Commission (EC), 'Public procurement for a better environment' SEC(2008) 2126, 16 July 2008. See also Commission (EC) 'Buying green – A handbook on environmental public procurement' (Office for Official Publications of the European Communities, 2004) 9 et seq.
32. For EC policies about small and medium-sized enterprises see: Commission (EC) ''Think Small First' A 'Small Business Act' for Europe', 25 June 2008.
33. R. Caranta 'Country Legal and Policy Review for SRPP in Italy – Study on social consideration in Public Procurement' March 20, 2008, 12 et seq.

## 5 Secondary considerations in the award criteria of central purchasing bodies and their effect in driving the market

The incorporation of secondary considerations in the definition of the subject-matter of the contract entails a precise choice of the public entity involving possible additional costs.[34] This might be considered a subsidy to producers. In Italy this choice made by central purchasing bodies influences and legitimizes the other procuring entities which are required not to exceed the same quality/price ratio. When a sustainable subject-matter can be defined without any additional costs, the central purchasing body's choice will influence the choice of other procuring entities anyway.

If secondary considerations are incorporated in the technical or professional capacity of the bidder or in the subject-matter of the contract, they will impose themselves to all participants. When procuring entities define a specific subject-matter with sustainable features, that will be obtained at the end of the awarding procedure. On the other hand, when secondary considerations are incorporated in the award criteria, they become part of the overall evaluation leading to the award, but the winning bid will not necessarily be the most sustainable one.

When they are foreseen as parameters for the evaluation of the offer of the bidders, they can influence the award of a contract according to the weight given to each evaluation criteria and the overall sum of the points awarded. The participant that presents an offer with social and environmental characteristics is not sure to win, nor is the procuring entity sure to choose an offer with these features. In fact, a lower price can lead to the victory of a bidder who did not include secondary considerations in his or her offer. Thus, the broad incorporation of secondary considerations by central purchasing bodies both in the qualitative selection criteria and in the definition of the subject-matter of the contract ensures the full pursuance of sustainable procurement policies.

To drive innovation from the demand side and orient the market towards sustainability, such clauses should be incorporated by central purchasing bodies in all their framework agreements, benefiting from their public procurement network synergies.[35]

34. For an analysis of economic impacts see. Commission (EC) 'Public procurement for a better environment' SEC(2008) 2124, 16 July 2008. See also Commission (EC) 'on the Sustainable Consumption and Production and Sustainable Industrial Policy Action Plan' COM(2008) 397 final, 16 July 2008, about incentives of Member States.
35. Commission (EC) 'Joint procurement – Fact sheet' (2008), 3 et seq.

This choice may influence, in turn, also individual contracting authorities that do not adhere to central purchasing bodies' frameworks agreements. In awarding their contracts they will be driven towards similar sustainable choices.

## 6 The 'congruence assessment' and the definition of a benchmark in public contracts defined with not purely economic values: a 'social' value for money

The Italian law prescribes a 'congruence assessment' (*valutazione di congruità*)[36] of the quality/price ratio, to be compared to the prices obtained by central purchasing bodies through their framework agreements.[37] In other words, to limit public expenditures, non-State procuring entities are free not to have recourse to framework agreements entered into by Consip s.p.a. only in so far as they are able to get better conditions than those provided in the framework agreements themselves. Such conditions define a sort of benchmark that must be complied with by all procuring entities, even when they decide to have recourse to their own awarding procedure with a view to try and obtain better conditions. The concern for financial stability is as such that the procuring officer might be held liable in front of the Court of auditors for 'incongruous' buying decisions.[38]

In so far as sustainable procurement might entail higher costs as compared with traditional best value for money, the 'congruence assessment' makes it

36. Art. 26, clause III, law 488 of 1999, in replacement, first, of art. 3, clause 166, of *Law no. 350 of December 24, 2003,* and later of art. 1, *L.D. no. 168 of July 12, 2004*, as amended by the relative law of conversion no. 191 of 30.7.2004: 'Public administrations may resort to the agreements stipulated pursuant to clause 1, or use its parameters of price-quality, as maximum limits, for the purchase of goods and services pursuant to *Presidential Decree no. 101 of April 4, 2002*. Stipulation of a contract in violation of this clause is cause of administrative liability; for purposes of calculation of the fiscal damage account shall be taken of the difference between the price foreseen in the agreements and that indicated in the contract'.
37. S. Ponzio 'La verifica di congruità delle offerte rispetto alle convenzioni Consip negli appalti pubblici di forniture e servizi' (2009) *Foro amm. – C. d. S.*, 2355 et seq.
38. Art. 26, clause III, law 488 of 1999: 'Public administrations may *(...)* use its parameters of price-quality, as maximum limits, for the purchase of goods'. 'Stipulation of a contract in violation of this clause is cause of administrative liability; for purposes of calculation of the fiscal damage account shall be taken of the difference between the price foreseen in the agreements and that indicated in the contract'.

more difficult – but not impossible – for Italian procuring entities to have recourse to it.

In this situation the best way to sustainable procurement is to include green and social considerations in the definition of the subject-matter of the contract and the technical specification. This may mean that the good or service procured is simply different from the one (eventually missing the same characteristics) bought under the framework agreements signed by Consip s.p.a. The 'congruence assessment' will instead come into play when including sustainable award criteria.

Normally, it is the same contracting authority that decides whether the offer is 'congruous' or 'incongruous' with reference to the conditions established in the framework agreement of Consip s.p.a. In this context having recourse to the most advantageous bid award criteria may lead to the identification of a winner whose offer does not ensure a better quality/price ratio than that set in the framework agreement. This may happen when the same quality specified in the framework agreement is obtained at a higher price than that found in the same framework agreement. If this is the case the contracting entity will either award the contract to the subsequent bidder whose offer has a better quality/price ratio compared to the one specified in the framework agreement, or cancel the procedure and have recourse to the framework agreement. Of course this may easily lead to litigation. Italian courts will limit their review to assess the coherence of this evaluation from a logical point of view.

For example, a private supplier recently challenged an Italian health agency's evaluation of 'incongruence' of its offer for 'diapers', but the court agreed with the public administration's assessment.[39]

39. State Council, Sect.V – February 2, 09-no. 557 *Artsana S.p.A. (Attorneys Longo, Patelli and Tumbiolo) vs. Local Health Service Unit of Ferrara (Attorney Pazzaglia Piccoli)* and S.I.L.C. S.p.A. et al (n.c.) – confirmation of the Regional Administrative Court of Emilia Romagna – Bologna, Sect. I, June 8, 2007, no. 1054) 1. The procuring entity was right in deciding not to assign the supply contract to the company declared the provisional winner due to lack of congruence of the offer price with respect to those of the agreement stipulated by Consip s.p.a., considering that art. 26, clause 3, of law no. 488 of December 23, 1999 establishes (with charging it with administrative liability in case of violation of the relative obligation) the requirement to purchase goods and services after assessing the congruence of the offer. The law also establishes the criteria for making such assessment, providing that it shall be made on the basis of the price-quality parameters of the agreements with the same subject already stipulated by the Ministry of the Treasury and Economic Programming, apply-

## 7 Conclusions as to the role of central purchasing bodies in fostering SPP in Italy

The 'congruence assessment' does not contribute nor drive individual contracting authorities to incorporate secondary considerations; actually, it is hampering trade unions, or consumer groups, efforts to promote such incorporation.

Consequently, the role of central purchasing bodies becomes more essential than ever in fostering SPP. It is true in Italy too that, in consideration of the overall amount of their purchases, central purchasing bodies can better influence and stimulate the market for sustainable products and services. In fact, they can award framework agreements assuring a 'social' value for money according with the discretionary choices of the Member States and in a more efficient way compared to individual procuring entities.[40]

Moreover, embracing sustainable clauses, Italian central purchasing bodies would legitimize the incorporation of the same clauses by individual contracting authorities, thus creating a new efficient 'model' that avoids claims and helps them to overcome difficulties and problems of compliance with EU Directives.

## Bibliography

C.H. Bovis, *EU Public Procurement Law* (Chaltenhan, 2008), pp. 94 and 315 et seq.

R. Caranta, '*Le centrali di committenza*', in M. A. Sandulli – R. De Nictolis – R. Garofoli (edited by) *Trattato sui contratti pubblici*, (Milano, 2008), Vol. II, pp. 607 et seq.

R. Caranta, 'Country Legal and Policy Review for SRPP in Italy – Study on social consideration in Public Procurement' March 20, 2008, 12 et seq.

ing the procedural methods and guarantees indicated in the first clause of the same art. 26. In all those cases in which the competition is not assigned to the competitor classified in first place (as in the case of offers ascertained as abnormally low in spite of the justifications), the contracting administration acts correctly in assigning the contract to competitors that follow in the classification. Legitimately, therefore, the contracting authority assigns the supply of some lots to the companies that follow the winner, which has been excluded because the offer is judged inappropriate, after having made the compulsory assessments of congruence of the relative offers.

40. S. Arrowsmith – P. Kunzlik (edited by) *Social and Environmental Policies in EC Procurement Law: New Directives and New Directions* (Cambridge, 2009), 34 et seq., where it is precised that the directive does not ensure efficient expenditure.

J. Chard – G. Duhs – J. Houlden, 'Body beautiful or vile bodies? Central purchasing in the UK' (2008) 1 PPLR NA26.

G. Della Cananea, '*Le alternative all'evidenza pubblica*', in P. Rescigno – E. Gabrielli (edited by) *Trattato dei contratti,* (Torino, 2007), Vol. I, pp. 381 et seq.

N. Dimitri – G. Piga – G. Spagnolo (edited by) *Handbook of Procurement* (Cambridge, 2006), pp. 47 et seq.

S. Arrowsmith, *Reform of the UNCITRAL Model Law on Procurement: Procurement Regulation for the 21st Century* (Danvers, 2009), pp. 204 et seq.

L. Knight – C. Harland – J. Telgen – K.V. Thai – G. Callender – K. McKen (edited by) *Public Procurement. International Cases and Commentary* (Oxford, 2007), pp. 176 et seq.

# VII. Sustainable Public Procurement in Poland

*by Marcin Spyra*

## 1 Introduction

The question of secondary considerations has never been at the centre of the debate about public procurement regulation in Poland. Due to the mandatory character of many environmental and social provisions, public procurement has never been immune from their influence. It is, however, clearly visible in practice that although the application of non- economical criteria to select candidates and to award contracts is evidently admissible under the Public Procurement Law of 2004 (PPL)[1] as it was under the old Public Procurement Act of 1994, a vast majority of public authorities in their contractual choices concentrate on limiting their expenses and on economic efficiency. There is a significant body of case law of the National Appellate Chamber (NAC)[2] decisions concerning non- financial considerations of an award. Most of them, however, pertain to technical merits and functionality characteristics. Cases involving a dispute about environmental or social considerations are rare. Similar conclusion has been prompted by the research performed in the course of preparation of the National Action Plan for Green Public Procurement for 2007 to 2009.[3] The reason for this phenomenon is not obvious. One

1. An English translation of PPL is available at www.uzp.gov.pl.
2. National Appellate Chamber (*Krajowa Izba Odwoławcza*) is a non-judicial body established by the President of the Public Procurement Office (*Prezes Urzędu Zamówień Publicznych*). The Chamber is competent at the first stage of the public and utility procurement review procedures. All decisions of NAC are published at www.uzp.gov.pl (in Polish).
3. According to the research performed by the Public Procurement Office (hereinafter PPO) only 4 % representatively chosen supply specifications and 6 % of works specifications include environmental criteria. The analysis of contract notices published in TED shows that 32 % of notices published by Polish awarding authorities in 2005 included environmental considerations. PPO: Action Plan for Green Public Procurement for 2007 to 2009. p. 5-7.

of the possible causes may be the rather usual tendency of many public authorities in Poland to muddle through their budget difficulties. Another reason may be found in the concern of public officials about the possible liability for the mismanagement of public funds. Even a non-deliberate abuse of prerogatives in the field of public finances which causes damage or creates a danger of damage to public assets may give rise to criminal investigations (Article 231 § 3 of Penal Code)[4] or public finances disciplinary action (Article 17 Liability for the Breach of the Public Finances Discipline Act of 2004).[5] Although an infringement of non-economic interests may also constitute a criminal offence, in practice a significantly higher attention is paid to infringements detrimental to the sphere of public finances. This mechanism fosters the tendency to apply predominantly economic criteria to an award.

Overcoming a traditional restraint of awarding authorities to apply secondary considerations has for several years been a part of the agenda of the Public Procurement Office (PPO), the Ministry of Environmental Protection and other governmental agencies. The development of sustainable procurement practice has recently been a subject of interest for the Government and the national legislator. The governmental agenda for combating the social and economical effects of the financial crisis includes several amendments of the PPL drafted to develop a practice of sustainable procurement in Poland. The Act of 7 May 2009 introduced several changes to the provisions on the definition of the subject-matter of the contract and technical specifications in order to encourage awarding authorities to include social requirements regarding reducing of unemployment and financing the professional training of employees. The second mayer development in this field has been the amendment of PPL of 5th November 2007. It aims to clear doubts about possibilities of applying secondary considerations in public procurement. The changes pertain to the definition of subject-matter of the contract and to tenderer qualification criteria. It is not possible yet to assess the impact of the current legislative changes on the development of sustainable public procurement in Poland. Nevertheless, expectations of major changes should be treated with a certain scepticism. According to the prevailing opinion a legal regulation

4. A. Barczak-Oplustil in A. Barczak-Oplustil, G. Bogdan, Z. Ćwiąkalski, M. Dąbrowska-Kardas, P. Kardas, J. Majewski, J. Raglewski, M. Rodzynkiewicz, M. Szewczyk, W. Wróbel, A. Zoll, *Kodeks karny. Część szczególna. Volume II. Komentarz do art. 117-277 k.k.*, Kraków 2006, S. Hoc: Odpowiedzialność karna za nadużycie władzy. WPP 2005/4.
5. M. Winiarz 'Odpowiedzialność za udzielanie zamówień publicznych w podsektorze samorządowym', FK 2007/9, p. 32.

does not constitute a significant barrier for the application of secondary considerations in public procurement practice in Poland.[6]

The objective of this paper is to analyse the legal environment of sustainable public procurement in Poland in the context of the implementation of the European Directives.

## 2 Definition of the subject-matter of the contract and technical specifications

The Article 29 section 1 PPL states that the object of the contract should be described in an unequivocal and exhaustive manner by means of sufficiently precise and comprehensive wording, taking into consideration all requirements and circumstances which could influence the preparation of a tender. The description cannot lead to restrictions of fair competition (Article 29 sec. 2 PPL).

Environmental considerations are one type of factors which may influence the content of definition of the subject-matter and technical specifications. Due to the mandatory character of environmental protection provisions their impact on the subject-matter of the contract is inevitable. Provisions on the accessibility of buildings to disabled persons have similar effect. It is possible to include also other social criteria if they are relevant and adequately related to the contract and the general requirements.

Social considerations as part of the subject-matter definition have been subject of the recent legislative amendment. The new section 4 of Article 29 PPL, which came into force on 16 July 2009 expressly admits employment and training considerations in the subject-matter of a public procurement contract. It provides that an awarding entity in definition of the subject-matter of the contract or in the technical specifications, may lay down the performance of a contract concerning employment of unemployed or juvenile persons for a vocational training referred to in the provisions on the promotion of employment and the labour market institutions, disabled persons referred to in the provisions on professional and social rehabilitation and on the employment of disabled persons or of other persons referred to in the provisions on social employment or in the applicable provisions of the Members States of the European Union or the European Economic Area. In the recommendation of the 20th October 2009 PPO point out that additional requirements may refer

6. PPO: Action Plan ..., p. 4-5.

only to the engagement of unemployed, juveniled or disabled persons in reforming the public contract. The requirements may pertain also to general employment policy of the bidder and characteristiscs of its staff not engaged in the performance of the contract.[7] The social requirement set forth in the may pertain also to creating a training fund, in the meaning of the provisions on the promotion of employment and the labour market institutions. Bidders contribution to this fund shall amount to not less than 1 % of their total employment costs. A training fund may be created by a bidder and other employees which do not take part in the awarding procedure. In such a case all employees contribute to the fund at least 1 % of their total employment costs. The article sec. 4. PPL refers to at training fund established according to provisions of polish law. According to the PPO recommendation an awarding authority in order not to discriminate foreign bidders is obliged to recognise equivalance training funds governed by foreign law provided they are financed in the same way and serve equivalance objectives.

The Article 22a which explicitly allows to include in the technical specifications a requirement pertaining to the number of unemployed or disabled persons engaged in the performance of the contract, or to young persons selected for vocational training, to the minimal period of engagement and to the evidence of the engagement of these persons. The contracting authority shall also have the possibility to determine in the specifications the control rights necessary to verify compliance with these requirements concerning social considerations.

## 3 Selection of candidates

### 3.1 Exclusion criteria

The secondary considerations may also play a role at the stage of exclusion of candidates. The list of the reasons of exclusions stated in Article 24 PPL is significantly shorter than the one provided in Article 45 of Directive 2004/18/EC. It is not possible to exclude a candidate on the grounds of grave professional misconduct proven by any means which the contracting authorities can demonstrate. It is always a judgment which has the force of *res judicata,* which is necessary as evidence of the relevant professional misconduct. According to Article 24 section 1 PPL relevant misconduct is an offence

7. Reccomendation of PPO and Regional Development Ministry on the "Social Causes" in Public Procurement – Warsaw, 20th October 2009. Available at www.uzp.gov.pl.

committed in connection with a contract award procedure, offence against rights of people performing paid work, offences against economic turnover, any offence committed with the aim of gaining financial profits, bribery, treasury offence and participation in organised crimegroup or in a union aimed at committing an offence or treasury offence.[8] Delay in payment of taxes, social insurance contributions or health insurance premiums is also a ground for a exclusion: Article 24 section 1 (3) PPL. The PPL amendment which came into form on 12 december 2009. Added to the this list offences Against the invironment. The regulation of the exclusion grounds in Polish public procurement law offers some possibilities of applying social considerations, e.g. exclusion for the reason of offences against the rights of people performing paid work. This brief overview of Article 24 section 1 PPL gives however a clear hint that the fiscal interests of the Treasury are much more in the foreground.

The described system is not very efficient in the international context. If a candidate has a registered office or place of residence outside Poland it shall submit a certificate regarding criminal offences issued by a competent judicial or administrative authority in the country of origin or residence of a person to whom the documents refer to: § 2 sec. 1 of the Regulation on the Types of Documents that May Be Requested by the Awarding Entity. Thus in the case of partnerships, corporations and other legal persons registered abroad, crimes committed by their partners and officers in Poland are irrelevant even if those partners and officers are domiciled in Poland. In the case of entities registered in Poland, a contracting authority may request only certificates issued by the Polish National Register of Criminal Records even if partners or officers of the entity governed by Polish law are domiciled abroad.[9] Regarding the broad scope of the freedom of establishment in the EU this model of documentation requirements offers many opportunities to devise evasive schemes.

8. A relevant offence proved by a judgment which has the force of res judicata is a reason for the exclusion of convicted natural persons, of partnerships (*spółka jawna*) whose members have been convicted, of limited partnerships (*spółka komandytowa*) and partnerships limited by shares (*spółka komandytowo- akcyjna*) whose unlimited partner (*komplemantraiusz*) has been convicted, of professional partnerships (*spółka partnerska*) whose partner or member of managing board has been convicted and of legal persons whose member of managing body has been convicted committing relevant offence.
9. The NAC award of 26th Sep. 2008, KIO/UZP 972/08, Lex 466568, also available at www.uzp.gov.pl

### 3.2 Technical capacity

A contracting authority may set down personal requirements relating to the necessary knowledge and experience, technical potential and personnel necessary to perform the contract: (Article 22 sec. 1 (2) PPL). It is of course possible to set out requirements related to capability and experience in the field of environmental protection and compliance with work safety standards.

Types of documents that may be requested by the awarding entity from the economic operator and forms in which these documents may be submitted are determined by the Prime Ministerial Regulation of 30 December 2009. § 1 section 2 of the Regulation transposes directly Article 48 of Directive 2004/18/EC into Polish legislation.

The possibility of environmental considerations checking the technical capacity of the tenderers to execute the tendered contract has never been a subject of controversy. Some doubts pertain to social considerations. NAC mentioned twice that it is possible to set down the requirement of engaging a certain number of staff only on the basis of employment contract (i.e. with the exclusion of engaging self employed persons).[10] In both cases the question of the criteria of qualitative selection was the obiter dictum of the decision. PPO arbitrators addressed this problem directly in an award of 7 March 2007.[11] They found the criterion of employment contracts unjustified and discriminatory. According to the arbitrators the nature of the relation between an economic operator and persons engaged to perform the contract remains irrelevant to the verification of operator's capacity to perform the contract as long as the engaged staff is bound to render necessary services by the performance of the contract.

### 3.3 Reserved contracts

The Article 19 Directive 2004/18/EC on sheltered workshops has not been implemented in Poland yet. According to the general principles of setting down qualitative criteria for candidates it is not possible to limit the right to participate in public contract award procedures to sheltered workshops or to provide for such contracts to be performed in the context of sheltered employment programmes. In most of situations the criterion of the employment of disabled persons was characterised as discriminatory. In practice many public authorities obliged to promote social and professional rehabilitation of disabled persons had established sheltered workshops as internal structures

10. Cf. the NAC awards of 30.1.2009 NAC/UZP 76/09, Lex 486391 and of 7.5.2008 KIO/UZP 383/08, Lex 428477.
11. UZP/ZO/0-204/07, Lex 286249.

without legal personality and directly award to them public contracts as to in-house entities. The PPL Draft Amendment of 5 November 2009 supplemented Article 22 PPL with the new section implementing Article 19 Directive 2004/18/EC. According to this provision of PPL, an awarding entity may stipulate in the contrac notice that only those economic operators may compete for a contract whose employed staff is in order 50 % composes of disabled persons within the meaning of the regulations on occupational and social rehabilitation as well as on employment of the disabled or relevant provisions of the European Union Member States or the European Economic Area Member States.

## 4 Award

### 4.1 Award criteria

According to Article 91 PPL tender evaluation criteria shall be price or price and other criteria linked to the subject-matter of the contract, in particular quality, functionality, technical parameters, use of best available technologies with regard to the impact on the environment, exploitation costs, after-sales service and period of contract performance (sec. 2). Where the best tender cannot be selected as two or more tenders represent the same balance of price and other tender evaluation criteria, the contracting entity shall choose from among those tenders the one with a lower price (sec.4). The list of possible assessment criteria is of course not exhaustive. In relevant cases it is also possible to apply social criteria related to employment, vocational training, rehabilitation of disabled persons etc. In some cases the application of additional, non- financial criteria is also possible.[12]

The decisions concerning secondary award criteria are not very numerous. They concentrate mostly on technical questions. In several decisions the arbitrators of the PPO, (competent at the first stage of the remedy proceeding before the NAC was established in 2007), recognised the possibility of applying award criteria based on a case-by-case and 'to some extent voluntary' assessment of a contracting authority. E.g. arbitrators accepted e.g. such award criteria specified as: 'evaluation of the concept of Internet information portal', 'evaluation of the concept of cooperation between a bidder and the con-

12 E.g. in the case of waste incineration it is necessary to take into account the distance between a wast inciniration plant and a place of waste origin (art. 9 of The Waste Act of 2001) Cf. the NAC Award of 5.12.2008 KIO/UZP 1362/08, LEX 48572

tracting authority',[13] 'evaluation of the Intranet system flexibility'.[14] On the other hand arbitrators rejected 'quality of the product criterion' as too unspecified and subjective.[15]

According to PPO Arbitrators, a contracting authority may use different evaluation criteria, including the application of the best available technologies regarding their influence on the environment, provided these criteria are linked to the subject-matter of the contract. The secondary criteria may be applied only to the whole subject-matter of the contract. Their application only to the part of the prospective object of performance may infringe the principle of non-discrimination.[16] This opinion was expressed in the procurement procedure aimed at the supply of police patrol cars by the Police Main Headquarter (*Komenda Główna Policji*). The contracting authority applied several evaluation criteria regarding functionality and technical characteristics of patrol cars. Some of them (e.g. volume of a boot) applied only to parts of the subject-matter of offers (estate type patrol cars). This limitation was favourable for one of the candidates. The Arbitrators found no reason for disregarding the boot volume criterion in the case of other police patrol cars. The decision is reasonable although the conclusion about the necessity of applying all award criteria to the whole subject-matter of the tenders seems too general.

### 4.2 Abnormally low offers and unfair competition

According to the Article 89 section 1 PPL a contracting entity shall reject a tender, if its submission is an act of unfair competition (subsection 3) or if it contains an abnormally low price in relation to the subject-matter of the contract (subsection 4). These two grounds for rejection of an offer could serve purposes of sustainable procurement. Although Article 90 section 2 PPL does not point out explicitly compliance with the provisions relating to employment protection and working conditions as a criterion for price justification, it is obvious that the catalogue of considerations is open and in most cases the labour costs may play an important role in price building. In several awards NAC explained its readiness to characterise an offer as abnormally low if there are reasons to believe that an economic operator is not likely to perform properly taking into account the level of outlays the economic operator in-

13. Award of 8.3.2007 UZP/ZO/0-212/07, Lex 286195.
14. Award of 3.6.2006 UZP/ZO/0-1879/06, Lex 209861.
15. Award of 6.4.2005 UZP/ZO/0-592/05, Lex 179374.
16. The Award of the Team of Arbitrators of the PPO of 25 June 2005, UZP/ZO/0-705/07; UZP/ZO/0-738/07, LEX nr 361041.

tends to take in connection with the performance of a public contract.[17] Based on this reasoning it would be possible to reject an offer not only due to the alleged infringement of minimal standards of wage or of minimal safety requirements but also reject an offer, e.g. due to inadequate number of employees, inadequate mesures for environment protection measures etc.

In practice social and environmental considerations are not in the foreground of abnormally low offer verification procedures. In the majority of NAC awards related to the abnormally low offer verification procedure, there are no considerations regarding employment protection and working conditions.[18] In a few cases the NAC stated that compliance with the minimum wage is enough to justify a labour factor in price building.[19] In a few other cases the NAC and courts took a position even more remote from the goals of sustainable public procurement. In the case decided on 7 May 2008 it was proved that the submitted offer had been based on the calculation of labour costs below the minimum wage.[20] The NAC observed that this fact was irrelevant to the characterisation of the offer as abnormally low. According to the NAC, the contracting authority could require performance of the contract by persons engaged by the economic operator on the basis of an employment contract.[21] Since in the analysed case the contract notice did not contain such a requirement, the operator could perform by means self-employed persons, which are not protected by the provisions on minimum wage. The Chamber concluded that minimising labour costs by engaging self employed persons could legitimise labour factors of an offered price.[22]

One cannot deny the coherence of the opinion of the NAC on the irrelevance of the minimum wage for the verification of abnormally low offers. Nevertheless the weakest point of this reasoning is that in practice many of the contracts with self-employed persons in fact deserve a re-characterisation

17. Compare e.g. NAC awards of 5.3.2009 KIO/UZP 196/09, Lex 488378, of 15.1.2009, KIO/UZP 1524/08, Lex 485643, of 23.12.2008 KIO/UZP 1443/08, Lex 485650 and the decision of the District Court in Warsaw of 8.6.2006 V Ca 459/06 (unpublished).
18. Only in 4 of 71 published NAC awards related to the abnormally low offer verification procedure refer to the minimal wages criterion, only 1 to work safety regulations, none to the costs of environmental protection.
19. NAC awards of 12.2.2009 KIO/UZP 126/09, Lex 487460 and of 13.3.2008 KIO/UZP 179/08, Lex 396215.
20. NAC award of 7.5.2008 KIO/UZP 383/08, Lex 428477.
21. This consideration is highly disputable in light of earlier awards. Cf. point 4.2.
22. This kind of reasoning has been approved also by courts. Compare the decision of the District Court in Katowice of 30.1.2007 XIX Ga 3/07 reported at www.bankier.pl

as employment contracts. It is not possible to take this fact into account in the proceedings before the NAC.

## 5 The question of contract performance clauses

Contract performance clauses are not a separate category under the provisions of the PPL. They are treated as a part of the subject-matter definition. Also under the provisions of the Polish Civil Code one cannot distinguish between performance conditions and a subject of the obligation.

## Bibliography

A. Barczak-Oplustil in A. Barczak-Oplustil, G. Bogdan, Z. Ćwiąkalski, M. Dąbrowska-Kardas, P. Kardas, J. Majewski, J. Raglewski, M. Rodzynkiewicz, M. Szewczyk, W. Wróbel, A. Zoll, *Kodeks karny. Część szczególna. Volume II. Komentarz do art. 117-277 k.k.*, Kraków 2006, S. Hoc: Odpowiedzialność karna za nadużycie władzy. WPP 2005/4.

M. Winiarz, 'Odpowiedzialność za udzielanie zamówień publicznych w podsektorze samorządowym', FK 2007/9, p. 32.

# VIII. Secondary Considerations in Public Procurement in Romania

*by Dacian C. Dragoş, Bogdana Neamţu, and Raluca Velişcu*

## 1 Introduction

This chapter provides an overview of the institutional and legal framework for public procurement in Romania and its influence on how environmental and social considerations may be taken into account. This situation is discussed in light of the Commission's initiatives that foster sustainable public procurements and of Directive 2004/18/EC. It also describes practical examples of the application of secondary considerations by contracting authorities and identifies possible situations in which breaches of both European Union (EU) and national law provisions occur. The paper is structured into three subsequent sections. Section 1 begins with a brief overview of the Romanian legal framework in public procurement in light of its conformity with EU law and principles. It focuses on the stages of the public procurement process where the law allows for secondary considerations to be included. It then discusses the institutional framework and various legal means for solving disputes in public procurement. Section 2 regards instances of both judicial and non-judicial applications of secondary considerations in the public procurement process. This section analyses the inclusion of secondary considerations in light of the distinction made in the comparative chapter – it questions which of these environmental or social considerations are truly secondary, not mandated by legislation on public procurements and/or other laws. Section 3 details policy initiatives in Romania aimed at fostering secondary considerations in public procurement and will assess their initial impact. This section refers mostly to green considerations and not to social ones.

The chapter is based on first hand research in the legal environment of Romania, referring to public procurement (scrutiny of national legislation on public procurement and other related acts and national case law); on interviews with representatives of local procuring entities and the National Authority for Regulating and Monitoring Public Procurement; on an empirical research conducted by using a legal software in order to determine whether or not contracting authorities actually include secondary considerations in their public procurement procedures; and on an inventory of policy initiatives at the national level in this field by using policy papers and strategies posted online by various central administrative authorities.

## 2 The legal framework of public procurement in Romania

### 2.1 Overview

Currently, public procurement in Romania is regulated by Government Emergency Ordinance no. 34/2006[1] (with all the subsequent amendments), which transposes most, if not all, of the provisions of the EC Directives in this field: Directive 2004/18/EC, Directive 2004/17/EC, Directive 1989/665/EEC, and Directive 1992/13/EEC. Romania thus has state of the art legislation in this field; however most challenges occur in practice. Several of the challenges that are going to be addressed in this chapter refer to: the lack of implementation capacity at the level of the contracting authorities; the poor monitoring capacity of the public monitoring bodies which are responsible for the general supervision of the public procurement system; uninformed economic operators (with regard to the legal procedures implied by the public procurement process); and the lack of a coherent body of national case law in this field.

This section discusses the current legal framework of public procurement; however a brief presentation of the recent evolution of the main legal provisions in this field is relevant. Prior to the adoption of Government Emergency Ordinance no. 34/2006, public procurement was regulated by Government Emergency Ordinance no. 60/2001[2] (with all the subsequent amendments) and also by a series of other legal acts regarding different components of the public procurement system, such as the public goods concession contracts regime (Law no. 219/1998), the electronic public procurement system (Government Ordinance no. 20/2002), and public-private partnership contracts (Government Ordinance no. 16/2002), etc. The first step made by the legislators with the adoption of Government Emergency Ordinance no. 34/2006 was

1. Published in the Official Monitor, Section I, no. 418 from 15/05/2006.
2. Published in the Official Monitor, Section I, no. 241 from 11/05/2001; For a commentary on this regulation, see DC Dragoş, 'Contractele de achiziţii publice' ('The public procurement contracts') (2002) 2 Curierul judiciar (Judicial Courier), Idem, 'Noua reglementare a achiziţiilor publice' (The new regulation of public procurement) (2001) 12 Dreptul (Law Journal).

to bring under the umbrella of one legal act the main provisions regarding public procurement in Romania.

In the 2001 Government Emergency Ordinance secondary considerations in public procurement are not included. The general principles governing the field of public procurement according to the 2001 regulation are similar to the current ones. The legal text shows concern for creating a framework that fosters competition, transparency and equal treatment of the economic operators. However, there is no reference to environmental or social considerations at any of the stages of the public procurement process: the description of the subject-matter of the contract, the drafting of the selection criteria, of the technical specifications, of the awarding criteria, and of the contract performance criteria. On the contrary, Article 37 refers to technical specifications that have to be drafted in such a way as to create non-discriminatory conditions for all tenderers by limiting the discretionary power of the contracting authorities in establishing technical specifications that are too narrow and therefore can lead to the distortion of competition and potential discrimination among tenderers.

Articles 59 through 61 of the 2001 Government Emergency Ordinance describe the drafting of the award criteria. As within the current legal provisions, there are two main award criteria, namely the lowest price or the most advantageous tender from a technical-economic point of view. The latter criterion can be defined by taking into consideration the following items: delivery or execution deadlines; running costs; cost/efficiency ratio; qualitative, esthetic, technical or functional characteristics; post-sale services and technical assistance, arrangements regarding long-term service for components, conditions regarding the employment of Romanian nationals or the use of national products/goods, and other elements considered relevant for the evaluation of the tenders, including the price. It can be remarked that there is no reference to environmental considerations.

Another observation regarding the criteria used for determining the most advantageous tender from a technical-economic point of view refers to the so-called 'margin of national preference', described in Article 108. Article 108 states that the contracting authority has the obligation to award public procurement contracts by taking into consideration: whether the tenderer employs Romanian nationals as a certain percentage of the total work force necessary to carry out the contract; whether there are goods of national origin involved in the contract as a certain percentage of the total value of the contract; whether the subcontractors, natural or legal persons, are of Romanian origin, as a certain percentage of the total value of the contract. Article 108 also states that the contracting authority needs to draft these criteria in such a way that competition and transparency are not affected. Also, this preference for internal workers and/or products is limited by the international agreements that Romania is part of, and it doesn't apply to the contracts financed by EU funds. This law was modelled following the UNICTRAL Model Law on the Procurement of Goods, Construction and Services, which in conformity with its non-binding nature, acknowledged the right of the States to restrict in some cases foreign participation in order to protect important sectors of the national economy. The 'margin of national preference' was considered at that time as an acceptable restriction as opposed to even more restrictive solutions. Under the margin of national preference, one aspect which refers to the employment of Romanian nationals could be assimilated to secondary (namely social) considerations. Currently, in light of ECJ case law (see *Beentjes*[3]) such provisions in the national legislation of the Member States would be a breach of EU law. The request to hire Romanian (national) workers could potentially be a case of discrimination on grounds of nationality and at the same time such a request could be difficult to satisfy by tenderers from other States. However, the provisions cited above were valid until 2006, a period in which Romania was not part of the EU. Therefore, this criterion could be considered as an early attempt to incorporate secondary (social) considerations into the public procurement legislation.

### 2.2 Current legal framework – Government Emergency Ordinance no. 34/2006

The legal framework in public procurement is currently represented by Government Emergency Ordinance no. 34/2006 which is accompanied by three subsequent Government Decisions comprising methodological norms for the implementation of the Government Emergency Ordinance no. 34/2006: Government Decision no. 925/2006 regarding the award of public procurement contracts, Government Decision no. 1660/2006 regarding the award of public procurement contracts by electronic means, and Government Decision no. 71/2007 regarding the award of concession contracts for public works and services.

3. Case C-31/87, *Beentjes* [1988] ECR 4635. See the chapter of Caranta on the EU for a discussion of the case.

### 2.2.1 *Secondary considerations in light of the definition of the object of public procurement contracts*

Similar to Directive 2004/18/EC, the Romanian legislation defines the public procurement contract as a contract for pecuniary interest concluded in writing between one or more contracting authorities on the one hand, and one or more economic operators on the other hand, and having as its object the execution of works, the supply of products, or the provisions of services within the meaning of the Ordinance – Article 3 (f). The national provision regarding the object of the contract offers no indication regarding whether or not green or social considerations may form the object of the contract, alongside with the execution of works, the supply of products, or the provisions of services.

The Romanian doctrine has always stated the existence and the importance of administrative contracts in the Romanian law, although the legislation has never given a clear definition of the concept and of its characteristics. Consequently, the theory of administrative contracts was inspired by French doctrine and jurisprudence. Its development was always regarded with reluctance by the courts, who considered themselves not quite bound by it. This tendency was augmented by the fact that in matters regarding contracts concluded by public bodies, legislation often gave jurisdiction to the ordinary courts and not to the administrative sections of the courts.

It is accepted that an administrative contract is an agreement between a public body and a private entity (or another public body), by which the private party takes upon the task of providing a public service or performing a public work that is normally the duty of the public body, in exchange for remuneration.[4] Academia agrees on several characteristics of such contracts, such as the inequality of the parties favouring the public body due to the existence of imposed clauses, and the pre-eminence of the public interest in executing the contract, compensated by the private party's right to damages in case of unilateral alteration of the contract terms by the public authority.

The courts have taken a slightly different and more vague approach to the issue of administrative contracts. This is shown also by the very succinct definition of the administrative contract given by the High Court of Cassation

4. For scholarly definitions of administrative contracts, see ED Tarangul, *Tratat de drept administrativ* (*Administrative Law Text Book*) (1936) 477; A Iorgovan, *Tratat de drept administrativ* (*Administrative Law Text Book*) (C. H. Beck Bucureşti 2006) 358; RN Petrescu, *Drept administrativ* (*Administrative Law*) (Hamangiu 2008) 276; A Vasile, *Prestarea serviciilor publice prin agenţi privaţi* (*The Provision of Public Services by Private Economic Operators*) (C. H. Beck Bucureşti 2003) 66.

and Justice, in spite of the elaborated theory endorsed by academia: a contract regulated by special provisions where one of the parties is a public body.[5]

The qualification of administrative contracts can be done by the legislator or by the courts. Since in most cases such a qualification is not expressly given by the legislator, one has to settle with an indirect qualification, drawn from the fact that the law empowers administrative sections of the courts to decide on litigation rising from a certain type of contract.

Thus, the Law on judicial review no.554/2004 assigns to the administrative section of the courts the competence to judge cases arising from contracts that have as their object the use of public property, public works, the provision of public services, and public procurement (Article 2). The jurisdiction of the administrative section of the courts is reiterated in the special legislation regarding public procurement and the concession of public goods (Government Emergency Ordinances no. 34/2006 and no. 54/2006[6]).

No special attention was paid by either academia or the courts to the object of administrative contracts. In the absence of a clear theory or case law on this issue, it can be concluded that it is possible to have administrative contracts with a mixed object as long as it is legal. Though these Romanian concepts are inspired by the French ones, so far the interdiction of having a non-nominated contract, with a mixed/multiple object has not been raised. Civil law, on the other hand, allows for contracts with a mixed object, which are legal. In light of these observations, in our opinion public procurement contracts under the Romanian legislation can incorporate secondary considerations – when they are the equivalent of a State aid.

#### *2.2.2 Stages in the public procurement process where secondary considerations are referred to by public procurement legislation*

As already mentioned, the Government Emergency Ordinance no. 34/2006 generally mirrors most of the provisions of Directive 2004/18/EC regarding secondary considerations; while the environmental considerations are similar, the Directive identifies and discusses more situations in which social considerations can be taken into account by the contracting authorities. In the Government Emergency Ordinance no. 34/2006 there is only one general provision in Article 39 which provides contracting authorities with the opportunity

5. Judgment no. 912/13.02.2007, High Court of Cassation and Justice, Division for Administrative and Fiscal Matters, in GV Bîrsan, B Georgescu, *Legea contenciosului administrativ adnotată* (*The Law of Judicial Review of Administrative Acts with Comments*) (Hamangiu 2008) 22.
6. Published in the Official Monitor, Section I, no. 569 from 30/06/2006.

to integrate social objectives into public procurement contracts at the stage of drafting conditions regarding the performance of the contract. Article 39 provides:

'The contracting authority has the right to impose within the tender documentation, to the extent that these are compatible with Community law, special conditions relating to the performance of the contract with the goal to obtain certain social effects or related to environmental protection and promoting the sustainable development'.

Recital 33 of the Directive states that social considerations may be included in contract performance conditions. Such considerations include but are not limited to favoring on-site vocational training, the employment of people experiencing particular difficulty in achieving integration, the fight against unemployment, etc. In addition, Recital 46 states, *inter alia*, that a

'contracting authority may use criteria aiming to meet social requirements, in response in particular to the needs – defined in the specifications of the contract – of particularly disadvantaged groups of people to which those receiving/using the works, supplies or services which are the object of the contract belong.'

This last indent was however considered to be particularly restrictive. The Romanian legislator has opted not to mention social considerations specfically in Ordinance no. 34/2006, such as those identified by the Directive. This is mainly due to the fact that at the EU level both the Commission and the ECJ have trod very carefully with regard to social considerations. The option of the Romanian legislator could be explained in the context of the existence of a limited implementation capacity and expertise among contracting authorities. As there is limited national case law in the field of public procurement, and in light of controversies at Union level as well, the option not to make specific reference to social considerations (besides the general provision of Article 39) seems justifiable.

Both the Directive (Recital 28 and Article 19) and the national Ordinance (Article 43) make reference to reserved contracts. The aim of this provision is to foster equal opportunities and integration in society for disadvantaged groups. The possibility for contracting authorities to set aside certain contracts for sheltered workshops or for tenderers who agree to perform the contract in the context of sheltered employment programs for protected employment is without doubt motivated by social considerations. Other national legal provisions detailing the conditions in which such contracts can be awarded to sheltered workshops will be further discussed in a subsequent section of this paper.

Environmental considerations can be incorporated at the following stages of the public procurement process: the technical specifications, the selection/qualification criteria, the award criteria, and the performance criteria. In addition, according to the classification made by the European Commission, these considerations could be included at the stage of drafting the subject-matter of the contract. Despite this delimitation made by the Commission, which is problematic in itself, the national law makes no clear reference to the drafting of the subject-matter.

*2.2.2.1 Technical specifications*

Article 35 (3) of the national Ordinance states that:

> 'Technical specifications define, if necessary, and without being limited to these, characteristics such as quality level, technical and performance level, requirements regarding the impact on the environment and safety for use as well as dimensions, terminology, symbols, tests and testing methods, packaging, marking and labeling, and instructions for the use of products, systems for insuring the quality, conditions and procedures for conformity certification with relevant standards or assessment and other such requirements'

Article 37 refers to eco-labels and states that the technical specification requirements, while including environmental characteristics, can be described by reference to national or European eco-labels. In order not to discriminate against tenderers and not to limit their participation in tendering procedures, the Ordinance, following the European legal provisions, states that any other means of proof that the products/services offered meet the technical requirements should be accepted. Such a means of proof is represented by the technical dossier of the producer or a certification/testing report issued by an accredited body. In the context of our country this last provision is important. While such a requirement may have boosted the debates about the eco-label certification in recent years, it also represents an alternative for most of the Romanian tenderers which do not have this certification: there were only six Romanian-based companies which received the EU eco-label until the beginning of 2010.

*2.2.2.2 Selection and qualification criteria*

Article 43 of the Ordinance no. 34/2006 establishes an important exception from the principle of non-discrimination, namely reserved contracts. Thus, the legal status of sheltered workshops or sheltered employment programs acts as a first instance of selection/qualification criteria.

With regard to the selection criteria, there are two kinds of relevant provisions: those listing possible reasons for exclusion from the procurement procedures and those concerning the technical capacity of bidders. Articles 180 through 186 of the Ordinance identify three broad categories of selection criteria that can be used to determine the exclusion of possible candidates. These are: the personal situation of the candidate/tenderer, the suitability to pursue the professional activity, and economic and financial standards.[7] Even though Directive 2004/18/EC allows wide scope for Member States to incorporate into these exclusion criteria a large array of secondary (social) considerations, the Romanian legislator has opted for minimal provisions related to social considerations. Following the provisions of Article 45 of the Directive, the national Ordinance states in Article 181(c) that the contracting authority has the right to exclude from the award of the public procurement contract any tenderer/candidate if the tenderer/candidate has not fulfilled his obligations relating to the payment of taxes to the State as well as the obligations relating to the payment of social security contributions in accordance with the legal provisions of Romania or of the country in which he is established.

Attention is also paid to environmental management as it relates to the technical capacity of the candidates. Article 176 (f) of the national Ordinance states that the contracting authority has the right to apply environmental management standards in the case of public works contracts and public services contracts. Article 188 states that the contracting authority may ask for information regarding the environmental protection measures that the economic operator can implement during the execution of the public works or services contract. If such a criterion is included in the selection procedure, Articles 194 through 196 list the means of proof that the economic operator shall refer to: either to the Community Eco-Management and Audit Scheme (EMAS); or to the environmental protection standards based on the relevant European or international standards certified by bodies in conformity with the EU law or the relevant European or international standards concerning certification. The contracting authority has the obligation to accept equivalent certificates issued by bodies established in Member States of the European Union. When the economic operator does not have an environmental management certificate as it is requested, the contracting authority has the obligation to accept any other evidences presented by the economic operator insofar as the presented evidence confirms the assurance of an appropriate level of environmental protection.

7. See, for these instances, the issue of applying the proportionality principle, DD Şerban, 'Principiul proporţionalităţii în domeniul achiziţiilor publice' ('The principle of proportionality in public procurement') (2007) 9 *Dreptul* (Law Journal).

*2.2.2.3 Award criteria*

The national Ordinance, following the provisions of Directive 2004/18/EC, lists in Article 198 two possible award criteria. Contracting authorities can use either the economically most advantageous tender or only the lowest price. When the award criteria is the economically most advantageous tender, the various factors used for the assessment of the tender can take into account the price, the characteristics of the quality level, the technical level or functional level, the environmental characteristics, the running costs, cost-effectiveness ratio, post-sale services and technical assistance, delivery date or execution date, other significant elements for the evaluation of the tenders. Again, similar to the Directive, the national Ordinance clearly spells out in Article 199 (3) the request for the existence of a specific link between the subject-matter of the contract and the award criteria.

With regard to the *abnormally low tenders*, recent evolutions in the national legislation have tried to address the issue of contracting authorities awarding contracts based on the criterion of the lowest price, even in situations in which there were clear indications that this price was abnormally low. Thus, in July 2009 an amendment was made to the legislation, more specifically, to the methodological norms[8] for implementation of the Government Emergency Ordinance no. 34/2006. The former provisions stated that a tender was abnormally low provided that the price was not the result of free competition and could not be justified by the tenderer. This wording offers enough discretionary power to the contracting authority since it did not state any precise thresholds. The new amendment states that a tender is abnormally low provided that the price is less than 85 per cent of the estimated value of the contract (without VAT) or, if there are at least five valid tenders, the price is lower than 85 per cent of the average of the other tenders. This does not automatically imply that the contracting authority has to exclude a tenderer with a lower tender; it rather implies that it has to carry out further inquiries with regards to how this price was established. This fact is confirmed by relevant case law.[9] An abnormally low tender does not always refer to the price,

8. Governmental Decision no. 834/2009 amending the Governmental Decision no. 925/2006, published in the Official Monitor no. 515 from 27/07/2009.
9. Judgment no. 2563/5.12.2008, Craiova Appellate Court, Division for Administrative and Fiscal Matters; Judgment no. 553/CA/15.12.2008, Iaşi Appellate Court, Division for Administrative and Fiscal Matters; Judgment no. 2775/12.12.2008, Bucureşti Appellate Court, Division 8 for Administrative and Fiscal Matters.

but also for example to the duration of the execution of works.[10] Sometimes abnormally low tenders are the result of a breach of various work-related rights, such as minimum wage, security measures at the work place, proper equipment, facilities provided to workers such as transportation to the work place, etc., which could be related to secondary (social) considerations. In one case, the Appellate Court ruled that the contracting authority must re-evaluate the tenders in light of the existence of one abnormally low tender based on the non-compliance of the operator with minimum wage and some proper safety measures for the workers.[11]

In the Romanian context, this new provision received mixed reactions. On the one hand, economic operators, at least the big companies, claimed that unlawful competition will be eliminated since small firms that do not have the ability to carry out contracts will face in the future more difficulties to get away with offering dumping prices. On the other hand, there were voices coming from the contracting authorities arguing that though this provision may bring more quality regarding the way in which contracts are executed and regarding contract performance, this will also mean higher prices. The general opinion is however that a 'safe' tender will be established at 85 per cent of the estimated value of the contract. From the perspective of secondary considerations, this provision brings about an important opportunity. If all tenderers will mainly offer the same price, then the contracting authorities will be forced to design award criteria based on the most economically advantageous tender, where, apart from the price, other considerations will have to be included.

With regard to contract performance criteria, the national Ordinance followed the provisions of the Directive, including performance criteria into the all-encompassing definition of technical specifications. It will be discussed in section four whether in practice contracting authorities make a distinction when drafting the tender documentation, between technical requirements and contract performance.

### 2.3 Institutional framework

This section provides a brief overview with regard to the institutional actors involved in the public procurement system in Romania. The institutional

10. Judgment no. 62/23.01.2009, Bacău Appellate Court, Division for Commercial, Administrative and Fiscal Matters.
11. Judgment no. 613/27.03.2008, Craiova Appellate Court, Division for Administrative and Fiscal Matters.

framework is discussed in light of the potential role of each institution in fostering sustainable public procurement..

### *2.3.1 The National Authority for Regulating and Monitoring Public Procurements (hereafter NARMPP)*[12]

The NARMPP was established by Government Emergency Ordinance no. 74/2005 (latter approved with amendments by Law no.111/2006[13]) as a public entity, subordinated to the Government, and directly coordinated by the Prime Minister. NARMPP is the public entity responsible for the management of the public procurement system in Romania, its major task consisting in drafting, promoting, and implementing public policy in the field of public procurement. The institution's role is to encourage the continuous development and evolution of the mechanisms through which the institutions and structures situated at the national level within the institutional framework of the public procurement system interact with contracting authorities throughout the country and the latter then interact with private companies. The main principles upheld are increasing efficiency, transparency and competitiveness of public procurement in Romania.

The NARMPP is responsible for fulfilling the following functions (Law no. 111/2006):

- The drafting of the strategy in the field of public procurements, in accordance with the provisions of the Community *acquis*;
- The initiation of legislation regarding public procurement procedures;
- The monitoring, the analysis and the evaluation of the award procedures of public procurement contracts;
- The representation of Romania within consultative committees, working groups, and communication networks organized by European institutions;
- Technical and methodological assistance for contracting authorities in the process of awarding public procurement contracts, in order to facilitate the proper enforcement of the legal framework in this field;
- The initiation/financing of training activities for the personnel involved in public procurement activities, acting as a support body for the development of the implementation and legal enforcement capacity at the level of contracting authorities.

12. Autoritatea Naţională pentru Reglementarea şi Monitorizarea Achiziţiilor Publice (A.N.R.M.A.P.) in Romanian.
13. Published in the Official Monitor, Section I, no. 379 from 3/05/2006.

In order to accomplish the above-mentioned functions, the NARMPP carries out the following activities (Law no. 111/2006):

- The assurance of a coherent national legal framework, harmonized with the Community *acquis* in the field of public procurement;
- The fulfillment of the correlative obligations derived from the implementation of the EU Directives in the field of public procurement;
- The maintenance of a permanent communication channel with the structures within the European Commission, with the similar bodies from the other EU member states, and with other national public bodies;
- The guarantee of a proper framework for the implementation and enforcement of the legal provisions in the field of public procurement;
- The development of implementation capacity at the level of contracting authorities.

The NARMPP, due to the functions it carries out, can be considered as the most important institutional actor in fostering sustainable public procurement and in advancing the use of secondary considerations in public procurement. Three main tasks are directly linked to sustainable procurement. The authors assessed how the institution carries out these tasks in light of two different surveys – one was addressed to contracting authorities (not a representative sample) and one to the NARMPP (the director of the Policy and Regulation Department, the main unit of the NARMPP).

*2.3.1.1 Policy initiation*

The contracting authorities acknowledge the importance of this institution but are nevertheless dissatisfied with its activity and with the lack of effective communication. The somewhat limited role played by NARMPP is also acknowledged by the institution itself. In the survey, it was stated that for the time being, the Authority has only published a text book with the EU case law in this field and some operational guidelines for the Romanian contracting authorities. It intends in the future to promote – together with the Ministry of the Environment and of Forestry – guidelines for including green considerations in public procurement. The Authority acknowledges that there is a latent potential for sustainable procurement in Romania in the future.

#### *2.3.1.2 Monitoring of the entire process of public procurement based on the data provided by the Operator of the Electronic Public Procurement (SEAP, see section 3.5)*

The representatives of local contracting authorities stated that the NARMPP acts as a first instance filter for the legality of the participation announcements. In other words, the NARMPP is the first entity which checks if the contracting authorities, in the process of setting selection and award criteria as well as in drafting the procedures for the awarding of the contract, meet the legal requirements (this process takes place before participation announcements are published). During informal discussions we were told that it is frequent for the NARMPP to ask contracting authorities to review the participation announcements – approximately 30 per cent of the participations announcements are rejected by NARMMP.[14] Thus, the NARMPP is the first to identify if the selection and award criteria are too vague, are not related to the subject-matter of the contract or violate the principle of non-discrimination. When asked to assess whether or not contracting authorities employ secondary considerations in public procurements procedures, the NARMPP stated that only a very small part of the contracting authorities use them, the main reasons being the lack of information and expertise with regard to the drafting of the tender documentation, to the potential benefits/advantages of sustainable procurement in general, and the lack of operational instruments that would assist them while carrying out the sustainable procurement procedures. Despite the fact that the Authority has general monitoring responsibilities with regard to how contracting authorities carry out procurement procedures and draft the tender documentation, the institution replied that for the time being it does not hold any relevant data about the use of secondary considerations in public procurement by contracting authorities.

#### *2.3.1.3 Monitoring of the entire process of public procurement based on the data provided by the Operator of the Electronic Public Procurement (SEAP, see section 3.5)*

With regard to technical assistance, NARMPP is cooperating with other public bodies (Ministry of the Environment and Forestry) in carrying out various training and dissemination programs that are meant to raise the awareness of

14. The Romanian Academic Society, 'O evaluare a eficienţei, integrităţii şi transparenţei sistemului de achiziţii publice din România' (An assessment of the efficiency, integrity, and transparency of the Romanian public procurement system), [Online] at http://www.sar.org.ro/do_download.php?file=files/paper-final.pdf, accessed March 2nd, 2010

contracting authorities with regard to the benefits of sustainable procurement and to increase their expertise level regarding the drafting of the tender documentation. The Authority plans to further this support, such new measures including: the development of operational tools; training for contracting authorities; policy and best practices dissemination; and the translation of some sustainable procurement documents drafted by the EU Commission.

In 2009, the monitoring role of the NARMPP came under questioning in the context of huge political corruption scandals related to public procurement. It was disclosed that in many situations, the legal provisions were ignored, this resulting in the awarding of public procurement contracts that are now found illegal and thus void. These contracts were all monitored and received at that time the approval of the Agency.[15]

*2.3.2 The National Council for Solving Legal Disputes (hereafter NCSLD)*[16]

The NCSLD is an administrative-jurisdictional body, independent from other structures with regard to its decisions, but functioning under the supervision of the Government. Its main role consists in deciding on complaints of tenderers dissatisfied with the decisions made by the contracting authorities with regard to public procurement procedures.

The NCSLD is formed of 33 members who are public servants and have special status. The position they hold is called councellor for solving contestations in the field of public procurement The Council is mandated to solve the contestations lodged during the award procedures, before an actual contract has been signed. The NCSLD adopts decisions in its activity of solving contestations. The NCSLD is made up of 11 units. The complaint is decided by a unit formed of three members, out of whom one is the president and has legal training. Each unit is assisted by technical experts.

Because the Council has a hybrid status, derived from being an administrative-jurisdictional body, it is interesting to see its relationship with the contracting authorities and with the courts of law. There is case law on exceeding the competences by the Council. From the case law, there are two main situations in which the Council has clearly exceeded its competences: a) the evaluation of tenders and the subsequent assessment of these tenders as non-

15. Transparency International Romania, 'Studiu asupra sistemului național de integritate 2009. Raport național asupra corupției 2009' ('Study regarding the national integrity system 2009. National report on corruption 2009') [Online] at http://www.transparency.org.ro/stiri/evenimente/2009/21octombrie/Prezentare %20NCR%20si % 20NIS %20final.pdf, accessed March 2nd, 2010
16. Consiliul Național de Soluționare a Contestațiilor (CNSC) in Romanian.

compliant with the requirements of the award documentation. In a case brought before a Court of Appeal,[17] the Court annulled the decision of the Council because the Council exceeded its competences by ruling that the tender of a bidder was abnormally low and therefore non-compliant with the legal requirements. It further stated that the contracting authority must continue the tender procedures, excluding the abnormally low tender. The Court ruled that the Council cannot substitute itself for the contracting authority in evaluating the tenders, more so without making any financial/economic inquiries.[18] The Court also ruled that the Council's decision represents a breach of the general principles of equal treatment and non-discrimination established by the Ordinance. b) When the Council, while responding to a contestation also identifies other possible breaches of the legislation, it cannot annul *ex officio* the award procedure, it can only ask the contracting authorities to remedy the breaches of legislation.[19] The literature considers this as a major set back of the national legal framework, since initially the national Ordinance stated that the Council could, *ex officio*, remedy certain illegalities arising from the acts of the contracting authorities, in cases when there were no complaints lodged against these acts. It is interesting to see how the national legislator envisions

17. Judgment no. 2775/12.12.2008, Bucureşti Appellate Court, Division 8 for Administrative and Fiscal Matters.
18. For doctrine opinions on this issue, see DD Şerban, 'Competenţa Consiliului Naţional de Soluţionare a Contestaţiilor de a atribui contracte de achiziţie publică şi de a obliga autorităţile contractante la încheierea acestora' ('The competency of the National Council for Solving Legal Disputes to solve the complaints regarding the awarding of PP contracts and to force the contracting authorities to conclude these contracts') (2008) 5 *Revista de Drept al Afacerilor* (Business Law Journal) 82; Idem, 'Discuţii pe marginea competenţei Consiliului Naţional de Soluţionare a Contestaţiilor. Contractele sectoriale' ('Discussions regarding the competency of the National Council for Solving Legal Disputes to solve complaints. Sectorial contracts') (2009) 2 *Revista de drept commercial* (Commercial Law Review) 38; Idem, 'Despre posibilitatea Consiliului Naţional de Soluţionare a Contestaţiilor de a anula, din oficiu, procedurile de atribuire a contractelor de achiziţie publică' ('Comments on the competency of the National Council for Solving Legal Disputes to annul, ex officio, the award procedures regarding PP contracts') (I) and (II), (2008) 4 *Revista de drept public* (Public Law Review) 85.
19. Judgment no. 780/3.07.2008, Timişoara Appellate Court, Division for Administrative and Fiscal Matters; Judgment no. 930/2.10.2008, Timişoara Appellate Court, Division for Administrative and Fiscal Matters.

the role of the Council – a court of law rather than an instance for offering remedies (in the spirit of Community law – Directive 2007/66/EC).[20]

*2.3.3 The Court of Auditors*

The Court of Auditors is the entity which conducts ex post financial audit regarding the generation, the management, and the use of public finances. In this context, it also inspects public procurement contracts.

*2.3.4 The Unit for the Coordination and Monitoring of Public Procurements*

The Unit for the Coordination and Monitoring of Public Procurement is organized as a department within the Ministry of Public Finances and its main role is the monitoring of the procedural aspects at all stages of the public procurement process. According to the Operations Handbook of UCMPP,[21] most of the activities performed are based on the assessment of the procedures using a checklist. With regards to the technical specifications, selection, and award criteria, on the checklist used there are questions regarding whether or not the criteria are present in the tender documentation and whether they are properly detailed, as required by law. In other words, it can be concluded that UCMPP does not monitor in-depth the content of the criteria, they rather focus on whether requirements such as deadlines, estimated value of the contract, the choice of the award procedure, etc meet the provisions of the law. The UCMPP issues interim reports containing recommendations for the contracting authorities regarding how to remedy the errors found and decisions which have non-binding status. These decisions are sent to the contracting authority and to the NARMPP. From an institutional perspective, there is a slight overlap of competences between these two institutions. It is not clear why the UCMPP, which mostly monitors financial issues involved in the procedures of public procurement (i.e. if the estimated value of the contract is properly established, if the financing sources are clearly stated, etc) conducts a separate procedure from that of the NARMPP, which is the main monitor-

20. The Romanian Academic Society, 'O evaluare a eficienței, integrității și transparenței sistemului de achiziții publice din România' (An assessment of the efficiency, integrity, and transparency of the Romanian public procurement system), [Online] at http://www.sar.org.ro/do_download.php?file=files/paper-final.pdf, accessed March 2nd, 2010.

21. The Unit for the Coordination and Monitoring of Public Procurements, 'Operations Handbook', 2007, [Online] at http://www.licitatiiblog.ro/ucvap-unitatea-pentru-coordonarea-si-verificarea-achizitiilor-publice/, in Romanian, accessed July 29, 2009.

ing authority. Initially, NARMPP was also part of the institutional structure of the Ministry of Public Finances, which could explain this overlap up to a certain extent.

*2.3.5 The Operator of the Electronic Public Procurements System (SEAP)*
The SEAP is represented by the National Management Center for the Information Society, created recently by the restructuring of a national agency. It is part of the hierarchical structure of the Ministry of Communication and Information Society. It implements and operates at the national level the IT systems designed to implement e-government in Romania. With regard to public procurement, the Center is the operator of the Electronic System for Public Procurement. More recently, after the drafting of the National Action Plan for Green Public Procurements 2009-2013, the Center became responsible for designing, implementing and operating the e-documents for green public procurement through the Electronic System for Public Procurement (ESPP). The specific responsibilities are detailed more in-depth in the last section of the paper.

Since 2009, all participation and award announcements need to be published online using this system. Since 2008, after an amendment brought to the methodological norms for implementation of the Ordinance 34/2006, it is mandatory for all contracting authorities to conduct at least 20 per cent of the total value of their public procurement contracts for one year through ESPP. This is meant to increase the transparency and the efficient dissemination within public procurement.

*2.3.6 Contracting authorities*
Contracting authorities are probably the most relevant actors in the process of including secondary considerations in the process of public procurement, in light of the fact that the inclusion of these considerations is voluntary and starts with the drafting of the public procurement plans at the local level and, more specifically, with the drafting of the tender documentation for each stage of the public procurement process. Currently there are approximately 11,000 contracting authorities. The contracting authorities bear the main responsibility regarding the legality of the documents and procedures in the procurement process. This explains up to a certain point their reluctance regarding the inclusion of secondary considerations – especially the social ones, into the procurement process.

The implementation of SPP has determined the inclusion into the institutional framework of the public procurements system of other public authorities responsible for the protection of the environment, one of the key elements of sustainable procurement and secondary considerations: the Ministry of the Environment and Forestry, the National Agency for the Protection of the Environment, and the National Environment Guard. As shown in the last section of the paper, with regard to sustainable procurement the institutions in the field of environmental protection have taken the lead in promoting, at least at the policy level, the concept and the benefits of sustainable procurement.

## 2.4 The regime of legal disputes in public procurement

This section briefly describes the legal means available to the economic operators or other interested parties who whish to complain against decisions/acts of the contracting authorities within the framework of a public procurement is procedure. An emphasis placed on how technical specifications, selection and award criteria can be contested as part of the tender documentation. Secondary considerations pertaining to the mentioned stages are included in the tender documentation.

Those who consider themselves aggrieved in their rights or legitimate interests by a decision of a contracting authority regarding the public procurement process can lodge a complaint with either the National Council for Solving Legal Disputes or with the competent court of law.[22] The claimant is

22. For the doctrine regarding this issue, see DD Şerban, 'Sinteză a practicii judiciare în materia achiziţiilor publice – studiu de caz' ('Synthesis of judicial practice in the field of public procurements – a case study'), (II, III, IV, V) (2008) 6/7/10 and (2009) 2 *Pandectele române* (Brochure comprising the opinion of jurists on various law issues); Idem, 'Contracte administrative. Achiziţiile publice şi contenciosul administrativ' ('Administrative contracts. Public procurements and the judicial review of administrative acts'), (2008) 5 *Pandectele române* (Brochure comprising the opinion of jurists on various law issues); Idem, 'Despre ordonanţa preşedinţială în materia achi-ziţ, iilor publice – studiu de caz' ('Comments on the president's decision in the field of public procurement') (2008) 9 *Pandectele române* (Brochure comprising the opinion of jurists on various law issues); Idem, 'Observaţii privind procedura de rezolvare a diferendelor juridice în legătură cu atribuirea contractelor de achiziţie publică, a contractelor de concesiune de lucrări publice şi a contractelor de concesiune de servicii' ('Observations regarding the solving of legal disputes related to the awarding of public procurements contracts, of concession of public works and public services contracts') (2009) 2 *Dreptul* (Law Journal); Idem, 'Contribuţii la corecta soluţionare a contestaţiilor în lumina dispoziţiilor Ordonanţei de Urgenţă a Guvernului nr. 34/2006 privind atribuirea contractelor de achiziţie publică, a contractelor de concesiune de lucrări publice şi a contractelor de concesiune de servicii' ('Observations regarding the correct solving of complaints in light of the provisions of Government Emergency

free to choose between these two; however the law states that it is forbidden to lodge the same complaint simultaneously with both the Council and the court of law. If this situation occurs, the procedure before the Council is suspended *de jure*. It is presumed that by lodging the same complaint with the court, the claimant renounces the administrative-judicial procedure in the Council. Though the administrative-judicial procedure before the Council is not mandatory, there are reasons and benefits associated with choosing it. In the first place, if such a complaint is lodged with the Council, then the contracting authority cannot proceed with awarding and signing the contract. The public procurement procedures are suspended *de jure* not just until the Council issues its decision but also for an additional 10 days (this is the timeframe in which the decision of the Council can be contested in front of a court of law). Thus, the tenderer, by approaching the Council first, and not directly a court of law, may 'gain' additional means for solving the legal dispute. In addition, if the tenderer lodges the complaint directly with the court of law, the contracting authority has the right to proceed with awarding and signing the contract. The court may order the suspension of the procedure, but only at the request of the party, and upon assessment of the reasons put forward. A special procedure – the presidential ordinance – can be used for that reason.

Ordinance no. 34/2006 regarding the awarding of public procurement contracts, of concession of public works and public services contracts') (2008) 7 *Dreptul* (Law Journal), no. 7/2008; Idem, 'Unele observaţii asupra căilor de atac prevăzute de Ordonanţa de Urgenţă a Guvernului nr. 60/2001 privind achiziţiile publice' ('Observations regarding the legal means for settling disputes according to the provisions of Government Emergency Ordinance no. 60/2001 regarding public procurement contracts') (2007) 2 *Dreptul* (Law Journal); Idem, 'Opinii despre recentele intervenţii asupra Ordonanţei de Urgenţă a Guvernului nr. 34/2006 cu relevanţă în privinţa procedurii de soluţionare a contestaţiilor în domeniul achiziţiilor publice' ('Opinions regarding recent changes in the text of Government Emergency Ordinance no. 34/2006 regarding the procedure for solving legal complaints') (2009) 1 *Revista de Drept Comunitar* (EC Law Review); E Albu, 'Propunere de lege ferenda pentru statornicirea legală a regulii divizării pe loturi a achiziţiilor publice' ('Proposal for changing the legal provision regarding the split into lots of public procurement contracts') (2007) 1 *Curierul Judiciar* (Judiciary Courier); I Deleanu, 'Poziţia favorizantă a operatorilor economici la procedurile de atribuire a contractelor de achiziţie publică' ('The advantage of some economic operators over others in the awarding of public procurement process') (2008) 3 *Dreptul* (Law Journal); VC Popescu, 'Concordanţa cu articolul 6 paragraful 1 din Convenţia europeană pentru apărarea drepturilor omului şi a libertăţilor fundamentale a procedurii de soluţionare pe cale administrativ-jurisdicţională a contestaţiilor privind achiziţiile publice' ('The procedure for solving legal complaints in public procurement interpreted in light of art. 6. par. 1 from ECHR') (2005) 6 *Dreptul* (Law Journal).

Statistical data confirms the fact that economic operators are motivated to use the Council as a first instance of legal mediation. This is reflected by the growing number of complaints the Council received in 2007, 2008, and 2009 respectively. By looking at the number of complaints lodged, an ascending trend is evident. Thus, if in 2007 there were 4,976 complaints, in 2008 their number had grown to 6,517, and in 2009 there were 9,019.[23]

After receiving a complaint, the Council needs to issue a decision within 20 days from the moment when it receives the tender documentation from the contracting authority, which has been notified in advance by the complainant. This deadline may be extended by a maximum of ten days in exceptional cases. Against the decision of the Council, the complainant can lodge a subsequent complaint with the Appellate Court in whose jurisdiction the premises of the contracting authority are. This complaint needs to be lodged within a 10 days framework. These very short terms for lodging complaints with different jurisdictions can be interpreted in two ways. On the one hand, they are intended to accelerate the award procedures as a response to the specific Romanian context where many of the actors involved in the system of public procurement complain that the procedures take too long. This situation however will not be solved by setting very short deadlines for lodging complaints. The problem is that once a complaint is brought to the court, the judicial review process takes very long. Thus, the very short deadlines established in the Ordinance do not necessarily address the entire issues. On the other hand, these deadlines can be viewed as restrictive, thus in certain situations limiting access to justice.

The general deadline for lodging a complaint with either the Council or the court is between five and ten days, depending on the estimated value of the contract, from the moment in which the tenderer is notified about any act/action of the contracting authority related to the public procurement procedures. When the tender documentation is published in the Electronic System for Public Procurement, the deadline starts with the day when the tender documentation is published and becomes available online.

With regard to secondary considerations, this deadline may prove to be restrictive for the potential tenderers. They can complain about the content of the technical specifications, and of the selection and award criteria only within a timeframe of a maximum of ten days from the moment when the

23. The National Council for Solving Legal Disputes, Statistical Data, 'Decisions issued by CNSC from its creation and until 31.12.2009' [Online] at http://www.cnsc.ro/ images/stories/rapoarte/2009/Contestatii_solutionate_dela_infiintare_31dec2009.pdf, accessed March 2nd, 2010.

economic operator receives the tender documentation. The deadline is shorter if the participation announcement is published in the Electronic System of Public Procurements. From the interviews conducted with representatives of local contracting authorities emanated that tenderers do not usually lodge a complaint with regards to technical specifications, selection and award criteria. This happens because they are either uninformed or do not pay sufficient attention to these criteria from the very beginning and often claim that they are allegedly illegal, discriminatory, unclear or vague later on into the tender procedures when it is too late to lodge such a complaint. During the interviews we were told that often tenderers attempt to complain against the content of these criteria at the moment when the contract is awarded to a different competitor based on the evaluation performed using these criteria. At this stage however, they can only complain about the way in which the contracting authorities assess the documents submitted by the economic operator in light of the already established technical specifications and award criteria. The case law confirms that this situation occurs in practice very often. In such a case,[24] brought before an Appellate Court, the tenderer contested, in the same complaint, both the award criteria and the award of the contract to a different competitor. The Appellate Court, stated, *inter alia*, that the tender documentation, including the award criteria, can only be contested within a five to ten days timeframe. Thus, the part of the complaint regarding the award criteria was overruled based on the grounds of its tardiness.[25]

Finally, it has to be stated that conducting legal research based on the decisions of the Council proves to be very difficult. This is due to the fact that the Council is breaching the law by refusing to publish on its website the motivation of its decisions or to communicate them to those interested. The law provides that within 10 days from the date when the decision becomes final, it has to be published on the website – Article 298 (4), with its motivation. The decision without motivation has to be published right away after it was issued. Initially, none of the motivated decisions issued by the Council start-

24. Judgment no. 458/R-C/25.04.2008, Piteşti Appellate Court, Division for Commercial, Administrative and Fiscal Matters.
25. For similar judicial instances see Judgment no. 970/CA/17.09.2008, Alba Iulia Appellate Court, Division for Administrative and Fiscal Matters; Judgment no. 1067/CA/8.10.2008, Alba Iulia Appellate Court, Division for Administrative and Fiscal Matters; Judgment no. 40/11.01.2007, Bucureşti Appellate Court, Division 8 for Administrative and Fiscal Matters; Judgment no. 629/R-C/20.06.2008, Piteşti Appellate Court, Division for Commercial, Administrative and Fiscal Matters; Judgment no. 453/6.03.2008, Craiova Appellate Court, Division for Administrative and Fiscal Matters.

ing with 2006 was posted online. Following the request for public information addressed by the authors of this chapter, the Council has started to publish a selection of these decisions for each year starting with 2006. The legal provisions are still not met and an administrative appeal lodged by the authors is pending.

### 2.5 Sustainable Public Procurement in other national legal acts

Apart from Ordinance no. 34/2006, there are additional legal acts which make reference to secondary considerations as they relate to public procurements. This section discusses several of these acts. The emphasis is on highlighting whether or not these national acts represent instances of breaches of the community law.

#### *2.5.1 Law no. 448/2006*

Law no. 448/2006 addresses the protection and the promotion of the rights of persons with disabilities.[26] Article 77 represents a general obligation for all legal persons, public or private, with the exceptions of military institutions, which employ more than 50 persons, to hire at least 4 per cent or more persons with disabilities from the total number of employees. However, if this general obligation cannot be satisfied, the law identifies two alternatives: (a) to pay to the state budget a monthly contribution representing 50 per cent of the minimum gross wage multiplied by the total number of job positions that should be occupied by the persons with disabilities; and (b) to procure goods or services from authorised sheltered entities of equivalent value.

From the perspective of conformity with EU law, this provision falls under the category of reserved contracts, which represent an admissible exception from the rules of free competition and non-discrimination stated both in Directive 2004/18/EC, Recital 28, and Article 19, respectively, and in the national legislation: Government Emergency Ordinance no.34/2006, Article 43.

During interviews with the representatives of the local contracting authorities, the authors were told that there were situations when such contracts could not be awarded because no sheltered entity responded to the invitation to participate. This could question the efficiency of such a provision in supporting the rights of persons with disabilities. Large public procurements contracts are generally not set aside for sheltered workshops. In order to have access to such contracts, sheltered workshops consider that the special provisions regarding the encouragement of SMEs to participate in public procure-

26. Published in the Official Monitor, Section I, no. 1006 from 18/12/2006.

ment should apply to them as well. The main incentives these entities suggest to be considered by procuring entities regard the division of procurements into lots and the use of subcontracting. Both measures are strongly contested, for reasons not related to secondary (social) considerations but rather because they may infringe the rules of free competition and transparency.[27]

### *2.5.2 Law no. 350/2005*

Law no. 350/2005 concerns the legal regime of grants awarded from public funds for non-profit activities of general interest.[28] The law states the general principles and the procedures for awarding grant contracts to NGOs based on the drafting of project proposals which are evaluated by the public financing authority via a selection process. The scope of such public contracts according to the Romanian legislation covers all non-profit activities that contribute to promoting actions or programs of general public interest, regional or local. With the exception of the general provision which refers to the public interest objective of such projects, including green and social considerations, there are no specific references which could be interpreted as fostering secondary considerations. This law does not refer to the concession or delegation of public services (for this see section c). It rather refers to activities of general interest financed by public funds. The contracting authority drafts the instructions based on which the NGOs will then draft their project proposals. The instructions include selection and award criteria. While the selection criteria evaluate the capacity of the NGOs to carry out the proposed activity, the award criteria assess the quality of the proposals and of the technical and the financial specifications. The award criterion is the most economically and technical advantageous proposal. It can be determined by using indicators underlying criteria that are precise enough and are related to the subject-matter of the contract. In practice however, complying with these requirements may prove challenging, to say the least. For example, when a municipality grants money to NGOs for services of general interest, without a more precise delimitation of the scope of these services, it may be quite difficult to set award criteria that are both general enough as to cover all the proposals and at the same time precise and specific enough as to be relevant for the subject-matter of the contract. One such instance regards a city council that awarded contracts for activities ranging from career development, sports, and culture to the protection of the environment based on the following criteria:

27. CECOP, 'Position paper on public procurements', Prague, 16 April 2009, [Online] at www.ucecom.ro/romana/bie/DocW/CECOPAP.doc, accessed March 2nd, 2010.
28. Published in the Official Monitor, Section I, no.1128 from 14/12/2005.

technical consistency, financial soundness, implementation capacity, expected results, involvement of the final beneficiaries, and the sustainability of the proposal.[29]

With regard to the general scope of the law, it could be argued that while still transparent, it limits competition, since the only eligible beneficiaries for such grants are the NGOs, even in instances when a for-profit company could carry out the same activity. Also, during interviews with NGOs representatives, the authors were told that this process had the tendency to be highly politicised. Since the public authority has a wide margin of discretion with regard to these funds, the award of the contract is based often, though informally, on political criteria.

### *2.5.3 Social criteria*

Currently, the provision of social services that are outsourced by public authorities is regulated by Government Ordinance no. 68/2003.[30] In addition to public bodies, private entities can also provide these services, based on an administrative contract with the public body. Based on this 2003 legal instrument, it is difficult to consider this administrative contract as being part of a public procurement procedure. Because the regulation is outdated, numerous NGOs and public officials are currently working to change it. The most recent proposal for updating the Ordinance states the possibility for contracting authorities to contract out social services to private providers, mostly NGOs (associations and foundations) but also to individuals authorized to work in this field. Contracting authorities can use three main tools: financing (State aid) of social services provided by private entities, concession, and procurement of social services. The proposed law states principles and the procedure for the procurement of these social services. It establishes a distinct procedure for this type of public contracts. The contracting authorities are drafting the documentation of the contract and carry out the award of the contract under the control/supervision of the Court of Auditors and the ordinary courts of law (responsible for reviewing all administrative acts).[31]

29. Award announcement for publicly funded grants for activities of general interest no. 45/31.618, City Hall of Hunedoara, published in the Official Monitor, Section VI, no. 354 from 6/06/2007.
30. Published in the Official Monitor, Section I, no 619 from 30/08/2003.
31. The Foundation for the Development of Civil Society, 'Legislative proposal regarding the provision of social services by NGOs', [Online] at http://www.fdsc.ro/documente/148.doc, accessed March 2nd, 2010.

## 3 Examples of application

This section describes examples of application, both judicial and non-judicial, of secondary considerations in public procurement in Romania. It has to be mentioned, however, that the number of judicial examples of application (national case law) is significantly lower than the non-judicial ones. Data made available by the National Council for Solving Legal Disputes shows that if we compare the total number of decisions issued by the Council, most of which are in response to complaints lodged by the tenderers, with the number of decisions further challenged in front of an Appellate Court, the former is significantly lower. Moreover, from the total number of complaints against a decision of the Council lodged with an Appellate Court, only a limited number was considered admissible. For 2009, for example, only 1.21 per cent of the total number of complaints against the decisions of the Council was declared admissible. This needs to be interpreted against an obvious increase of the total number of complaints lodged with the Council. If in 2007, the Council received 4,976 complaints, the number increased in 2008 to 6,517 and to 9,019 in 2009. Table 1 below presents the statistical data supporting these claims. It can be concluded that the Council represents an efficient alternative means for solving the disputes related to public procurement procedures.

*Table 1: Decisions issued by the Council and challenged in court*

| Year | Decisions issued by the Council | Decisions challenged in court | Complaints declared admissible by the courts |
|---|---|---|---|
| 2006 | 338 | 28 | 5 |
| 2007 | 4119 | 416 | 75 |
| 2008 | 6275 | 788 | 129 |
| 2009 | 7360 | 784 | 89 |

Source: The National Council for Solving Legal Disputes, Statistical Data 'Decisions issued by the Council, total decisions challenged, complaints admitted by the Court of Appeal until 31 December 2009', [Online] at http://www.cnsc.ro/index.php/ro/rapoarte, accessed 26 February 2010.

The methodology for determining judicial and non-judicial instances of application of secondary considerations in public procurement included:

- A scrutiny of the National Council for Solving Legal Disputes decisions. According to the legislation, all the decisions of the Council need to be made public, after the identification data regarding both the case and the parties are eliminated. However, the Council is currently breaching this provision by providing online only a limited number of motivated decisions for the time frame 2006-2009. The total number of decisions with motivation currently available and examined during our research is 545.[32]
- The case law of the Appellate Courts and of the High Court of Cassation and Justice. In Romania the courts do not have a legal obligation to make available or publish all their decisions. Therefore, in our research we only scrutinised those decisions posted online by the courts and those included by authors in brochures comprising commented jurisprudence.
- Non-standardised interviews with representatives of local contracting authorities. Specific issues related to the inclusion of secondary considerations were addressed based on the expertise of each contracting authority.
- A scrutiny of the participation and the award announcements as well as of the tender documentation (if available online) of the contracting authorities starting with 15 May 2006 (the date when Ordinance no. 34/2006 was published in the Official Monitor of Romania) to the present (February 2010). In order to conduct this inquiry, the authors used the legal software called LEGIS which incorporates, among others, all the announcements related to public procurement contracts that are also published in the Official Monitor of Romania and in the Electronic System for Public Procurement. There was a multi-stage filtering process involved: First, from all the announcements related in any way to public procurement procedures, we selected the participation and award announcements because it is mandated by law that they include the selection and award criteria. We then used relevant keywords which describe secondary considerations such as 'environmental protection', 'ISO 14001', 'environmental management', 'creation of new jobs', 'sheltered workshops/entities', 'unemployment', 'local workforce', 'social objectives', etc. There are three main limits to this exploratory research: first, it is possible that during the filtering process some announcements were ignored. The likelihood of this happening is greater with regard to social considerations, because it is almost impossible to identify all instances of how social objectives are defined by the contracting authorities. Another major limit refers to the fact that, when the criteria used is the economically most advantageous tender,

32. This is the situation on February 26th, 2010.

some of the announcements do not include details about the evaluation criteria. These criteria are only detailed in the tender documentation which is not available free of charge and is not posted online. Third, when the tender documentation was not available, we could not examine the technical specifications. Even though, due to these limits, the actual numbers obtained are not precise, they offer a general image of the use of secondary consideration in public procurement in Romania.

### 3.1 Green and social considerations – primary or secondary?

In light of the distinction made between primary and secondary considerations in PP contracts in the comparative chapter, the following situations may occur in practice:

In the first type of situation, the contracting authority defines the subject-matter or the technical specifications so as to include green or social standards that are required by law in order for the work, the product or the service to be legally used by the procuring entity. In these cases the green or the social standards can hardly be labeled as secondary. This is confirmed by national case law and by what contracting authorities do in practice. In a number of cases, the Courts have ruled that, if a specific certification or standard is legally required for a certain good or in order for the economic operator which provides the works/services to function, then the contracting authority does not even have a legal obligation to mention in the tender documentation or in the contract that specific requirement. The courts' reasoning implied that if a certain standard or certification is required to legally function in a field of activity, then the said standard or certificate is fundamental for the very existence of that good/work/service.[33] The representatives of a contracting authority also mentioned to the authors that for example they do not expressly require an environmental authorisation. However, it is presumed that all economic operators will have it, because otherwise they cannot function legally in Romania.

Though this situation appears to be clear-cut in theory, in practice, especially with regard to social considerations, the boundary between primary and secondary considerations is blurred. Law no. 519/2002[34] regarding the special protection and the creation of work opportunities for disabled persons re-

33. Judgment no. 1038/16.09.2008, Piteşti Appellate Court, Division for Commercial, Administrative and Fiscal Matters; Judgment no. 1601/16.06.2008, Constanţa Appellate Court, Division for Commercial, Maritime and Fluvial, Administrative and Fiscal Matters.
34. Published in the Official Monitor, Section I, no. 555 from 29/07/2002.

quires that all public transportation vehicles should be equipped so as to allow access of disabled persons. In light of this provision, is a contracting authority which intends to buy buses and includes in the technical specifications requirements regarding the existence of equipment which facilitates the access of disabled persons, employing primary or secondary social considerations? In Romania, because of cost constrains, most contracting authorities ignore these legal requirements and buy vehicles which do not meet the standards for disabled people. In this context, a contracting authority which requires buses to have elevators for disabled people is in fact employing secondary considerations. When we are in the presence of a legal requirement of a general character, such as the facilitation of access for disabled people, the contracting authority cannot require only a specific equipment/fabrication process; it has to allow for equivalent solutions which lead to the same result. In a case brought before the Council, a contracting authority was accused of restricting competition by requiring a certain mechanism for elevation in order to facilitate the access of disabled people to public buses. The Council ruled that a mention in the tender documentation should be made regarding the acceptance of similar technical solutions.[35]

In the second type of situation, the contracting authority includes among the selection criteria (reliability of the tenderers) that are related to green or social considerations. The Romanian national law on public procurement does not establish any additional criteria that could be related to green or social considerations. The text of the national law follows closely the provisions of the Directive in this respect, see Article 176 through 196 and section I.2 of this chapter. However, starting with 2009, contracting authorities have included as part of the qualification criteria, the technical and/or professional standing of the tenderer, a standard/certificate related to social considerations, namely SA 8000:2001 (or newer). This standard measures social responsibility in terms of some performance requirements such as: discrimination, working hours, wages, disciplinary measures, union-related rights, and health and security at the workplace. The Romanian law on public procurement does not expressly mention the possibility for contracting authorities to require this type of certification. Theoretically, if these social considerations are not stated in the public procurement legislation, they cannot be used by the contracting authorities. The economic operators have contested these 'new' qualification criteria in the Council. There are several 2009 decisions of the

35. The motivated decision of the Council is available [Online] at http://www.cnsc.ro/images/stories/ bo/2006/BO2006_0143.pdf, accessed February 26th, 2010.

Council regarding this issue. At the time being they are made public without motivation; however from the rulings of the Council it could be concluded that in some cases the Council required contracting authorities to eliminate the SA 8000 certification requirement[36] while in other cases it ruled that the complaint was unsubstantiated.[37]

In the third type of situation, the contracting authority includes in the tender documentation green or social standards other than the ones resulting from the public procurement legislation. Because there is limited capacity/expertise at the level of the Romanian contracting authorities, the NARMPP has provided standard contracts to be used by the contracting authorities. Though contracting authorities can create their own contracts, most of them use the standard format provided by NARMPP since it minimises the chances of legal disputes. In the standard contract for works there are two sections where we can find references to special legislation on green and social issues. The first reference is found in the section referring to the obligations of the economic operators:

> 'The economic operators have the obligation to make sure that all the authorised personnel, the site of the work, and the work-related activities are conducted in such a manner as to avoid any potential harm of the personnel' (*social considerations*).
>
> The economic operators have the obligation to take all reasonable measures in order to protect the environment on and outside the work site and to ensure to avoid all damages and inconveniences to people or properties resulting from pollution, noise or other factors related to work activities' (*green considerations*).

The second reference is found in a section called 'standards' which refers to the execution of the contract:

> 'The economic operator guarantees that he will meet the legal requirements regarding work conditions, work security and environmental protection according to Law no. 319/2006 – work-security and work-health, Government decision no. 1091/2006 – minimal requirements for security and health at the work place, Government Emergency Ordinance no. 195/2005 – environmental protection with all subsequent changes, Law no. 307/2006 regarding fire hazards'.

The breach of any of the obligations included in the contract may represent a ground for the termination of the contract. However, several remarks have to

36. Decision no. 2230/150/C11/1939/2238 from 03.06.2009, [Online] at http://www.cnsc.ro /d/2009/ decizie_2230.pdf, accessed February 27th, 2010.
37. Decision no. 3331/C1/3444/3733 from 23.07.2009, [Online] at http://www.cnsc.ro/d/2009/decizie _3331.pdf, accessed February 27th, 2010.

be made. First, as seen above, the policy objectives in the field of social security or environmental protection are worded very broadly. In fact, the clause in the contract is very general and not oriented towards any specific policy objective in this field. This is confirmed by representatives of the contracting authorities. They admit that they include these obligations in the contract because this is the recommended format by NARMPP. However, the authors were told that the contracting authorities are not interested in terminating the contract if violations related to social or environmental legislation occur. The economic operators will be sanctioned by the agencies responsible for these fields based on the specific legislation outside public procurement, in most cases without any consequence regarding the contract.

This interpretation seems to be supported by the relevant case law as well. An economic operator filed a complaint with the Council and then with the court, complaining against tender documentation that included technical specifications that were drafted in accordance with special legislation, the law regarding the protection of industrial designs and models. The court ruled that the complaint was inadmissible since it exceeds the competence of both the Council and the Court, which are supposed to examine the documentation in light of public procurement law. Any further complaints should be lodged and addressed according to the provisions of the special legislation.[38]

Though this case doesn't involve social or green considerations, it questions the fact that by including provisions related to special legislation in the contracts two tears of control are created. The tendency, at least thus far, seems to be of allowing special bodies outside the realm of public procurement legislation to assess the completion of these provisions.

In the fourth type of situation, the contracting authority introduces green or social considerations in the tender documentation on a discretionary basis without a connection to any existing law. Based on both judicial and non-judicial instances of application of secondary considerations in public procurement, it can be concluded that examples for this type of situation are limited.

One municipality asked in a contract whose subject-matter regards street cleaning services that all the vehicles used should have as minimal equipment Euro 3, in order to prevent environmental pollution. The national legislation does not require vehicles to meet this requirement in order to be used on pub-

38. Judgment no. 376/31.03.2008, Alba Iulia Appellate Court, Division for Administrative and Fiscal Matters.

lic roads if they meet some standards that are verified during an annual technical inspection.

Another instance identified refers to the procurement of monitoring equipment for the polluting emissions of smoke stacks. The contracting authority required in the tender documentation/technical specifications that the measurement error of the equipment should be less than 1 per cent – this is higher than what is legally required, therefore it can be considered a secondary consideration related to the environment. The Council in its ruling confirmed that it is allowed for contracting authorities to set higher standards than what is legally required.[39] In the same case another issue related to secondary considerations was raised. Sometimes, the contracting authorities who require higher than legal standards realise during the award procedure that the costs are higher than what they can pay for. Thus, the contracting authorities decide to accept lower standards than the ones initially described in the tender documentation. Both the Council and the courts have ruled that it is illegal to accept an offer that is not compliant with the tender documentation even if it complies with the minimal legal standards.

By looking at participation announcements and tender documentation we also identified other instances when secondary considerations not linked to any existing law were introduced. Such considerations refer to the use of a local workforce or to the promotion of sustainable development. It is very hard to assess the legality of such considerations because all of the case law identified referring to these secondary considerations introduced on a discretionary basis by contracting authorities were in fact overruled on grounds of tardiness. The court did not therefore rule on whether or not they were appropriately drafted.

### 3.2 Stages in the PP process where environmental and social considerations are included

A few general observations can be made regarding whether and how contracting authorities include both primary (required by law) and secondary (required by contracting authorities in addition to existing legislation) considerations in their procurement procedures. A first observation is that environmental and social considerations are not very frequently included in the tender documentation. Although, as already mentioned, the absolute numbers are not accurate and cannot be said to be relevant from a statistical point of

39. The motivated decision of the Council is available [Online] at http://www.cnsc.ro/images/ stories /bo/2006/BO2006_0075.pdf, accessed February 26th, 2010.

view, a general trend is evident. Thus, from some 34,480 participation and award announcements, the authors found 125 that included references to environmental or social considerations. As a result, the conclusion that can be drawn is that contracting authorities are not too keen to include social or environmental objectives in their public procurement procedures, since they have the potential of creating technical and legal complications for the authorities. Also, in the interviews conducted with some representatives of the local authorities, the authors were told that including such considerations results in attracting a different type of tenderer (usually larger companies are environmentally and quality certified), and usually their tenders (in terms of the price offered) are higher. Thus, the costs of public procurement increases. Also, one representative of a small municipality commented that the local public authority is aware of the general business environment in their region and that they try, within legal limits, to attract tenderers from their region, thus trying to support local companies. In many instances these companies are SMEs which do not have either certificates proving quality or environmental management standards or do not offer green services/products.

The remaining part of this section looks in more detail to the instances when secondary considerations were used by the contracting authorities.

*3.2.1 Secondary considerations included in the subject-matter*

Though secondary considerations are usually included in the definition of the subject-matter of the contract via the technical specifications, there are examples, though limited, when the object of the contract itself makes explicit reference to secondary considerations. For example, a local authority defined in a participation announcement the object of the contract in terms of the construction of a social apartment building for evicted tenants.[40] Such a definition includes social objectives from the outset. Another similar instance occurred when a small municipality, in the process of granting a concession of the public waste management service, defined the object of the contract as selective waste collection, waste management, and the reuse of recyclable waste.[41] This definition clearly includes reference to environmental consid-

40. Participation announcement for public works no. 38/46.647, City Hall of Caransebeş, published in the Official Monitor, Section VI, no. 646 from 4/09/2007.
41. Participation announcement for service concession no. 70/74.119, City Hall of Borsec, published in the Official Monitor, Section VI, no. 202 from 22/04/2008.

erations. Other examples include:[42] works regarding the environmental rehabilitation of brownfields, design services regarding the environmental rehabilitation of agricultural sites, and environmentally-friendly incinerators.

### *3.2.2 Secondary considerations included in technical specifications*

In general, technical specifications should be drafted in such a way that equal treatment, non-discrimination and free competition between tenderers are ensured. This raises the question of how detailed technical specifications should be. If contracting authorities define them narrowly, in some cases even indicating a specific model, it could be presumed that the principles listed above are violated. However, based on the national case law, the courts have ruled that contracting authorities can define technical specifications in a precise and narrow way, even if this means that some obstacles are created with regard to free competition. The contracting authorities can do this in light of the fact that more detailed technical specifications are necessary in order to satisfy their needs better.[43] Thus, the courts usually decide whether or not such detailed technical specifications are legal in light of the arguments put forth by the contracting authorities who have to justify why certain narrower technical specifications ensure the fulfillment of their needs in a better way. Based on the existing case law, the courts have ruled in favour of contracting authorities in this matter.

This type of reasoning could be interpreted as a favourable context for fostering secondary considerations. Contracting authorities may draft technical specifications which appear restrictive because of the secondary considerations included. However, this could be justified in view of the specific needs of the contracting authorities.

### *3.2.3 Secondary considerations included in selection/qualification criteria*

As a general remark, it can be said that contracting authorities often include secondary considerations (environmental) in the drafting of the selection/ qualification criteria regarding the technical and professional capacity of the tenderers. In many cases, the contracting authorities require tenderers to hold

42. Taken from Council's motivated decisions, no identification data available; see the Council's motivated decisions [Online] at http://www.cnsc.ro/index.php/ro/buletinul-oficial/deciziibo/2006, accessed February 26th, 2010.
43. Judgment no. 1280/CA/3.12/2008, Alba Iulia Appellate Court, Division for Administrative and Fiscal Matters; Judgment no. 1546/9.06.2008, Bucureşti Appellate Court, Division 8 for Administrative and Fiscal Matters; Judgment no. 612/22.05-2008, Timişoara Appellate Court, Division for Administrative and Fiscal Matters.

an ISO 14001/2005 environmental management certificate. It is also common for contracting authorities to accept a simple declaration of the tenderer regarding the environmental management measures. Though both the Directive and the national Ordinance allow for such a practice, in the Romanian context it may not be the best alternative. The contracting authorities often choose this option because it establishes a minimal requirement, thus allowing all companies, environmentally certified or not, to participate in the tender procedures. Though this may be regarded as an example of good practice regarding non-discrimination, because of the weak enforcement capacity of the contracting authorities, it is not clear how they will monitor the fulfillment of the stated measures.

The authors identified several situations which could be considered as examples of incorrect drafting of the selection criteria. A rural municipality, in a participation announcement for the concession of the waste management service, stated that the tenderers who hold an environmental management certificate (a criterion clearly related to the technical capacity of the tenderers, and thus a selection/qualification criteria) will be awarded additional points for this during the awarding stage.[44] This is an example of a violation of the national law since a tenderer can be excluded for lack of technical capacity, but during the award stage this criterion cannot be used. In a similar case, the Appellate Court ruled that it is illegal for contracting authorities to use qualification criteria (ISO 9001 certificate) also for the award of a contract As part of the award criteria, the said authority included the requirement for tenderers to hold the ISO 9001 certificate and awarded 10 points for meeting this requirement. The certificate was included among the award criteria as an indicator/measure for evaluating the quality program proposed by the tenderers in the execution of the contract. The court ruled that the contracting authority used an evaluation system that lacked transparency and accuracy, which leads to the possibility of an arbitrary interpretation of the said criteria.[45]

One situation that often occurs in practice and is related to the use of secondary considerations at the stage of selection/qualification criteria refers to pending environmental/quality control certifications of the tenderers. In other words, at the stage when the tender is evaluated by the contracting authority, the tenderer is still undergoing the process of certification and cannot produce the actual certificate but rather a document stating that the said certification is

44. Participation announcement for service concession no. 2/78.919, City Hall of Garoafa, published in the Official Monitor, Section VI, no. 441 from 10/12/2008.
45. Judgement no. 2082/15.10.2008, Craiova Appellate Court, Division for Administrative and Fiscal Matters.

pending. Unfortunately, neither the contracting authorities nor the courts have been able to produce a unitary practice with regard to this situation. In most cases, the courts have ruled that a pending decision regarding environmental certification cannot be considered the equivalent of an environmental management system that is already in place.[46] In another case, however, the court ruled that such alleged equivalent means of proof should be accepted since they provide a guarantee with regard to the environmental management implemented by the economic operators.[47]

*3.2.4 Secondary considerations included in award criteria*

First, it is interesting to determinine which award criterion is used more often by the contracting authorities. In a recent study,[48] based on data provided by NARMMP, it was concluded that from the total procurement procedures, contracting authorities have used the criterion of the economically most advantageous tender in approximately 40 per cent of the cases, thus creating the premise for including secondary considerations. Based on our own analysis of participation announcements, it can be said that the number of the tenders using only the price criterion has decreased in the last two years and the trend is likely to continue in light of the new provisions discussed above.

With regards to award criteria, the authors identified several examples of non-compliance with EU and national provisions on sustainable procurement. One such example refers to the inclusion of the promotion of employment as an award criterion. A local contracting authority, in a concession procedure of a land field for surface mining, included an additional award criterion, namely the employment of a local workforce.[49] The participation announcement listed as award criterion for the contract the most economically advantageous tender, apart from the employment of a local work-force, other criteria related to the protection of the environment, economic and financial aspects, performance and quality monitoring, etc. In light of the ECJ case law

46. Judgment no. 407/29.05.2008, Bacău Appellate Court, Division for Commercial, Administrative and Fiscal Matters.
47. Judgment no. 1166/23.10.2007, Ploieşti Appellate Court, Division for Commercial, Administrative and Fiscal Matters.
48. The Romanian Academic Society, 'O evaluare a eficienţei, integrităţii şi transparenţei sistemului de achiziţii publice din România' (An assessment of the efficiency, integrity, and transparency of the Romanian public procurements system), [Online] at http://www.sar.org.ro/do_download.php?file=files/paper-final.pdf, accessed March 2nd, 2010
49. Participation announcement for concession of public goods, no. 8/45.591, City Hall of Bata, published in the Official Monitor, Section VI, no. 571 from 20/08/2007.

prior to Directive 2004/18/EC Directive (*Beentjes* and *Concordia Bus*[50]), criteria related to employment can be accepted as long as they have no direct or indirect discriminatory effects on tenderers from other Member States and are made sufficiently public (clear reference to this criterion in the participation announcement). In addition, such a criterion must be linked to the subject-matter of the contract and should not confer an unrestricted freedom of choice to the authority, and must comply with all the fundamental principles of EU law, in particular the principle of non-discrimination. The award criterion set by the contracting authority, is, in light of these considerations, a breach of the Directive's provisions as well as of the national Ordinance because there is no link between the employment of a local workforce and the subject-matter of the contract; this criterion also represents a possible example of discrimination of tenderers, who are required to hire a local workforce and may not be able to fulfil this condition. The use of such a criterion is not rare. The research of the authors identified similar examples regarding the use of social considerations – namely the promotion of employment, as an award criterion.[51]

Another possible breach of the legal provisions regarding the drafting of the award criteria was found in several instances when they were too vague and hard to quantify – for example the overall sustainability of the tender, the financial situation of the tenderer, the expected outcome, the involvement of the beneficiaries, etc. Such a vague reference to the general soundness of the tenderer, where the contracting authority is not able to evaluate the fulfillment of the requirement, infringes the principle of equal treatment, because such a criterion does not ensure the objectivity and the transparency of the tender procedure. In a concession contract for the delegation of the public waste management service,[52] the contracting authority set as a criterion in the framework of the economically most advantageous tender, the solving of certain social problems. Again, the criterion is too vague and tenderers cannot be objectively evaluated based on it. In addition, this vague reference makes it impossible to even start an inquiry regarding whether or not it is related to the

50. Case C-513/99, *Concordia Bus*, [2002], ECR I-7213.
51. Award announcement for concession of public goods, no. 17/77.446, County Council Argeş, published in the Official Monitor, Section VI, no. 5 from 3/01/2008; Award announcement for concession of public goods, no. 27/16.598, Moreni Industrial Park Authority, published in the Official Monitor, Section VI, no. 52 from 5/02/2007.
52. Participation announcement for concession of public services, no. 23/66.767, City Hall of Constanţa, published in the Official Monitor, Section VI, no. 16 from 8/01/2008.

subject-matter of the contract. These aspects are summarized in the ECJ ruling in the *EVN* case.[53] The Court stated that the principle of equal treatment implies that tenderers must be in a position of equality both when they prepare their tenders and when those tenders are being assessed by a contracting authority.

In a number of cases brought before the Appellate Courts, the courts decided that vague and unclear factors used for the evaluation of the economically most advantageous tender represent grounds for the annulment of the award procedure.[54] Such criteria include: the way in which environmental and social problems will be addressed by the tenderers during the execution of the contract; the willingness to implement certain services that are the object of the contract in other locations than the capital city; the technical level etc. The grounds mentioned by most of these courts are related to the impossibility to accurately and objectively assess the different tenders by the members of the Commission for awarding public contracts. The principles of transparency, equal treatment and efficiency in the spending of the public funds were thus infringed. In general, the sanction given by the courts is the annulment of the award procedure. In one case, however,[55] the court decided that since some of the evaluation criteria were vague enough as to allow discretionary interpretation by the members of the Commission, the plaintiff's score for the tender was recalculated. The winning tender was given the maximum points for the criteria defined too vaguely. Also, the courts ruled that when contracting authorities are notified by monitoring authorities with regard to the vagueness of the criteria used, the elimination of those criteria cannot represent a legal solution; rather, the contracting authorities are supposed to clarify the evaluation criteria by offering specific indicators-measurements.[56]

53. Case C-448/01 *EVN and Wienstrom* [2003] ECR I-14527.
54. Judgement no. 764/13.11.2008, Bacău Appellate Court, Division for Commercial, Administrative and Fiscal Matters; Judgement no. 302/R/22.04.2008, Braşov Appellate Court, Division for Administrative and Fiscal Matters; Judgement no. 496/R/29.07.2008, Braşov Appellate Court, Division for Administrative and Fiscal Matters; Judgement no. 366/CA/10.07.2008, Iaşi Appellate Court, Division for Administrative and Fiscal Matters; Judgement no. 355/7.03.2008, Ploieşti Appellate Court, Division for Commercial, Administrative and Fiscal Matters.
55. Judgement no. 764/13.11.2008, Bacău Appellate Court, Division for Commercial, Administrative and Fiscal Matters.
56. Judgement no. 666/CA/13.08.2008, Constanţa Appellate Court, Division for Commercial, Maritime and Fluvial, Administrative and Fiscal Matters.

Secondary considerations, when included, sometimes represent a small percentage in the overall evaluation of the most economically advantageous tender. Instances were found where environmental considerations accounted for only 4 per cent of criteria used.[57]

## 4 Policy initiatives addressing SPP in Romania

This section provides an overview of the various national policies aimed at fostering sustainable procurement, mainly green considerations related to the characteristics of the goods/works/services. Though many of these efforts are disparate, in the last two years significant steps have been made toward the integration of sustainability considerations into different policy areas. Policy efforts in this field can be divided into five main categories[58]: (1) informational or endorsing instruments (e.g. campaigns, guidelines, trainings), (2) partnering instruments (e.g. networks, partnerships, dialogues), (3) financial or economic instruments (e.g. economic incentives, subsidies, grants), (4) mandating instruments (e.g. regulations and laws), and (5) hybrid instruments (e.g. strategies, action plans, platforms, centers). They range from a soft-law approach to more traditional, regulatory approaches.

### 4.1 The National Action Plan for Green Public Procurement[59]

The European Commission proposed that by 2010, 50 per cent of all public procurement contract would become green. The 50 per cent threshold has a voluntary character and was stated in the Commission's Communication to the European Council and the European Parliament.[60] In Romania, this initiative will prove difficult to implement because the market for ecological goods and services is underdeveloped. However, the National Action Plan for Green Procurement 2009-2013 details several of the thresholds set by the Romanian authorities in response to the Commission's initiative as well as several

57. Award announcement for public works, no. 81/51.339, City of Coşna, published in the Official Monitor, Section VI, no. 756 from 11/10/2007.
58. T Fox, H Ward, and B Howard, *Public Sector Roles in Strengthening Corporate Social Responsibility: A Baseline Study* (The World Bank 2002), [Online] at http://www.iied.org/pubs/pdfs/16017IIED.pdf, accessed March 2nd, 2010.
59. Planul Naţional de Acţiune pentru Achiziţii Publice Ecologice (National Action Plan for Green Public Procurement 2009-2013), [Online] at http://www.sgg.ro/ nlegislativ/docs/2009/07/hrq 4xkp7jd23tb518mf9.pdf, accessed July 27th, 2009.
60. COM (2008) 400.

measures to be taken in order to encourage the growth of sustainable procurement in Romania.

In the plan there are eight groups of products and services of interest for the public administration. For each group, thresholds, both voluntary and mandatory, are set. For many groups of products and services the thresholds are lower than in the case of other Member States and also not mandatory. The only group for which the Plan sets a 50 per cent threshold is lighting equipment. For the other groups, the thresholds range from 9 per cent to 19 per cent. In light of the fact that most of these thresholds are voluntary, policy efforts should consider the development of incentives rather than regulations.

*Table 2: Thresholds for green public procurement (Romania)*

| **Categories of products/ services** | **2010** | **2011** | **2012** | **2013** |
|---|---|---|---|---|
| Products and services for cleaning | 9 % Voluntary threshold | 11 % Mandatory threshold | 11 % Mandatory threshold | 13 % Mandatory threshold |
| Construction works | 9 % Voluntary threshold | 9 % Voluntary threshold | 11 % Voluntary threshold | 11 % Voluntary threshold |
| Lighting equipments (on the streets and interior) | 50 % Voluntary threshold | 50 % Mandatory threshold | 50 % Mandatory threshold | 50 % Mandatory threshold |
| Food and beverage items obtained from ecological agriculture | 9 % Voluntary threshold | 9 % Mandatory threshold | 11 % Mandatory threshold | 11 % Mandatory threshold |
| Furniture | 9 % Voluntary threshold | 11 % Voluntary threshold | 11 % Voluntary threshold | 13 % Voluntary threshold |
| IT equipment | 15 % Voluntary threshold | 17 % Mandatory threshold | 17 % Mandatory threshold | 19 % Mandatory threshold |
| Copying paper | 15 % Voluntary threshold | 17 % Mandatory threshold | 17 % Mandatory threshold | 17 % Mandatory threshold |
| Buses, services for buses | 5 % Voluntary threshold | 7 % Voluntary threshold | 7 % Voluntary threshold | 10 % Voluntary threshold |

Source: National Action Plan for Sustainable Public Procurement 2009-2013

In order to meet these thresholds, the Plan lists three electronic tools that will be used in order to monitor how these obligations are fulfilled:

When public works, services or goods are bought directly (public procurement whose value is below €15,000), the operator of the Electronic System for Public Procurement will organise a database with all the works/services/goods offered by the registered operators by the system and which meet the required ecological conditions. The data base will be called 'ecological products and services'.

When the value of the public procurement is above €15,000, it will be mandatory to fill out a Green Form.

Because not all public procurement are carried out by using the Electronic System, the public procurements carried out outside this framework will also be monitored. A self-reporting document will have to be completed by the contracting authorities for each year. This document is called the Green Report.

The adoption of the Plan is still pending. In 2008 an interim draft was launched. Since then, the title was changed in order to cover the 2009-2013 timeframe as opposed to the initial draft where the stated timeframe was 2008-2013.

### 4.2 Initiatives and projects of the Ministry of the Environment and Forestry[61]

Once the concept of sustainable public procurement was integrated into the national legislation and policy, the Ministry of the Environment has become a key actor in the system. All of the Ministry's projects in the field of sustainable production and consumption are financed through EU funds. In this way the pressure on the State budget is reduced in light of the significant costs associated with the process of fostering sustainable procurement. There are three such projects, out of which two are directly related to sustainable public procurement while the third one addresses industrial symbiosis (the use of a company's waste as input for the production process of another company).

#### *4.2.1 The creation of a favorable environment for the training of the contracting authorities in the field of green public procurement*

This project represents a collaborative effort between the Ministry of the Environment and Forestry and the National Institute for Administration, with a

61. A Stroia, I Degeratu, 'Toward sustainable models of production and consumption', *EcoMagazin, [Online] at* http://www.ecomagazin.ro/catre-modele-durabile-de-productie-si-consum/, accessed July 27th, 2009.

value of approximately €1,000,000, financed through the Operational Sectorial Program for Enhancing the Administrative Capacity (also known as PODCA in Romania). The aim of the project is to train and certify a number of 40 representatives of the contracting authorities with regard to how secondary considerations can be included in the public procurement process. Other outcomes included the drafting of a handbook regarding how to conduct training sessions (the initial 40 trainees are then supposed to train their colleagues) and the creation of a network of public contracting authorities specialised in green public procurement.

*4.2.2 The development of emergent green markets in Romania*

This project represents a partnership with the Norwegian Ministry of the Environment. The project is part of the Norwegian Cooperation Program (Innovation Norway), having an approximate value of €2,000,000. The project strives to create the framework for sustainable production and consumption in Romania by developing an emergent green market, in which both the producers and the consumers are educated and informed with regard to the benefits of the production/consumption of green products and technologies. Sustainable procurement are an important part of this project, which has two main components:

*4.2.2.1 EcoTechnoNet*

A study consisting in the evaluation of the Romanian market for environmental technologies and the identification of methods and tools aimed at enhancing it in the future. This includes the creation of an electronic national platform for information and technological transfer (a data base with the providers of environmental technologies and with the R&D entities whose activity is relevant in this field); the organization of eight regional dissemination seminars of the best practices and technologies with low environmental impact (at least 200 innovative entities included in the national network of eco-innovators and 200 R&D entities trained in the field of technological transfer). The seminars will include details regarding EMAS registering and the eco-label; and increasing the access of the companies to the financing tools/sources for eco-innovative technologies as a result of their participation in the seminars.

*4.2.2.2 Green Procure*

Informing of at least 200 producers, distributors, consumers, and the scientific community with regard to the green thresholds established in the Action Plan for Green Public Procurement. This includes the training of 400 contracting authorities from the eight regions of Romania with regard to green public procurement through training workshops and the establishment of a monitoring scheme of green public procurement which will be part of the National Action Plan for Green Public Procurement.

### 4.3 The eco-label

The European eco-label provides precise scientific information regarding 24 groups of products from different sectors of activity, including computers and home appliances, as well as two activities in the field of services. The eco-label is not issued, however, for food and beverage items, and for medical products. In Romania, the competent authority for issuing the European eco-label is the National Commission for Granting the Eco-Label, which functions under the coordination of the Ministry of the Environment. At the national level, the revised system for granting the European eco-label was transposed by Government Decision no. 236/2007. Other Government Decisions transposed the community provisions for specific groups of products (Government Decision no. 175/2004 regarding the granting of the eco-label for laptops).

The fee for the processing of the application for obtaining the eco-label is €300, and the annual fee for using the label is 0,15 per cent of the total sales for the products which carry the eco-label. SMEs can obtain a fee reduced by 25 per cent. In addition, SMEs can obtain, due to an initiative of the Ministry of the Economy (the Program for the enhancement of the competitiveness of the industrial products), discounted fees, with up to 65 per cent, of the total costs covered by the eco-labeling process. The fee for the granting of the eco-label does not include, however, the costs regarding the testing/verification of the products in the process of assessing their performances, in accordance with the criteria for the granting of the eco-label. These costs prove in many cases to be restrictive for the Romanian SMEs.

## 5 Conclusions

In recent years the field of public procurement has received attention both from within the public, the private and non-profit sectors. The main issues of interest concern the combat against corruption/illegal or unethical practices, fostering transparency of the public procurement process, and making the entire procedure more time-efficient. These problems are not necessarily specific to the public procurement sector but rather characterise the entire Romanian public sector. In this context, sustainable procurement is merely a secondary concern, seen most of the time as a trendy policy promoted by the EU. It is also perceived as being too costly for Romanian contracting authorities, a 'luxury' that most of these authorities cannot afford. Therefore, it is expected to see a limited interest and impact with regard to sustainable procurement, beyond what is mandated by the Commission. This is the problem in general with a top-down approach to public policy.

In 2006, the new national legislation adopted, transposed almost, if not all, of the provisions of Directive 2004/18/EC. Regarding environmental and social considerations mandated by procurement legislation or other acts, it can be argued that in general contracting authorities make use, at least formally, of these provisions. However, looking at environmental and social considerations beyond what is legally required, contracting authorities are reluctant to use their discretionary powers and to include these considerations in their procurement procedures in order to achieve specific policy objectives. Also, because of numerous corruption problems, contracting authorities are reluctant to include too high environmental requirements because they could be accused of setting aside the contract for a certain tenderer. There have been cases when contracting authorities have required a specific certification, irrelevant in the context of the subject-matter of the contract, knowing that only one specific tenderer will be able to comply with it.

Other challenges exist as well. In those instances when environmental and social considerations are used in public procurement, the success of these measures needs to be assessed. To successfully follow the path of sustainable procurement into the future, the already existing systems for monitoring and reporting will have to be further enhanced as to play the role prescribed for them by the law.

Recently there has been a tendency of policy makers to restrain the application of the lowest price criterion, which has proved to be rather unsuccessful for selecting quality offers. This tendency can be an incentive for applying more secondary considerations, as well.

Moreover, the inclusion of secondary considerations in public procurement could be further enhanced by the existence of a unitary and coherent case law at the level of both the Council and the courts. Untill now, they have ruled in an inconsistent manner with regard to similar legal issues, some of them including the drafting of the technical specifications, selection and award criteria. This inconsistent ruling has affected the willingness of contracting authorities to include secondary considerations in their procurement procedures. The inconsistent case law makes the effects of the inclusion of such considerations unpredictable. A more consistent case law will then result in basic guidelines which the contracting authorities can follow.

## Bibliography

G. V. Bîrsan, B Georgescu, *Legea contenciosului administrativ adnotată* (*The Law of Judicial Review of Administrative Acts with Comments)* (Hamangiu 2008)

D.C. Dragoş, 'Contractele de achiziţii publice' ('The public procurement contracts') (2002) 2 *Curierul judiciar* (Judicial Courier),

D.C. Dragos, 'Noua reglementare a achiziţiilor publice' (The new regulation of public procurements) (2001) 12 *Dreptul* (Law Journal).

National Authority for Regulating and Monitoring of Public Procurements, Operational Handbook for the Awarding of Public Procurements Contracts, vol I (Bucureşti 2009).

D.D. Şerban, *Jurisprudenţă comentată în materi achiziţiilor publice* (*Annotated jurisprudence in the field of public procurements*) (Wolters Kluwer Bucureşti 2009).

D.D. Şerban, 'Despre posibilitatea Consiliului Naţional de Soluţionare a Contestaţiilor de a anula, din oficiu, procedurile de atribuire a contractelor de achiziţie publică' ('Comments on the competency of the National Council for Solving Legal Disputes to annul, ex officio, the award procedures regarding PP contracts') (I) and (II), (2008) 4 *Revista de drept public* (Public Law Review)

D.D. Şerban, 'Sinteză a practicii judiciare în materia achiziţiilor publice – studiu de caz' ('Synthesis of judicial practice in the field of public procurements – a case study'), (II, III, IV, V) (2008) 6/7/10 and (2009) 2 *Pandectele române* (Brochure comprising the opinion of jurists on various law issues).

The Romanian Academic Society, 'O evaluare a eficienţei, integrităţii şi transparenţei sistemului de achiziţii publice din România' (An assessment of the efficiency, integrity, and transparency of the Romanian public procurements system), [Online] at http://www.sar.org.ro/do_download.php?file=files/paper-final.pdf, accessed March 2nd, 2010.

# IX. Sustainability and Public Procurement in the Spanish Legal System

*by Julio González García*

## 1 Introduction

The problem of so-called 'secondary objectives' in public procurement has given us an insight into a complete overhaul of the parameters traditionally taken into account when awarding public contracts, in accordance with current economic and social needs. Therefore, it is submitted, it is not so much a question of what the so-called 'primary objectives' are, by comparison, but one of understanding the process through which a public contract is defined, awarded, and performed, as a complete whole, in which the final outcome – the service received by the public authority – is as important as the instruments by which public contracts are carried out. To view it in any other way would be to deny the role of public procurement as an instrument for bringing about the change needed in how productive processes are configured.

It is precisely for this reason that it now seems appropriate to pose the question that will be tackled in this chapter from the point of view of sustainability in public procurement, which is more in line with the current content of the provisions of the Spanish legal system. What the idea of sustainability seeks is to advance the principles of the welfare state, and in respect of social clauses, to advance public policies for the attainment of full employment, environmental protection, or cultural protection. Ultimately, these are structural principles of our constitutional order which have to be projected into all aspects of public policy. As such, public procurement is one way of achieving certain political objectives.

In the Spanish legal system, the change that must be faced when it comes to examining public procurement must be seen as part of a more complex process, i.e. that of the change to the productive model which must be faced as we enter the new millennium. In effect, given the problems that have arisen in the productive model when examined from an economical point of view, the Prime Minister's Office of the Spanish Government has tabled a *Sustainable Economy Bill*,[1] which defines public policies with the aim to make them an instrument for ensuring that the economy is not a slave to the same ideas it served in the past: the financial economy should not outweigh the productive economy; the economy measured in accounting terms should not overshadow the real economy; the construction industry should not predominate over the economy based on research, development, and innovation; and the rights of citizens should not be overlooked in a welfare state. All of this sits within an overall process, underway since the election victory of Prime Minister Rodríguez Zapatero in 2004, of strengthening and widening citizens' rights. This has its effect on public procurement. The case of the law on equality between men and women, for example, directly creates a focus of action in relation to public procurement, as shall be seen below, which leads us to the inclusion of social clauses.

In any event, Spanish legislation covers the introduction of sustainable elements as a substantive element within the public procurement process in great detail. The Preamble to Law 30/2007 of 30 October, on Public Sector Procurement[2] (hereinafter, the Public Sector Procurement Law) acknowledges the significant weight that these aspects have:

> 'by including, in accordance with their own terms and without any reservations, the guidelines set forth in Directive 2004/18/EC, the Public Sector Procurement Law contains substantial innovations in respect of the preparation and award of those procedures it regulates. In summary, the main innovations are that it sets up mechanisms that allow social and environmental considerations to be included within public procurement, configuring them as special conditions affecting the performance of the contract, or as criteria in the evaluation of bids, outlining a structure that allows for the inclusion of guidelines on how well the contracts comply with new ethical and social requirements, such as the extent to which the services provided meet the standards of fair trade with underdeveloped or developing countries, as envisaged by the Resolution of the European Parliament on Fair Trade and Development 2005/2245 (INI), and which allow public demand for goods and services to be adjusted to fit the actual availability of natural resources'.

1. The Spanish Government's entire strategy in respect of sustainability can be viewed on the following website, on which the Sustainable Economy Bill is also published: http://www.economiasostenible.gob.es.
2. Bernal Blay, M.A., 'Hacia una contratación pública socialmente responsable: las oportunidades de la Ley 30/2007, de 30 de octubre, de contratos del sector público', in the journal *Revista Aragonesa de Administración Pública*, (2008) pp. 211 *et seq.*. Prior to the Public Sector Procurement Law, see Gosálbez Pequeño, H.; 'Clásulas sociales en la selección de los contratitas de las Administraciones Públicas?'; in the journal *Justicia Administrativa* no. 20 (2003), pp. 27 *et seq.*.

Thus, social, environmental, and justice-related elements in the globalisation process appear as elements to be taken into account in public procurement. Nevertheless, none of this amounts to anything other than abiding by the content of the provisions of the European public-procurement regime, in particular Directive 2004/18/EC, which is explained in another chapter of this work.

If the general legislation on procurement and the regulations that are to configure public and private activity in the future acknowledge the weight of sustainable elements within procurement, it is no less important to point out that special rules for the recognition of rights go one step further and require that certain values should be present in the award and performance of the contracts, as is clearly the case with Organic Law 3/2007 of 22 March, on effective equality between men and women,[3] which contains a host of elements that complement the general principles in this area. It is precisely for this reason that this question shall be specifically examined further below.

## 2 The idea of sustainability and its effect on public procurement

The idea of sustainability – in its social, economic, and environmental forms – has a direct effect on public procurement procedures, and for this reason, the forthcoming Sustainable Economy Law, which is just beginning its enactment process, includes certain precepts which extend its applicability in the public arena. However, as we shall see, certain aspects of sustainability, specifically those of an environmental nature, and some of a social nature, are sufficiently well backed up by laws that are already in force and are applicable to public contracts, either as a result of the provisions of Law 30/2007 on Public Sector Procurement, or other rules of a more general nature, which pervade public activities and as such affect procurement.

The idea of sustainability is pervasive, and it seeks to be the driving force that will allow the productive system to be altered to encompass criteria that are more reasonable from all points of view. The Sustainable Economy Strategy features

'amongst its guiding principles the promotion and protection of fundamental rights and intra- and inter-generational solidarity, as well as principles of care and the requirement that

3. In respect of the impact of the regulations on equality between men and women, see Zambonino Pulito, M.; 'La igualdad efectiva de mujeres y hombres y la contratación de las Administraciones públicas en la Ley Orgánica 3/2007, de 22 de marzo', in the journal *Revista de Administración Pública*, no. 175 (2008), pp. 463 *et seq.*.

polluters pay in those areas affecting public health and the environment. The cornerstone is encouraging participation by citizens, businesses, and social mediators in decision-making processes'.

In this regard, the Law will perform a dual role: on the one hand, with the specific measures that it implements. And secondly, it has a role in defining principles, i.e. it is a norm that sets principles and objectives that constitute instruments for programming public and private activities. Ultimately, it forms a part of these rules which, as has been stated from within our ranks by *Parejo Alfonso,* conform to the principle of the teleological programming which defines the general guiding principles of the Public Authorities, whilst at the same time referring to numerous decisions, even in this field, to the administrative level.[4]

It is precisely because of this principle-defining function attributed to the Sustainable Economy Law that it is convenient to recall the general principles that it will apply to administrative functioning, which have a special field of application in public procurement procedures, with a requirement that procurement procedures be configured in such a way as to allow these principles to be fulfilled, and secondly, requiring contractors to perform the contract in accordance with the said principles. The structural principles would be as follows: Improved competitiveness; Stability of public finances.[5] Stimulation of the innovative capacity of businesses. Energy savings and efficiency. Promotion of clean energies, lower emissions, and effective waste management. Rationalization of residential building; extension of and improvement to quality of education, and encouragement of continuous training; strengthening and safeguarding of the welfare state. All of this is envisaged under Article 31 of the Bill, pursuant to which

'all statutory and regulatory provisions, all administrative acts, all contracts and co-operation agreements, and any other activities undertaken by the public authorities must assess their repercussions and effects, in order for budgetary sustainability to be guaranteed.'

4. Parejo Alfonso, L., '*Crisis y renovación en el Derecho público*', Centro de Estudios Constitucionales, Madrid (1991), p. 49.
5. In respect of the European principle of budgetary stability and its impact on public procurement, see González García, J.V.; Financiación de infraestructuras públicas y estabilidad presupuestaria, Tirant lo Blanch, Valencia (2007).

Bearing in mind the significance of public procurement in public economic efficiency and in the improvement of the productive structure as a whole, Article 38 of the Bill provides that

> 'all bodies, organizations, and entities within the public sector shall ensure the efficiency and the attainment of the terms agreed in the performance of public procurement processes, shall encourage the streamlining of procedures, and shall promote the participation of small and medium-sized enterprises, and cost-free access to information, within the terms laid down in Law 30/2007 of 30 October, on Public Sector Procurement, as amended by the eighteenth final provision of this Act'.

These are measures which pursue a variety of objectives, all of which are linked to different aspects of sustainability, and which in the Sustainable Economy Law, as has been stated, go beyond environmental concerns.

In effect, improvement of the economic stability of public finances – with the direct effect that this has on the regime for the amendment of contracts or with the enhanced productivity of public bodies and improved attainment of the principles of efficacy and efficiency; development of the innovative capacity of businesses with a direct impact in particular on procedures for public-private partnerships; energy efficiency as part of the content of construction and supply contracts; clean energy aimed at supply contracts for public authorities and so on. There is even a provision for allocating parts of the procurement budget for executing contracts with innovation-led businesses, which are those which, in principle, will provide the technical sustenance for the change of productive models towards another model founded on a knowledge-based economy. Within these, those executed with Technologically-Based Businesses have a primary role.[6]

As may be seen from these examples, which are in no way exhaustive, the principles of sustainability to be contained in the Sustainable Economy Law have a direct impact on public procurement. With the boost provided by this law once it will enacted, and with the current weight given to the social criteria within the framework of the activities of central and regional governments, with the exception of some led by the Popular Party, it is reasonable to think that the impact will be even greater as time goes by. On this point, it

6. In respect of the forthcoming Sustainable Economy Law and the boost to the Technology Based Company, see Petit Lavall, M.V.; 'El anteproyecto de Ley de Economía Sostenible y la transferencia de resultados de la actividad investigadora de las Universidades públicas mediante la constitución de Empresas de Base Tecnológica' *Homenaje al Profesor Fernández Novoa,* (2010), to be published.

would be convenient to re-consider the very wide-ranging role played by competition law in public procurement.

However, it would be convenient to specify how the idea of sustainability is currently configured in the rules governing public contracts.

## 3 The aim of the contract: primary elements and sustainability?

As stated above, the introduction of clauses aimed at ensuring sustainability has a greater effect on the productive processes of the goods or services than on the actual subject-matter of the contract. In this regard, it will not matter whether the subject-matter of the contract, defined in accordance with one of the seven standard contracts recognised by Spanish law,[7] is too narrow to provide for these kinds of elements. It is precisely for this reason that the sustainability stimulus should occur at other stages of the procurement procedure, as important as the definition of the subject-matter itself, given that in public activities the means are as important as the means with which they are put into effect.

## 4 Social and sustainability clauses in public procurement

The general framework has been described above. In the remainder of this chapter, the question how the principle of sustainability manifests itself in the process for the award and performance of contracts within the Spanish legal system, in the various stages for the preparation, award, completion, and execution of the contract, will be examined. However, as a preliminary matter, it would be convenient to examine which sustainability clauses allow restrictions to be imposed on qualifying as a contractor, which will in turn have an effect on the possibility of being able to bid, and on the types of contracts which can be won.

It is worth remembering that the inclusion of these clauses amounts to a ray of light within the *dictatorship* of competition law, and that the dazzle so created currently distorts the execution of public policies. The rules on public procurement, when correctly interpreted, must seek a balance between the in-

7. Under Spanish law, contracts defined as being standard within the Public Sector Procurement Law are as follows: public works contracts, contracts for the management of public services, service contracts, supply contracts, public-works concession contracts, and public-private partnerships.

troduction of sustainability criteria, and the defence of the principle of competition. This balance must manifest itself in the reasonableness of the clauses included and in the interpretation they are given. In our legal system, their inclusion and their enforcement by public bodies is none other than a consequence of the welfare state clause, which configures the State in accordance with the provisions of Article 1.1. of the 1978 Constitution.

### 4.1 Contractors and the performance of the requirements of sustainability in public procurement

Pursuant to the Public Sector Procurement Law, not only must contractors be technically and economically capable of performing the contract, which amounts to the essential aspect of qualification as a contractor, as required in the Public Sector Procurement Law, but they must also meet other requirements of a social nature which will improve their credentials. On the one hand, these criteria require certain quality assurance standards to be met, to be verified by the bodies in charge of approving them, and on the other they require certain environmental standards to be met. These are new criteria which derive directly from Articles 49 to 51 of Directive 2004/18/EC.[8]

First of all, we encounter eco-management criteria compliance. The contracting authorities have the power to

> 'require the production of certificates drawn up by independent bodies attesting the compliance of the contractor with certain environmental management standards, with reference to the Community Eco-Management and Audit Scheme (EMAS) or to environmental management standards based on the relevant European or international standards certified by bodies conforming to Community law or the relevant European or international standards concerning certification' (Article 70 of the Public Sector Procurement Law).[9]

Secondly, there is compliance with the rules governing quality. From this point of view, contractors may be required to

8. This concern over the acquisition of green products is not limited to the legal framework, but has already been developed by the Resolution of the Cabinet Meeting of 11 January 2008, which approves the Green Public Procurement Plan for Central Government and its Public Bodies and the bodies in charge of managing the Social Security.
9. This concern has given rise to the approval of provisions on environmental requirements in schedules of special administrative clauses, such as those contained in the Order of the Environment Minister 2116/2007 of 10 July, published in the Official State Gazette of 13 July 2007.

'produce certificates drawn up by independent bodies attesting the compliance of the economic operator with certain quality assurance standards, they must refer to quality assurance systems based on the relevant European standards series certified by bodies conforming to the European standards series concerning certification' (Article 69 of the Public Sector Procurement Law"

In addition to the above, certain restrictions on participation are imposed for reasons of sustainability. The first of these is that the contractor should not be disqualified from contracting, given that the intention is that contractors should be sufficiently worthy in order to perform contracts for a public body. The regime governing disqualification opens the door to elements of an economic nature – linked to the actual performance of other contracts – and to others which, in contrast, affect the performance of requirements of a social nature envisaged in the legislation: failure to pay social security contributions, which is a necessary element in all remuneration for labour, or having been found guilty of offences against workers' rights or environmental protection.

It is also appropriate to refer to the new possibility introduced by the Seventh Additional Provision to the Public Sector Procurement Law of restricting the scope of the possible bidders in the procurement procedure, either on the basis of the contract or the businesses that seek to participate. Thus, from the first point of view, it is provided that

'participation in tendering processes may be restricted to Special Employment Centres, or its execution may be reserved to fall within the framework of subsidised-employment programmes, where at least 70 % of the affected employees are disabled, and given the nature or severity of their disability, they are unable to perform a professional activity under normal conditions. The invitation for tenders must refer to this provision'.

The special characteristics of Temporary Recruitment Agencies lead to the rule that, pursuant to the Fifth Additional Provision of the Public Sector Procurement Law

'no service contracts may be executed with Temporary Recruitment Agencies unless there is a requirement for temporary staff for the performance of surveys, compilation of data, or similar services'.

In this case, the function this rule performs derives from the view that employment stability should be one of the public policies that ought to be pursued through public procurement.

Beyond those tendering processes that are subject to European guidelines, in those contracts where the award may be given following restricted or negotiated procedures, the Authorities have even greater powers to choose socially responsible contractors; either by way of the pre-qualification process or by way of the criteria established in the contract conditions.

### 4.2 Preparation of the contract and sustainability criteria

The preparation of the contract features a series of preliminary stages prior to the start of the award process, in which the conditions that are to govern the award and the subsequent performance are outlined. Basically, it is composed of the schedules of general administrative clauses, the schedule of special administrative clauses, and the schedule of technical conditions which are to govern the contract. At this point the principle of freedom to draft the conditions in public procurement should be mentioned, which has been included throughout all articles of the Public Sector Procurement Law, and which will allow a wide margin for the inclusion of sustainability clauses, which will therefore depend on the Public Authority in question. It is when drafting the schedules listing the general and special administrative clauses that sustainable elements and the protection of bidders are included in the contract, to the extent that the sustainable clauses are also subject to the principles of competition law.

Despite the importance given by the legislation to the schedules of general administrative clauses, the reality is that it is difficult to get them approved, given that in theory they are a general framework for many different kinds of standard contracts. In any event, it is in these schedules that the rights and duties of the parties to the contract should be defined, within which sustainability elements should be included, given that this is the framework within which the contracts should be awarded.

Given the difficulty that has just been described, an instrument that is much more flexible shall be examined, viz. the schedule of special administrative clauses, the function of which, pursuant to the provisions of Art. 99 of the Public Sector Procurement Law, consists in including

> 'the warranties and conditions that define the rights and duties of the parties to the contract, and any other points required by this Act or its implementing provisions.'

As can be seen, this is the basic instrument for the performance of the contract. Added to this is the fact that the conditions for the award of the contract must define those elements in accordance with which the process for identifying the best bid for the public authority is to be carried out. It is precisely for all of the above that approval must take place at the same time as the expenditure is authorized, and in any event, prior to the commencement of the award procedure.

For this reason the schedule, in accordance with the provisions of the General Regulations of the Spanish Contracts Act, may establish 'rights and duties specific to the parties to the contract', and 'criteria for the award of the tender, in decreasing order of importance, and the weighting given thereto'. Aspects affecting the manner in which the contract is to be performed and to be configured in accordance with sustainable criteria may be established as additional elements of the contract.

These are not merely generic considerations that are left to the whim of the contracting authority, to decide whether or not they are included. The gender clause, for example, constitutes a compulsory feature of many public contracts, as we shall see below. Beyond this, consideration should also be given to the relative weight to be attached to this in the award procedure, given that it may be one of the relevant elements for the performance of the contract, as we shall see below, which shall have an effect on the possibilities of revoking the contract in the event of a breach.

The difficulty that compliance with certain sustainability requirements could entail is reduced by way of providing guidelines in order to be able to determine the exact scope of the requirements:

> 'the contracting authority may stipulate in the schedule the body or bodies from which candidates or bidders may obtain the relevant information concerning the duties pertaining to tax requirements, environmental protection, and the provisions in force regarding employment protection, working conditions, and health & safety at work, which shall be applicable to works carried out at the building site or to the services provided during the performance of the contract'.

Such enquiries made in cooperation with bodies external to the public authority itself are encouraged given that a right is acknowledged for a certificate to be obtained in respect of any such enquiry, which may be taken into account, notwithstanding the possibility of any particular offer being deemed to be an abnormally low bid, something which is not affected thereby. However, the fact that these bodies are external to the public authority might give an impression of objectivity, despite the fact that, in accordance with the provisions of Article 103 of the 1978 Constitution, this is a general mandate for the functioning of all public authorities.

As may be seen from the above, the introduction of sustainability requirements in tendering schedules must comply with a formal requirement, the advance publication prior to the opening of the procurement procedure, which amounts to a requirement for the purpose of complying with the principle of competition that also applies to this area. Further to these criteria of a general nature, we should also add four specific items which are all envisaged in the law: first, the preference for companies in which over two per cent of the staff is disabled, or second, those businesses specifically dedicated to assisting and providing employment to persons deemed to be in a situation of social exclusion, as defined in the law: i) persons receiving the minimum social-integration benefit, or any other benefit of the same or similar nature in accordance with the different terminology of each Autonomous Region; ii) persons who are unable to claim the benefits referred to in the foregoing section, on the grounds that they do not comply with the minimum time requirements or residency or registration, or for the creation of the recipient unit, or because they have exhausted the maximum term allowed for the receipt of the said benefit; iii) young people aged between eighteen and thirty who have come from child protection institutions; iv) persons with drug or alcohol addiction problems who are undergoing rehabilitation or participating in social-integration programmes; v) prison inmates whose prison regime allows them to seek employment, as well as persons released on parole and ex-offenders; and finally vi) disabled persons.

Moreover, for contracts relating to services of a social or welfare nature a preference is given for bids submitted by non-profit organisations with legal personality, provided that their aim or activity is directly related to the subject-matter of the contract.

The fourth possible preference is provided in the Sixth Additional Provision of the Spanish Contracts Act and concerns businesses that manufacture

> 'products where there is a Fair Trade alternative for bids submitted by entities acknowledged as being Fair Trade Organizations, provided that the terms of the said bids can match the most advantageous from the point of view of the criteria that serve as the basis for the award'.

Finally, it is necessary to make a brief reference to the impact of sustainability on the schedules of technical conditions, which are an essential element in order for the performance of the project to be reasonable from this perspective. Article 101 refers specifically to this matter, where it provides that

> 'the technical conditions shall be defined, in so far as is possible, taking into account criteria of universal accessibility and design for all, in accordance with the definition of these terms contained in Law 51/2003 of 2 December, on equal opportunities, non-discrimination, and universal accessibility for disabled persons, and wherever the subject-matter of the contract affects or may affect the environment, applying sustainability and environmental protection criteria, in accordance with the definitions and principles governed by

Articles 3 and 4, respectively, of Law 16/2002 of 1 July on the integrated prevention and control of pollution.'

The importance of these criteria is underlined by the fact that where it is not possible to define the technical conditions taking into account criteria of universal accessibility and design for all, adequate justification must be given.

This reference to the criteria of sustainability and environmental protection are particularly detailed in the rules governing schedules of technical conditions. Firstly, it is provided that the technical conditions may be established

'in terms of performance or functional requirements, and wherever the subject-matter of the contract affects or may affect the environment, the latter may include the imposition of environmental characteristics. The parameters used should be precise enough in order to allow the determination of the subject-matter of the contract by the bidders and the award of the said contract by the contracting authorities.'

This general provision is complemented by the fact that

'where environmental characteristics are prescribed in terms of performance or functional requirements, they may use the detailed specifications, or if necessary, parts thereof, as defined by European or (multi-) national eco-labels, or any other eco-label, provided that: (i) those specifications are appropriate to define the characteristics of the supplies or services that are the subject-matter of the contract, (ii) the requirements are drawn up on the basis of scientific information, (iii) all stakeholders have been able to participate in the procedure for their approval, such as governmental bodies, consumers, manufacturers, distributors, and environmental organizations, and (iv) they are accessible to all interested parties.'

As may be seen, sustainability values constitute an essential element of both the conditions of the tendering process, composed of the schedules of special and technical conditions, which affects very specific elements which refer precisely to environmental protection. All of these shall serve as the defining elements in the process for awarding the contract.

### 4.3 Sustainability and the tendering processes

Based on the underlying schedule of special administrative clauses, the procedure for awarding the contract must be set out. Obviously, sustainability criteria may be included in those procedures where the price is not the only determining factor in the award decision, which entails the requirement that, in accordance with the terminology used by the law, reference should be made to the 'most advantageous offer' taken as a whole. This should not mean, however, that where contracts do have to be awarded solely on the basis of price, sustainability criteria are irrelevant. On the contrary, in those cases, which are not in the least infrequent, where two bidders are tied on price, account must be taken of the way in which social requirements are met in order to award the contract to the more sustainable of the two.

As has been seen above, the schedules may include all elements deemed appropriate, provided that they are configured in an objective manner, are non-discriminatory, and are suitable for the type of contract to be awarded. In this regard, it is the schedule of conditions that must configure the procurement procedure, selecting from all the different options. Article 134.3 of the Law gives a precise outline of the tendering formula, *inter alia*, in those cases where

> 'the performance of the contract may have a significant impact on the environment, in which case the award shall take into account measurable environmental conditions, such as a lower environmental impact, the saving and efficient use of water and energy and materials, the environmental life-cycle cost, eco-production procedures and methods, waste generation and management, or the use of recycled or re-used materials or eco-friendly materials.'

If we find ourselves here with an essential impact of environmental protection, we cannot overlook the fact that at section b of the same rule, one of the elements for resorting to tendering is defined as being

> 'where the contracting authority considers that the definition of the service is open to improvement by way of other technical solutions, to be proposed by the bidders by way of submitting alternatives.'

It is clear that beyond these situations affecting the subject-matter of the contract, the evaluation of the bids is directly linked to the introduction of sustainable criteria. This is the idea contained in Article 134 of the Public Sector Procurement Law:

> 'In order to evaluate the bids and determine the offer that is economically most advantageous, criteria that are directly linked to the subject-matter of the contract shall be taken into account, such as the quality, the price, the formula used to review remuneration linked to the use of the works or the provision of the service, the deadline for the performance or the delivery of the service, the cost of use, the environmental characteristics or those linked to complying with social requirements concerning needs defined in the contractual specifications pertaining to those particularly deprived sections of the population to which the beneficiaries of the services offered for tender belong, cost-effectiveness, the technical merit, the aesthetic or functional characteristics, the availability and cost of spare parts, maintenance, technical assistance, after-sales service, or other such like'.

It should be noted here that certain social conditions do not appear as criteria to be taken into account, such as, for example, in respect of compliance with the regulations on health and safety at work, which is a statutory requirement. However, the inclusion of the clause of Article 134 does not open the door in general terms to the inclusion of these kinds of clauses, but rather it is imposing additional conditions to the requirements already laid down by European law.

As will be seen below, there is a wide margin for the introduction and consideration of criteria of a social nature within public contracts. This fact could give rise to excessive discretion on the part of the contracting authorities, which could always be counter-balanced by providing sufficient reasons, both for the criteria to be included, which ought to be suitable in accordance with the nature of the contract, and for the relative weight they are given, and ultimately, for the consideration of the bids submitted by the candidates for the public contract. But the fact that discretion may turn into arbitrariness is not something that can only happen in relation to sustainability criteria in contracts, and the positive effects that these bring mean that it is important to continue down this path.

In this regard, it is worth bearing in mind that the inclusion of these elements is providing a response, on the basis of the values of the welfare State, in three different directions: a) firstly, this is not a mechanism to restrict competition, but rather, on the contrary, it is regulating competition and relegating mere economic factors to a less important position, given that their relative weight is overrated; b) it is allowing the inclusion of public policies in the areas of social and environmental protection, and c) it is favouring the implementation of European law containing these principles, and as such, it is devaluating those laws which, due to the differing powers of the different legal systems, do not give the necessary weight to these criteria, and as such it is becoming an indirect way to fight back against business offshoring.

## 5 Changes to the productive system and procedure for the award of contracts

As can be seen, one of the concerns of the moment is to configure the economy in such a way that it ceases to be dominated by the construction industry, replacing this model with a knowledge-based economy. It is precisely for this reason that both the legislation in force and the forthcoming Sustainable Economy Law introduce certain changes to the tendering processes in order to favour those businesses that carry out research tasks.

Currently, 'service and supply contracts executed by State Public Research Bodies and similar bodies of the Autonomous Regions that have as their aim services or products that are necessary for the execution of technological research, development, and innovation projects or technical services' are excluded from the technical public tendering rules 'where the presentation and attainment of results deriving from them is linked to scientific, technological, or industrial returns capable of being handled by the legal process and the performance thereof has been entrusted to the said bodies' research teams by way of competitive tendering processes'. This possibility has been specifically devised for the commissioning of services from public universities.

The forthcoming Sustainable Economy Law provides an equivalent possibility for all other entities dedicated to research, which is excluded from the scope of the Public Sector Procurement Law. In this manner, the following shall be excluded from the provisions of the said Law:

> 'Research and development contracts funded in full by the contracting authority, provided that said body shares, together with the successful bidders, the risks and benefits of the scientific and technical research necessary in order to develop innovative solutions that surpass those available on the market. The award of these contracts must ensure that the principles of publicity, competition, transparency, confidentiality, equality, non-discrimination, and selection of the economically most advantageous bid are respected.' (Nineteenth Final Provision of the Sustainable Economy Law).

The evaluation of the offers likewise includes elements that allow sustainability factors to be taken into consideration. Initially, the actual regime governing bids with 'abnormal or disproportionate values', which leads us in principle to the traditional regime governing abnormally low bids. Here, the rule requires, amongst other factors with regard to which the bidder must provide information during the procedure that must be followed in order to decide whether or not the bid is abnormal (and as such, whether it should be excluded), the following:

> 'the technical solutions adopted and the exceptionally-favourable conditions that it enjoys in order to provide the service, the originality of the services proposed, respect for the provisions governing employment protection and working conditions in force at the place where the service is to be provided, or the possible award of State funding' (Article 136.3 of the Public Sector Procurement Law'.

## 6 Sustainability conditions in the execution of the contract

Article 102 of the Public Sector Procurement Law also provides, furthermore, for the possibility of the introduction of sustainability elements in the performance of the contract. As may be seen from what has been set forth so far, this is the fourth stage at which these objectives may be introduced into public contracts: the first is at the determination of the subject-matter of the contract; the second is at the drafting of the technical specifications, the third is at the stage for the selection of the contractor by way of the set of requirements that contractors must meet, and the fourth is now upon the performance of the contract.

Article 102 of the Public Sector Procurement Law provides in this regard as follows:

> 'the contracting authority may establish special conditions in relation to the performance of the contract, provided that these are compatible with European law and are stated in the invitation for tenders and in the schedule or contract. These performance conditions may refer, in particular, to considerations of an environmental nature or of a social nature, with the aim of (i) promoting the recruitment of persons with particular difficulties for entering the labour market, (ii) eliminating inequality between men and women within the said market, (iii) reducing unemployment, (iv) encouraging on-site vocational training, or any other aims that may be established with reference to the co-ordinated employment strategy defined in Article 125 of the Treaty establishing the European Community, or (v) ensuring that basic labour standards are respected throughout the production chain by way of the requirement that the fundamental conventions of the International Labour Organization are met.'

These clauses are also applicable in other countries, given that the last of them is specifically designed to introduce the requirements of so-called fair trade and to adjust the demand for goods to fit the actual availability of natural resources.

These clauses are subject to a series of requirements, one of a formal nature and others of a substantive nature. First, they must be included in the invitation to tender and in the schedule or in the contract itself. If this last option is used they must appear in the last two, the shedule and the contract itself.

As has just been shown, the rule requires that the said clauses should be compatible with European law. On the basis of the provisions of the Interpretative Communication on Contracts, the areas within which these clauses have been developed are those of the duty to find employment for those persons who are in a legal situation of unemployment – especially for members of those groups who have the greatest difficulty in entering the labour market;

the duty to perform activities that serve to encourage equal opportunities, both in respect of gender and ethnic problems; respect for the conventions of the International Labour Organisation, even where they have not been subscribed, and lastly, the recruitment of disabled persons in excess of the quotas set by the national legal system. In the Spanish legal system, the duties deriving from the Directive on the displacement of workers, or the Directive on the maintenance of workers' rights in cases of transfers of undertakings, all form part of these duties.

Within the area of environmental law, we find clauses such as the use of re-usable packaging, the collection, re-cycling, and re-use of waste to be borne by the contractor, the delivery of goods by weight and not in units, or even the possibility of requiring a specific form of transport because this is more environmentally friendly, or forms for delivering supplies of goods that are more efficient from an energy perspective.

From a formal point of view, we have just seen the connection that exists with the provisions contained in the letter of the contract. From a material point of view, the authority has powers to interpret the contract and also powers of management, inspection, and control, which allow the contracting authority to issue such instructions as may be appropriate in order to achieve a performance that is particularly suited to the principle of sustainability.

It could possibly be particularly important to bear in mind that the breach of these clauses is especially envisaged in Article 102 of the Public Sector Procurement Law itself. In accordance with the provisions of its second paragraph:

> 'The schedules or the contract may establish penalties, pursuant to the provisions of Article 196.1, in the event of the breach of these special performance conditions, or they may be deemed to be essential contractual conditions for the purposes laid down at Article 206.g. Where the breach of these conditions is not deemed to go to the root of the contract resulting in its termination, the breach may be deemed to be a serious infringement for the purposes of Article 49.2.e, either pursuant to the schedules or the contract, within the terms laid down by regulation.'

Pursuant to the precept, they may be deemed to be essential clauses for the purpose of the termination of the contract, and as such two of the legal precepts are being specified. At the same time, where the said clauses are deemed to be essential contractual provisions, this shall mean that those contractors breaching them are barred from contracting with the public authorities. If they are not essential, performance of the contract may continue, with a penalty being imposed on the contractor not exceeding ten per cent of the contract price.

## 7 Subsidies for the performance of the contract: the case of public works concessions

Within the regime governing public contracts, public works concessions[10] are particularly significant due to the fact that the Authorities provide funds for the performance of the contract. Article 237.1 expressly envisages this where it provides that

> 'Public authorities may partly fund the financing of the works by way of contributions to be made during the performance stage of the works, as provided for at Article 223 of this Act, once these have been concluded or upon the expiry of the concession, and the value thereof shall be determined in the corresponding schedules of conditions or by the bidders in their bids where the said schedules should require this.'

The basic reason for this, as is stated at Article 236 of the Public Sector Procurement Law, is due to the fact that 'where there should be reasons of economic or social cost-effectiveness, or there should be unique requirements arising from the public aim or the general interest of the works subject to the concession, the public authority may also provide public resources towards its financing, which shall take the form of joint financing of the works, by way of refundable subsidies or loans, with or without interest, in accordance with the provisions of Article 223 and this section, and pursuant to the provisions of the corresponding schedule of special administrative clauses, but under all circumstances the principle of the risk being borne by the concessionaire shall be upheld'.

There is a second factor that ought to be pointed out. Beyond any direct contributions that may be provided by the public authorities, one of the most important elements is that of public guaranties for the grant of the private funding, which would be deemed to be indirect subsidies for the performance of the contract. This is an aspect for which

> 'in Spain we have a long and negative experience. Public guaranties can have a truly perverse effect and be a serious impediment to the proper evolution of both the productive

10. In respect of the régime governing public works concessions in the new public procurement regulations, see Herranz Embid, P. '*Concesión de obra pública*', in the collective work directed by J.R. Fernández Torres, Concesiones administrativas, to be published soon. A more succinct view, by the same author, may be found in 'Régimen general de las obras públicas', in J. V. González García, *Derecho de los bienes públicos*, Valencia (2009), pp. 213-260.

sectors involved in public works concessions and the financial system as a whole. Hence the importance of the sensible configuration and application of award criteria.'[11]

In this regard, participating loans are particularly significant, given that they are especially damaging, in my opinion, to the protection of the general interest and the very essence of public works concessions, in accordance with the provisions of the Interpretative Communication.

This regime replaces the one that was in force during the tenure of the previous regulations, and which gave rise to a multitude of extreme cases during the mandate of the Popular Party Government in power between 1996 and 2004 and based on a clause concerning the social value of the public works granted. The problem is that neither then nor now does there exist a clause capping the value of the public contribution, as exists, for example, under French law, and therefore the nature of the concession is distorted, and furthermore there are negative effects on the public deficit given that in accordance with the Eurostat criteria, there is an insufficient transfer of risks from the Public Authority to the contractor.[12]

## 8 Consequences of failure to comply with the sustainability clause in public procurement

In addition to the specific problem of breaches in the performance of the contract, we must also consider the general problems arising when performance of the service fails to live up to the sustainability clauses included in the contract.

First, Article 49 of the Public Sector Procurement Law provides that where companies have been found culpable in situations of breach of contract, they should be barred from contracting with public authorities. Causes of a social nature are fully covered under this range of possibilities open to the public authority in order to declare debarrment. Thus, being found guilty of

11. Ruiz Ojeda, A., *La concesión de obra pública*, Ed. Civitas (2006) p. 533.
12. With regard to the principle of budgetary stability and the ESA 95 rules in relation to public works, see my monograph *Financiación de infraestructuras públicas y estabilidad presupuestaria*, Tirant lo Blanch, Valencia (2007), the conclusions of which remain valid.

'the offences of conspiracy, corruption in international economic transactions, undue influence, bribery, fraud and extortion, offences against the Tax Authorities, and the Social Security, offences against the rights of workers, embezzlement and receiving and similar offences, and offences relating to environmental protection.'

Offences against social rights and environmental protection are therefore the first area.

Secondly, we find those situations where companies have been penalised by way of a final decision for serious offences in relation to matters of market discipline, in professional matters or in matters concerning labour integration and equal opportunities and non-discrimination against persons with disabilities, or very serious offences in social matters, including offences in matters of health and safety at work or environmental matters. There is no need for a criminal conviction; an administrative penalty is sufficient.

The third reason linked to the breach of social undertakings directly refers to duties with respect of the workers; for instance those economic operators who are not up to date in the performance of their tax or social security duties shall be barred from future contracts, within the terms laid down by the regulations.

In the performance of the contract itself, any breach of the sustainability elements considered to be essential to the performance of the contract shall be sufficient ground for the public authority to terminate the contract, in accordance with the provisions of Article 206 of the Public Sector Procurement Law. The discretionary powers of the contracting authority include the right to define other conditions which might not be essential but which entail the termination of the contract. From amongst these, clearly one of the elements that can most often be used is precisely that of sustainability elements.

A second less aggressive possibility – which will depend, ultimately, on the nature of the breach – would be to impose a penalty of up to 10 per cent of the total contract price, with disqualification of the contractor from contracting with public authorities for a period of up to one year.

## 9 Economic sustainability and public procurement

As has been pointed out from the very beginning of this chapter, sustainability does not just affect the inclusion of social clauses in procurement. It has a direct economic content that affects the effects the award of a contract has on the economic solvency of the public authorities, which may be the determining factor for actually commencing the procurement procedure. It is a manifestation of the principle of efficiency in public expenditure.

This is a principle arising under Article 31.3 of the forthcoming Sustainable Economy Law, where it provides that

> 'statutory and regulatory provisions, administrative acts, contracts and co-operation agreements, and any other activities by the public authorities must assess their repercussions and effects in a manner that ensures budgetary sustainability.'

## 10 The inclusion of social sustainability elements into special legislation: the case of the gender clause

Out of all clauses of a social nature, the one that has taken centre stage since 2004 is the one on protection against inequality between men and women, which has been backed by the enactment of Organic Law 3/2007 of 22 March, on effective equality between men and women (hereinafter the equality law). The principle of gender equality is transformed into an element that pervades all public policies, by the application of the law, which is nothing more than an extension of the constitutional principle of equality. This pervasive element, however, has two specific points of significance in respect of public procurement, possibly because the possibility of obtaining a public contract may be a suitable mechanism for achieving a higher degree of acceptance of gender equality in economic relations. It is precisely for this reason that it is structured as a special objective for public contracts in general and for Central Government in particular, and which complements the measures that have been envisaged in general terms in the above sections.

First, Article 33 of the Equality Act provides that

> 'Public Authorities, within the scope of their respective powers, and by way of their procurement bodies, and in relation to the performance of any contracts they execute, may establish special conditions with the aim of promoting equality between men and women within the labour market, in accordance with the provisions of the legislation on public sector procurement.'

As this refers to the performance of the contract, what the Equality Law is allowing is the inclusion of gender-related sustainability clauses in the schedules of special administrative clauses that are to govern the life of the contract. But to the extent that reference is made to special conditions, what this is in effect allowing is the inclusion of the implementation of affirmative action measures in the schedules of conditions.

For its part, Art.icle 34, with reference to Central Government, has a broader scope. It provides as follows:

'The Cabinet, in view of the progress and impact of equality policies in the labour market, shall determine, on an annual basis, those contracts of Central Government and its public bodies that are to necessarily include within their performance conditions measures aimed at promoting the effective equality of men and women in the labour market, in accordance with the provisions of the legislation on public sector procurement.

The Resolution referred to in the above paragraph may establish, where appropriate, the characteristics of the conditions that must be included in the schedules in accordance with the nature of the contracts and the sector of activity where the services are generated.

2. The contracting bodies may establish in the schedules of special administrative clauses a preference, when awarding the contracts, for bids submitted by those companies which, upon proof of their technical or professional solvency, comply with the guidelines of the above section, provided that the terms of these bids match those of the most advantageous from the point of view of the objective criteria that serve as the basis for the award, and always respecting the order of priority established at section one of the Eigth Additional Provision of the Recast Text of the Public Authority Procurement Act, approved by Royal Legislative Decree 2/2000 of 16 June. [13]

The content of this precept is broader. On the one hand, acknowledging some former practices of the Zapatero Government, the State is allowed to approve rules of a regulatory nature in which it is compulsory to include gender clauses in public contracts. Secondly, that gender clauses should amount to a criterion for the selection of contractors, which would have to be configured in accordance with the criteria that have been described previously.

## Bibliography

Bernal Blay, M.A., *'Hacia una contratación pública socialmente responsable: las oportunidades de la Ley 30/2007, de 30 de octubre, de contratos del sector público'*, in the journal Revista Aragonesa de Administración Pública, (2008) pp. 211 et seq..

13. This Act has been repealed and the reference should be understood as being to the Public Sector Procurement Law.

Gimeno Feliu, J.M. *"La adjudicación de los contratos: la oferta económicamente más ventajosa"*, in the jounal Revista Aragonesa de Administración Pública, Monográfico X pp. 155 sq.

González García, J.V.; Financiación de infraestructuras públicas y estabilidad presupuestaria, Tirant lo Blanch, Valencia (2007).

Gosálbez Pequeño, H.; *"¿Cláusulas sociales en la selección de los contratistas de las Administraciones Públicas?"*; in the journal Justicia Administrativa no. 20 (2003), pp. 27 et seq..

Herranz Embid, P.; *'Concesión de obra pública'*, in J.R. Fernández Torres, Concesiones administrativas, forthcoming.

Herranz Embid, P., *'Régimen general de las obras públicas'*, in J.V. González García, Derecho de los bienes públicos, Valencia (2009), pp. 213-260.

Parejo Alfonso, L., Crisis y renovación en el Derecho público, Centro de Estudios Constitucionales, Madrid (1991)

Petit Lavall, M.V.; *'El anteproyecto de Ley de Economía Sostenible y la transferencia de resultados de la actividad investigadora de las Universidades públicas mediante la constitución de Empresas de Base Tecnológica'* in the collective work Homenaje al Profesor Fernández Novoa, (2010).

Petit Lavall, M.V.; *"Las empresas de base tecnológica en las Universidades públicas"*, in González García, J.V.; Comentarios a la Ley Orgánica de Universidades, Civitas, Madrid (2009), pp. 1365-1412.

Zambonino Pulito, M.; *'La igualdad efectiva de mujeres y hombres y la contratación de las Administraciones públicas en la Ley Orgánica 3/2007, de 22 de marzo'*, in the journal Revista de Administración Pública, no. 175 (2008), pp. 463 et seq.

# X. Sustainability and Value for Money: Social and Environmental Considerations in United Kingdom Public Procurement Law

*by Martin Trybus*

*'[...] sustainability policy is consistent with Government's policy on value for money, as environmental and other sustainability costs and benefits are an important part of the value for money obtained by the buyer.'*

Office of Government Commerce,
*Environmental Sustainability*, June 2009

## 1 Introduction

The use of public procurement as an instrument to promote 'secondary' or 'horizontal' objectives[1] has never been as extensive in the United Kingdom as in other European countries. Value for money and efficient procurement

1. The term 'secondary objectives' separates certain industrial, social, and environmental policies pursued through public procurement from its 'primary objective', which is to provide the government with the goods, works, and services it needs to operate. Related to this primary objective is the consideration to achieve value for money in government purchasing: to acquire goods, works, and services at the best possible terms. The use of the terms 'primary' and 'secondary' does not imply a ranking of importance. All government policies are on an equal footing. Thus the terms 'functional' instead of 'primary' and 'horizontal' instead of 'secondary' have been suggested as more neutral expressions. See: Arrowsmith and Kunzlik (eds.), *Social and Environmental Policies in EC Procurement Law: New Directive and New Directions* (CUP, 2009), at 12. This chapter will use the more traditional term 'secondary' rather than the term 'horizontal'.

outcomes are the dominant objectives of British procurement law and policy. Nevertheless, a look into the legal history of the jurisdictions of the United Kingdom[2] and the policies of its central Government reveals that the discussion about these issues has been as fierce as elsewhere. Various schemes to use public procurement as a tool to promote different secondary policies, industrial, social, and environmental, were in place in the past. Moreover, it appears that the discussion about the importance of secondary considerations is far from over. Certain polices, for example in the context of the sustainability agenda of the central Government, have gained importance in recent years. However, these are defined within the legal limits of European Union (EU) public procurement law and are perceived to be generally in line with the value for money and efficient procurement objectives.

This chapter will discuss the treatment of secondary objectives in the procurement law of the United Kingdom. First, the analysis will provide a historical perspective. This will look at how the laws of the United Kingdom dealt with secondary considerations from the 19th century until and during the period of the 1980s and 1990s, before this area was increasingly affected by 'Thatcherism' and became largely determined by European Community (EC) public procurement law. An understanding of the legislative initiatives and political context is important for the understanding of the treatment of secondary considerations in the current statutory and policy framework. Second, in it's main parts the chapter will consider the treatment of secondary objectives in the statutory instruments transposing the Public Sector Directive 2004/18/EC in the United Kingdom, namely the Public Contracts Regulations SI 2006/6 (UKPCR) applicable in England, Wales, and Northern Ireland and the separate Public Contract (Scotland) Regulations SI 2006/1 (SPCR) applicable north of the border. The latter are very similar to the earlier. References will also be made to the statutory instruments transposing the Utilities Procurement Directive 2004/17/EC, the Utilities Contract Regulations SI 2006/5

2. The United Kingdom is divided into three main jurisdictions: England and Wales, Scotland, and Northern Ireland. Essential fields of law, contract, torts (damages), criminal, and public (including local government) are separate, including separate court systems. In addition, there are central Government laws and policies. It needs to be understood that since the devolutions (from 1997) the Government in Whitehall and the Parliament in Westminster are both responsible for the United Kingdom as a whole and for the jurisdiction of England. The devolved governments for Scotland, Wales, and Northern Ireland do not all have the same powers and the degree to which the legal systems are separated differs considerably. Unless otherwise indicated, this chapter will refer to laws applicable to the United Kingdom as a whole or to laws applicable to England, including Wales if appropriate.

(UKUCR) for England, Wales, and Northern Ireland and the Utilities Contracts (Scotland) Regulations 2006 (SUCR) for Scotland.[3] The latter instruments are also very similar. All these Regulations entered into force on 31st January 2006. With the further progress of the devolution of government in the United Kingdom, separate public procurement regulations for the devolved assemblies (governments) in Wales and Northern Ireland are possible. The current United Kingdom and Scotland Regulations apply only to public and utilities contracts within the field of application of the Directives, most importantly to contracts above the value thresholds of these instruments.

Unfortunately, leading cases from the highest courts of the United Kingdom cannot be discussed. Secondary objectives have never been a central issue in the public procurement case law of any the jurisdictions, although public procurement litigation has been growing considerably over the last few years. The chapter will, however, refer to a number of Government documents on the use of public procurement as a tool to promote social and environmental objectives. While not legally binding, these documents clarify how the executive understands the relevant legal limits and aims to shape procurement practice. However, due to a lack of reliable empirical material, procurement practice regarding secondary objectives cannot be discussed.

The chapter is aimed at providing an overview of the current legal situation on secondary considerations in the laws of the United Kingdom. It will be shown that the limits of using public procurement as an instrument to promote secondary polices are largely based on and meeting the requirements of the relevant EU law.

3. See: www.opsi.gov.uk/si/si200600.htm (accessed in May 2010). SSI 2006/1 at: http://www.opsi.gov.uk/legislation/scotland/ssi2006/20060001.htm (accessed in May 2010); SSI 2006/2 at: http://www.opsi.gov.uk/legislation/scotland/ssi2006/20060002.htm (accessed in May 2010). The OGC web site (www.ogc.gov.uk) also contains associated guidance, including guidance on central purchasing bodies: (2006) 15 PPLR NA82-90. For detailed commentary on implementation for England, Wales, and Northern Ireland see Arrowsmith, 'Implementation of the New EC Procurement Directives and the Alcatel Ruling in England and Wales and Northern Ireland: a Review of the New Legislation and Guidance' (2006) 15 PPLR 86.

## 2 Historical overview

In the past public procurement was used as an instrument to promote secondary considerations in the United Kingdom for a long time.[4] This started in the 19th century with the payment of fair wages to workers employed on government contracts. In the 1970s it even included the use of procurement as a means to reduce sex and race discrimination. The 1980s are seen as a watershed in this context because the general approach changed during those years. This was caused by two important factors. First, the Conservative governments from 1979 to 1997 favoured a value for money approach in public procurement and did not want to use it as a policy tool.[5] Second, the new set of public procurement directives of the early 1990s and the case law of the European Court of Justice was interpreted as largely excluding the possibility to use public procurement as a tool to promote social and environmental objectives. The limitations imposed by EC law became clearer and were increasingly enforced by the European Commission during the 1980s.[6]

For the period before the 1980s, secondary considerations in United Kingdom public procurement law can be subdivided into six broad groups of schemes: rules relating to fair wages, general preference schemes for depressed regions, the wage settlements of the 1970s, contract compliance and contract performance, rules relating to ex-servicemen, prisons and disabled workshops, and even general economic policy.

A formalised policy on fair wages through public procurement in government contracts was first introduced with the 1891 Fair Wages Resolution of the House of Commons and later developed in other instruments.[7] These rules contained fair wages clauses to ensure that in the award of public con-

4. This historical section of the chapter draws heavily on the leading general work on United Kingdom public procurement law, namely Arrowsmith's 2nd edition of *The Law of Public and Utilities Procurement* (Sweet & Maxwell: London, 2nd ed. 2005) hereinafter 'Arrowsmith', and on McCrudden's extensive and detailed monograph *Buying Social Justice: Equality, Government Procurement, and Legal Change* (OUP: 2007), hereinafter 'McCrudden'.
5. Arrowsmith, ibid., at 1226. As pointed out by McCrudden at 334:
'The election of Margaret Thatcher as British Prime Minister in 1979 and the rise of 'Thatcherism' in Britain had profound effects on the debate about the appropriate relationship between procurement regulation and procurement linkages.'
6. Arrowsmith, *supra* note 4, at 1226.
7. Working Hours Resolution of 1909, the Local Government Act 1933, the Sugar (Subsidy) Act 1925, the Sugar Industry (Reorganisation) Act 1936, and the Road Traffic Act 1930.

tracts contracting entities '[made] every effort to secure the payment of wages at a level generally accepted as current for a competent workman in his trade.'[8] This was later extended to other working conditions, including the right to join a trade union in 1946.[9] The policy was not undisputed. The main arguments against it were based on the freedom of contract and free trade. Moreover, Arrowsmith, Bercusson, and Kahn-Freund consider the policy to be largely ineffective due to inadequate enforcement mechanisms.[10] Local authorities followed similar policies, including training and labour-only subcontracting.[11] The Conservative governments of the 1980s favoured free labour markets and pursued a policy of market testing and contracting out. Hence the Fair Wages Resolutions were abolished in 1983. The Local Government Act 1988, which generally severely limited the use of public procurement to promote secondary policies, put an end to the similar policies of local governments.[12]

From the 1930s preference schemes for depressed regions were introduced in the United Kingdom. There was a General Preference Scheme for Depressed Regions in the 1930s, a General Preference Scheme and Special Contracts Preference Scheme to assist 'development areas' in the 1950s,[13] and a Northern Ireland Contract Preference Scheme in the 1970s. McCrudden summarised the contents of these schemes:

> '[They] required that government departments (and certain other public bodies) had to give preference to a tender received from a firm based in one of the eligible areas in cases where such a tender was equal in terms of price, quality, delivery, and other relevant criteria to a tender made by a firm located in a non-qualifying area. [In addition], 25 per cent of an available contract may be offered to firms in development areas in cases where, if the lowest tender was accepted, such firms would not otherwise receive this proportion provided it will not increase the total cost of a contract above that of the lowest tender submitted.'[14]

8. Citation in Arrowsmith, *supra* note 4, at 1240.
9. Arrowsmith, ibid.; McCrudden, *supra* note 4, in detail at 42-63.
10. Arrowmith, *supra* note 4, at 1240 citing Bercusson, *The Fair Wages Resolutions* (Mansell, 1978) and Kahn-Freund, 'Legislation through Adjudication: the Legal Aspects of the Fair Wages Clauses and Recognised Conditions' (1948) 11 *Modern Law Review* 274.
11. *Contract Compliance: the United Kingdom Experience* (Institute of Personnel Management, 1987), at 25-26, as cited by Arrowsmith, ibid., at 1242.
12. *Supra* note 4, at 1241.
13. Arrowsmith, ibid., at 1240.
14. McCrudden, *supra* note 4, at 30-31.

The Northern Ireland Contract Preference Scheme contained a five per cent price preference for bids benefiting employment in Northern Ireland.[15] The preference schemes for depressed regions were abolished in 1991, but a commercial approach was generally followed in public procurement since 1983.[16] While the preference schemes did not fit in with the commercial approach of the Conservative governments, their abolishment or phasing out was also due to the limitations of then EC law and the Government Procurement Agreement of the World Trade Organisation.

A prominent feature of social considerations in public procurement in the history of England and Wales is the policy of contract compliance in the 1980s which 'became a prominent part of local government activity [...] particularly, if not exclusively, among Labour Party controlled local authorities.'[17] Contract compliance involved the attachment of contract conditions which sought to reinforce statutory prohibitions such as race and sex discrimination or safety at work, the attachment of conditions to resist deregulation of central government, the attachment of conditions related to general policy aims, such as Apartheid in South Africa and nuclear weapons, or the attachment of local labour requirements. The Greater London Council and the Inner London Education Authority 1983-1986 were particularly active in this field and served as a model for others.[18] Local authorities often based some of these policies on section 71 of the Race Relations Act 1976[19] The case law on contract compliance concerned the question whether local authorities had the power to adopt such policies under this provision. In *Wheeler v Leicester City Council*[20] a ban of the City of Leicester on a rugby football club for not having done enough to prevent its players from playing in Apartheid South Africa was held 'unreasonable and a misuse of its statutory powers.' In *R v Lewisham LBC, ex p Shell UK Ltd*[21] the local authority decided on the basis

15. Arrowsmith, *supra* note 4, at 1228.
16. Ibid.
17. McCrudden, *supra* note 4, at 337.
18. McCrudden, ibid., at 339-346.
19. Section 71 of the Race Relations Act 1976 provided:
    'Without prejudice to their obligation to comply with any other provision of this Act, it shall be the duty of every local authority to make appropriate arrangements with a view of securing that their various functions are carried out with due regard to the need (a) to eliminate unlawful racial discrimination and (b) to promote equality of opportunity, and good relations between persons of different racial groups.'
20. [1985] AC 1054.
21. [1988] 1 All ER 938.

of section 71 that trade with Shell should stop because of the latter's links with Apartheid South Africa. The Court held that

'[...] though the scope of s.71 of the 1976 act is wide and embraces all the activities of the council, a council cannot use its statutory powers in order to punish a body or person who has done nothing contrary to English law.'

Since the ban was designed to pressure Shell to stop trading with Apartheid South Africa generally, it was not restricted to improve race relations in Lewisham. In addition to this case law, the Local Government Act 1988 basically put an end to the practice of contract compliance.

Related to the contract compliance regime of many local authorities was a contract performance regime of the central Government from 1969. Central government contracting entities inserted requirements into contracts for providers to refrain from unlawful racial discrimination. These contract performance clauses were criticised since there were no attempts to monitor compliance and sanctions had never been imposed.[22]

The use of a procurement to support the disabled and prison workshops also has a tradition in the United Kingdom. This started with ex-service men in the Royal Proclamation of 1919 'King's Roll' which provided for a 'scheme to assist the re-employment of ex-servicemen by appealing to employers to employ a specific quota, normally 5 per cent of the existing workforce'.[23] The subsequent 1926 House of Commons and Lords Resolutions provided:

'[...] it is the duty of the Government in all Government contracts to make provision for the employment to the fullest possible extent for disabled ex-service men, and to this end to confine such contracts, save in exceptional circumstances, to employers enrolled on the King's National Roll'.[24]

The 'appeal for voluntary action [was] reinforced by a substantial inducement in the form of a preference for enrolled firms in the allocation of government contracts.'[25] A compulsory system, however, was not introduced.[26]

22. Carr, *New roads to Equality: Contract Compliance in the United Kingdom* (Fabian Society No.517, 1997), at 9 as cited by Arrowsmith, *supra* note 4, at 1236.
23. McCrudden, *supra* note 4, at 56.
24. *Hansard*, vol 190, col 1830 (16 February 1926).
25. 1943, cmd 6415, para 68, as cited by McCrudden, *supra* note 4, at 57.
26. Ibid.

Moreover, more than 120 factories and workshops approved under the Disabled Persons (Employment) Acts 1944 and 1958 for the provision of employment under special (sheltered) conditions for disabled persons were advantaged in the 'Priority Suppliers Scheme' which ran from 1979 to 1994. This also included the company employing most disabled people 'Remploy' and the Prisons Services Industries and Farms. Generally:

> '[...] registered workshops were given preferential treatment, where they could supply at a commercial rate. This meant that with low-value contracts not put out to tender, departments purchased selectively from Priority suppliers whose products were available on 'commercial terms.'[27]

Where one of these workshops could provide the required good or service it was to be given every opportunity to bid. Contracting authorities should award the contract to the approved workshop if the cost was no greater than the most economically advantageous commercial tender. Moreover, if the approved workshop was not able to compete on price alone there was an 'offer back' policy: the priority supplier was 'offered back' the contract, if he was able to match the lowest offer, a revised offer should be accepted.[28] This policy was abolished in 1994 as it was considered in violation of the then EC Treaty and the EC Procurement Directives.[29] It was replaced by a policy limited to contracts below the thresholds and open to workshops from other Member States.[30]

Finally, public procurement was used as an instrument to promote general economic policy. For example, the White Paper 'The Attack on Inflation' of 1975[31] suggested procurement as one of many instruments to fight inflation: companies who breached the government pay guidelines were blacklisted.[32] Comparable measures have not been taken since the 1970s.

As explained above, the Conservative governments of the 1980s and 1990s largely put an end to the use of public procurement as an instrument to

27. Arrowsmith, *supra* note 4, at 1237.
28. McCrudden, *supra* note 4, at 60.
29. Arrowsmith, *supra* note 4, at 1238.
30. Ibid.
31. Cmd 6151, HMSO 1975.
32. McCrudden, *supra* note 4, at 31 and R. Williams and R Smellie, 'Public Purchasing: An Administrative Cinderella' (1985) 63 *Public Administration* 23-39; Arrowsmith, *supra* note 4, at 1231 citing *inter alia* Daintith, 'Legal Analysis and Economic Policy' (1982) 9 *Journal of Law and Society* 191; Daintith, 'Regulation by Contract: the New Prerogative' [1979] 32 *Current Legal Problems* 41.

promote secondary policies. However, under the Labour governments from 1997 to 2010 there has been a gradual resurgence of procurement as a policy tool, especially in support of environmental policies and the 'sustainability agenda'.[33] For example, the Joint Report on SMEs 2003[34] sees procurement-specific measures relating to SMEs as 'often but one aspect of a broader policy of SME development.' At the level of the central government the framework for using procurement to support environmental objectives forms part of the Government's broader strategy for sustainable development, set out in the 1999 White paper *A better quality of life – a strategy for sustainable development*. This document sets out that with regard to central government the Governments broader strategy for sustainable development should include the use of public procurement to support environmental objectives.[35] However, as the Government pointed out:

33. Arrowsmith, ibid., at 1227. There is a multitude of publications on this issue, see: See: http://www.defra.gov.uk/sustainable/government/publications/index.htm: *Sustainable Development Indicators in Your Pocket*, 2009 edition of the annual publication that measures the UK progress on sustainable development: http://www.-defra.gov.uk/sustainable/government/progress/data-resources/sdiyp. htm; *Securing the Future:* the UK sustainable development strategy (2005): http://www.-defra.gov.uk/sustainable/government/publications/uk-strategy/index. htm; *One Future Different Paths – The UK's shared framework for sustainable development* (2005): http://www.defra.gov.uk/sustainable/government/publications/uk-strategy/frame-work-for-sd.htm. The Devolved Administrations are producing their own strategies: *'Choosing our future: Scotland's Sustainable Development Strategy'* was published in December 2005: http://www.scotland.gov. uk/Topics/ Environment/Sustain-ableDevelopment (all accessed in April 2010). The Welsh National Assembly has a legal duty to develop a Scheme setting out how they will promote sustainable development in exercising all their functions. Their first two Schemes were launched in November 2000 and March 2004. Their programme for putting the new Scheme into effect is set out in their 'Sustainable Development Action Plan', published in October 2004. Northern Ireland's first sustainable development strategy, *'First Steps towards sustainability'*, was published on 9 May 2006 (all web sites accessed in May 2010).
34. Better Regulation Taskforce/Small Business Service, *Government: Supporter and Customer*? (May 2003) at 2.3.1. as cited by Arrowsmith, *supra* note 4, at 1229.
35. Cm 4345, HMSO 1999 on http://www.defra.gov.uk/sustainable/government/ (accessed in May 2010). See also Arrowsmith, ibid., at 1232. See also the Department for Environment, Food, and Rural Affair's *Procuring the Future: Sustainable National Action Plan*, June 2006, at: http://www.defra.gov.uk/sustainable/government/documents/full-document.pdf (accessed in May 2010).

'The mechanisms for implementing this policy are those available within the constraints of EC law: drafting specifications, contract conditions, award criteria ...'[36]

Thus changes in law and policy concerning the use of public procurement as a tool to promote secondary objectives have to stay within the limits set by EU law. Consequently, the implementation of the Public Sector Directive 2004/18/EC and the Utilities Sector Directive 2004/17/EC in the United Kingdom is the starting point for the assessment of the current national regime on secondary considerations in public procurement.

Following the Directives, the 2006 Regulations mentioned above include provisions on disabled and other workshops, the inclusion of social and environmental considerations in finalising the specifications, in the selection of candidates, the award of the contract, and contract performance. In line with the general United Kingdom policy of transposition of procurement directives, the wording of the implementing Regulations 2006 closely follows that of the 2004 Directives. As pointed out in the introduction above, there is currently no authoritative case law on the application of these provisions in the jurisdictions of the United Kingdom.

## 3 Social considerations

Even after the recent implementation of the new Directives, government documents suggest that social considerations are of great importance in public procurement. The *Social Issues in Purchasing Guide*,[37] a 53 pages long guidance document prepared by the Office of Government Commerce (OGC),[38] was published shortly after the entering into force of the 2006 Regulations. It suggests the following twelve relevant social considerations: (1) community benefits, (2) core labour standards, (3) disability equality, (4) employment and training issues, (5) fair trade, (6) gender equality, (7) race equality, (8) small and medium size enterprises, (9) including social enterprises, (10) women's businesses, (11) disabled-owned businesses, and the

36. *Framework for Sustainable Development on the Government Estate* at: http://www.defra.gov.uk/sustainable/government/ (accessed in May 2010). See also Arrowsmith, *supra* note 4, at 1233-1244.
37. OGC, February 2006: http://www.ogc.gov.uk/documents/Social_ Issues_in_Purchasing.pdf (accessed in April 2010).
38. This is an independent office under the Her Majesty's Treasury (the United Kingdom Ministry of Finance), inter alia responsible for national procurement policy including the implementation of the EU Directives, see www.ogc.gov.uk.

voluntary and community sector, as well as (12) workforce skills, including adult basic skills.[39] Social issues in procurement in general and particular aspects of it are also the subject of various other government documents.[40]

Following the implementation of the Public Sector Procurement Directive 2004/18/EC in the UKPCR and the SPCR and of the Utilities Sector Procurement Directive 2004/17/EC in the UKUCR and the SUCR, social considerations can only be taken into account on the basis of the Regulations, which closely follow the requirement of the Directives. Thus there are rules on reserved contracts for supported businesses, supported employment programmes, and supported factories (3.1.), the possibility of taking social considerations into account when defining the subject-matter of the contract (3.2.) and in the technical specifications (3.3.), indirectly in the award of the contract through the rules on abnormally low tenders (3.5.) and in the contract conditions (3.6.). There appears to be no possibility to take social considerations into account at the qualification stage (3.4.). Finally, the Regulations do not apply outside the field of application of the Directive, most notably below the thresholds of the latter. With regard to these contracts contracting authorities appear to retain considerable flexibility in taking social considerations into account (3.7.).

Government documents such as the OGC *Social Issue Purchasing Guide* recognise the limitations set by EU law.[41] Moreover, they emphasise that social considerations must be relevant to the subject-matter of the contract, must be consistent with the government's procurement policy based on value for money, and must be approached from a whole life cycle cost perspective.[42] Hence for the OGC there is no conflict between social considerations and value for money. The earlier 'can be consistent with achieving' the latter, a position that also includes the environmental considerations discussed below.[43] It is submitted that what emanates especially from the *Social Issues*

39. Ibid., at 3.
40. OGC document *Make Equality Count*, http://www.ogc.gov.uk/documents/ Equality_Brochure.pdf, OGC 2008 (accessed in April 2010); OGC *Skills through Public Procurement*, http://www.ogc.gov.uk/documents/ Promoting_ skills_ through_ public_procurement.pdf, OGC 2009 (accessed April 2010); OGC document *Guidance on Fair Trade*, http://www.ogc.gov.uk/documents/ Guidance_on_Fair_and_Ethical_Trading.pdf, OGC 2008 (accessed in April 2010).
41. OGC, *Social Issues in Purchasing Guide supra* note 38, at 3; OGC *Government and Fair Trade*, ibid., at 2; *Skills through Public Procurement*, ibid., at 6.
42. *Social Issues in Purchasing Guide*, ibid.; *Government and Fair Trade, supra* note 41, at 2; *Skills through Public Procurement, supra* note 41, at 6.
43. OGC, *Social Issues in Purchasing Guide, supra* note 38, at 4.

*Purchasing Guide* published during the month right after the entering into force of the new Regulations is that the Government only wants to pursue social considerations within the limits of EU procurement law and only without compromising value for money. The reserved contracts discussed under the next heading below are to a certain extent an exception to this basic policy.

### 3.1 Reserved contracts

Following the introduction of this possibility in the 2004 EU Directives, the 2006 United Kingdom and Scottish Procurement Regulations now contain special rules on reserved contracts. For example Regulation 7 (2) of both UKPCR and SPCR read:

> 'A contracting authority may reserve the right to participate in a public contract award procedure, framework agreement or dynamic purchasing system to economic operators which operate supported factories, supported businesses or supported employment programmes.'

Regulation 10 UKUCR and SUCR contain similar provisions. On behalf of the central Government the OGC has produced guidance on these rules.[44] The institutions these contracts are reserved for, i.e. supported factories, supported businesses or supported employment programmes, are defined in Regulations 7 (1) UKPCR and SPCR and 10 (1) UKUCR and SUCR respectively:

> ''supported business' means a service where more than 50 % of the workers are disabled persons who by reason of the nature or severity of their disability are unable to take up work in the open labour market and 'supported businesses' shall be interpreted accordingly;
>
> 'supported employment programme' means a scheme under which work is provided for disabled persons and where more than 50 % of the workers so supported are disabled persons who by reason of the nature or severity of their disability are unable to take up work in the open labour market [...]; and
>
> 'supported factory' means an establishment where more than 50 % of the workers are disabled persons who by reason of the nature or severity of their disability are unable to take up work in the open labour market [...].'

44. Supported Factories and Business: OGC Guidance on reserved contracts in the new Procurement Regulations (January 2006), http://www.ogc.gov.uk/documents/ Supported_Factories_Businesses.pdf (accessed in May 2010).

The United Kingdom term 'supported employment programme' corresponds to the EU term 'sheltered employment programme'.[45] In the United Kingdom these are usually operated through the Department of Work and Pensions' WORKSTEP programme, which provides individually tailored and flexible support for people with disabilities at the workplace.[46] A disabled person is defined by Section 1 of the Disability Discrimination Act 1995 as a person with

> 'a physical or mental impairment which has a substantial and long-term adverse effect on his or her ability to carry out normal day-to-day activities.'[47]

However, being classed as one of the three types of economic operators favoured by the reserved contracts scheme does not lead to an automatic contract award: 'Contracts cannot [...] be reserved for a specific organisation.' Hence the term 'reserved contracts' used in the Regulations is slightly misleading. The favoured operators still have to compete in tendering procedures as explicitly provided in Regulation 7 (3) UKPCR and SPCR:

> 'Where a contracting authority has reserved the right to participate in a public contract, framework agreement or dynamic purchasing system in accordance with paragraph (2), it shall follow the contract award procedures set out in these Regulations.'[48]

This clarifies what appears to be the position under Directive 2004/18/EC.[49] What is envisaged is a competition between reserved contract providers at the end of which the tenders are assessed on a value for money basis with the contract being awarded to the tender offering best value for money.[50] Hence value for money is not replaced by the social objectives of the reserved contracts scheme. The Regulations rather aim to reconcile the contradictory objectives. The *OGC Guidance Supported Factories and Businesses* 2009 appears to be aware of the contradiction between the objectives but advocates

45. Ibid., at paragraph 3.4.
46. OGC Guidance, *supra* note 45, at paragraphs 3.4. and 3.5.
47. Schedule 1 of the Disability Discrimination Act 1995 contains provisions, which supplement the definition of disability in Section 1, for example it provides definitions for impairment and disfigurement, etc.
48. Regulation 7 (4) continues:
'(4) When seeking offers in relation to a public contract, a framework agreement or dynamic purchasing system, a contracting authority shall specify in the contract notice if it is using the approach referred to in paragraph (2).'
49. On the Directives: Arrowsmith, *supra* note 4, at 1238.
50. OGC Guidance *Supported Factories and Businesses*, *supra* note 45, at paragraph 5.1.

that 'Value for money and the use of reserved contracts can go hand in hand.'[51] Contracting authorities should compare value for money considerations such as quality, price and the capacity potential of reserved contract providers with the rest of the market and against previous similar contracts.[52] However, as part of this comparison, they should also 'bear in mind the wider benefits to society where these are relevant to the procurement process.'[53] This means that both costs and wider social benefits should be taken into consideration. While it is appreciated that it is not always possible to place a market value on some of these wider social benefits, they should be considered in terms of the actual benefits that they bring against any costs. Benefits could include:

'– Contributing to the wider Government commitment to enable greater access to employment opportunities for disabled people to help achieve equality for disabled people by 2025;
– Increasing the diversity of the public sector supplier base to help to deliver better public goods and services that meet the needs of those who use them;
– Drawing on the wider pool of talent and skills in the workforce that are currently under utilised;
– Increased social inclusion and interaction of disabled people in the labour market and their communities.'[54]

The *OGC Guidance* continues by arguing that because the beneficiaries of reserved contracts often operated within niche markets their specialised products could often be reflected in the quality of the goods they produce. Because of this specialised nature many of these enterprises were flexible in what they can offer to contracting authorities and thus doing business with them 'is often a cost effective way of contracting'.[55]

This line of argument mixes value for money considerations and social policy considerations, such as employment opportunities for the disabled, diversity, and social inclusion in a way which is only partly convincing. If the award of contracts to supported businesses represented value for money, then these businesses would win tender competitions against non-supported businesses in a competitive market based on economic criteria, without the reserved contracts tool being necessary. The argument, that including busi-

51. Ibid., at paragraph 8.3.
52. OGC Guidance *Supported Factories and Businesses*, *supra* note 45, at paragraph 8.3.
53. Ibid.
54. OGC Guidance *Supported Factories and Businesses*, *supra* note 45, at paragraph 8.4.
55. Ibid, at paragraph 8.5.

nesses that have been overlooked in the past can widen the supplier base and thus increase competition and improve value for money in government contracts makes perfect sense. However, the *OGC Guidance* appears to gloss over the basic conflict underlining the reserved contracts scheme and the presence of most social considerations in public procurement generally: the benefits of social considerations such as diversity and social inclusion are not fully quantifiable for value for money purposes; it is difficult to put a price on it. The *OGC Guidance* is of course partly designed to encourage the use of the reserved contract tool by contracting authorities. Moreover, it is argued here that the policy behind the scheme is worthwhile and might well reach its objectives. Finally, in many cases the costs with regard to value for money might be lower than expected. However, the reserved contracts scheme artificially limits competition by excluding tenderers who do not qualify as supported businesses, thereby in most cases inevitably compromising value for money. Many if not most of these institutions work less efficiently and this is precisely the reason why they are privileged through the reserved contracts instrument. It can be assumed that most contracting authorities in the United Kingdom will know that and not easily believe the *OGC Guidance* that 'Value for money and the use of reserved contracts can go hand in hand.' If they use the reserved contract tool they will champion the relevant social objectives over value for money. If this will happen very often, then the introduction of the reserved contracts scheme represents a small revolution against the dominant value for money gospel in the United Kingdom. The historical overview above shows that this would not be without precedent in the legal history of Great Britain. The main change brought about by the 2006 Regulations is the application of the reserved contract regime to contracts above the thresholds.

### 3.2 Definition of the subject-matter of the contract

Even within the field of application of the EU Directives and United Kingdom and Scotland Regulations, contracting entities remain largely free regarding the decision on what to buy. This decision is closely related but separate from that on technical specifications which have to be defined at the beginning of open and restricted tendering procedures and which are subject to Treaty, Directive, and Regulation requirements. The *OGC Principles: Social Issues in Procurement*[56] adequately call this 'pre-procurement, when consid-

56. OGC 2008, http://www.ogc.gov.uk/documents/Policy_principles_-_Social_Issues.pdf (accessed in April 2010), at 4. This approach is also in line with the EU Directives, see: Arrowsmith, 'Application of EC Treaty and Directives to horizontal poli-

ering the need, approaches and considering the market.' In contrast, the definition of the specifications already forms part of the procurement process for open and restricted procedures.

Both the *OGC Principles: Social Issues in Procurement*[57] and the OGC document *Buy and Make a Difference: How to Address Social Issues in Public Procurement*[58] suggest considering social issues 'when indentifying the need and considering the market. The earlier points out: 'Think about social issues from the outset.' The case studies provided suggest awareness of the social agenda and the legislative requirements such as the Race Relations Act, the Disability Act, and the Sex Discrimination Act, testing the affordability of social considerations, and measures ensuring the openness to bodies such as SMEs, social enterprises, and Black, Asian and Minority Ethnic (BAME) owned businesses as the means to consider social aspects in the pre-procurement definition of the subject-matter of the contract. The only more concrete example given is a service specifically catering for ethnic minorities, unfortunately without giving further details. This makes it somewhat difficult to see the dividing line between pre-procurement decision of the subject-matter of the contract and the drawing of technical specifications discussed under the next heading below. Not surprisingly, the OCG documents do not suggest any activities that would violate the requirements of the EU Directives or the United Kingdom or Scotland Regulations.

### 3.3 Technical specifications

According to Arrowsmith, the technical specifications remain '[t]he main approach used in the UK' for supporting many secondary objectives, in particular the environmental objectives discussed below but also including certain social objectives.[59] Regulation 9 UKPCR reads:

> '(1) In this regulation – [...] 'technical specifications' means
> (a) in the case of a public services contract or a public supply contract, a specification in a document defining the required characteristics of materials, goods or services, [...] , design for all requirements (including accessibility for disabled persons) [...]

cies: a critical review', in Arrowsmith and Kunzlik, 'Social and Environmental Policies' in *EC Procurement Law: New Directive and New Directions*, *supra* note 1, at 198; McCrudden, *supra* note 4, at 522-524.

57. OGC 2008, ibid., at 1.
58. http://www.ogc.gov.uk/documents/Social_Issues_in_Public_Procurement.pdf (accessed in April 2010) at 5.
59. Arrowsmith, *supra* note 4, at 1243.

(b) in the case of a public works contract, the totality of the technical prescriptions contained, in particular, in the contract documents, defining the characteristics required of the work, works, materials or goods, which permits the work, works, materials or goods to be described in a manner such that it fulfils the use for which it is intended by the contracting authority and these characteristics shall include – (i) [...] design for all requirements (including accessibility for disabled persons [...].'

The design of all users and accessibility for disabled persons considerations are reiterated in Regulation 9 (3) UKPCR which provides:

'(3) When laying down technical specifications in accordance with paragraph (2), a contracting authority shall, wherever possible, take into account accessibility criteria for disabled persons or the suitability of the design for all users. [...]"

Regulation 12 UKUCR, Regulation 9 SPCR, and Regulation 12 SUCR contain provisions with exactly the same wording. Hence it could be said that, based on the wording of the Regulations, in compliance with the requirements of the Treaty on the Functioning of the European Union (TFEU) and Procurement Directives,[60] the possibilities to promote social objectives through technical specifications are actually very limited indeed. Only accessibility criteria for disabled persons represent an important exception.

The OGC document *Buy and Make a Difference: How to Address Social Issues in Public Procurement*[61] suggests wider possibilities to use social considerations in technical specifications:

'Social considerations can be a core requirement and reflected in the specifications provided it is central to the subject of the procurement and consistent with the public procurement regulations.'[62]

However, the example following this statement suggests that the statement refers to the pre-procurement definition of the subject-matter of the contract, a stage where social considerations may be taken into account as explained above, rather than technical specifications which form part of the procurement process for open and restricted procedures. Moreover, the wording of the Regulations and EU law do not back such a wider use of social considerations in technical specifications, but a rather limited use to promote design for

60. See also: Weber, 'Development promotion as a secondary policy in public procurement' (2009) 4 PPLR 171, at 193.
61. *Buy and Make a Difference, supra* note 59, at 7.
62. Ibid.

all users and accessibility of disabled persons. Nevertheless, the OGC continues:

> 'It is also possible to describe specifications in terms of performance/ functional requirements and to specify production processes provided, in both cases, that they are relevant, if in doubt, seek legal advice.'[63]

The reservation at the end of this statement indicates that the OGC does recognise the difficulty to draft such specifications in a way consistent with the Regulations and EU law. This is reiterated by the following sentence of the statement:

> 'Any social requirement reflected in the specification should be transparent and should not discriminate against suppliers, such as SMEs or those from outside the UK.'

The three examples following this statement are either not clearly referring to social considerations or not explaining how the specifications should accommodate the social consideration. One of the examples refers to a police service procurement contract for the supply of body armour in which the specifications require the contractor to accommodate the different requirements of men and women, including different requirements of ethnic minority men and women. However, it is submitted that technical specifications for equipment which is suitable for women and minority employees are not using the technical specifications as a means to promote social considerations, if the entity has women and minority employees it needs to equip. These specifications simply respond to the identified need of the entity. They do not use the procurement function for social purposes. If the equipment is only suitable for white and Christian men, it is simply not suitable for parts of the workforce thus not providing the entity with what it needs to operate. Providing the entity with what it needs to operate, however, is the primary and not a secondary function of public and utilities procurement. The design for all users and accessibility for disabled persons considerations which are actually expressly accommodated in the Regulations and EU law are similar. If, for example, some of the users of a public building and service are disabled, then a building or service which does only provide access to able bodied persons would not provide the entity with what it needs to operate. Thus these are considerations related to the subject-matter of the contract and not social considerations *strictu sensu*. The disabled access to a building, for example, is akin to the re-

63. *Buy and Make a Difference, supra* note 59, at 7.

quirement to have windows letting in air and light or a requirement to have stairs to allow the access of able bodied persons. A building with windows and stairs will also be more expensive than one without. The windows and stairs will cost extra money just as a ramp for wheelchair users, for example. Hence allowing disabled persons access to a public building or service is referring to social public services not to the use of the procurement function to further social objectives.

In this context it might be helpful to introduce a differentiation. Public procurement is only used to promote social considerations when this affects competition and value for money, as in the case of reserved contracts discussed above. Design for all users and accessibility for disabled persons requirements in the technical specifications make the procurement more expensive but do not affect competition. All tenderers have to meet these requirements since otherwise their tender will be rejected as non-compliant. The same point can be made about many environmental features of a contract, as will be discussed below. However, as some of the other chapters in this volume show, this confusion of social procurement and social public services emanates from the Directives and is not a specifically British problem.

### 3.4 Qualification

The United Kingdom and Scotland Regulations do not allow social considerations to be used as a qualification criterion. Regulations 23 UKPCR and SPRCR and Regulations 26 UKUCR and the SUCR do not contain social considerations as qualification criteria, unless the failure to pay social security contributions as a de-selection criterion in Regulations 23 (4) (f) UKPCR and SPCR and 26 (5) (f) UKUCR and SUCR is considered a social consideration.

The OGC document *Buy and Make a Difference*[64] is also cautious on the issue of qualification and points out that the Regulations 'contained an exhaustive list of references and evidence that potential suppliers can be required to provide.' However, it continues:

> 'If a contract requires specific know-how in the 'social' field, specific experience may be used as a criterion to prove the suitability of potential suppliers in regard to technical or professional ability. Contracting authorities can ask potential suppliers for relevant evi-

64. *Supra* note 59.

dence of technical and/or professional ability, for example, language skills or cultural awareness.'[65]

This statement is followed by a positive and a negative example. The first example, where the skills of the staff involved in the contract are used as a qualification criterion, is not a specific social consideration case at all. The skills of the relevant staff are a legitimate selection criterion related to the subject-matter of the contract, even if it relates to, for example, knowledge of a minority language or experience in caring for disabled persons. It does not relate to the use of the procurement function to promote social considerations. In contrast, the second and negative example in which the manner 'in which imbalances in job applicants and employees according to gender, ethnicity and disability' are used as a criterion for the selection of bidders, is a clear case of a specific social consideration, but clearly illegal under both the Regulations and EU law. What remains unclear in the OGC document is how to legally use the procurement function to promote social considerations. As outlined above, the Regulations and EU Law do not allow social considerations to be taken into account when they are not related to the subject-matter of the contract. Hence, as stated in the opening sentence of this section above, the Regulations do not allow social considerations to be used as a qualification criterion.

### 3.5 Award criteria

Social considerations do not feature as award criteria in the United Kingdom and Scotland Regulations. Regulation 30 of both UKPRC and SPCR read:

'(1) Subject to regulation 18(27) and to paragraphs (6) and (9) of this regulation, a contracting authority shall award a public contract on the basis of the offer which—
  (a) is the most economically advantageous from the point of view of the contracting authority; or
  (b) offers the lowest price.'

Regulation 30 of both UKUCR and SUCR contain a similar provision. The criteria linked to the subject-matter of the contract which the contracting authority or entity shall use to determine that an offer is the most economically advantageous are listed in Regulation 30 (2). They do not contain social considerations.

65. Ibid., at 8.

However, according to Regulations 30 (6) a contracting authority or utility may reject an offer for a public or utilities contract which is abnormally low. In assessing whether an offer is abnormally low, Regulation 30 (7) (d) also allows the contracting authority to take 'compliance with the provisions relating to employment protection and working conditions in force at the place where the contract is performed' into account. Thus a lack of compliance with these labour law standards can lead to a tender being considered abnormally low and therefore rejected at the award stage. This rule on abnormally low tenders complies with the requirements of the Directives; see for example Article 55 (1) (d) Directive 2004/18/EC. However, the use of the abnormally low tool to promote employment protection and working conditions carries a litigation risk. This litigation risk will deter contracting officers and limit the use of this tool in practice. On the other hand there have been no relevant court cases yet.

Notwithstanding the limited possibilities to accommodate social criteria at the award stage based on an interpretation of the wording of the Regulations and the EU law they are based on, the OGC document *Buy and Make a Difference: How to Address Social Issues in Public Procurement*[66] suggests a wider use. First, as with reserved contracts above, social considerations appear to be understood as economically quantifiable in certain circumstances and thus also a value for money consideration:

> 'Criteria involving social considerations may be used to determine the most economically advantageous tender where they provide an economic advantage for the contracting authority which is linked to the product or service which is the subject-matter of the contract.'[67]

This would need more detailed explanation: which social considerations can provide an economic advantage linked to the product or service and under which circumstances? The basic conflict between value for money and social considerations appears to be glossed over by this unexplained statement, possibly slightly misleading contracting entities on the issue of social considerations at the award stage.

Another role for social considerations at the award stage arises, according to the OGC document *Buy and Make a Difference*, when two tenders are economically equal:

66. *Supra* note 59, at 9.
67. Ibid.

'Where there are two or more bids which are equal on value for money grounds, it is possible to use 'additional social award criteria' to determine between them [...]'[68]

The OGC recognises both the fact that this would be quite a rare occurrence and that contracting authorities applying this secondary social evaluation after the economic evaluation are risking litigation:

'[...] legal advice should be sought first, as it is very rare for bids to be equal in this way.'

Thus, while this technique would be legal under the Regulations and EU law, it is submitted that meeting the requirement of two economically equal bids and the high risk of litigation make it unlikely to be used in practice.

### 3.6 Contract conditions

The accommodation of social considerations in the contract conditions has gained importance in recent years as it is considered one of the few remaining mechanisms legally possible under the Directives.[69] The term used in the United Kingdom is also 'social clauses', which the OGC document *Buy and Make a Difference* defines as: 'conditions relating to the performance of the contract which address social issues.'[70] The same document lists conditions regarding on-site vocational training, the employment of people experiencing difficulty achieving integration and the fight against unemployment as examples.[71] Regulation 39 UKPCR and SUCR read:

'(1) A contracting authority may stipulate conditions relating to the performance of a public contract, provided that those conditions are compatible with Community law and are indicated in –
   (a) the contract notice and the contract documents; or
   (b) the contract documents.
(2) The conditions referred to in paragraph (1) may, in particular, include social and environmental considerations.'

68. *Buy and Make a Difference, supra* note 59, at 9.
69. Arrowsmith, *supra* note 4, at 1249. See also: *Buy and Make a Difference*, ibid., at 10, referring to 'a wide range of possibilities for determining the contract clauses on social issues.' Weber, *supra* note 61, at 197, emphasises the wider range of possibilities to accommodate social considerations in EU law with the fact that the Directives do not regulate the execution stage of public contracts.
70. *Supra* note 59.
71. *Buy and Make a Difference*, ibid., at 10.

Regulations 36 UKUCR and SUCR contain similar provisions. Hence (1) compatibility with Community law and (2) stipulation in the contract notice or documents are requirements for the use of social clauses. *Buy and Make a Difference* clarifies and elaborates these requirements: the clauses have to (3) relate to the performance of the individual contract in question, (4) be relevant, (5) be able to be met by whoever wins the tender from the time at which the contract starts, (6) must not be disguised technical specifications, selection, or award criteria, and (7) not represent direct or indirect discrimination against foreign or national tenderers.[72] Moreover, (8) contract clauses 'that require changes to the organisation, structure, or policy of a supplier in another Member State might be considered discriminatory or a barrier to trade.' These are simply requirements that repeat and elaborate the basic requirements relating to the performance of the contract and the compatibility with EU law. The compatibility with EU law is also featuring prominently in the example case study provided in the document, which describes a contract clause requiring 10 per cent of the works to be completed by new entrants to the labour market. This would be proportionate in contrast to a similar 50 per cent requirement.[73] Furthermore, (9) blanket clauses should be avoided since they may be considered burdensome and deter suppliers. Finally, (10):

> 'Value for money should be maintained, contract clauses should be supported by the benefits they accrue set against the cost of achieving them.'[74]

Similar to the other stages discussed above where consistency between value for money and social objectives is required, this could be interpreted as glossing over the basic conflict between these objectives. Social clauses will cause extra costs and therefore compromise value for money. The social benefits of including social conditions will often not be convincingly quantifiable so as to reconcile them with value for money. However, value for money through competition is still achieved, since all tenderers have to meet the requirements defined in the social clauses. Overall, in contrast to the other possible stages of the procurement process, the inclusion of social objectives in the

72. Ibid.
73. *Buy and Make a Difference*, *supra* note 59, at 10: '10 % of the person-weeks required to complete all of the works is to be delivered by new entrants that have an apprenticeship, trainee or employment contract with the contractor or subcontractor and are engaged in a trainee programme that is accepted by the employer.'
74. *Buy and Make a Difference*, ibid., at 10.

contract conditions appears to be the safest way to do it, with a relatively small risk of litigation.

The old *Standard General Terms and Conditions of Contract,* clause B2.1 issued by the OGC require providers to refrain from unlawful discrimination on any ground in employment, whether on the basis of race, gender, religion, disability, sexual orientation or otherwise.[75] This reflects the extension of general anti-discrimination legislation to cover discrimination on these grounds.[76] The new *Model Terms and Conditions of Contracts for Goods* of November 2009,[77] clause D3.1, also issued by the OGC, require:

> 'The Contractor shall not unlawfully discriminate either directly or indirectly on such grounds as race, colour, ethnic or national origin, disability, sex or sexual orientation, religion or belief, or age and without prejudice to the generality of the foregoing the Contractor shall not unlawfully discriminate within the meaning and scope of the Sex Discrimination Act 1975, the Race Relations Act 1976, the Equal Pay Act 1970, the Disability Discrimination Act 1995, the Employment Equality (Sexual Orientation) Regulations 2003, the Employment Equality (Religion or Belief) Regulations 2003, the Employment Equality (Age) Regulations 2006, the Equality Act 2006, the Human Rights Act 1998 or other relevant or equivalent legislation, or any statutory modification or re-enactment thereof.'

The new *Model Terms and Conditions of Contracts for Services* of November 2009,[78] clause D3.1 has the same wording. The Guidance provided by the OGC in 2010 explains that a new Equality and Human Rights Commission[79] will bring together the powers of its three predecessors[80] as well as more powers to enforce legislation.[81] The problem with these clauses is that bidders

75. General Terms and Conditions of Contract, B2.1 issued by the OGC, available at www.ogc.gov.uk as part of the Successful Delivery Toolkit. The Employment Equality (Sexual Orientation) Regulations 2003 and the Employment Equality (Religion or Belief) Regulations 2003 have introduced prohibitions on discrimination in employment, vocational training and pension schemes on grounds of sexual orientation, religion and belief.
76. Arrowmith, *supra* note 4, at 1236.
77. Available at: http://www.ogc.gov.uk/documents/Model_Goods_Contract_Final_Nov_2009(1).DOC (accessed in April 2010).
78. Available at: http://www.ogc.gov.uk/documents/Model_Services_Contract_Final_Nov_2009.DOC (accessed in April 2010).
79. Website: http://www.equalityhumanrights.com. (accessed in May 2010)
80. Commission for Racial Equality, Disability Rights Commission, and the Equal Opportunities Commission.
81. For goods available at: http://www.ogc.gov.uk/documents/Goods_Guidance_Final_Nov_2009.pdf, at 12; for services at: http://www.ogc.gov.uk/documents/Services_Guidance_Final_Nov_2009.pdf, at 15 (accessed in April 2010).

may commit to these conditions without either the ability or the intention to abide by them. Thus the crucial question is if and how these requirements are enforced in practice. In the Fair and Equal Treatment Order (Northern Ireland) 1998[82] debarment from future contracts through the Northern Ireland Equality Commission is one sanction for non-compliance.[83] However, this regime has to be seen in the rather special context of the history of sectarian conflict in Northern Ireland and a general policy to overcome it. This context does not apply to the other parts of the United Kingdom.

The *Model Contracts Terms and Conditions of Contracts (for Goods and Services* respectively) do not contain any immediate sanctions. According to condition D3.2 contractors shall take all reasonable steps to secure the observance of clause D3.1 by all Staff. In the new *Model Terms and Conditions of Contracts for Services* 2009, the usual 'remedies in the event of inadequate performance' (clauses F.5) could be used in theory to enforce clause D3.1, including partial or complete termination (clauses H.2). However, there is no evidence on whether these rather drastic measures are used to enforce the anti-discrimination clause in practice. Hence these contract clauses might suffer from the same problems as the contract compliance regime applied from 1969 and discussed in the historical overview above – that there are no attempts to monitor compliance and that no sanctions are ever imposed. The clause will be mainly effective as a reminder and emphasis of the general anti-discrimination legislation. However, the clause is made part of government contracts and thus subject to the same enforcement mechanisms as any other part of the contract, at least in theory. Hence to a certain extent the policy makers have done their work.

### 3.7 Outside the field of application of the Directives and Regulations

A considerable part of the procurement activities of United Kingdom procurement authorities and entities is conducted outside the field of application of the Regulations and Directives, most notably below their contract value thresholds. Since no specific binding rules apply, contracting entities retain

82. Fair and Equal Treatment (Northern Ireland) Order 1998, SI 1998/3162 (N.I. 21) as amended, in particular by the Fair and Equal Treatment (Amendment) Regulations (Northern Ireland) 2003, Statutory Rule 2003 No. 520, as cited by Arrowsmith, *supra* note 4, at 1237.
83. Ibid. See also: McCrudden, 'Country Legal and Policy Review for SRRP in Northern Ireland' (March 2008), *European Commission Study on Social Considerations in Public Procurement*, 2008, at: http://ec.europa.eu/social/main.jsp?catId=331&langId=en&newsId=417&furtherNews=yes (accessed April 2010).

considerable flexibility, although the rules of the TFEU still apply to these contracts. The case law of the European Court of Justice[84] and the Interpretative Communication[85] issued by the European Commission based on that case law provide guidance on how to promote social considerations in the context of these contracts. The basic rule is that the TFEU principles of non-discrimination, equal treatment, and transparency have to be observed.

According to the OGC's *Guidance on Reserved Contracts in the Procurement Regulations*[86] a similar approach to sheltered programmes within the field of application of the Directives and Regulations can be applied for below the threshold contracts, provided reserving such a contract can be justified on public policy grounds and all other European Union principles are observed.[87] The *Guidance* also suggests publication of such a contract on the United Kingdom government portal www.supply2gov.uk. This approach ap-

84. Requirements for contracts outside the field of application of the Directives have been formulated by the Court of Justice. A selection: Case C-76/81, *Transporoute et Travaux SA* v. *Ministère des traveaux publics* [1982] ECR 417; Case C-263/85, *Commission* v. *Italy* [1991] ECR I-2457; Case C-45/87, *Commission* v. *Ireland* ('Dundalk') [1988] ECR 4929; Case C-3/88, *Commission* v. *Italy* ('Re Data Processing') [1989] ECR 4035; [1991] CMLR 115; Case C-/21/88, *Du Pont de Nemours Italiana* v. *Unita Sanitara Locale di Carara* [1990] ECR 889; Case C-11389, *Rush Portuguesa* v. *Office national d'immigration* [1990] ECR I-1417; Case C-234/89, *Commission* v. *Denmark* ('Storebaelt'), *supra* note 27; C-360/89, *Commission* v. *Italy* [1992] ECR I-3401; Case C-272/91, *Commission* v. *Italy* ('Lottomatica') [1992] ECR I-3929; Case C-87/94, *Commission* v. *Belgium* ('Walloon Buses') [1996] ECR I-2043; Case C-359/93, *Commission* v. *The Netherlands* ('UNIX') *supra* note 27; Case C-275/98, *Unitron Scandinavia* [1999] ECR I-8291; Case C-324/98, *Telaustria* [2000] ECR I-10745; Case C-470/99, *Universale Bau AG* [2002] ECR I-11617; Case C-59/00, *Bent Mousten Vestergaard* v. *Spøttrup Boligselskab*, *supra* note 27; Case C-358/00, *Buchhändler Vereinigung*, [2002] ECR I-4685; Case C-231/03, *Coname*; [2005] ECR I-7287; Case C-234/03, *Contse and others*, [2005] ECR I-9315; Case C-264/03, *Commission* v. *France*, [2005] ECR I-8831; Case C-358/03, *Parking Brixen*, [2004] ECR I-12055; Case C-535/03, *Commission* v. *Italy*, [2006] ECR I-2689.
85. *Commission Interpretative Communication on the Community law applicable to contracts not or not fully subject to the provisions of the Public Procurement Directives*, 1 August 2006, OJ [2006] C-179/02. See also: Trybus, '*Public Contracts in European Union internal market law*', and Craig and Trybus, '*Public Contracts: England and Wales*'in Nogouellou and Stelkens (eds.) *Traité de droit comparé des contrats publics/Comparative Law on Public Contracts Treatise* (Bruylant: Brussels, 2010), forthcoming.
86. January 2009: http://www.ogc.gov.uk/documents/Supported_Factories_Businesses (1).pdf (accessed in April 2010).
87. Ibid. at 8.

pears sensible and in compliance with the requirements of EU law.[88] The Directives allow the instrument of reserved contracts even for contracts above the thresholds and according to the case law of the European Court of Justice these contracts do not have to be published in the Official Journal but can be published on a national web site. This is important since the majority of the relevant contracts will have a value below the thresholds. As explained in the historical overview above, the United Kingdom had a regime for sheltered programmes for contracts below the thresholds of the Directives and Regulations in place since 1994.

Overall, the use of public procurement for contracts below the thresholds of the Regulations will be legal at least within the limits in which they are allowed for contracts above the thresholds. Going beyond these limits carries a certain litigation risk, since the principles of the TFEU have to be observed. However, this litigation risk might be reduced by the low value of these contracts. Finally, as pointed out above, there have been no cases on social considerations in the British public procurement law generally, which puts all litigation risks into perspective.

## 4 Environmental considerations

Similar to the social considerations discussed above, Government documents suggest that environmental considerations are of great importance in public procurement. The June 2009 OGC document *Environmental Sustainability* informs central Government departments of the Government's policy on environmental issues in public procurement.[89] This policy requires departments to seek to promote sustainable development activities through procurement. Five environmental priorities are defined as mandatory for central Government departments 'to deliver through their procurement spend'. These are: (1) contributions to the Sustainable Operations on the Government Estate (SOGE)[90] and commitments (including the Sustainable Procurement Action Plan Commitments), (2) always buying products that at least comply with

88. See also Arrowsmith, 'Implementation', *supra* note 3, at 127-128.
89. OGC, http://www.ogc.gov.uk/documents/Environmental_Sustainabilityv2.pdf, (accessed in April 2010).
90. Department for Environment, Food and Rural Affairs, http://www.defra.gov.uk/sustainable/government/gov/estates/index.htm#sustainableprocurement, (accessed in April 2010).

mandatory environmental standards,[91] (3) buying timber and timber products from legal and sustainable or Forest Law Enforcement Governance and Trade sources only,[92] (4) buying low emission cars,[93] and (5) considering the energy efficiency of products required by the Energy Services Directive.[94] Environmental issues in procurement in general and particular aspects of it are also the subject of various other government documents.[95]

However, following the 2006 implementation of the 2004 Directives in the United Kingdom and Scotland, above their thresholds, environmental considerations can only be taken into account on the basis of the implementing Regulations. These Regulations closely follow the requirement of the Directives. There are possibilities in taking environmental considerations into account when defining the subject-matter of the contract (3.1.) and in the technical specifications (4.2.), and in the contract conditions (4.5.). There appear to be only very limited possibilities to do this at the qualification stage (4.3.) or the award stage (4.4.). Finally, again, flexibility exists as the Regulations do not apply outside the field of application of the Directives, most notably below their thresholds (4.6.).

Government documents such as the 2009 OGC's *Buy Green and Make a Difference* and *Social Issues in Purchasing Guide* recognise the limitations

91. Department for Environment, Food, and Rural Affairs, http://www.defra.gov.uk/sustainable/government/advice/public/buying/index.htm, (accessed in April 2010).
92. Central Point for Timber Procurement, http://www.cpet.org.uk//uk-government-timber-procurement-policy, (accessed in April 2010).
93. See the 'Energy White Paper' of the Department of Transport: http://www.dft.gov.uk/pgr/scienceresearch/technology/transportewp, (accessed in April 2010).
94. Directive 2006/32/EC of the European Parliament and of the Council of 5 April 2006 on energy end-use efficiency and energy services and repealing Council Directive 93/76/EEC, OJ [2006] L-114/64.
95. See: OGC, *Sustainable Operations on the Government Estate Targets: 2008/9 Guidance*, OGC 2008, http://www.ogc.gov.uk/documents/SOGE_Guidance.pdf (accessed in April 2010); OGC, *Buy Green and Make a Difference: How to Address Environmental Issues in Public procurement,* OGC 2008, http://www.ogc.gov.uk/documents/Environmental_Issues.pdf (accessed in April 2010); OGC, *Top Quartile Guidance 2010: Procuring Buildings for the Government Estate in the Top Quartile of Energy Performance*, OGC 2009, http://www.ogc.gov.uk/documents/tq_Guidance_2010.pdf (accessed in April 2010); OGC and DEFRA, *Joint Note on Environmental Issues in Purchasing*, OGC and Department for Environment, Food, and Rural Affairs, October 2003, http://www.ogc.gov.uk/documents/Environmental_Issues_In_Purchasing.pdf (accessed in April 2010); OGC, *Considering Energy Efficiency in Procurement: Guidance Notes*, OGC 2009, http://www.ogc.gov.uk/documents/ESD_-_Guidance.pdf (accessed in April 2010).

set by EU law.[96] Moreover, they emphasise that environmental considerations must be relevant to the subject-matter of the contract, must be consistent with the government's procurement policy based on value for money, and must be approached from a whole life cycle cost perspective.[97] Hence for the Government there is no conflict between environmental considerations and value for money, the earlier 'can be consistent with achieving' the latter.[98] Again, what emanates especially from the *Social Issues in Purchasing Guide*, published during the month right after the entering into force of the new Regulations, is that the Government only wants to pursue secondary considerations within the limits of EU procurement law and only without compromising value for money.

### 4.1 Definition of the subject-matter of the contract

As already discussed in the context of social considerations above, even within the field of application of the EU Directives and United Kingdom and Scotland Regulations, contracting entities remain free regarding the decision on what to buy.[99] This decision is not mentioned in or covered by the Regulations. The OGC documents *Environmental Sustainability*[100] and *Buy Green and Make a Difference*[101] and the 2003 OGC and DEFRA *Joint Note on Environmental Issues in Purchasing*[102] suggest considering environmental issues at an early stage when there is most scope for them. The case studies provided in both *Buy Green* and the *Joint Note* suggest awareness of the environmental agenda, such as the Sustainable Operations on the Government Estate (SOGE) targets or the DEFRA guidance on the 'shadow price on car-

96. OGC, *Buy Green and Make a Difference*, ibid., at 3 and 4; *Social Issues in Purchasing Guide*, *supra* note 59, at 3; as pointed out on page 3 of the *Buy Green* document with reference to the *Social Issues* document: 'It is useful to read these two documents together and consider the whole range of environmental and social issues when planning a procurement exercise'. See also: OGC *Government and Fair Trade*, *supra* note 41, at 2; *Skills through Public Procurement*, *supra* note 41, at 6.
97. OGC, *Buy Green and Make a Difference, supra note 96, at 4; Social Issue in Purchasing Guide*, ibid.;
98. OGC, *Buy Green and Make a Difference*, ibid., at 4; OGC, *Environmental Sustainability*, *supra* note 90, at 2; OGC and DEFRA, *Joint Note on Environmental Issues in Purchasing*, *supra* note 96, at 3 and 4.
99. See: OGC and DEFRA, *Joint Note on Environmental Issues in Purchasing*, ibid., at 7.
100. *Supra* note 90, at 1.
101. *Supra* note 96, at 3.
102. *Ibid.*

bon'.[103] Examples provided by Barbara Morton and cited in the *Joint Note* include the installation of video conferencing instead of a business travel contract, installing IT computer faxing facilities rather than new fax machines, or installing shared printing facilities including the most up-to-date energy and paper saving features rather than new printers for every desk.[104] The OCG (and DEFRA) documents do not suggest any activities that would violate the requirements of the EU Directives or the United Kingdom or Scotland Regulations.

A question related to that on what to buy is how to buy. The OGC document *Sustainable Operations on the Government Estate Targets: 2008/9 Guidance* suggests that 'framework agreements enable departments to access energy saving assets without having to run their own.'[105] Within the confines on the general requirements regarding the choice of method of procurement, environmental considerations may therefore also contribute to, for example, the use of framework agreements.

### 4.2 Technical specifications

It is only when the decision on what to buy is implemented in the technical specifications or contract conditions that EU law and the Regulations can be affected. As pointed out by Arrowsmith, the specifications remain '[t]he main approach used in the UK for supporting many secondary objectives.'[106] Consequently, the OGC documents *Environmental Sustainability*[107] and *Buy Green and Make a Difference*[108] as well as the OGC and DEFRA *Joint Note on Environmental Issues in Purchasing*[109] suggest building relevant environmental objectives into the specifications. The limits for doing so are stipulated in Regulation 9 UKPCR. Regulation 12 UKUCR, Regulation 9 SPCR, and Regulation 12 SUCR contain provisions with exactly the same wording. Regulation 9 (1) UKPCR and SPCR already include environmental considerations as part of the very definition of technical specifications:

103. http://www.defra.gov.uk/environment/climatechange/research/carboncost/index.htm
104. *Supra* note 96, at 5 citing examples of ©Barbara Morton.
105. *Ibid.*
106. Arrowsmith, *supra* note 4, at 1243.
107. *Supra* note 90, at 1.
108. *Supra* note 96, at 3.
109. *Ibid.*

'In this regulation – [...] 'technical specifications' means

(a) in the case of a public services contract or a public supply contract, a specification in a document defining the required characteristics of materials, goods or services, such as [...], environmental performance levels, [...]

(b) in the case of a public works contract, the totality of the technical prescriptions contained, in particular, in the contract documents, defining the characteristics required of the work, works, materials or goods, which permits the work, works, materials or goods to be described in a manner such that it fulfils the use for which it is intended by the contracting authority and these characteristics shall include [...] environmental performance levels [...]"

Hence the Regulations specifically define the notion of technical specifications as including environmental performance levels. The OGC document *Buy Green and Make a Difference* explains that environmental considerations should be included in the specifications where they are relevant to the subject-matter of the contract and where they relate to the characteristics of the good or service. This includes 'core requirements' regarding the composition of the product or how a product performs its function and environmentally friendly production processes, provided they help to characterise the product. The environmental requirements need to be visible in the end product. Requirements that relate to the wider operation of the supplier will generally not be relevant.[110] Positive examples are organically produced food, timber from sustainably-managed forests, electricity from renewable sources, or products made in an energy and water efficient way. Negative examples are requiring that the supplier uses recycled office paper, buys energy from renewable sources, has an established environmental management scheme for all its operations, or serves organic food in its canteen.[111] More detail is added by Regulations 9 (7) UKPCR and SPCR which provide:

'A contracting authority may define the technical specifications [...] in terms of performance or functional requirements (which may include environmental characteristics) provided that the requirements are sufficiently precise to allow an economic operator to determine the subject of the contract and a contracting authority to award the contract.'

*Buy Green and Make a Difference* and the *Joint Note on Environmental Issues in Purchasing* emphasise the advantages of defining specifications in terms of environmental output and outcomes, such as offering flexibility and allowing innovative solutions.[112] However, they also stress that specifications

110. *Supra* note 96, at 7.
111. Ibid.
112. *Supra* note 96, at 9 and *supra* note 96, at 8.

have to be transparent and non-discriminatory, that it is clear to bidders what is required, and that specifications are not framed in a way as to limit competition.[113] Further detail is added in Regulations 9 (12) UKPCR and SPCR which read:

'Where a contracting authority lays down environmental characteristics in terms of performance or functional requirements as referred to in paragraph (7), it may use the detailed technical specifications, or if necessary, parts thereof, as defined by European, national or multi- national eco-labels or by any other eco-label, provided that –

(a) those technical specifications are appropriate to define the characteristics of the materials, goods or services that are the object of the contract;
(b) the eco-label requirements are drawn up on the basis of scientific information;
(c) the eco-label is adopted using a procedure in which all stakeholders, such as government bodies, consumers, manufacturers, distributors and environmental organisations, are able to participate; [...]'

In compliance with the relevant EU law, the *Joint Note on Environmental Issues in Purchasing*, a 2003 document written before the new Directives and Regulations, points out that as with any other standard contracting authorities must be prepared to accept other means of proof that the product or service offered meets the specifications.[114]

The OGC's *Sustainable Operations on the Government Estate Targets: 2008/9 Guidance* outlines a set of product specifications for procurement by central Government describing sustainable and environmental criteria for a range of product groups. They comprise of both revised mandatory requirements and voluntary best practice criteria.[115] The mandatory specifications ensure that products will be chosen with the minimum energy efficiency performance required to reduce energy consumptions and emissions to sustainable levels and reduce the waste of water and of waste in general. This emphasises the crucial importance of the definition of the technical specifications stage for the promotion of environmental objectives in the procurement law of the United Kingdom.

Hence, based on the wording of the Regulations, in compliance with the requirements of the TFEU and EU Procurement Directives, the possibilities to promote environmental objectives through technical specifications are limited yet considerable. The relevant government documents emphasise that the

113. Ibid.
114. *Supra* note 96, at 9.
115. *Ibid.*, at 11, 14, 28 and 33.

inclusion of environmental criteria in the specifications can and must be in line with value for money and competition objectives.[116] Considering the life cycle costs of many products and services, energy efficiency, disposal costs, the costs of environmental damage, and health implications, it appears that value for money and environmental considerations can more easily be squared than value for money and some of the social considerations discussed above. This requires that the principles of transparency, equal treatment, and value for money are observed. Moreover, the requirement that the specifications have to relate to the subject-matter of the contract implies that the environmental consideration refers to the primary objective of providing the contracting authority with what it needs to operate, rather than to a secondary objective. Competition and market access are not compromised *per se* since all tenderers bid on the basis of the same specifications.

### 4.3 Qualification

The United Kingdom and Scotland Regulations do not expressly allow environmental considerations to be used as a qualification criterion.[117] However, according to for example Regulation 23 (4) (d) UKPCR a bidder can be de-selected if he or she 'has been convicted of a criminal offence relating to the conduct of his business or profession.' Moreover, according to Regulation 23 (4) (f) UKPCR and SPCR he or she can be de-selected if they 'committed an act of grave professional misconduct in the course of his business or profession.' According to the OGC document *Buy green and make a difference* and the DEFRA and OGC *Joint Note on Environmental Issues in Purchasing* this includes a breach of environmental law.[118] Hence environmental considerations can lead to de-selection if violations of environmental law occurred. This is a relatively high threshold. Moreover, the latter document points out that:

> 'Care should be taken to ensure that candidates are treated equally and that the decision to reject a candidate is proportionate to the seriousness of their misconduct and the profile of

116. DEFRA and OGC *Joint Note on Environmental Issues in Purchasing*, supra note 96, at 8; OGC *Buy Green and Make a Difference*, supra note 96, at 9; OGC *Environmental Sustainability*, *supra* note 90, at 1.
117. Regulations 23 of the United Kingdom Public Contracts Regulations 2006 and the Public Contracts (Scotland) Regulations 2006 and Regulations 26 of the United Kingdom Utilities Contracts Regulations 2006 and the Utilities Contracts (Scotland) Regulations 2006 do not contain environmental considerations as qualification criteria.
118. Both *supra* note 96, at 10 and 10 respectively.

a particular contract. Candidates should be given opportunity to describe any steps they have taken to prevent recurrence.'

This suggests that misconduct will not automatically lead to de-selection. Especially the second sentence implies that in many cases bidders will be able to stay in the competition by convincing the contracting authority that they will not breach the relevant rules again. This will discourage many contracting authorities from de-selecting on the basis of environmental criteria in the first place. On the other hand it may well lead to stopping violations of environmental law.

Moreover, according to Regulation 25 UKPCR and SPCR information as to technical and professional capability can be collected.[119] According to Regulation 25 (2) (h) this includes:

'[...] the environmental management measures evidenced in accordance with paragraph (4), that the services provider or contractor is able to apply when performing a contract, but only where it is necessary for the contract, [...].'

This rule is only relevant for works and services and not for supplies. The OGC document *Buy Green and Make a Difference* emphasises that contracting authorities may only ask for evidence that relates to the specific contract itself and not to that of the entire business of the tenderer.[120] A case study provided in the document uses environmental management standards (EMS) in a works contract for an office building as an example. Contracting authorities shall accept EMS as one form of proof that the bidder can carry out the contract according to their environmental management standards. They may not, however, require EMS as such since that would go beyond the requirements of the contract. Regulation 25 (4) adds detail relating to the evidence for environmental management standards:

'The evidence referred to in paragraph (2) (h) is –
(a) a certificate –
  (i) attesting conformity to environmental management standards based on –
    (aa) the Community Eco-Management and Audit Scheme (a); or
    (bb) the relevant European or international standards, and
  (ii) from an independent body established in any relevant State conforming to Community law or the relevant European or international standards concerning certification; or

119. Regulations 28 of the United Kingdom Utilities Contracts Regulations 2006 and the Utilities Contracts (Scotland) Regulations 2006.
120. *Supra* note 96, at 10.

(b) any other evidence of environmental management measures which are equivalent to the standards referred to in sub-paragraph (a) (i).'

The DEFRA and OGC *Joint Note on Environmental Issues in Purchasing* emphasises that these are voluntary schemes, that contracting authorities may accept the holding of a relevant label as evidence of compliance with the specification, and that they must also accept other means of proof.[121]

Overall, the United Kingdom and Scotland Regulations implement the generally quite restrictive approach to the use of environmental consideration at the qualification stage of the Directives.

### 4.4 Award criteria

As discussed in the context of social considerations above, Regulation 30 of all procurement Regulations provide that contracts are to be awarded to the lowest or the economically most advantageous offer. With respect to environmental considerations Regulation 30 (2) provides:

'A contracting authority shall use criteria linked to the subject-matter of the contract to determine that an offer is the most economically advantageous, including [...] environmental criteria [...]'

This could be understood as giving environmental criteria a certain importance at the award stage.[122] However, the OGC document *Buy Green and Make a Difference* clarifies that 'at this [the award] stage you can't consider wider benefits to society.'[123] Contracting authorities need to make sure that at the specifications stage 'the winning bid will provide the environmental benefits you need.'[124] In the DEFRA and OGC *Joint Note on Environmental Issues in Purchasing* resource consumption and disposal costs are listed as examples for possible award criteria. However, apart from the fact that these are economical as well as environmental criteria, it also emphasises the relevance to the subject-matter of the contract, giving a benefit to the contracting authority and consistency with basic Treaty principles as requirements for the lawful use of environmental criteria at the award stage and that their maxi-

121. *Supra* note 96, at 7.
122. See also the DEFRA and OGC *Joint Note on Environmental Issues in Purchasing*, ibid., at 10: 'Awarding contracts on this basis provides scope for consideration of relevant environmental issues.'
123. *Supra* note 96, at 11.
124. Ibid.

mum impact is better achieved at the specification stage.[125] Hence the relevant Government documents discourage the use of environmental considerations as award criteria.

### 4.5 Contract conditions

As discussed above in the context of social considerations, Regulations 39 UKPCR and SPCR allow contracting authorities to stipulate conditions relating to the performance of a public contract, which 'may, in particular, include [...] environmental considerations'.

The new *Model Terms and Conditions of Contracts for Goods* of November 2009[126] issued by the OGC, clause D5 require:

> 'The Contractor shall, when working on the Premises, perform its obligations under the Contract in accordance with the Client's environmental policy, which is to conserve energy, water, wood, paper and other resources, reduce waste and phase out the use of ozone depleting substances and minimise the release of greenhouse gases, volatile organic compounds and other substances damaging to health and the environment.'

The new *Model Terms and Conditions Contracts for Services* of November 2009[127] D3.1 contains exactly the same provision. As outlined in the context of social considerations above, the *Model Contracts Terms and Conditions* do not contain any immediate sanctions for non-compliance with the 'client's environmental policy'. According to the new *Model Terms and Conditions of Contracts for Services* 2009, for example, the usual 'remedies in the event of inadequate performance' (clauses F.5) could be used in theory to enforce clause D5, including partial or complete termination (clauses H.2). There is no evidence on whether these rather drastic measures are used to enforce the environmental policy clause in practice. The clause will be mainly effective as a reminder and emphasis of the general environmental policy. However, the clause is made part of central Government contracts and thus subject to the same enforcement mechanisms as any other part of it.

The possibility to include and enforce environmental polices through contract conditions is separate from the question whether this is actually done in practice. Both the OGC document *Buy green and make a difference* and the DEFRA and OGC *Joint Note on Environmental Issues in Purchasing* indicate a rather negative position towards the inclusion of environmental considera-

125. *Supra* note 96, at 10.
126. *Supra* note 78.
127. *Supra* note 79.

tions in the contract conditions. First, they emphasise that contract conditions should be relevant to the performance of the contract and the achievement of value for money, that contract conditions should not be disguised technical specifications, selection, or award criteria, that the need for transparency requires that conditions of contract should be advertised in advance to all candidates, and that they need to be compatible with the basic principles of the then EC Treaty, especially the principle for non-discrimination.[128] Second, both Government documents express doubt about the use of contract conditions to further environmental objectives in general. The DEFRA and OGC *Joint Note* stipulates that:

> 'As a general rule, contract conditions should be used sparingly, as they will be unlikely to contribute to cost effectiveness or affordability.'[129]

The OGC document *Buy Green and Make a Difference* almost issues a warning against the use of contract conditions as potentially compromising value for money. Suppliers will pass extra costs on the contracting authorities, compliance with extra conditions could distract suppliers from the main business of the contract, the conditions may put off smaller suppliers from bidding and 'fewer bids means reduced competition' thereby threatening value for money, and finally, requiring changes to the basic organisation 'of a supplier established in another Member State might be considered discriminatory or a barrier to trade.'[130] Hence the relevant Government documents discourage the inclusion of environmental considerations in the contract conditions.

### 4.6 Outside the field of application of the Directives and Regulations

As explained in the context of social considerations above, a considerable part of the procurement activities of United Kingdom procurement authorities and entities is conducted outside the field of application of the Regulations and Directives, most notably below their thresholds. Since no specific binding rules apply, contracting entities retain considerable flexibility. Nevertheless, crucial for the legality of any of such practices and polices is their compatibility with the requirements of the TFEU. The case law of the European Court of Justice[131] and the Interpretative Communication[132] issued by the

128. *Supra* note 96 and *supra* note 96, both at 12.
129. Ibid.
130. *Supra* note 96, at 13.
131. See the case law listed in *supra* note 83.

European Commission based on that case law provide guidance on how to promote social considerations in the context of these contracts.

Neither *Buy green and make a difference* nor the *Joint Note on Environmental Issues in Purchasing* refer to contracts below the thresholds in a specific section in a way comparable to the documents on social considerations discussed above. This suggests that the promotion of environmental considerations below the thresholds should stay within the limits set for contracts above the thresholds. If they go beyond these limits they have to comply with the public procurement principles of the TFEU, namely non-discrimination, equal-treatment, and transparency.

## 5 Conclusions

There is a long and rich history of promoting secondary objectives, especially social considerations, through public procurement in the United Kingdom. This ranges from the payment of fair wages to workers on government contracts, to sex equality and the fight against Apartheid. However, since the Conservative governments of 1980s and with the increasing adaptation of British public procurement laws to the requirements of EU law, many of these schemes gradually disappeared. Today, the Procurement Regulations of the United Kingdom and Scotland allow the promotion of social and environmental consideration through procurement only within the strict limits set by EU law. This allows taking them into account in the context of the decision on what to procure and also to an extent when drafting the technical specifications. Their use as a qualification or award criterion and in the contract conditions is discouraged. Not only due to the current financial constraints and the limits of EU law, a drastic change of the current value for money emphasis of British public procurement law and policy is unlikely.

## Bibliography

Sue Arrowsmith, John Linarelli, Don Wallace Jr., *Regulating Public Procurement: National and International Perspectives* (Kluwer Law International: London, 2000).

132. *Commission Interpretative Communication on the Community law applicable to contracts not or not fully subject to the provisions of the Public Procurement Directives*, *supra* note 87.

Sue Arrowsmith, *The Law of Public and Utilities Procurement* (Sweet & Maxwell: London, 2nd ed., 2005).

Sue Arrowsmith, 'Implementation of the New EC Procurement Directives and the Alcatel Ruling in England and Wales and Northern Ireland: a Review of the New Legislation and Guidance' (2006) 15 *Public Procurement Law Review* 86.

Sue Arrowsmith and Peter Kunzlik (eds.), *Social and Environmental Policies in EC Procurement Law: New Directive and New Directions* (Cambridge University Press, 2009).

Sue Arrowsmith, 'Application of EC Treaty and Directives to horizontal policies: a critical review', in Arrowsmith and Kunzlik, *Social and Environmental Policies in EC Procurement Law: New Directive and New Directions* (Cambridge University Press, 2009).

Brian Bercusson, *The Fair Wages Resolutions* (Mansell, 1978).

Christine Boch, 'The Implementation of the Public Procurement Directives in the United Kingdom: Devolution or Divergence?' (2007) 16 *Public Procurement Law Review* 410

John Carr, *New roads to Equality: Contract Compliance in the United Kingdom* (Fabian Society No.517, 1997).

Paul P. Craig and Martin Trybus, 'Public Contracts: England and Wales', in R. Nogouellou and U. Stelkens (eds.) *Traité de droit comparé des contrats publics/Comparative Law on Public Contracts Treatise* (Bruylant: Brussels, 2010) 399, forthcoming.

Terence Daintith, 'Legal Analysis and Economic Policy' (1982) 9 *Journal of Law and Society* 191.

Terence Daintith, 'Regulation by Contract: the New Prerogative' [1979] 32 *Current Legal Problems* 41.

Sir Otto Kahn-Freund, 'Legislation through Adjudication: the Legal Aspects of the Fair Wages Clauses and Recognised Conditions' (1948) 11 *Modern Law Review* 274.

Peter Kunzlik, 'Environmental Issues in International Procurement' in Arrowsmith and Davies, *Public Procurement: Global Revolution* (Kluwer Law International: London, 1998).

Christopher McCrudden, 'Social Policy Issues in Public Procurement: A Legal Overview' in Arrowsmith and Davies, *Public Procurement: Global Revolution* (Kluwer Law International: London, 1998), chapter 12.

Christopher McCrudden, *Buying Social Justice: Equality, Government Procurement and Legal Change* (Oxford University Press, 2007).

Martin Trybus, 'Public contracts in European Union internal market law', in R. Nogouellou and U. Stelkens (eds.) *Traité de droit comparé des contrats publics/Comparative Law on Public Contracts Treatise* (Bruylant: Brussels, 2010) 81, forthcoming.

Rolf. H. Weber, 'Development promotion as a secondary policy in public procurement' (2009) 4 *Public Procurement Law Review* 171.

R. Williams and R Smellie, 'Public Purchasing: An Administrative Cinderella' (1985) 63 *Public Administration* 23.

# XI. Green and Social Considerations in Public Procurement Contracts: A Comparative Approach

*by Mario E. Comba*

## 1 Introduction: the role of comparative law in the interpretation of EU law

The aim of this chapter is defined in the Foreword of the Editors to the first volume of this series.[1] The principle of supremacy by which European law prevails over the national laws of the Member States must realistically take into account that national laws are part of the legal traditions of each country and as such are not easily pushed aside. Unsurprisingly, what results after the penetration of EU law in the different national legal orders is often a mixture, which does not always guarantee the uniform application of EU law throughout the Europe. This is a good reason for studying and describing national legal systems in relation to specific issues of EU public procurement law, such as in-house procurement contracts or green and social considerations in public procurement, which is the subject of the other chapters of this book. It is in fact

> '[...] valuable for practitioners in the member States to be aware of practices, regulations, case law and interpretations of procurement law throughout the European Union as this can assist them in understanding the rules applicable and in developing best practices.'[2]

In other words, knowing other Member States' ways of implementation of the EU procurement Directives can help to implement them in one's own national legal system, and to implement them in a way that aims to foster the

1. R. Caranta & S. Treumer 'Foreword by the Editors of the European Procurement Law Series', in M. Comba & S. Treumer (eds) *In House providing in European Law* (Copenhagen, DjøfPublishing, 2010) 9-10.
2. Caranta & Treumer, above fn. 1, at 10.

uniform application of EU law. Circulating the interpretations of the Directives provided by national Courts and administrations is a useful tool for making their application uniform throughout the Union.[3] This is already a challenging objective.

However, there is a further possible use of comparative law, one even more ambitious: trying to pick up the common trends developing at national level, if any, give them a proper theoretical reconstruction, and propose them as possible solutions to legal problems not yet tackled – or not yet solved – by the Court of Justice. European institutions cannot ignore these common trends developing at national level – a sort of '*spontaneous ius commune*',[4] especially when they develop in fields, such as green or social considerations in public procurements, where legal issues surrounding sustainable public procurement in European law are still very much in need of further clarification.[5]

Comparative law is not limited to the study of foreign law, which is only a first step, but requires a further and deeper analysis in order to identify common trends and to build legal models, to classify legal systems, to determine if different legal systems have given common answers to common problems. In the field of green and social considerations in public procurement, this comparative law approach is at the same time particularly difficult and useful.

Particularly difficult, because it focuses mainly, as we will see in the following paragraphs, on the subject-matter of public procurement contracts which is one of the most controversial problems in comparative law. This is a problem going directly to the crucial question about the existence of an EU law definition and a set of rules about the 'contract'. There is no unitary definition of the notion of 'contract' at European level and there is no common definition of the notion of 'contract' within the national laws of the Member States: on the contrary, the 'contract' itself is one of the traditional examples utilised by private comparative law scholars in order to emphasise the incompatibility of legal terms in the various European legal systems.[6]

3. M. Derlén *Multilingual interpretation of European Union Law* (Leiden, Wolters Kluwer, 2009) analyzes the usage by Danish, English and German judges of EU directive in languges different from their national ones, which could lead to the introduction of interpretation 'attached' to national languages, but concludes that this is done on a casual basis and only limited to English and French (at 341-356)
4. Caranta & Treumer, above fn. 1, at 10.
5. R. Caranta, *Sustainable Public procurement in the EU*, in this book, par. 7.
6. R. Sacco *Introduzione al diritto comparato* (Torino, Utet, 1993) 75-89; Id., *Il contratto nella prospettiva comparatistica*, in *Europa e diritto privato*, 2001, 479. For exemple, marriage is considered a contract in French law, but not in German, Italian

Particularly useful because the problems linked to the introduction of green and social considerations in public procurement belong to a yet under-researched field and, above all, they require the definition of the framework within which the question has to be approached. This is easier if it can be done in comparison with the same framework at national level. As we will see in the following paragraph, the question which underlies the problem of green and social considerations in public procurement can be different depending on the principle used to address the problem. And the different ways of framing the question can be put in evidence only if the question is examined with the technique of the 'as opposed to': for example, the EU framework 'as opposed to' the United Kingdom or the Romanian or the Spanish one.

In the following paragraphs of this chapter, the methodological premises briefly described here will be applied. Therefore the structure will be as follows: (i) an analysis of the common trends developed at national level, if any, and an attempt to build one or more legal models, and (ii) a comparison of these legal models with the law as it stands in the EU in order to (iii) suggest a possible interpretation of EU law, in cases of a lack of a consolidated case law, which could be consistent with the common trends developed at national level. This analysis will be conducted on the basis of the national reports and of the EU report published in the other chapters of this book, as well as on the basis of the discussion with the authors during the workshop held in Orta San Giulio, Italy in September 2009.

and English law; see B. Pozzo, *Multilinguismo, terminologie giuridiche e problemi di armonizzazione del diritto privato europeo*, in Jacometti – Pozzo (editors) *Le politiche linguistiche delle istituzioni comunitarie dopo l'allargamento* (Milano, Giuffré, 2006) pag. 3- 26, spec., pag. 10-11. See also G. Ajani – M. Ebers (editors) *Uniform Terminology for European Contract law* (Baden-Baden, Nomos-Verlag, 2005); G.Ajani, '*A Better Coherence of EU Private Law and Multilingualism*', in R. Schulze (ed.), *Common Frame of Reference and Existing EC Contract Law* (Munchen, Sellier, 2008, pp.33-46; S. Prechal (ed.) *The coherence of EU law: the search for unity in divergent concepts* (Oxford, OUP, 2008).

## 2 Definition of the problem: sustainability vs. value for money or sustainability vs. competition?

### 2.1 Value for money and competition

A correct comparative approach requires first of all the definition of the problem (the so called 'problem based' method): the researcher must identify the legal problem in the most accurate way possible to compare the different legal solutions to that problem found by different legal systems. The definition of the problem is therefore a very delicate state of the analysis because it has to be done at the same time with a common language, in order to avoid as far as possible the translation risks, but also in an accurate and specific way, to avoid misleading comparisons such as comparing issues which are entirely different and can therefore not be compared. The identification of the problem often consists of the most demanding part of the entire task.

In our case, the identification of the problem is in itself problematic because, from the national reports and the EU report emerge a basic difference. Provided that green and social procurement can be considered as fostering the goal of 'sustainability', the problem consists of competing objectives, a competition between sustainability on the one hand and what ever happens to be the dominating principle governing public procurement in a particular system on the other hand. However, if we look deeper, in some cases, namely the United Kingdom, this competition is between sustainability and value for money, while in other cases, namely the EU, it is between sustainability and competition law. This situation leads to the basic question of what the main objective of public procurement legislation is: if it is aimed at imposing on the contracting authority the obligation to seek best value for money, or if it is aimed at guaranteeing the position of economic operators in order to foster competition and the internal market.

Traditionally, the first position is common to Member States, whose legislation on public procurement prior to the EU intervention was aimed at regulating the activity of contracting authorities imposing on them the pursuit of certain aims, first among them efficiency in purchasing works, goods and services. The protection of competition was only an instrument to facilitate the main interest of the contracting authorities. In contrast, the second position is typical of the EU.[7] It is inscribed in the first articles of the TFEU

7. The main reason for EU regulation of public procurements is to bring their markets on line with to the operation of private markets on the demand side – that is the public side – which can be altered because it pursues the public interest instead of the maximization of profits: C. H. Bovis *EU Public Procurement Law*, (Cheltenham, Elgar,

which foster competition and the internal market. The economic interest of the contracting authorities, in this case, is only a by-product of the competition rule and of the creation of the internal market.

The two different positions largely overlap. Competition is in fact often instrumental to obtaining best value for money in the sense that putting economic operators in competition allows the contracting authority to get the best offer. This would hardly be the case had only one economic operator been sure to be the only possible provider of the good or of the service in question. It follows that rules aimed at guaranteeing competition often are also useful for getting best value for money, notably transparency and equal treatment.

It is in fact possible to have situations in which competition rules are complied with, yet the best value for money principle is compromised. This can be the case when a contracting authority decides to buy goods which are completely useless or luxurious, for example luxury cars instead of ambulances for a hospital, following a correct public procurement procedure. In this case, the interest of the common marked is fulfilled, but not the interest of the purchasing administration.

On the other hand, it may happen that rules are applied from a 'best value for money' perspective and not from the 'competition' perspective. For example, the power of the contracting authority to automatically exclude abnormally low offers below the thresholds can be considered consistent with the need of the contracting authority to get best value for money because it is an efficient way to eliminate unrealistic offers, but according to Court of Justice case law this clashes with EU rules about competition and freedom of establishment.[8]

This latter case of rules which are good for best value for money but not for competition becomes very important when considered in the context of green and social public procurement. Sustainability reacts differently if put in opposition to the best value for money rule or with the competition rule.

To a certain extent, the 'best value for money' rule, if interpreted loosely, can be consistent with a great part of the green and social considerations. Since the best value for money rule considers the problem from the point of view of the procuring entity's needs and interests, one could simply say that

2007) at 11 – 16. Best value for money is an important objective of most national regimes on public procurement but it is not an objective of EC rules: S. Arrowsmith & P. Kunzlik, *Social and environmental Policies in EC Procurement Law*, (Cambridge, Cambridge University Press, 2009) at 31 – 33.

8. Joined Cases C-147/06 and C-148/06 *SECAP and Santorso* [2008] ECR I-3565

inserting green or social considerations in public procurement is a way for the procuring entity to purchase goods or services which it should purchase anyway. For example, imposing on the contractor an obligation to hire a certain number of unemployed people, much higher than what would be effectively necessary for providing the service, can be considered by the contracting authority as consistent with the best value for money rule. The contracting authority should spend money for providing social assistance to the unemployed anyway and it might find it more convenient to do so through a public procurement procedure. The costs for social policy are thus borne by the contractor who will certainly find a way to shift them back to the contracting authority, but possibly allowing the contracting authority to benefit from the lower price resulting from the competitive award procedure.

In other words, if one public law entity, considered as a whole, has for example (i) to buy cleaning services for the roads of the municipality and (ii) to provide social assistance to 100 unemployed people, it can follow two different routes. First, it can organise a public procurement procedure for awarding the contract to the best company on the market and, at the same time, pay benefits to unemployed people or provide them with re-qualification courses. Second, it can organise a public procurement procedure for awarding the same contract but adding to the subject-matter, or in the performance conditions, the provision that the winner should employ those specific 100 unemployed.[9] The second hypothesis will be chosen if considered more convenient than the first on the basis of economic considerations.

It can be said that a public law entity behaving like that is a rational one pursuing the best value for money objective, even if in a broad sense; that is considering all its institutional objectives. But it is easy to say that a situation like that would probably be considered not compatible with EU law by the Court of Justice, because in conflict with competition rules and freedom of establishment.

9. This example is drawn, with some modifications, from the case decided by the TAR Lazio – Roma, sez. II quater, decision 7512/09 of 23 july 2009 (in www.giustizia-amministrativa.it). The administrative Tribunal held a call for offer issued by the Ministry for Culture for a public procurement in the field of cultural services, which required the winner to hire a high number of unemployed people, analytically listed in the call. The TAR declared that the 'social clause' was not so much a secondary clause, but a part of the subject matter because it was however pursuing a public interest that is proper to the Goverment – the assistance to unemployed people – and which the Government would have been bound to pursue with other means.

### 2.2 The national approaches: UK, Spain and the others

If we consider the national chapters in this book, the United Kingdom situation is very interesting since the Office of Government Commerce (OCG) documents, for example the *Social Issues Purchasing Guide* tend to affirm that 'there is no conflict between social considerations and value for money.'[10] This is even more the case for green considerations, since they are more easily quantifiable[11] while social considerations are not. However, the United Kingdom Government committed itself to pursue social considerations within the limits of EU procurement law and only without compromising value for money, which means that value for money is the 'driving' value, while green or social considerations can be inserted only as far as they do comply with it. The only admitted exception are reserved contracts, but also in this case value for money is not replaced by the social objectives of the reserved contract scheme so that 'Value for money and the reserved contracts can go hand in hand'.[12]

The opposite position can be found in the Spanish legislation on public procurement. The new *Sustainable Economic Bill* is reshaping the system of public procurement as a whole, imposing the total predominance of sustainability over competition considerations in the public procurement legislation. It seems in fact that in the new law:

> '[...] the idea of sustainability is pervasive and it seeks to be the driving force that will allow the productive system to be altered to encompass criteria that are more reasonable from all points of view'.[13]

The particular position of the Spanish system seems to be one that considers the productive process of the goods or services at least as important as the result of the selection procedure for awarding the contract, and this is because the production process is where the introduction of sustainability clauses has a greater effect. On the other hand, even if the inclusion of social clauses 'amounts to a ray of light within the dictatorship of competition law' it is, however, true that 'the rules on public procurement, when correctly inter-

10. M. Trybus 'Sustainability and value for money: social and environmental considerations in United Kingdom public procurement law' above, para. 3.
11. M. Trybus above, para. 4
12. M. Trybus above para. 3.1
13. J. González García 'Sustainability and public procurement in the Spanish legal system' above, para. 2.

preted, must seek a balance between the introduction of sustainability criteria and the defence of the principle of competition'.[14] In conclusion, in Spain

> '[...] it is not so much a question of what the so-called 'primary elements' are, by comparison, but one of understanding the process through which a public contract is defined, awarded and performed, as a complete whole, in which the final outcome – the service received by the public Authority – is as important as the instruments which public contracts are carried out. To view it in another way would be to deny he role of the public procurement as an instrument for bringing about the change needed in how productive processes are configured.'[15]

In a sense, the two 'extreme' positions of the United Kingdom and the Spanish systems have something in common: they both reduce and somehow trivialise the possible contrast between sustainability, on the one hand, and best value for money or competition on the other hand. But they reach that conclusion following opposing paths: in Britain the tendency is to reduce sustainability to best value for money, in the sense that the introduction of sustainability clauses must be reconciled with the quest for best value for money. On the other hand, the Spanish picture sees the application of competition rules almost as pre-empted by the preponderant needs of sustainability, which are fostered by the recent *Sustainable Economic Bill* so that the subject-matter of the contract is not so important any more, if compared with the production processes of the goods or the services.

A third position, explicitly shared by other national chapters, such as the German and the Romanian ones but implicitly recognisable also in others, such as the Italian and the French, admits the impossibility to reconcile the two positions – sustainability and value for money/competition – and try to build a theory in order to justify the 'coexistence' or 'cohabitation' of these two principles in the public procurement legislation. This is how the problem of the distinction between primary and secondary considerations arises. It will be addressed in the following paragraph.

### 2.3 The EU law approach

EU law approaches the problem of social and environmental considerations in public procurement in terms of a conflict between sustainability and competition. EU case law seems pretty clear on the point: secondary considera-

14. J. González García above, para. 4.
15. J. González García above, para. 1.

tions can be inserted into public procurement contracts as far as they do not hamper competition rules: environmental considerations can be inserted

> '[...] provided that they are linked to the subject-matter of the contract, do not confer an unrestricted freedom of choice on the authority, are expressly mentioned in the contract documents of the tender notice and comply with all the fundamental principles of Community law, in particular the principle of non-discrimination.'[16]

And the definition of the subject-matter is a question for the contracting authority to address. The contracting authority is free to buy whatever it wants, provided that the definition of the subject-matter is not contrary to competition and internal market rules.

Of course this does not mean that the Court is promoting or even endorsing sustainable public procurement. It can rather be said that only the traditional EU concerns of non-discrimination and free movement are very much at the heart of this case law.[17] As a consequence, the EU law position seems to be more like the British and Spanish ones, since it does not admit in principle to a conflict between sustainability and competition rules: sustainability may be pursued only if fully complying with the latter. If a conflict arises, competition must prevail.

## 3 What are primary and secondary considerations? The quest for the subject-matter of the public procurement contract

### 3.1 Defining the problem of 'secondary' considerations

The problem of defining 'secondary' considerations as opposed to 'primary' ones implies a distinction between primary and secondary objectives of public procurement. However, the question is controversial, since green and social considerations can well fit into the 'primary' objectives of public procurement. The point is to understand if the subject-matter of the public procurement contracts is only one or more than one.

Article 1 (2) (a) of Directive 2004/18/EC states that public procurement contracts have 'as their object the execution of works, the supply of products

16. Case C-513/99 *Concordia Bus Finland* [2002] ECR I-7213. For a comment on the evolution of EU case law, see R. Caranta 'Sustainable Public Procurement in the EU' above, para. 1.1.
17. R. Caranta above, para. 1.1.

or the provision of services.'[18] Therefore, strictly speaking, everything that is not necessary for the execution of works, the supply of products or the provisions of services is a 'secondary consideration'.

18. From a comparative law point of view, an interesting analysis could be done on the different definitions of public procurement contract given by the different linguistic versions of Article 1(2)(a) of Directive 2004/18/EC. They read as follow, in the national languages of the reports present in this book:

'Public contracts' are contracts for pecuniary interest concluded in writing between one or more economic operators and one or more contracting authorities and having as their object the execution of works, the supply of products or the provision of services within the meaning of this Directive.

Les 'marchés publics' sont des contrats à titre onéreux conclus par écrit entre un ou plusieurs opérateurs économiques et un ou plusieurs pouvoirs adjudicateurs et ayant pour objet l'exécution de travaux, la fourniture de produits ou la prestation de services au sens de la présente directive. Un marché public ayant pour objet la fourniture de produits et, à titre accessoire, les travaux de pose et d'installation est considéré comme un 'marché public de fournitures'.

'Öffentliche Aufträge' sind zwischen einem oder mehreren Wirtschaftsteilnehmern und einem oder mehreren öffentlichen Auftraggebern geschlossene schriftliche entgeltliche Verträge über die Ausführung von Bauleistungen, die Lieferung von Waren oder die Erbringung von Dienstleistungen im Sinne dieser Richtlinie.

'Contractele de achiziţii publice' sunt contracte cu titlu oneros, încheiate în scris între unul sau mai mulţi operatori economici ş i una sau mai multe autorităţi contractante ş i care au ca obiect execuţia de lucrări, furnizarea de produse sau prestarea de servicii în sensul prezentei directive.

Son 'contratos públicos' los contratos onerosos y celebrados por escrito entre uno o varios operadores económicos y uno o varios poderes adjudicadores, cuyo objeto sea la ejecución de obras, el suministro de productos o la prestación de servicios en el sentido de la presente Directiva. productos y, de forma accesoria, obras de colocación e instalación se considerará un 'contrato público de suministro'.

Gli 'appalti pubblici' sono contratti a titolo oneroso stipulati per iscritto tra uno o più operatori economici e una o più amministrazioni aggiudicatrici aventi per oggetto l'esecuzione di lavori, la fornitura di prodotti o la prestazione di servizi ai sensi della presente direttiva.

Ved »offentlige kontrakter« forstås gensidigt bebyrdende aftaler, der indgås skriftligt mellem en eller flere økonomiske aktører og en eller flere ordregivende myndigheder, og som vedrører udførelsen af arbejde, levering af varer eller tjenesteydelser, der er omfattet af dette direktiv, som også accessorisk omfatter monterings- og installationsarbejde, betragtes som en »offentlig vareindkøbskontrakt«.

The problems here are multifarious: can we say that a 'public contract' is the same thing as a 'contrat public' and 'Öffentliche Aufträge'? By the way, why 'Öffentliche Aufträge' instead of 'Öffentliche Verträge'? And what is the meaning of '*for pecuniary interest*' in the different linguistic versions and – a different but related question – in the different national legal systems? It is not even possible to

One could say that 'what is necessary for' is up to the procuring entity, so that if the procuring entity decides that it is necessary for its needs to buy fair trade coffee instead of non-fair trade coffee, this is still the subject-matter of the contract and therefore there are no secondary considerations involved, which means that no secondary considerations are ever conceivable, thus eliminating the problem. In fact most national chapters stressed that contracting authorities remain largely free regarding the decision on what to buy[19] and EU law could hardly curtail this freedom of the national contracting authorities.[20]

However, to such formalistic approach it can easily be replied that, on the contrary, 'what is necessary [...]' can be defined with a certain degree of accuracy in objective terms. For example, fair trade coffee and non-fair trade coffee, are objectively the same product and can be used without substantial differences in the canteen of a municipality. Of course one can always imagine the exceptional case in which, for example, a special situation led the local unions to impose the use of fair trade coffee, which will turn out to be an obligation for the municipality to buy fair trade coffee instead of regular coffee, but this is in fact an exception.

In certain cases, particularly with green clauses, it is possible that what can appear to be a secondary consideration is on the contrary part of the subject-matter. For example, when buying buses for urban transportation, a procuring entity has to put into the technical specifications all the green devices which are required in order for the buses to run legally according to EU, national and local legislation. If the Euro 4 standard is required by the national legislation for buses in order to operate, the procuring entity has no choice but to require the Euro 4 standard in order to have running buses and therefore the Euro 4 requirement is not a secondary consideration, but a primary consideration. Requiring the Euro 4 standard is like requiring a bus with engine, seats and wheels.

Secondary considerations are therefore something which is required by the procuring entity even if not objectively necessary in order to reach the aim of the public procurement contract, i.e. the execution of the works, the supply of products or the provision of services, something additional and unnecessary, in respect of the object of the contract, as defined by the Directive.

define all the these problems in this chapter, but it is important to stress the existence of a grey material which requires to be studied and systematized.

19. M. Trybus above, para. 3.2; M. Burgi above, para. 2. 2.
20. R. Caranta above, para. 2.

### 3.2 Secondary considerations as State aids

The next question is to ask why the procuring entity asks something additional and unnecessary with respect to the subject of the contract. As far as green and social clauses are concerned, the reason lies in the pursuit of public objectives which are different from those typical of the public procurement contract: a municipality has also competence over the fight against pollution and therefore may ask for buses with Euro 5 standards, even if Euro 4 only is required by the law; or the Ministry for Labour has also competence over equal opportunity policies and therefore asks for cleaning services provided by companies with high standards of equal opportunity integration.

This situation implies at least two consequences:

(1) Under domestic administrative law the procuring entity cannot pursue an objective which is not provided for by law and therefore it would be illegal for a procuring entity to insert in a public procurement contract a secondary consideration related to an objective other than those given to that procuring entity by national law. This could be a problem, e.g., for justifying fair trade secondary considerations, because it implies pursuing the objective of fair labour conditions abroad. But, as it was seen in the previous paragraph, it would not be a problem, under domestic law, for a public law entity to pursue through a public procurement procedure an objective (e.g. helping unemployed people) which falls within the scope of its competencies.

(2) More importantly, the reason, the 'causa', the 'consideration',[21] the 'Grund' of secondary considerations is substantially different from that of primary considerations. For primary considerations, the reason of the contract lies in the need of the procuring entity to procure works, products or services for itself, for its own use. For secondary considerations, the reason is the pursuit of the general welfare or happiness (clean environment, better working conditions, equal opportunities, fair trade). For primary consideration, the procuring entity acts as a *consumer*, while for secondary considerations it acts as a *regulator*.[22]

The different roles of the procuring entity influence the legal nature of the act it is performing: when the procuring entity acts as a regulator, paying money to a company not for purchasing something for itself but with the objective to

21. Here 'consideration' is used in its technical – contract law meaning.
22. McCrudden *Buying social justice: Equality, Government Procurement and Legal Change* (Oxford, OUP, 2007) Chapter 17.

award a prize for a behaviour useful for the community, it is not making a contract, it is awarding a subsidy or State aid.[23] Therefore, a public procurement contract with secondary considerations could be seen as a contract plus a State aid in the sense that the procuring entity is paying something more not for a better product, but in order to foster a general interest. It can happen through admitting to the procedure only tenderers with green or social standards higher than the normally required standards, or giving to these tenderes a higher point score in the award stage. In any case, the procuring entity gives a 'prize' to tenderers who deserve it because they contribute in pursuing a specific public interest.

### 3.3 The legality of inserting a State aid in a public procurement contract in national legal systems

According to McCrudden,[24] different answers could be found along the divide between common law and civil law systems. In the first case the principle of freedom of contracts leaves a complete autonomy to the contracting authority, while in the latter case (McCrudden refers to the French system) the principle of 'nominate' contracts could prevent contracting authorities from signing contracts with multiple objectives. But this does not seem to be the case because in civil law systems the 'causa' or 'Grund' of the contract is the economic reason of the contract and it is not 'nominate': its only limit is that it must not be illegal. The 'type' of the contract is on the contrary 'nominate'

23. See the definition of 'subvention' as opposed to 'marché public' given by Ministère de l'économie, des finances et de l'industrie, *Circulaire du 3 août 2006 portant manuel d'application du code des marchés publics, point 2.4.1: 'Les marchés publics se distinguent des subventions. Les contrats que l'administration signe fréquemment avec différents partenaires, notamment des associations, ne sont pas obligatoirement des marchés publics. C'est le fait de répondre à un besoin exprimé par l'administration qui permet de différencier les marchés publics des conventions qui accompagnent, par exemple, certaines décisions d'octroi de subventions. Le marché public se différencie de la subvention, qui constitue une contribution financière de la personne publique à une opération justifiée par l'intérêt général mais qui est initiée et menée par un tiers. Il s'agira d'une subvention si l'initiative du projet vient de l'organisme bénéficiaire et si aucune contrepartie directe n'est attendue par la personne publique du versement de la contribution financière. Dans le cas contraire, il s'agira d'un marché public. La notion d'initiative implique non seulement l'impulsion du projet mais aussi sa conception et sa définition'.* For the EU case law, see Case C- 25/03/2010, *Helmut Müller*, nyr, which draws a line, in public works, between a public procurement and a public intervention legally based on different grounds.
24. McCrudden above fn. 22, at 259.

and the civil codes usually lists all the typical contracts, but also allows 'atypical' contracts which do not fall into any specific contractual type. It is therefore possible to have a typical contract with illegal 'causa' as for example the purchase of a slave, or an atypical contract with a legal 'causa', like the contract of leasing which, before a specific law was enacted in order to regulate it, was considered somewhere in the middle between a sale contract and the lease contract. It is also possible to have contracts with mixed 'causa', like in the case of a father who sells a house to his daughter at a price considerably lower than the market price: it is a sale mixed with a gift, which is perfectly legal.

From the analysis of the national chapters, the lawfulness of a public procurement contract coupled with a State aid is explicitly admitted in Germany[25] and Romania[26] and seems to be admissible in Italy.[27] The other national chapters do not seem to address the question explicitly, but it can be implicitly inferred from the case law cited that secondary considerations are admitted as such and therefore they can co-exist with primary considerations in the same contract.[28]

### 3.4 The legality of inserting a State aid in a public procurement contract under EU law

Since Article 1(2) (a) Directive 2004/18/EC provides that public procurement contracts have 'as their object the execution of works, the supply of products or the provision of services',[29] the first question for the EU contributor is what Directive 2004/18/EC means with the abovementioned definition which could be read at least in the following two meanings:

(1) Under EU law, public procurement contracts cannot have any other object than the one specified and therefore EU law prevents contracting au-

25. Burgi above, para. 2.2 says that secondary considerations '*make an appearance as subventions*', even if he warns that: '*the transition between purely primary and secondary considerations is definitely smooth*'.
26. D. Dragos – B. Neamtu – R. Veliscu 'Secondary considerations in public procurements in Romania' above, para. 2.2.1, say that: '*civil law, on the other hand, allows for contracts with a mixed object, which are legal. In light of these observations, in our opinion, PP contracts under the Romanian legislation can incorporate secondary considerations – when they are the equivalent of a subvention*'.
27. According to the decision of TAR Lazio-Roma, sezione II quater, n. 7512/09 of 23 july 2009, above fn. 9.
28. See f. eg. Vidal above, para 4.1, about subject matter.
29. For the various different linguistic versions see above fn. 18.

thorities from concluding mixed contracts, i.e. contracts having as their object anything different from the execution of works, supply of products or the provision of services and, in particular, having as its objet also a State aid;

(2) The EU Directives only regulate contracts having as their object the execution of works, the supply of products or the provision of services; therefore mixed contracts are not forbidden, but they do not fall under the EU Directives in the part in which they regulate a State aid.

The case law appears to have followed the latter interpretation. The recent *Loutraki* case[30] deals with the hypothesis of a mixed contract not in the sense of Article 22 Directive 2004/18/EC, but in the sense of a contract possibly having as subject-matter partly a public procurement and partly a non-public procurement (namely a concession). The rule to be applied is that, if it is not possible to follow two different legal regimes for the two contracts, the criterion of the main purpose of the contract has to be applied:

> '[...] therefore, where a mixed contract relates to both a transaction within the scope of a procurement directive and a transaction otherwise outside its scope, the contract as a whole will not fall within the scope of the directive if the former is merely incidental to the latter.'[31]

This judgement is not entirely satisfactory.[32] Perhaps, when deciding it, the Court was not completely aware of its possible systematic consequences, also because the case decided was about a mixed contract where the non-public procurement contract was a public concession, which is not far from the logic of public procurement. Had the non-public procurement contract been a different one, such as for example a State aid, perhaps the conclusion would have been different. In any case, it must be said that, according to present EU law, public procurement contracts can have objectives 'other' than those described in the Directive and when those different objectives are the main purpose of the contract, then their legal regime will affect the whole contract. In our case, a contract made up of a public procurement and a State aid will be regulated by the State aids legal regime if it is clear that the granting of a State aid is to be characterised as the main reason for the contract.

30. Joined Cases C-145/08 and C-149, nyr.
31. Caranta above, para. 2.
32. For critical considerations see Caranta above, para. 2.

This is not a contradiction to the situation described in paragraph 2.3, since competition rules always prevail, without any possibility for sustainability to breach or even reduce them. However, here the point is (1) to admit that contracts with mixed objectives exist and (2) to determine the legal regime of these contracts, when it is not possible to apply two different regimes to the same contract.

### 3.5 Conclusions on secondary considerations

It seems clear that the problem of secondary considerations in public procurement contracts goes directly to the core question about the existence of an EU law definition and set of rules about the 'contract'. This question has been studied by private comparative law scholars for decades. The contribution of public procurement comparative lawyers can consist, in the present case, in helping to clarify the dividing line between public procurement contracts and State aid, which seems to be the heart of the definition problem about secondary considerations. No solution could be found, if any, without deepening the polyphonic dialogue between national laws and EU law.

## 4 Technical questions on the process for inserting green and social considerations into public procurement procedures

If in the distinction between primary and secondary considerations in public procurement contracts, it is accepted, the latter can be qualified as a State aid, it is then necessary to proceed with the next step and analyse some specific and more technical aspects in the process of inserting secondary considerations in a public procurement procedure. In particular, three points will be addressed: (1) at what stage(s) of the public procurement procedure can secondary consideration be inserted; (2) what is the relation between secondary considerations inserted in public procurement contracts and those provided for in existing legislation, if any, fostering those same secondary considerations, and (3) is there a substantial difference between green and social considerations or, on the contrary, can they be treated with the same legal tools?

### 4.1 The different stages of the public procurement procedure at which green and social considerations can be inserted

The public procurement procedure consists of various stages. The point here is to analyse what the legal consequences of inserting the secondary consideration in one stage instead of in another are. Generally speaking, it is possible to distinguish the stages which are linked to the subject-matter from those which are not[33]: the first being mainly selection criteria, award criteria and abnormally low tender; the latter being sheltered workshops, domestic employment laws and special contract conditions.

Almost all the national chapters have followed this indication, examining the insertion of green and social considerations in the different stages of the public procurement procedure. Even if the dividing line between stages linked with the subject-matter and stages not linked with it can not been always been clearly drawn, what derives clearly from the national chapters is the peculiarity of sheltered workshops as opposed to the subject-matter (and to the selection and award criteria). Sheltered workshops are different because this has to do with a specific *a priori* choice of the contracting authority which decides to reserve the procedure to them, thus excluding all other economic operators. Italy seems to be the country where the discipline of sheltered workshop, as applied to social cooperatives, is the most generous, sometimes even risking to be inconsistent with European law,[34] but Spain has similar provisions.[35]

The definition of the subject-matter is certainly one of the central points of the whole issue: it is a common idea that the contracting authority has a wide discretion in deciding what to buy and therefore this is a phase where green and social considerations can easily be inserted. But this is the case for EU law, which is mainly concerned with competition law and therefore with equal treatment. If we consider national law principles on procurement we face the principle of efficiency and therefore we see that the discretion of the contracting authority on what to buy is reduced. A contracting authority is obliged, before launching a public procurement procedure, to define its needs in some detail and to buy only what is necessary for its needs. If it buys something which exceeds its needs it can be considered liable for misuse of public money. Therefore it can be said that, under this perspective, national law is generally more restrictive about secondary considerations than EU law.

Selection and award criteria are very much connected to the subject-matter because they have to be linked with it, both under national and EU law. It is precisely about the award criteria question that the principal EU case law was developed[36] and it is not by coincidence that the Court's main decisions always repeat that the first requirement for the award criterion to be legal is its

33. McCrudden above, chapter 17.
34. R. Caranta – S. Richetto 'Sustainable Procurements in Italy: of light and some shadow' above, para. 4.
35. J. González García above, para. 4.2.
36. Caranta above, para. 1.2.

linkage with the subject-matter. In national legislation, it has been asserted that satisfaction of the public interest alone is not sufficient to justify the legality of a criterion.[37]

It is not easy to draw a line between the subject-matter, technical specifications and contract performance clauses.[38] However, it can hardly be denied that contract performance clauses are the best place where to insert social clauses connected with the process of producing the good or the service to be purchased by the contracting authority, because they relate to the execution phase (with the exception of supply contracts when the goods already exist). On the other hand, even if contract performance clauses have to be coordinated with the subject-matter, they are not necessarily linked to it[39] and therefore they have a higher flexibility if compared to selection and award criteria.

### 4.2 Green and social considerations compared to existing green and social legislation

From the analysis of the national chapters,[40] it can be said that differences exists among the following different situations.

(1) The procuring entity requires in the definition of the subject-matter or in the technical specifications that the work, the product or the service has to meet certain green (or social) standards necessary in order for the work, the product or the service to be legally used by the procuring entity (e.g. the subject-matter requires Euro 4 buses, because national legislation requires Euro 4 standards for all buses to be legally used). This case is clearly out of the discourse about secondary considerations: it is simply like requiring the buses to have wheels and brakes. The same can be said for social considerations already imposed by national legislation, like the prohibition of child labour.

(2) The procuring entity requires in the definition of the subject-matter or in the technical specifications that the work, the product or the service has to meet certain green or social standards which are required by EU and national public procurement legislation, as criteria for qualitative selection. This is basically, for EU law, Article 45(2) (e) of Directive 2004/18/EC with reference to the payment of social security contributions, which can be seen as a social consideration. But this can not be considered a secondary consideration, in the sense of a State aid, if it is as an indication of the suitability and reliability

37. Vidal above, para. 2.2.
38. Caranta above. para. 2 and 5.
39. Vidalabove, para. 2.2.
40. E.g. Burgi above, para. 3.1.2, 3.1.3, 3.1.4 and 3.1.5; Dragos, B. Neamtu and R. Veliscu. above, section 2.

of the tenderer. In other words, the line between the subject-matter of the public procurement contract and a State aid can be difficult to draw. The point is to verify what the additional criteria for qualitative selection added by national legislation are. For example, in Italy the tenderer has to prove to be compliant also with legislation on disabled persons: is this a reliability criterion or a secondary consideration/State aid?

(3) The procuring entity requires in the definition of the subject-matter or in the technical specifications that the work, the product or the service has to meet certain green or social standards which are required by EU or national legislation other than public procurement legislation. This is the typical case of secondary consideration/State aid because the standard is neither objectively linked to the subject-matter, nor imposed for reliability reasons, and therefore the reason why the contracting authority is requiring it is exclusively for fostering green or social policies. The legal mechanism is the following: national legislation pursues a specific social policy, such as, for example, forbidding night work for women and provides a criminal sanction for employing women at night. If this prohibition is inserted as a secondary consideration/State aid in a public procurement award procedure, this means that the undertaking breaching the prohibition will incur both (i) the criminal sanction and (ii) the 'sanction' of public contract law for breach of contract. If, on the contrary, the prohibition is not inserted as a secondary consideration/State aid in the award procedure, the undertaking violating the prohibition will incur the criminal sanction, but the public procurement contract will not be terminated.

An additional advantage of this scheme is that control over compliance with the secondary consideration is (or at least should be) already performed under the non public procurement national legislation.

(4) The procuring entity requires in the definition of the subject-matter or in the technical specifications that the work, the product or the service has to meet certain green or social standards which are defined discretionarily by the same procuring entity without any connection to any existing law. This is again a typical case of secondary consideration/State aid which has to be distinguished from the previous case only because of legal technical reasons. Namely: (i) there is no mechanism of a double sanction and (ii) it requires an autonomous control procedure set up by the contracting entity. It seems from the national chapters that this case of secondary consideration is not used very much.

### 4.3 Green vs social considerations

Almost all national chapters report a structural distinction between green and social considerations. First, green considerations are more easily quantifiable than social ones and therefore they are more suitable to be taken into account for the application of the best value for money principle.

In addition, green considerations are more linked to the product (green bus, recycled paper), while social considerations are more linked to the producer's internal organisation (working conditions, equal opportunities), or with the production procedure (fair trade coffee). Therefore green clauses are more easily linked to the subject-matter, while social ones find their natural place in the contract performance conditions.

As a result, it can be said that green and social considerations require different legal techniques for their application and, in general, green considerations are easier to use and less problematic than social ones: this is a common feature in national legal systems as well as in EU law.

Finally, it has to be emphasised that this book is voluntarily limited to green and social considerations, leaving out other possible beneficiaries of secondary considerations. This choice left out the clauses in favour of small and medium sized enterprises (SME's), which, however, in the German legislation are considered to be social clauses because they favour employment and development of small economic entities.

## 5 Quantitative data

From a comparative point of view, it is very important to analyse quantitative data about the actual national policies aimed at fostering sustainable public procurement.[41] This is the only way to get a realistic idea of what the kinds of green and social considerations most often used are. It is evident that a study focusing on cases brought in courts is insufficient because it is subject to the selection imposed by the parties' decision to litigate or not. This study was, however, also very difficult because, being a classification operation, it required to set common definitions and, before that identify common problems, according to the comparative methodology.

41. Dragos, B. Neamtu and R. Veliscu. above, para. 3; Treumer above, para 4; Caranta – Richetto above, para. 4.

## Bibliography

G. Ajani – M. Ebers (Editors), *Uniform Terminology for European Contract law* (Baden-Baden, Nomos-Verlag, 2005).

G.Ajani, '*A Better Coherence of EU Private Law and Multilingualism*', in R. Schulze (ed.), *Common Frame of Reference and Existing EC Contract Law* (Munchen, Sellier, 2008).

S. Arrowsmith & P. Kunzlik, *Social and environmental Policies in EC Procurement Law*, (Cambridge, Cambridge University Press, 2009).

C.H. Bovis, *EU Public Procurement Law*, (Cheltenham, Elgar, 2007).

R. Caranta & S. Treumer, 'Foreword by the Editors of the European Procurement Law Series', in M. Comba & M. Derlén *Multilingual interpretation of European Union Law* (Leiden, Wolters Kluwer, 2009).

McCrudden, *Buying social justice: Equality, Government Procurement and Legal Change* (Oxford, OUP, 2007).

B. Pozzo, *Multilinguismo, terminologie giuridiche e problemi di armonizzazione del diritto privato europeo*, in S. Prechal (ed.) *The coherence of EU law: the search for unity in divergent concepts* (Oxford, OUP, 2008).

Jacometti – Pozzo (editors) *Le politiche linguistiche delle istituzioni comunitarie dopo l'allargamento* (Milano, Giuffré, 2006).

R. Sacco, *Introduzione al diritto comparato* (Torino, Utet, 1993);.

R. Sacco, *Il contratto nella prospettiva comparatistica*, in *Europa e diritto privato*, 2001, 479.

S. Treumer (edds) *In House providing in European Law* (Copenhagen, Djøf Publishing, 2010).

# List of Cases

**EU**

Case C-76/81, *Transporoute et Travaux SA* v. *Ministère des travaux publics* [1982] ECR 417
Case C-263/85, *Commission* v. *Italy* [1991] ECR I-2457
Case C-45/87, *Commission* v. *Ireland* ('Dundalk') [1988] ECR 4929
Case C-31/87, *Beentjes* [1988] ECR 4635
Case C-3/88, *Commission* v. *Italy* ('Re Data Processing') [1989] ECR 4035; [1991] CMLR 115
Case C-21/88, *Du Pont de Nemours Italiana* v. *Unita Sanitara Locale di Carrara* [1990] ECR 889
Case C-11389, *Rush Portuguesa* v. *Office national d'immigration* [1990] ECR I-1417
Case C-243/89, *Commission* v. *Denmark* ('Storebaelt'), [1999] ECR I-3353
Case C-360/89, *Commission* v. *Italy* [1992] ECR I-3401
Case C-272/91, *Commission* v. *Italy* ('Lottomatica') [1992] ECR I-3929
Case C-359/93, *Commission* v. *The Netherlands* ('UNIX')
Case C-87/94, *Commission* v. *Belgium* ('Walloon Buses') [1996] ECR I-2043
Case C-275/98, *Unitron Scandinavia* [1999] ECR I-8291
Case C-324/98, *Telaustria* [2000] ECR I-10745
Case C-470/99, *Universale Bau AG* [2002] ECR I-11617
Case C-513/99, *Concordia Bus Finland [*2002] ECR I-7213
Case C-59/00, *Bent Mousten Vestergaard* v. *Spøttrup Boligselskab*
Case C-358/00, *Buchhändler Vereinigung*, [2002] ECR I-4685
Case C-448/01 *EVN and Wienstrom* [2003] ECR I-14527
Case C-231/03, *Coname*; [2005] ECR I-7287
Case C-234/03, *Contse and others*, [2005] ECR I-9315
Case C-264/03, *Commission* v. *France*, [2005] ECR I-8831
Case C-358/03, *Parking Brixen*, [2004] ECR I-12055
Case C-535/03, *Commission* v. *Italy*, [2006] ECR I-2689
Case C- 346/06, *Rüffert* [2008] ECR I-1989
Case C-532/06, *Lianakis* [2008] ECR I-251
Case C-119/06, *Commission v. Italy*, [2007] ECR I-168
Case C-357/06, *Frigerio*, [2007] ECR I-12311
Cases C-147/06 and C-148/06 *SECAP and Santorso* [2008] ECR I-3565
Case C-305/08, *CoNISMa*, nyr.
Cases C-145/08 and C-149, nyr.

**Denmark**

ISS Facility Services A/S and Danish Industri against Silkeborg Kommune. Judgment of 15 May 2009 from the Court of Appeal (V.L. B-0257-08)
Ruling of 16 October 1996, Danske Vognmænd against Stevns Kommune
Ruling of 6 August 2001, Oxford Reseach against Faaborg Kommune
Ruling of 15 December 2005, Air Liquide Danmark A/S against Roskilde Amt, Storstrøms Amt and Vestsjællands Amt

Ruling of 24 April 2007, Konkurrencestyrelsen against Silkeborg Kommune
Ruling of 10 December 2008, Nordjysk Kloak- og Industriservice A/S against Aalborg Kommune
Ruling of 14 July 2009, Updata Danmark A/S against Lyngby-Taarbæk Kommune
Ruling of 26 August 2009, Barslund A/S against Københavns Kommune
Ruling of 1 October 2009, Cimber Air A/S against Forsvarskommandoen
Complaint of 5 April 2006 concerning the municipality of Silkeborg's termination of a tender procedure without an award
Complaint of 3 December 2008, Jobcenter Odenses udbud af beskæftigelsesopgaver
Complaint of 29 October 2009, Swedlock AB's klage over Servicestyrelsens udbud af låseenheder

**French**

Constitutional Act No. 2005-205 of 1 March 2005, *Official Journal of March* 2, 2005
Council of State, 10 May 1996, *National Federation of Building*, Appl. No. 159.979, conclusions by Stephane Fratacci
Council of State, July 25 2001, Municipality of Gravelines, Appl. No. 229.666.Council of State, April 28, 2006, *City of Toulouse*, Appl. 280197
Council of State, May 10, 2006, *Society Bronzo*, Appl. No. 281976
Council of State, January 25, 2006, *Department of Seine-Saint-Denis*, Appl. No. 278115
Council of State, Section, January 30, 2009, *National Agency for Employment*, Appl. No. 290236
Administrative Tribunal of Nimes, injunction, July 10, 2009, *Ocean Company*, No. 091712
Administrative Tribunal of Caen, injunction, January 5, 2010, No. 0902741, *Company Les Champs Jouault*
Council of Modernization of Public Policies December 12, 2007

**Germany**

Appellate Court Saarbrücken, Ruling of 13th November 2002, 5 Verg 1/02
Appellate Court Düsseldorf, Ruling of 16th April 2003, Verg 64/02= 2003 ZfBR 721
Procurement Chamber Südbayern, Ruling of 17th June 2009, Z 3-3-3194-22-05/09
Procurement Chamber Saarland, Ruling of 7th September 2009, 3 VK 01/09

**Italy**

Corte cost., 26 giugno 2001, n. 207, *Urbanistica e appalti*, 2001, 987
Corte cost., 7 novembre 2003, n. 331, *Foro it.*, 2004, I, 1364
Corte cost., 23 novembre 2007, n. 401, *Giorn. dir. amm.*, 2008, 624
Cass. Lav., 14 marzo 2005, n. 5472, *CED Cassazione*, 2005
Cons. Stato, Sez. V, 15 giugno 2001, n. 3185, *Foro Amm.*, 2001, 1561
Cons. Stato, Sez. V, 30 agosto 2001, n. 4580, *Foro Amm.*, 2001, 2044
Cons. Stato Sez. V, 17 aprile 2002, n. 2010, in *Foro Amm. CDS*, 2002, 929
Cons. Stato Sez. V, 25 giugno 2002, n. 3451, *Foro Amm. CDS*, 2002, 1470
Cons. Stato, Sez. V, 8 luglio 2002, n. 3790, *Giust. Civ.*, 2002, I, 2956
Cons. Stato, Sez. V, 28 aprile 2003, n. 2128, *Foro amm. CDS*, 2003, 1324
Cons. Stato, Sez. IV, 27 ottobre 2003, n. 6640, *Giur. it.*, 2004, 1285
Cons. Stato, Sez. V, 12 luglio 2004, n. 5049, *Giur. it.*, 2005, 407
Cons. Stato, Sez. V, 18 novembre 2004, n. 7555, in *Foro Amm. CDS*, 2004, 3244
Cons. Stato, Sez. V, 24 gennaio 2007, n. 256, in www.giustizia-amministrativa.it

Cons. Giust. Amm. Sicilia, 2 marzo 2007, n. 86, www.giustizia-amministrativa.it
Cons. Stato, Sez. VI, 27 febbraio 2008, n. 716, www.giustizia-amministrativa.it
Cons. Stato, sez. V, 7 ottobre 2008, n. 4901 in *Ambiente e sviluppo*, 2009, 4, 374
Cons. Stato, Sez. V, 21 gennaio 2009, n. 278, *Giur. It.*, 2009
Cons. Stato, Sez. V, 2 febbraio 2009, n. 558 www.giustizia-amministrativa.it
Cons. Stato Sez. V Sent., 25 febbraio 2009, n. 1128, *Giornale dir. amm.*, 2009, 532
Cons. Stato, Sez. VI, 16 giugno 2009, n. 3897, *Giur. It.*, 2009, 2787
Cons. Stato, Sez. V, 19 giugno 2009, n. 4028, in *Giur. It.*, 2009, 456
Cons. Stato, sez. V, 19 novembre 2009, n. 7255, in www.giustizia-amministrativa.it.
T.A.R. Marche, 14 maggio 1999, n. 565, in *Trib. Amm. Reg.*, 1999, I, 2662
T.A.R. Marche, 7 aprile 2000, n. 521, *Urbanistica e appalti*, 2000, 6, 674
T.A.R. Puglia, Bari, Sez. I, 27 maggio 2000, n. 2307, *Riv. It. Dir. Pubbl. Comunitario*, 2000, 1485
T.A.R. Veneto, Sez. I, 26 febbraio 2002, n. 957, *Foro Amm. TAR*, 2002, 425
T.A.R. Puglia, Bari, Sez. I, 7 maggio 2002, n. 2265, *Foro Amm. TAR*, 2002, 1731
T.A.R. Campania, Salerno, Sez. I, 3 luglio 2002, n. 641, *Foro Amm. TAR*, 2002, 2651
T.A.R. Liguria, Sez. II, 23 dicembre 2002, n. 1206, *Urbanistica e appalti*, 2003, 703
T.A.R. Lazio, Sezione III *quater*, 18 luglio 2006, n. 5993, *Giur. It.*, 2006, 2421, and *Sanità pubbl.*, 2006, 6, 79
T.A.R. Lazio, Latina, Sez. I, 15 novembre 2007, n. 1211, www.giustizia-amministrativa.it
T.A.R. Liguria, Sez. II, 15 maggio 2008, n. 1012, in www.giustizia-amministrativa.it
TAR Lombardia Brescia, sez. I, 27 ottobre 2008, n. 1440 in www.giustizia-amministrativa.it
T.A.R. Calabria, 24 novembre 2008, n. 1503, in www.giustizia-amministrativa.it
T.A.R. Lazio Roma, 9 dicembre 2008, n. 11093, in www.giustizia-amministrativa.it
T.A.R. Piemonte, Sez. I, 11 dicembre 2008, n. 3130, in *Urbanistica e appalti*, 2009, 248
T.A.R. Puglia, Lecce, 15 aprile 2009, n. 724, in *Urbanistica e appalti*, 2009, 1015
T.A.R. Veneto, Sez. I, 26 maggio 2009, n. 1601 www.giustizia-amministrativa.it
TAR Lazio-Roma, sezione II quater, 23 July 2009 n. 7512/09 in www.giustizia-amministrativa.it
T.A.R. Puglia Lecce, Sez. III, 29 gennaio 2010, n. 372, in www.giustizia-amministrativa.it

**Poland**

NAC,13.3.2008 KIO/UZP 179/08, Lex 396215
NAC, 7.5.2008 KIO/UZP 383/08, Lex 428477
NAC, 26.9. 2008, KIO/UZP 972/08, Lex 466568, also available at www.uzp.gov.pl
NAC, 5.12.2008 KIO/UZP 1362/08, Lex 485672
NAC 23.12.2008 KIO/UZP 1443/08, Lex 485650
NAC,15.1.2009, KIO/UZP 1524/08, Lex 485643
NAC, 30.1.2009 NAC/UZP 76/09, Lex 486391
NAC, 12.2.2009 KIO/UZP 126/09, Lex 487460
NAC, 5.3.2009 KIO/UZP 196/09, Lex 488378
UZP/ZO/0-592/05, 6.4.2005 Lex 179374
UZP/ZO/0-1879/06, 3.6.2006 Lex 209861
UZP/ZO/0-204/07, Lex 286249
UZP/ZO/0-212/07, 8.3.2007, Lex 286195
UZP/ZO/0-705/07
UZP/ZO/0-738/07, LEX nr 361041

KIO/UZP 383/08, 7.5.2008, Lex 428477
District Court in Warsaw of 8.6.2006 V Ca 459/06 (unpublished).
District Court in Katowice of 30.1.2007 XIX Ga 3/07 reported at www.bankier.pl

**Romania**

Judgment no. 40/11.01.2007, Bucureşti Appellate Court, Division 8 for Administrative and Fiscal Matters
Judgment no. 912/13.02.2007, High Court of Cassation and Justice, Division for Administrative and Fiscal Matters
Judgment no. 1166/23.10.2007, Ploiesti Appellate Court, Division for Commercial, Administrative and Fiscal Matters
Judgment no. 453/6.03.2008, Craiova Appellate Court, Division for Administrative and Fiscal Matters
Judgment no. 355/7.03.2008, Ploieşti Appellate Court, Division for Commercial, Administrative and Fiscal Matters
Judgment no. 613/27.03.2008, Craiova Appellate Court, Division for Administrative and Fiscal Matters
Judgment no. 376/31.03.2008, Alba Iulia Appellate Court, Division for Administrative and Fiscal Matters
Judgment no. 302/R/22.04.2008, Braşov Appellate Court, Division for Administrative and Fiscal Matters
Judgment no. 458/R-C/25.04.2008, Piteşti Appellate Court, Division for Commercial, Administrative and Fiscal Matters
Judgment no. 612/22.05-2008, Timişoara Appellate Court, Division for Administrative and Fiscal Matters
Judgment no. 407/29.05.2008, Bacau Appellate Court, Division for Commercial, Administrative and Fiscal Matters
Judgment no. 1546/9.06.2008, Bucureşti Appellate Court, Division 8 for Administrative and Fiscal Matters
Judgment no. 1601/16.06.2008, Constanţa Appellate Court, Division for Commercial, Maritime and Fluvial, Administrative and Fiscal Matters
Judgment no. 629/R-C/20.06.2008, Piteşti Appellate Court, Division for Commercial, Administrative and Fiscal Matters
Judgment no. 780/3.07.2008, Timişoara Appellate Court, Division for Administrative and Fiscal Matters
Judgment no. 366/CA/10.07.2008, Iaşi Appellate Court, Division for Administrative and Fiscal Matters
Judgment no. 496/R/29.07.2008, Braşov Appellate Court, Division for Administrative and Fiscal Matters
Judgment no. 666/CA/13.08.2008, Cnstanţa Appellate Court, Division for Commercial, Maritime and Fluvial, Administrative and Fiscal Matters
Judgment no. 1038/16.09.2008, Piteşti Appellate Court, Division for Commercial, Administrative and Fiscal Matters
Judgment no. 970/CA/17.09.2008, Alba Iulia Appellate Court, Division for Administrative and Fiscal Matters
Judgment no. 930/2.10.2008, Timişoara Appellate Court, Division for Administrative and Fiscal Matters

Judgment no. 1067/CA/8.10.2008, Alba Iulia Appellate Court, Division for Administrative and Fiscal Matters
Judgment no. 2082/15.10.2008, Craiova Appellate Court, Division for Administrative and Fiscal Matters
Judgment no. 764/13.11.2008, Bacău Appellate Court, Division for Commercial, Administrative and Fiscal Matters
Judgment no. 1280/CA/3.12/2008, Alba Iulia Appellate Court, Division for Administrative and Fiscal Matters
Judgment no. 2563/5.12.2008, Craiova Appellate Court, Division for Administrative and Fiscal Matters
Judgment no. 2775/12.12.2008, Bucureşti Appellate Court, Division 8 for Administrative and Fiscal Matters
Judgment no. 553/CA/15.12.2008, Iaşi Appellate Court, Division for Administrative and Fiscal Matters
Judgment no. 62/23.01.2009, Bacău Appellate Court, Division for Commercial, Administrative and Fiscal Matters
Judgment no. 669/9.03.2009, Bucureşti Appellate Court, Division 8 for Administrative and Fiscal Matters

**United Kingdom**
*Wheeler v Leicester City Council* [1985] AC 1054
*R v Lewisham LBC, ex p Shell UK Ltd* [1988] 1 All ER 938
Order 1998, SI 1998/3162 (N.I. 21)

# List of Authors

Professor Martin Burgi, Ruhr Universität Bochum, Germany
Professor Roberto Caranta, University of Torino, Italy
Professor Mario Comba, University of Torino, Italy
Professor Dacian C. Dragoş, Babeş-Bolyai University, Cluj-Napoca, Romania
Professor Julio González García, Universidad Complutense de Madrid, Spain
Bogdana Neamţu, Lecturer, Babeş-Bolyai University, Cluj-Napoca, Romania
Professor Gabriella M. Racca, University of Torino, Italy
Dr. Sara Richetto, Torino, Italy
Professor Marcin Spyra, Uniwersytet Jagielloński Kraków, Poland
Professor Steen Treumer, University of Copenhagen, Denmark
Professor Martin Trybus, University of Birmingham, United Kingdom
Raluca Velişcu, Assistant professor, Babeş-Bolyai University, Cluj-Napoca, Romania
Professor Laurent Vidal, University of Paris I Panthéon Sorbonne, France

# Index